Parenting
Your
Internationally
Adopted
Child

Parenting Your Internationally Adopted Child

From Your First Hours Together Through the Teen Years

Patty Cogen

THE HARVARD COMMON PRESS

Boston, Massachusetts

The Harvard Common Press
535 Albany Street
Boston, Massachusetts 02118
www.harvardcommonpress.com

Copyright © 2008 by Patty Cogen
Cover illustration copyright © 2008 by Hugh Dunnahoe

Printed in the United States of America

Printed on acid-free paper

Library of Congress Cataloging-in-Publication Data
Cogen, Patty.
    Parenting your internationally adopted child : from your first hours
together through the teen years / Patty Cogen.
        p. cm.
    ISBN 978-1-55832-326-1 (pbk.) — ISBN 978-1-55832-325-4 (hardcover)
    1. Intercountry adoption—United States. 2. Parenting—United States.
    I. Title.
    HV875.5.C634 2008
    649'.157—dc22

                                                                2007047233

Special bulk-order discounts are available on this and other Harvard
Common Press books. Companies and organizations may purchase books
for premiums or resale, or may arrange a custom edition, by contacting the
Marketing Director at the address above.

Cover design by Night & Day Design
Interior design by John Kramer
Cover illustration by Hugh Dunnahoe

10 9 8 7 6 5 4 3 2 1

To my brother, David

Contents

Part III As Your Adopted Child Grows Up

ACKNOWLEDGMENTS

If I thanked everyone involved with the development of this book, the acknowledgments would be longer than the book itself. The short version I offer here is only a slim reflection of the immense amount of daily support I have received over the past ten years from family and friends as well as professional colleagues and clients with whom I have worked. Thank you to all who remain anonymous, but whose names are in my heart.

Both my mother and my daughter lost birth parents at an early age and my relationship with each of them has given me a close-up view of what such loss means to a child throughout a lifetime. My daughter, Sun-Jia, whom we brought home from China when she was three years old, has been exceedingly frank, open, and articulate about what it means to grow up as an internationally adopted child. She has been both an inspiration for me and a model for what I have to say in the pages of this book. In addition, Ying Johnstone and her mother, Barbara, have contributed a great deal of information that is incorporated here, and I am grateful for their openness and enduring friendship.

I began dreaming about the possibility of this book in the late 1990s during conversations with Nina Berson, Sue Betts, Karen Delshad, Lois Langland, Aimee Liu, and Michelle Thoreson. Insightful readers of early drafts included Rhonda Bolton, Judy Challoner, Jan Faull, Gail Hudson, Barbara Johnstone, Jeri Jenista, Roberta Wilkes, and Linda Ziedrich. I am grateful to Jeannette Dyal and other members of the Child Therapy Association of Seattle who invited me to speak about my work more than once.

Thanks to my writing teacher, Nick O'Connell, who taught me to appreciate critiques. Deep thanks to my insightful and indefatigable agent, Elsa Dixon, who helped me to stay true to my original vision. Special thanks go to my editor, Dan Rosenberg, for his unfailing insight into my meaning and the exceptional kindness that accompanied each of his queries. I was exceedingly fortunate to have Dan as an editor. Thanks to Barbara Wood for her final polish on the manuscript. Thanks to publisher Bruce Shaw and the staff at the Harvard Common Press for their support of and confidence in this project, and for their patience. A special word of appreciation is owed to the book's cover artist, Hugh Dunnahoe.

Deep thanks to my old friends from Scripps College—Sam, Merrilee, Lucille, Joanne, Mari, Deirdre, and Dale—who restored my flagging energy as the final editing drew to a close. Thanks also to Deborah Lodish and Judy Rothman for their compassion and insight. I owe much gratitude to my brother and sister-in-law, David and Dove Cogen, who took over the care of David's and my mother in the last year of her life and as I completed the writing of this book.

Special love and thanks for daily support, home-cooked meals, help with editing, and constant inspiration go to my children, Robin and Sun-Jia. Thank you, Robin, for encouraging me to take the big step of enrolling in my first non-fiction writing course and for your steadfast belief in me. Finally, profound thanks are due to my husband and co-parent, Larry Stein, for taking care of our family while I was up to my eyeballs in writing and for sharing the unfolding adventure of parenthood and international adoption.

Patty Cogen
Seattle, Washington

Proactive Parenting

RAISING AN INTERNATIONALLY ADOPTED CHILD is both a challenge and an adventure. It is a challenge because it requires an adoptive family to face and overcome obstacles. It is an adventure because it is filled with surprises, excitement, and new learning. I hope that what you read in this book will help you to overcome the challenges you face and to experience your family life as a series of wondrous adventures.

There is one all-important concept behind this book, and it is the concept of *proactive parenting*. A proactive parent is the *initiator* of interactions with a child, as opposed to being merely a *responder* to a child's communication. Proactive parenting is effective in any family, but it is particularly important in adoptive families. In the pages of this book you will see how recent research—about how internationally adopted children behave, about the most effective parenting strategies for this group of children, and about the family traits that integrate an internationally adopted child most successfully into a new family—all point in the direction of a proactive parenting style. A proactive approach, in which you are knowledgeable about your child's needs and are able to anticipate problems before they occur, keeps you ahead of, rather than behind, your child. When the inevitable challenges arise, the proactive parent is able to address them before they get out of control.

WHAT IS PROACTIVE PARENTING?

In 1991 Vera Fahlberg published an important book entitled *A Child's Journey through Placement*, which focused attention on the child's experience of being

1

placed in a new family setting. Fahlberg describes the cycle of arousal and relaxation that occurs when a child fusses (is aroused), a parent responds with care, and, as a result, the child calms and relaxes. Fahlberg makes use of the psychiatrist John Bowlby's observations that a child's attachment is based on the speed and intensity of a parent's caregiving response, and also that a child's trust grows as the parent responds with empathy to the child's distress. Fahlberg describes how a newly adopted child, regardless of age, needs to experience *contingency parenting*—that is, responsive, empathetic parenting—in order to become attached to his adoptive parent.

Since 1991, contingency parenting has been a primary focus of many adoptive-parenting classes. The concept of contingency parenting helps parents recognize that responding quickly and fully to a child's distress, either physical or emotional, is important and appropriate following adoption and will not result in bad habits or a spoiled child. The concept reassures parents that they do not need to worry about giving "too much attention."

I have found that most adoptive parents view contingency parenting as a temporary parenting approach that can be set aside, once trust and attachment are established, in favor of a more traditional parenting approach that centers on parents' age-appropriate expectations about how the child must learn to control himself and must learn to wait to have his needs met.

In the years since Fahlberg's book appeared, researchers have learned that the trust and attachment that develop after adoption are not in all cases stable and permanent. The same researchers have identified as well some of the factors that interfere with trust and attachment as an adopted child matures. In this book you will discover how a lack of *resiliency*, which appears as an inability to exert self-control, and struggles with *identity*, when the adopted child wonders who he really is and whether he truly belongs anywhere, can disrupt trust, attachment, and connection within an adoptive family. You will also see examples of how internationally adopted children, even when they are otherwise quite mature and articulate, often express their difficulties with resiliency, identity, and connection indirectly, with mixed or contradictory messages or even with outright rejection of their parents' attempts to reach out to them.

Proactive parenting expands upon contingency parenting in two ways. First, it provides guidelines that work for eighteen-plus years of parenting, not just the first year home. Second, it helps parents to anticipate as well as respond to a child's distress. Proactive parenting is vital because internationally adopted children are vulnerable to being derailed from their development by what often are, for non-adopted children, ordinary experiences of stress. At these times a child of, say, nine, twelve, or fifteen years of age may revert to survival and coping behaviors (see chapters 4 and 5)—behaviors that kept the child alive, despite neglectful and changing caregivers, in his early months or years abroad but which are inappropriate and counterproductive in a loving adoptive family. When an adopted preteen or teenager regresses to rejecting, negative behavior to communicate needs, proactive parenting provides the strategies for response.

A proactive parent has two toolkits with which to respond to a school-age child who, for example, continually misbehaves when playing with friends in the backyard. The first is made up of traditional strategies, such as a lecture on good behavior or a time-out. The second is a proactive approach that recognizes that the child is likely to be struggling with larger issues, having to do with self-control, identity, and adoption, and that encourages parents to intervene not just with disciplinary measures but also with specific strategies that foster better self-control and that ease the child's underlying concerns. When an internationally adopted child, to use another example, refuses to go to school and repeatedly shouts, "I hate school," traditional kinds of strong encouragement may very well not help him move forward. Instead, parents may need to uncover what adoption or separation issues may have been triggered at school the day before.

PROACTIVE PARENTING PROVIDES . . .

- a complement to contingency parenting and other traditional parenting strategies.
- long-term parenting strategies that reach all the way to young adulthood.
- techniques for responding to negative and rejecting behaviors.
- strategies for managing regressed behaviors.
- ways to overcome and decode mixed-message communications.

In the chapters that follow you will also learn about the concept of *family age*, which refers to the length of time a child has been in an adoptive family. An adopted child's family age is always less, and sometimes considerably less, than his chronological age. You will also learn about how children from complex backgrounds, such as internationally adopted children, often engage in negative behaviors that I call *reactive coping behaviors* and *survival skills*. An adopted child's low family age relative to chronological age, and his tendency to use coping behaviors and survival skills, can interfere with his ability to communicate needs clearly and to deal calmly with the challenges of everyday life. In addition, adopted children who have come from abroad may simply not even know the right words for what they are feeling. A two-year-old child who has recently joined his adoptive family, for example, might spit out his food because it does not taste familiar. But he cannot communicate this; he does not know how to say, in his new family's language, "This tastes strange to me. I would rather have food I know and like." Beyond his language barrier, he may not even be aware that a child is allowed to choose his own food or even to express food preferences. At six years old the same child may come home from school angry and reject his mother's embrace, shouting, "We gotta bring a baby picture tomorrow," unable to explain, "I don't have a picture of me as a baby and I'm deeply worried about what to do and say in school about my adoption." Parents must be proactive in cases such as these, trying to see the world through their child's eyes, in the context of the child's past, and asking the kinds of questions that will draw out the child's underlying concerns. In the course of reading this book, you will learn to recognize many situations that are likely to be the occasions for unclear communication on the part of your internationally adopted child. You will learn that while some situations, such as a two-year-old spitting out food, are relatively easy to interpret or "decode," other situations—especially as your child matures toward the preteen and teen years—are more complex and will require that you become a detective of sorts, in order to deduce what needs and concerns lie behind your child's confusing communications.

Children with complex backgrounds do not communicate clearly about their needs. Parents must behave *as if* the child has expressed those needs.

Proactive parenting might well be called *"as if" parenting.* By this I mean that a parent must often use his or her intuitions, experiences, and innate skills in order to behave *as if* a child has expressed certain feelings or needs. Parents, especially parents of children from complex backgrounds, often need to provide and offer care despite the fact that the child does not consciously expect it or has not explicitly asked for it.

FIVE FAMILIES: THE FIRST YEAR HOME GROUP

In this book I follow five internationally adopted children to illustrate how the world of a new family appears to an internationally adopted child; the challenges such a child faces in adjusting, first, to the new family, and then, over time, to the wider world; and the tools and strategies you can use to help your own adopted child meet these challenges. The examples of behavior and parent-child interaction are drawn from real children and parents who have participated over the years in an education and support group for internationally adopted families, the First Year Home Group, which I have led for the past decade. To preserve the privacy of actual individuals and families, each of these five children, and each of their parents, is a composite of many individuals. (When I report on my own interactions with members of the group, on the other hand, I am just myself—not a composite.) The First Year Home Group has allowed me to observe the emotions and behaviors, and the growth process, of children from all over the world in many different kinds of adoptive families. Other families who have consulted me over the years outside the context of the First Year Home Group provide additional examples in the pages that follow.

I have chosen to follow the families in the First Year Home Group especially closely for three reasons. First, the children illustrate a range of ages at adoption, as well as a variety of pre-adoption experiences. Second, each child has a unique way of coping with overwhelming stress. Third, by following these children from their adoption through their teen years, we can discern how age at adoption, pre-adoption experiences (orphanage, foster care, or both), and coping styles unfold over time and affect development.

In the first part of the book I define core concepts and issues, including survival, coping and adjustment behaviors, and the psychological issues of identity, separation, and emotional/behavioral control that almost always first appear in early childhood. Understanding and recognizing these behaviors when your child is an infant, a toddler, or a preschooler will enable you to recognize these same behaviors when they appear in school-age or teenage form. Therefore, even if your child is six or ten or thirteen years old, reading the early chapters is important. In them you will find descriptions and explanations of behaviors and of underlying psychological or behavioral issues that may only recently have become apparent to you but that have been enduring features of your child's life ever since she was a baby or toddler. The second part of the book is chronological; I describe how these behavior patterns and issues play out as the children mature and how parents can adjust their proactive parenting strategies to older children and teens.

More so than with non-adopted children, missed developmental steps of adopted children need to be addressed. If your child has always had difficulty with eye contact, or has seemed overly mature for her age, or has persistently had trouble with transitions from one activity to another, it is vital to remedy the developmental gaps that have led to these behaviors. Simple problems in the early years create a cascade of problems as a child grows up. For example, very precocious behavior at three years old may be viewed as cute, but at ten or twelve it may manifest itself as defiant independence, and the child may associate inappropriately with older teens or even adults as peers. In older children it may be hard to see the roots of a problem. Social difficulties for a teen may stem from earlier difficulties with eye contact and from other kinds of disconnection from parents, but these early origins may be lost among a multitude of other possible causes.

Parenting books and magazines often lay out a set of simply defined problems and quick solutions, but few of the core issues that confront parents of internationally adopted children can be handled in this breezy manner. I hope that the examples provided by the five children offer real-life snapshots that help you to see the true complexity of child development. I hope, too, that the First Year Home Group provides a coherent narrative anchor that makes these complexities understandable.

Do you have to keep track of all the details about each child in the group? No, that is not necessary. I have picked names that reflect each child's country of origin. I provide reminders of basic facts about the children—age, gender, length of time since adoption, and so on—as the book proceeds.

Most parents, whether they adopt or not, are "on-the-job learners."

Can you pick out a later chapter focused on older children and read it? Of course! You many find, however, that reading about your older child's challenges sends you back to the beginning of the book, to discover new parenting strategies to help get you and your child on track.

ON-THE-JOB TRAINING

Few parents of internationally adopted children begin with a full toolbox of proactive-parenting skills. Most parents are "on-the-job learners." This book is intended to be your guide to proactive parenting and the skills that you need to raise an internationally adopted child successfully. Do not despair if you feel that you are starting out with few of the tools or skills I describe. Your willingness to learn, like your child's, is more important than how accomplished you are at the start. If you can do it, so can your child. Take heart, and read on. This parenting experience will be an adventure: *Bon voyage!*

Part I

Understanding Your Child's Behavior— and Misbehavior

"Are You My Mommy? Are You My Daddy?"

The Beginnings of Identity

IT IS A MONDAY MORNING in February, just before ten, and a new session of the First Year Home Group is about to begin. This Group offers support, education, and early intervention to families with internationally adopted children. A child and family therapist and child-development specialist who works primarily with families with internationally adopted children, I founded the Group to help parents develop connection with their children and to help the children with issues of identity and resiliency. You, the reader, are my guest, an invisible observer in my office playroom, able to watch what the children do and hear what the parents say.

I am busy arranging the room to welcome the five children who will arrive shortly, accompanied by their parents. I have put away the blocks and the playhouse and covered the shelves full of dolls of a variety of races, and I have set out five baby toys in a circle on the green rug: a soft cloth ball, a squishy plastic ball, a wooden rattle, two interlocking plastic rings, and a plastic box with five levers that make five individual boxes pop open. I want the room to be inviting but not overwhelming to the children, who range from infancy to preschool age. Only one month ago each child came from another country and joined his or her new family.

FIVE FAMILIES

Following are thumbnail sketches of the families in my Group. I include the initial behavioral and psychological issues each child faces, along with the coping behaviors he or she most commonly uses. (I describe these behaviors, which I call *reactive coping behaviors*, in more detail in chapter 5, where I also offer additional parenting strategies to address them.)

1. **Charlotte and Joe** adopted **Soon An**, now a seven-month-old girl, from a foster home in Korea. They already have one birth child, Lars, who is nine years old. Soon An seems to come from the ideal situation: foster care since birth and adoption at a young age. Her coping style is to withdraw or shut down into sleep. Her parents call her the "Warm Rock."

2. **Carolyn and David** are coming with their daughter, **Sonia**, who is thirteen months old. They adopted her from a foster home in Guatemala and she is their first child. Because David is Latino and speaks Spanish and English, the family is bilingual. Sonia is also from a seemingly ideal foster care situation. Her coping style is another form of withdrawal, a sort of stunned shock as she realizes her losses. She is the "Stunned Rag Doll."

3. **Denise** is bringing her son, **Demetri**, now nineteen months old, who was born in Russia. He has lived most of his life in a hospital or orphanage. Demetri exhibits many of the typical survival behaviors of a child who comes from an orphanage. He is independent and charming but lacks emotional and behavioral control. He is the "Dizzy Performer."

4. **Meg and Laura** accompany their daughter, **Mu Ling**, who is just over two and a half years old. She lived in a Chinese orphanage. Clara, her older sister, was also adopted from China and is now six years old. Mu Ling copes with change and stress by taking control, and she too has problems with self-control. Mu Ling manages life by being the "Royal Boss."

5. **Nina and Kenji** have the oldest child in the Group, **Yi Sheng**. He lived in a Chinese orphanage and a Chinese foster home during his first four and a half years of life. His parents have two birth daughters, Aiko and Rivka, who are both teenagers. Yi Sheng has had the most complex and confusing pre-adoption background. He personifies the feelings of many older children who feel trapped by and angry about their adoption. Yi Sheng copes as an "Unwilling Guest," which interferes with his ability to connect with his new family.

THE FAMILIES ARRIVE

Charlotte and Joe are the first to arrive with Soon An. Her black hair is standing straight up in the air, except where Charlotte has pinned a small pink barrette. Soon An quickly turns her head away from me, closes her eyes, and begins to squirm in her mother's arms. Demetri, who toddles in next with his blond, bowl-shaped haircut, immediately reaches out to me with both arms, as if I were a familiar caregiver. He gives me an extra-large nineteen-month-old grin, showing four teeth as he leans into my legs, expecting me to pick him up.

"He's so friendly to everyone!" Denise comments proudly.

"*This* is your mommy," I tell Demetri as I gently turn him around to face his mother.

Kenji and Nina arrive next with their son, Yi Sheng, who looks quite mature for four and a half years old. He walks in sturdily beside his mother. His penetrating, dark, almond-shaped eyes watch me greeting people; he comes over, takes my hand, and then gazes blankly into space.

Nina looks to me for guidance. "He does this a lot, and I'm not sure what to do."

"We'll talk about this in group," I reassure her. "For now, just take his hand and encourage him to stay with you and explore the playroom."

Two-and-a-half-year-old Mu Ling has her black hair in tiny pigtails tied with red bows. She trots in ahead of her parents and heads into the playroom without a look at her family or me. She goes to each toy on the floor, picks it up, and, after a brief look, tosses it over her shoulder. Her mother Meg runs in and scolds her while her other mother, Laura, looks at me helplessly and shrugs. "She's always two steps ahead of us," she comments.

David and Carolyn arrive carrying Sonia, who is just over a year old. Sonia's round brown eyes gaze at the other parents and children, and then she shakes her head of thick, wavy dark hair and hides her face in her father's shirt, beginning to cry. I back away and say, "Sonia, you will *stay* with your Daddy and *you will go home with Daddy* after we play together."

The behavior of the children reveals, in different ways, how fragile their sense of connection with their parents truly is. Each child either avoids or reaches for me, depending on what his or her past experience has been with strange adults. How the children behave upon meeting a stranger is a clue to their past experience and their memories of their recent international adoption. Those who avoid me usually come from foster homes and are frightened of strangers, who they believe will remove them from their familiar caregivers (in this case, their new parents). Children who come from an orphanage tend to greet me as a new caregiver or to ignore me completely.

A non-adopted child with a secure background would react quite differently. He would look at his parent's face to gauge Mom or Dad's reaction to me. When a child does not look at his parent to get a "read" on a new person or situation, I know that child does not feel completely connected with Mom or Dad. None of my new arrivals has checked in by looking at a parent's face. They all still feel as if they are "on their own," despite their adult "chaperones." Each child has behaved in a way that reveals uncertainty about who the primary caregiver is. (We will talk more about developing a child's parent recognition later in this chapter.)

Virtually all internationally adopted children feel "on their own" during their first year home. Having had and then lost several caregivers already, the children are not sure who will take care of them or for how long. Your first goal as a parent is to see the world from your child's viewpoint, in this case to understand that he may not at first perceive you as someone who will be with him consistently for a long time.

I do simple things to convey this information to the child as well as the parent. I step back from anxious Soon An, point to myself, and say, while shaking my head, "I am not Soon An's mommy. I am Soon An's *teacher*." Then I encourage Charlotte to reassure her daughter, with words and with pantomime, that the two of them will go home together after visiting in my playroom.

"Soon An," I explain to her parents, "doesn't know what to expect. Not too long ago her trusted foster mother handed her to a stranger who escorted her on the plane, and most recently she was handed over to other strangers, the two of you. Soon An may think you are going to hand her to me."

When Demetri reaches out to me, I step back to make a gap between us to reinforce that I am not taking him away from Denise. He begins to self-soothe by rubbing his ear. Again I repeat, "I am *not* your mommy. *This* is Demetri's mommy," and I point to Denise. "I am the *teacher*." Denise, who overheard my comments to Charlotte, follows Charlotte's lead, reassuring Demetri that she is his mom and that they will play here and then go home together. He turns and looks first at me, and then at his mother. He stops rubbing his ear and both of his arms fold into the middle of his body, covering his belly. He begins to suck his lower lip. This little boy is trying to soothe himself on his own, using the earliest methods of an infant: sucking, rubbing his ear, and bringing his arms together. Having come from an orphanage in Russia, he is used to lots of caregivers, none much more important or primary than another, and therefore he assumes that everyone is a caregiver—including me as well as the other parents in the Group.

A child who treats someone other than a parent as a primary caregiver needs to be gently directed back to the parent. A child who ignores the parent, as Mu Ling has done, should not be left with the conclusion that the parent is unimportant. I tell Meg that Mu Ling needs to hear that they are *together* and that Meg wants to be with Mu Ling. Meg takes the cue and runs into the playroom after Mu Ling to restore their connection.

TEACHING PARENT RECOGNITION THROUGH SONG

The families seat themselves in a circle on the green rug in my playroom. "Welcome to the first meeting of your First Year Home Group!" I tell them. "Everything we do in the Group has a purpose. The first thing we do each week is sing the 'Hello Song.' This is a song about parent-child recognition and connection as well as a greeting. The words of the song are designed to help your child recognize his or her own name, which may still be somewhat unfamiliar, and to recognize Mom or Dad. Think of this song as a parenting strategy to answer the questions 'Who am I?' and 'Who are you?'"

To demonstrate, I take a doll, Mary, from my shelf to serve as my child. I sit her on my lap and begin to sing to the tune of "Mary Wore Her Red Dress":

Mary and her mommy, her mommy, her mommy,
Mary and her mommy came to play at Group.

I touch the doll when I sing her name. I point to myself and make the doll look at me when I sing the word *mommy*. The three children who are cruising the room, Demetri, Mu Ling, and Yi Sheng, stop and watch me. The two younger girls, Soon An and Sonia, peek out from their parents' arms to see what is happening.

The parents join me as we sing to one child and parent at a time. I pause and narrate the behavior of each child to help the parents understand how little their child really relates to his or her name or to the words *mommy* or *daddy*. No child looks at or touches his or her parent during the song. In a few weeks' time, with practice, the children will put a hand on a parent's arm as we sing, but it will be another two weeks or more before they make eye contact spontaneously.

To address the pervasive disconnection I direct the parents to teach their children how to connect. When we sing to Soon An, for example, I encourage

Charlotte to touch Soon An's chest to help her daughter recognize that we are singing to her. When we sing the word *mommy* I ask Charlotte to touch Soon An's hand gently to Charlotte's body. "Look right into your child's face," I encourage the parents from the first moment onward. "Make eye contact happen."

The first time we sing there is a blank, stone-faced look on each child's face. No one moves. Some children may associate singing with the party that preceded their leaving the orphanage. After we sing to several children, Mu Ling stands up and claps in a bid for attention, although we are not singing to her yet.

We will sing this song each week when Group begins. Over time we will see dramatic changes in how a child responds to hearing his or her name sung and hearing his or her parent mentioned. By week four we will see genuine smiles and waves, and the children will snuggle into their parents' arms. When the eighth week of Group rolls around, the children will hug their parents and gaze into their eyes. Each child will recognize his or her own name and point to himself or herself at the appropriate time. The performances for attention, such as Mu Ling's, will diminish.

As the children become more secure in their grasp of the basics of identity— Who am I? Who is Mommy or Daddy?—their next challenge is to develop a deeper attachment to their parents. The next chapter addresses "attachment" concerns, which I have found to be at the center of most adoptive parents' thoughts, and defines the specific developmental challenges of internationally adopted children.

Differences
in Development

Identity, "Attachment,"
Connection, and Resiliency

ATTACHMENT IS A CONCEPT that seems simultaneously to scare and to fascinate parents. Some therapists, counselors, and even parents use the term to explain many behaviors of the internationally adopted child. If the child has a problem, it is attributed to the absence of attachment.

I avoid focusing on attachment, which is a static construct. People envision attachment as a rope, with a child holding one end and the parent holding the other. You either have it or you do not, and there is no middle ground. But this vision misses the point.

Parenting an internationally adopted child is a *process of building connection* on many levels, including sensory, emotional, cognitive, and physical. The process includes not just building connection but also *recognizing and repairing* tangled or disrupted parts of the parent-child relationship. Therefore, I prefer the more inclusive and process-focused word *connection* to describe this vital aspect of parenting.

> **Parents need to know how to build connection and how to recognize and repair tangled or disrupted parts of the parent-child relationship.**

You and your child are creating a relationship, just as a weaver creates a weaving. Think of connecting as the process of weaving, whereas attachment is the completed piece of cloth. In this book I will talk about *how to parent to create connection continuously.* Although connection is just one component of development, it is an especially important one.

Children from overseas face unique challenges in their development. Adoption experts once believed that attachment was the key to normal (or abnormal) development. Many years of intensive research on the developing brain has shown that healthy childhood development is the result of three interrelated areas of development. The first area is the *connection* between a parent and child, including any changes that affect that connection. The second area, *resiliency*, is the child's ability to remain emotionally balanced and her ability to regain control when faced with any sort of change or stress. The third area is *identity*, or how the child answers the questions "Who am I, and who are you, and where do I fit in this world?" Not surprisingly, these three areas develop together, not as separate pieces.

The unique developmental challenges that internationally adopted children face are the result of disruptions of these three areas, not only because of difficulties in the child's pre-adoption life, but also because of the international adoption process itself. Parenting your child effectively begins with an understanding of how connection, resiliency, and identity interrelate; how they become disrupted; and what parenting strategies can do to reorganize disrupted development.

THE BEDROCK OF DEVELOPMENT: THE BRAIN

When a baby is born, the mother's protective care and her relationship with her infant replace the protective barrier of the womb and the mother's body. Maternal care and the mother-infant relationship begin to build specific types of brain structure in human babies. We now know that the brain of an infant develops differently when the relationship with the birth mother is interrupted, terminated, neglectful, or abusive. I use the metaphor of two colts to describe these two different developmental paths. One colt is raised by its mother in a warm barn with plenty of food, and the other colt is raised in a wild herd on the open, sparsely vegetated plains. Eventually the brain of each colt has expectations and responses built into it, based not just on the brain with which it was born but also on its experiences since birth. Recent research tells us that the development of the human brain, like that of the colt, is to a surprising degree *experience dependent*.

Immediately after birth, an infant's brain relies on the fight-or-flight stress response to enable the infant to survive. As the child's relationship with the birth mother builds, the mother consistently and reliably controls the baby's environment, making sure that it is neither overstimulating (with an overattentive parent) nor understimulating (with a neglectful parent). As a result, the infant's brain learns to *expect* care and help from a specific caregiver to manage responses to the baby's experience. This expectation leads the baby to anticipate a safe, trustworthy environment and to respond to others accordingly.

Even a newborn infant can tell when its birth mother vanishes and a new person takes over. The change in this special relationship, a relationship of nine months' duration by the time of the child's birth, is a significant stress for the baby. Overwhelming stress of this type, the trauma of separation, loss, or neglect, activates the brain's fight-or-flight reaction not once but repeatedly and, if there is enough repetition, forever thereafter. The baby and eventually the growing and grown child will have this fight-or-flight response to anything his brain perceives as "dangerous," including many ordinary events—especially ones that remind the child of an early loss. New events, changes in expected routines, surprises, or just spontaneous interactions with others can trigger the stress response in a child who has early separation trauma. For example, if the final time such a child saw his birth mother she wore red, the color red could in later years be a signal to him of an impending loss of care. Repeated instances in childhood of the high-strung fight-or-flight response literally lead to the growth of a brain that is different from one built through the experience of (relatively) uninterrupted care. The stress responses of a child who has this background are reminiscent of a wild colt that is spooked by every little movement or noise when confined in the barn. High-strung, easily spooked colts are notoriously difficult to tame and train.

THE STRESS-SHAPED BRAIN

A child whose brain has been shaped by stress expects danger and reacts immediately, without conscious thought. These expectations and reactive behaviors persist regardless of how nurturing and loving subsequent caregivers may be. Having a stress-shaped brain is like seeing through eyeglasses that make the whole world look threatening. The condition also interferes with a child's autobiographical and other types of memory and her ability to "make sense of the world" through rational thought and understanding such concepts as cause and effect. Stress responses interfere with attention, visual and auditory focus, and learning abilities generally. This is the "simple" explanation for why internationally adopted children have difficulty with identity, connection, and emotional and behavioral self-control, the cornerstones of development.

Fortunately, brain and early-childhood researchers in recent years have made important discoveries about ways that parents (as well as therapists and other professionals) can teach children the means to counteract the habitual reactivity and negativity that traumatic early experience can cause. These are significant discoveries for many parents, but especially for parents of internationally adopted children. In brief, these researchers have determined that it is possible to recruit the consciously directive front part of the brain, the frontal lobes, which act like the brain's supervisor, to intervene in and temper the reactive fight-or-flight behaviors. Some researchers and clinicians have begun referring to behavior that follows the actions of the conscious brain as "taking the high road," as opposed to out-of-control "low road" behavior. Although this book is not primarily about the brain and nervous system, the parenting strategies I introduce throughout are consistent with this new area of scientific research, and the various strategies I recommend lead to ways your child can use her front brain to control fight-or-flight and other stress-shaped responses. The books by Daniel Hughes, Daniel Siegel, and David Ziegler that are listed in the Bibliography provide much more detail about the effects of early trauma on the brain and also about why we now believe these effects can be reduced and brought under control.

THREE CORNERSTONES OF DEVELOPMENT: IDENTITY, CONNECTION, AND RESILIENCY

Brain structure is the bedrock of development. When the brain is organized by traumatic loss, a child has beliefs and behaviors that are suitable for survival in a more or less dangerous environment but not in family life in a loving home. The foundation stones of identity, connection, and resiliency appear almost magically in the brains of most children. But these critical foundation pieces are either missing or distorted in the stress-shaped brain. Consequently, parents must actively teach a stress-shaped child to create identity, connection, and resiliency, and to do so in that order.

Identity issues begin the moment a child parts from his first set of parents, the genetically related ones. The basic question "Who am I?" is derailed by the loss. With each new set of caregivers, whether foster parents or orphanage workers, and then with adoptive parents, a child's identity and life story grow more complex. Often a child with such a wild-colt-like background concludes that he is a "nobody."

It is unwise to wait until the teen years, or even until age five or six, to discuss identity with your child. Talking about your infant or toddler's names, assuming he has an old one and a new one, is one of the best ways to start the discussion. Mention explicitly that you know someone else used to care for your child. Such talk about identity begins to build a bridge to connect the two of you. Ignoring early identity issues is equivalent to leaving a chasm between you and your child. Adult adoptees refer to this original and unbridged chasm when they talk about what their adoptive parents never understood.

Connection is everything that keeps a parent and child interacting in positive ways and that makes the child want to "come back for more." When a child comes to an adoptive home with a stress-shaped "wild colt" brain, he must be taught to connect, consciously and continuously, by a persistent parent. Connection begins with you teaching your child to stay close to you, as opposed to following strangers, and teaching him to look at your facial expressions to learn what is going on in new situations. Connection includes teaching your child to ask you for help and to get your attention appropriately, and to distinguish among parents, friends, and strangers. Connection is when you and your child learn to have fun playing interactively, in order to release vital hormones (discussed later in this chapter) that are known to reinforce both feelings of closeness and a child's emotional resiliency. In fact, connection with a parent provides and nurtures resiliency in a child.

Resiliency is the ability to bounce back from a stressful situation, without getting stuck in stress-based reactivity and the fight-or-flight response. Resiliency is needed to manage or control strong feelings—hunger, fatigue, excitement, joy, anger, and grief. Resiliency includes behavioral and emotional self-control. It helps a child to calm down after a fall, to wait patiently when hungry or tired, and to handle separation.

Resiliency in the "child next door" is the result of the child having been well protected and well supported by a parent. Resiliency in a child adopted from overseas is that and more. Beyond providing support and care, parents of an internationally adopted child must teach the child's brain to override its automatic stress responses. The child must learn how to use the most advanced, conscious part of his brain, where rational choice and the conscious ability to self-soothe reside. In short, parents must help create and activate the "brain supervisor"—the part of the brain that uses conscious choice and reason—which can soothe the overreactive, negative, fight-or-flight "workers."

BRAIN DEVELOPMENT AND
THE INTERNATIONAL ADOPTEE

What we know about how the stress-shaped brain operates comes from many studies of neglected, abused, or traumatized children. This research has demonstrated that cortisol, a hormone that calms the stress response, is significantly lower in such children. Thus these children have difficulty calming or remaining calm under even minimally stressful conditions. To expand on this line of investigation a group of researchers recently looked at internationally adopted children. In 2005 Seth Pollak and his colleagues published important work that examined adopted children from Romania, all of whom had been with their U.S. families for three or more years, and compared the levels of soothing chemicals emitted by the children's brains to the levels in non-adopted children.

Pollak showed that even after three years with their adoptive families, the Romanian children had significantly lower levels of oxytocin and vasopressin than their non-adopted peers. These hormones are critical to a person's ability to form emotional connections with others and to recognize familiar people. When a baby is born, the mother and child have high levels of oxytocin in their systems, leading to a deep sense of connection. Touch and physical play between parent and child release more oxytocin. In the adoptees in Pollak's study, however, touch and play with a parent released less of these connection chemicals— the children were experiencing less connective "bang" for their "buck" of play. Pollak's research demonstrates why parents of internationally adopted children have to work harder and play longer than their neighbors with non-adopted children to get a happy, connected response from their children.

Other researchers have shown that high levels of oxytocin and vasopressin help to "inoculate" a child against stress and emotional and physical pain. Higher levels of these chemicals enable a child to soothe and calm rapidly. We see this when a mother picks up a crying child and her touch and voice seem to calm her. What we do not see is the mechanism by which this interaction works: the release of hormones, triggered by the physical and emotional connection of the two, that act like a shot of morphine to the child's pain. When a mother picks up a crying child and the child fails to soothe, the child is not getting the "feel-good" hormone release. This shortage of soothing hormones makes managing behavior and emotions more difficult. If a child cannot calm down, she is more likely to fuss, cry, scream, or throw tantrums, and for longer periods of time.

In sum, stress changes the brain in two ways. First, the stress-shaped brain puts out abnormal levels of cortisol, which allows the reactive fight-or-flight response to continue unchecked. Second, children subjected to repeated stress, such as those adopted from overseas, fail to respond with the same level of "connection" chemicals as their nonstressed peers. As a consequence, an adopted child often feels that a parent "isn't doing enough to help me," which in turn confirms the child's belief that the world is a negative, unsafe place. All this can happen even when that child is in the arms of an actively soothing, devoted parent.

GUIDANCE ON PARENTING STRATEGIES

Once you know what you are up against (a very frightened brain!), you need to know how to counteract, subvert, and derail this powerful stress response in your child while boosting the effects of your soothing efforts. Researchers have identified some powerful means by which you can respond to this challenge.

According to Alicia F. Lieberman and her colleagues, in their book *Losing a Parent to Death in the Early Years*, a child is never "too young" to remember losing a primary caregiver who represented the world and safety when he was an infant, baby, or toddler. Even living birth parents have nonetheless essentially died in the adopted child's mind. The same may be said of other caregivers the child had in his earliest years.

Lieberman and her colleagues demonstrate that the best way to establish an integrated identity is to tell the child's story *with* the child, incorporating his perspective, feelings, and perceptions. Identity repair begins when a parent answers the child's question "What happened to me?" Lieberman's research demonstrates that a child's posttraumatic stress symptoms, including explosive and uncontrolled emotions, are significantly reduced when he hears the parent tell the story of the traumatic events, specifically acknowledging the child's feelings and perceptions about them.

Posttraumatic stress is a fancy clinical term that refers to a loss of resiliency and of behavioral and emotional control. It includes a numbing of feelings and an injured or shattered sense of temporal continuity and personal identity. In young children posttraumatic stress often looks like hyperactivity, accompanied by exaggerated startle responses, or like a propensity to "deer in the headlights" expressions and responses. Here is how this syndrome appears in my office:

A child's posttraumatic stress symptoms are significantly reduced when he hears the parent tell the story of the traumatic events, specifically acknowledging the child's feelings and perceptions.

A mother and her child come to see me, and the mother reports, "I think my child must be hyperactive! He never stops unless it's to have a tantrum." After hearing the mother's story of the adoption, I begin telling the child's story to the mom, using dolls to act out the events. Within moments the child has slowed down and has come over to watch the "play." If he is old enough, he begins to contribute information about what happened. Frequently the child picks up the doll that represents himself and throws it away in the trash can or "loses" it under the bookshelf. Only through play can the child express how alone, lost, and worthless he feels.

When parents see this behavior they begin to understand that identity is in need of repair from the start, beginning with answers to the most basic questions—"Who am I?" "Who are you?" "What happened to me?" Constructing identity and telling the child's own story are the keys to building both connection and resiliency.

Identity changes and takes on new meanings as a child matures. In *Beneath the Mask: Understanding Adopted Teens*, Debbie Riley, who has extensive clinical experience with teens who were adopted, maps out some of the unique challenges teens face in understanding and establishing their own identities. Whereas young children work on their life story from the past to the present, older children look to the future and begin to incorporate race and ethnic concerns into their identity work. This

Answering questions of identity and telling the child's own story are the keys to building both connection and resiliency.

added layer makes it necessary for older children to rethink their connections to their adoptive parents and to their birth family and birth country. Issues of family loyalty and questions about the permanence of family emerge. The normal developmental focus on identity in the teen and young adult years is more intense and more complex for international adoptees, often leading to extreme emotions and actions. Once again, parental support and assistance are necessary to help a teen's "brain supervisor" consciously choose "high road" behaviors over stress responses.

Talking openly and regularly about a child's past, present, and future recruits the brain supervisor to build an integrated sense of identity and maintain connection between parent and child. Simply telling "the adoption story" a few times is not enough. Your child needs your help to connect the adoption story to his own reactive behavior. As you read this book you will learn how to incorporate your child's pre-adoption and adoption story into his understanding of identity and into the resiliency that results from that understanding.

Pollak, Lieberman, and Riley help us to know what to expect of, and how to respond to, a child with a stress-shaped brain. Stress-shaped brains work on an unconscious, reactive level. I call the way a child with a stress-shaped brain sees the world, as if through a pair of stress-colored glasses, *trauma vision*. The antidote to trauma vision comes from a parent's more mature brain, with its conscious understanding of what is happening to the child. Telling your child's story, relating your child's behavior to real past events, and offering support and soothing are all part of reducing posttraumatic stress behaviors and helping your child remove his trauma-vision glasses.

For example, when Soon An withdraws and rejects her mother by sleeping, or at an older age shouts, "You're not my mother!" Charlotte can understand that Soon An is seeing the world through her own traumatic, if unconscious, experience. Charlotte can use her more mature, nonreactive brain power to articulate this: "I know you are trying to sleep [are shouting that I'm not your mother] because of what happened to you when you were taken away from your foster mother." As Lieberman and Riley explain, when a parent recognizes the child's experience and verbalizes it to the child, the child is able to see beyond trauma vision and stress-based reactive behavior. "You don't know how I feel," Soon An shoots back, and her mother responds soothingly, "Why don't you tell me?" Talking about rather than acting out feelings is the primary way children gain control of themselves. These lines of research are powerful because they demonstrate that there is hope for children with stress-shaped brains.

STRESS-SHAPED BRAINS REACT
NEGATIVELY TO NURTURING CARE

The more parents understand about the stress-shaped brain and reactive behavior, the more they can help change their child's trauma vision. Mary Dozier and her colleagues provide valuable insights into how stress-shaped behavior pushes away the very person a child needs most. Dozier's research with foster children and their parents has defined three areas of connection that are consistently disrupted. First, foster children fail to behave in ways that elicit nurturance from caregivers or parents. A hungry, cold, or hurt child does not call a parent or ask for help. A child may even reject the caregiver most intensely when she is most needy. Second, when a foster child provides little or no positive response to an act of nurturing, parents or caregivers begin to feel uncomfortable providing more nurturing. Third, foster children have significant and ongoing difficulties regulating their response to stress. This means that a child who has tantrums or shuts down in rapid response to even small stressors puts up a wall of negative behavior that makes it much more difficult for a caregiver to attend to her inner needs. As an adoptive parent you need to anticipate these negative responses and understand what lies behind them. Once you do so, you are on the way to being able to change them.

Dozier designed a ten-session intervention for parents that significantly improves all three problem areas. Parents learn to recognize a child's negative behavior as the result of past failed relationships with caregivers and not to take the child's behavior personally. Parents learn to read a child's indirect cues regarding needs and to respond quickly to them. Parents learn that this rapid response is not spoiling the child but enabling her to experience care as contingent on her inner need, not her angry behavior. Finally, parents learn to recognize their own needs or feelings that interfere with their nurturing behavior. I have incorporated the specific elements of Dozier's intervention into several of the chapters later in this book; they are techniques that all parents of internationally adopted children can and should use.

LEARNING TO BE ATTUNED, EVEN WHEN YOUR CHILD IS NEGATIVE OR WITHDRAWN

Parents frequently assume that if they feel connected to their child, the child feels connected in return. This is not a safe assumption, especially with internationally adopted children. Connection may break down in the first hours, days, and months after a child is adopted, and the breakdown may continue for years. One day in the preteen or teen years, and seemingly out of the blue, the child explodes. "I hate you," he says. "You're not my real mother. I don't have to listen to you." If we look carefully, we see that the signs of disconnection have been there for years.

Let us look at an example from the First Year Home Group. Sonia's father, David, assumed that his thirteen-month-old daughter was "attached" or connected to him because she clung to him when meeting strangers. Dad felt connected to his daughter and assumed that her feelings mirrored his. In fact, Sonia clung to David because she was fearful that she might be given away to another stranger. David happened to be slightly more familiar than strangers, in part because he was Latino and spoke Spanish. But that did not make him her parent in Sonia's eyes.

We can think of this relationship as a mismatched duet. Dad is singing a song, "She Loves Me, Yeah, Yeah, Yeah," his own version of the Beatles' song. Sonia is singing the old Negro spiritual "I'm Going Down the Road Feeling Bad." Research on parent-infant relationships tells us that the only way to get the duo together, as it were, is for the parent to understand what it is like to sing the child's song. When a parent expresses this understanding, or sings the child's song back to him, the child realizes that the parent knows how he feels. This process is called *attunement.*

Early research on attunement studied eye contact, and the mirroring of body movements and voice tone, between parent and child. More recently researchers have looked at neurons and neurotransmitters in the brains of parents and children as they interact, and at their hormonal activity as well. We now know how attunement happens on a biochemical level and what chemical "cocktail" keeps a child "coming back for more" to a parent. When attunement occurs, special connection hormones and chemicals are released, including oxytocin, vasopressin, and dopamine. Touch and eye contact are also vital to attunement. Having a child's left eye and a parent's left eye connect is a way that two right brains can "talk" together through eye contact. (Remember that each side of the brain controls the opposite side of the body.) Why is right-brain conversation so important? Because the right side of the brain controls emotions and behavior; it is the side that gives us resiliency. It is no surprise, then, that nursing mothers tend to hold babies on the left side, putting the two right brains in conversation through the left-eye connection. The skills of attunement are disrupted when a child has multiple caregivers, either simultaneously (as in an orphanage) or sequentially (as with a child who spends a few months with his birth mother, several months in foster care, and then is adopted). As you read this book, you will see that many of the parenting strategies I recommend are based on building attunement— simply put, getting your brain talking to your child's brain.

HOW LONG DOES IT TAKE TO CHANGE A BRAIN?

Some parents wonder, "Can you really change a child's brain?" The answer is yes and no. Brains are not erasable. That is not a change parents can make. But parents can build new pathways that compete with and override the old reactive responses to stress. How long does such a process take? One answer comes from the work of a Dutch researcher, Frank Verhulst.

In 2005 Verhulst and his collaborators completed a study that tracked more than two thousand international adoptees, matched with nearly one thousand non-adopted children from the general population. The study followed most of these children for about sixteen years, until they were in their late teens or early twenties. The study revealed that internationally adopted children struggled with "externalizing behavior" more than their non-adopted peers. Externalizing behavior is what teachers call "not using your words." It includes yelling, crying, having tantrums, throwing things, and generally acting out rather than talking about feelings or needs. The non-adopted children in the study engaged in externalizing behavior, too, of course, but by five or six years of age it was reined in by self-control and replaced by verbal interaction. Many adopted children did not reach this benchmark until the later teen years or early adulthood. In short, it took the internationally adopted children four times longer on average to develop the same level of behavioral and emotional self-control as their non-adopted peers.

Surprisingly, this slower development of resilient and well-controlled behavior was not correlated to age at adoption or to the type of pre-adoption experience. The startling conclusion was that the children who did best had adoptive families with a moderate, rather than high, socioeconomic status (SES). The researchers concluded that families with higher status (extensive education, high-prestige jobs, and high income) had higher expectations for their children and consequently put more pressure on them to achieve. Children from moderate SES families did better in school from early on and were less likely to engage in substance abuse. Thus for internationally adopted children with a lot on their developmental plate, lower parental expectations and less stressful lifestyles paid off in greater resiliency.

Slower development of resilient and well-controlled behavior was not related to age at adoption or to pre-adoption experiences but to the socioeconomic level of the adoptive parents.

If we look at the parents in the Verhulst study who had more moderate expectations of their children, we can hypothesize that the energy and time they were able to put into connecting with their children, rather than devoting themselves to demanding, high-status jobs, resulted in their children developing a connection and resiliency more quickly. High academic and social expectations for internationally adopted children may stand in the way of those children achieving resiliency, and this is true regardless of the child's actual intelligence. Intelligence cannot flourish without emotional stability. Parents need to incorporate this reality into their expectations, both for themselves as parents and for their child.

AGE-APPROPRIATE STRATEGIES
VERSUS STARTING AT THE BEGINNING

What does all this tell us? We now know that connection, identity, and resiliency are disrupted and made more complex for internationally adopted children. We also know that when parents understand the situation, teach specific strategies, and offer extra support for a longer time, and when they maintain reasonable expectations for success, their children can develop successfully.

Every child must learn to walk before she can run. If you expect your child to run right away, your expectations are too high and you are setting you and your child up for disappointment. Verhulst's research provides ample warnings about this—you may actually slow down the pace of development by expecting too much too soon. My advice is simple: Avoid using an ages-and-stages schedule (or comparing your child with the child next door of the same age) to guide and evaluate your child's progress.

TWO STEPS FORWARD, TEN STEPS BACK

One of the realities of development in real children (as opposed to those idealized in some books and magazine articles) is that they have setbacks. When a child is tired, ill, or stressed he reverts to younger behavior. This can also happen just as a child enters a new developmental stage, such as walking, reading, entering a new grade at school, and the like. More important, for a child with a stress-shaped brain even seemingly small and ordinary events can trigger stress responses that negate previously mastered positive behaviors and bring back disruptive fight-or-flight reactions. When this happens, you must actively help your child rebuild his capacity for rational, controlled responses rather than expect him to recover on his own.

A new developmental stage almost always triggers a setback in behavior.

At stressful or transitional times an internationally adopted child may do more than revert to younger behavior. He may fall apart completely. Some parents describe how their child of six, seven, or even the early teen years suddenly wants to be fed, carried, and tended to like a baby. What is going on here?

When internationally adopted children have difficulty with resiliency, they frequently and extensively revert to younger behavior. Sometimes this reverted behavior is connected with the age at which the child experienced trauma (such as separation from birth or foster parent, or even the adoption itself). Instead of taking one or two steps back, your child may fall back ten steps. This may happen several times in a single day! We know that such extreme reversions are the result of a stress-shaped brain. In fact, a whole range of behaviors, from extra-mature to babyish, is typical of internationally adopted children who have experienced loss and trauma. With help, these children can ultimately gain control and learn to avoid extreme regression. But "with help" is the key; your child cannot do this alone.

WHAT KIND OF HELP DOES MY CHILD NEED?

Let us return briefly to the wild-colt metaphor. It is well known that harsh, punitive training results in a colt with a broken spirit that reveals itself in sneaky, mean, or skittish behaviors. In a similar way, harsh parenting of a child with a lot of built-in stress responses produces a child with abundant negative (and often angry) energy, which is returned to the parent tenfold.

A child who has a negative, untrusting view of the world and an automatic, highly reactive response to parenting can learn and grow only if she is willing. Finding the way to connect and to gain your child's willingness to override the stress response is the first and most important adoptive parenting strategy. As Mary Dozier has pointed out, parents have to read the real needs behind a child's negative, off-putting behavior. First you need to understand your child's reactive coping behaviors. Sometimes a child reacts to a "reasonable" consequence as if it were abuse. Telling the child to "snap out of it" retriggers the stress response, making it even less likely she will respond as you wish.

By becoming attuned to your child's fearful, negative feelings, you can begin to connect with her. When a parent understands that a child is afraid that she will be "given away again" and speaks to that fear, the child learns about identity and connection. Once the child recognizes that the parent is on her side, which includes helping with control of overwhelming emo-

Children need our help most when they are at their worst.

tions, she becomes a partner in learning. But this recognition must be earned daily, if not more often. Once parents understand a child's true feelings, they can begin working on the foundation stones of development, beginning with identity and the child's life story.

Identity and Your Child's Complex Background

MAKING A LIST OF WHAT YOUR CHILD has experienced, from birth or even from conception forward, is an excellent way to begin to understand his identity issues. True, most adoptive parents have only a few pieces of information about their child's past. Some parents have conflicting information. Do your best to create a coherent time line, beginning as early as possible in your child's history.

If you find yourself angry, puzzled, frustrated, sad, and ultimately defeated by even the thought of this task, you are not alone. In fact you have just joined with your child in understanding how it feels to be internationally adopted. How can a child answer the question "Who am I?" if these are the feelings he has when contemplating the past? Only with your help can your child construct a secure and positive sense of self.

In order for your child to construct a positive identity, he must be able to tell his own story. You will model how to do this, using the information you have or are able to gather. As Dr. Spock said in the opening line of *Baby and Child Care*, "You know more than you think you do." This chapter will help you collect and organize what you know about your child's life before adoption. The first thing to note is how many and what kinds of changes your child has experienced. For example, Soon An was adopted from Korea at six months of age. She had more than one change of parents and of other caregivers. First she was with her birth mother; then there may have been a period with one or more unknown caregivers at the police station or orphanage before she settled with her foster mother;

next the escort on the plane cared for her; and finally she had her adoptive parents, Charlotte and Joe. Although Soon An had one of the simpler and shorter pre-adoption histories, she had *four* changes of caregivers.

A child with a complex background has experienced many changes. Such a child expects change; it is the norm. As Yi Sheng, adopted at four and a half years of age, explained when he was nine years old, "*Anything* can happen in life. It did happen—to me."

In the chart below you will find a list of some of the kinds of changes that internationally adopted children have experienced. You may want to add others. Take a moment to circle all the ones that apply to your child. Then go back over the list and indicate how often a given change happened.

A COMPLEX BACKGROUND CHECK

Type of Change	Number of Changes
Change of caregivers	_____
Change of parents: birth, foster, adoptive	_____
Change of living place	_____
Change of daily routines	_____
Change of country and culture	_____
Change of diet and nutrition	_____
Change of access to health care and education	_____
Change of language	_____

It helps to write down the key changes in your child's life and your child's age (or your best guess of his age) at the time of the change. Now that you have tallied up the major changes in your child's life, the next chart will help you draw a more complete portrait of your child's background.

MY CHILD'S COMPLEX BACKGROUND

Current name: _____

Previous name(s): _____

Age in earliest photograph or video: _____

Present chronological age: _____

Family age (length of time with present family): _____

Age at birth: _____ preemie   _____ full-term   _____ unknown

Location of birth: _____ home   _____ hospital   _____ unknown

Age at separation from birth mother: _____

Second caregiver's name and location: _____

Age at separation from second caregiver(s): _____

Third caregiver's name and location: _____

Age at separation from third caregiver(s): _____

Fourth caregiver's name and location: _____

Age at separation from fourth caregiver(s): _____

Continue listing information through the child's adoptive parent(s).

_____

_____

Languages or dialects child's caregivers used: _____

Illnesses, injuries, scars, birth defects, disabilities, abuse information:

_____

_____

THE SOCIAL ASPECTS OF IDENTITY

Keeping your child's complex background in mind can be difficult, especially when people around you are unaware of all she has experienced. A father I know came up with the idea of posting a list of "reality statements" on the refrigerator to educate relatives, friends, and guests. "After all, our child's identity is not just what we know, or what our child knows about himself, but how others see him," he commented. The box below lists a variety of reality statements, which you can tailor to your own child's experiences.

REALITY STATEMENTS ABOUT MY CHILD'S IDENTITY AND BACKGROUND

1. My child lived nine months (or less) in utero with her birth mother and possibly longer with her birth family. My child heard her birth mother's voice every day during that time.
2. My child's birth parent(s) or grandparents decided to separate her from the birth family permanently, or the birth country had reasons to separate parent and child. (Assume that this is true, unless you have evidence to the contrary.)
3. My child has lived in different residences: hospital, orphanage, foster family, or even a previous adoptive family. (Choose the appropriate ones from the list.)
4. My child experienced an abrupt transition to each new residence and a sudden immersion in a new environment with new caregivers. Changes included food, clothing, daily routines, and child-care methods.
5. Because of these experiences, my child has learned to expect change, loss, and discontinuity, and these experiences are reflected in her behavior.
6. My child is having an involuntary "immersion experience" with the English language and with the culture of my family.

INCORRECT, MISSING, OR CONFUSING INFORMATION

There is no country so poor or illiterate that it cannot keep accurate records, assuming officials want to do so. Typically, when a child is available for adoption, a photo is taken and a file opened. The age of your child in the youngest referral photo should match the age when he was first available for adoption. A discrepancy suggests that a parent is not receiving the full story. Gaps or discrepancies in record-keeping are not uncommon, and they suggest that a child's true experience is being hidden from someone. That someone may be you, the adopting parent.

There are three basic reasons to hide the truth about a child's background. First, the majority of adoptive parents from the United States must swear to immigration officials that the child is a "true" orphan, with no living parents, in order to obtain a visa to bring the child home. If adoptive parents know that the birth parents are alive, they could not honestly comply with the U.S. visa requirements.

Second, the child's birth parents may be involved in "placing" their child for adoption. Some parents leave their infant in a conspicuous location to be found and placed in an orphanage; others in the community may know this, making the "abandonment" an open secret. Parents with power or connections to arrange things through back-door methods may actually keep a young child at home until just before the adoption occurs. In either case the birth parents are alive. Records may say that the child has been in foster care or has gone home with an orphanage worker at night. Some orphanage workers have been known to place their own children for adoption abroad. Again, adoptive parents are kept in the dark in order that they can swear that the child is truly an orphan.

Third, the child's true background may be hidden because the child was part of illegal trafficking in women and children. One adoptive mother told me that while she was at the orphanage picking up her child, she overhead the agency facilitator talking to orphanage officials. The officials openly stated that the "babies are brought in and the orphanage gives the delivery person two or three hundred dollars [or the equivalent in the country's own currency]." When the facilitator asked how many children lived at the orphanage and were not adopted, the orphanage official replied that *all* the children were adopted; only the physically handicapped ones remained in the orphanage. Undoubtedly this "orphanage" had become part of a child-trafficking operation. The Hague Convention on Intercountry Adoption is an attempt to control this problem.

I bring up such unsavory information here because I have found that nearly every internationally adopted child fears that he was kidnapped, sold by someone (possibly birth parents), and purchased by adoptive parents. Every internationally adopted child is riveted by the large amount of money that changes hands in order for him to be brought to a new home. Of course there are many explanations that make sense to adults, but it takes a child many years to reach that level of understanding. Meanwhile, the child's sense of identity is linked to these grim realities.

TELL THE STORY DESPITE YOUR FEARS

Before a child can make sense of these facts and suppositions, the parents themselves must do so. Fears, suspicions, or outright knowledge of illegal dealings are important to uncover and discuss. Parents who harbor these feelings find that they interfere with their own comfort in forming a relationship with their child. Parents often tell me that they dread the day, albeit years in the future, when their child will ask, "How did you get me?" These parents struggle to tell the child the adoption story, and in turn the child senses from the beginning that something is wrong. The parents' fears and suspicions contaminate the child's earliest sense of identity.

If as an adopting parent you find yourself overwhelmed with fears and suspicions about your child's past, get help from a counselor or adoption professional to unravel and come to terms with your concerns. By doing this you can also create ways to talk to your child that include age-appropriate comments or explanations that prevent you from having to keep a secret. Mu Ling's mother Meg told me that the orphanage caregiver had explained that Mu Ling always played with a six-year-old boy at the orphanage. Meg was even introduced to the boy, the son of the orphanage bookkeeper. The incident disturbed Meg and she later shared her concern with me. We agreed that it was odd for a six-year-old boy to play with a specific girl orphan, especially one who was more than four years younger than he was. Could the reason be, we wondered, that the bookkeeper was the mother of both children but had chosen to keep her son? When we came to this conclusion, Meg relaxed. "This makes sense," she admitted. "The orphanage wanted me to know but couldn't tell me directly."

You may find it difficult to communicate this type of information to your child; however, it is important that you do so. Otherwise it becomes a family secret, ultimately destructive because, like other family secrets, it will undermine the child's trust in you. Mu Ling's adoptive mother had photographs of Mu Ling and the boy with whom she played, showing the birth mother in the background. Meg decided to tell her daughter, "We think this is your mother. If it is, we know that she used her connection at the orphanage to give you what *she thought* would be a better life for you." As Mu Ling grew up, she was alternately angry with her birth mother for relinquishing her and keeping her brother, yet happy to have a photo of her first family. Meg emphasized how educated Mu Ling's birth mother was, capable of working as a bookkeeper and smart enough to find a good family for her daughter. Using this small piece of information, the little girl was able to construct a positive identity for herself, relating her own talent in math to her birth mother's skills.

Whereas many people might feel that Meg confabulated the story, there is sufficient evidence to make it a genuine possibility, and it validates some of Mu Ling's earliest memories. It is important to understand, however, that if a child has no information about a birth parent, he will construct or confabulate information on his own. Having no information about one's past is like trying to imagine the endpoint of an infinite universe. One tries and tries, but it is literally mind-boggling. This is where many children get stuck. They cannot mourn the loss of a completely unknown parent, yet without mourning they cannot move on with their own lives.

A complex background includes many losses and other experiences that shape a child's future identity. The more you are aware of your child's complex background, and the more openly you communicate your awareness to the child, the more he will benefit.

Connection, Survival Skills, and Family Skills

A CHILD DEVELOPS *survival skills* in response to neglect or deprivation, which most internationally adopted children have experienced to some degree. Deprivation is a lack of the physical necessities of life: food, warmth, and shelter. Neglect is the lack of consistent, nurturing attention from, and social interaction with, an adult. A child acquires survival skills in order to make the best of a poor situation.

A child develops *family skills* when she has a nurturing and consistently available caregiver or parent. Family skills as a rule grow gradually, but survival skills must develop rapidly or a child will die or acquire an environmentally induced form of autism, sometimes called institutional autism.

Family skills are based on connections between a child and an adult, usually a parent. A child using family skills assumes that Mom or Dad is there to help, to nurture, and to understand and explain the world. There is a sense of interdependency. A child using family skills communicates, cooperates, and shares.

Survival skills are based on what a child can manage to do alone. A child using survival skills expects neglect, expects to be independent, and assumes control of what is happening. Connections are important only for the purpose of acquiring basic necessities or temporary nurturance. Children using survival skills are often manipulative.

> **Family skills are group-centered and based on cooperation and communication. Survival skills are self-centered and based on manipulation with little communication.**

This summary suggests how family and survival skills differ in terms of connection. Let us look at how they differ in terms of identity. Family skills involve being a member of a group, even if the group is just a two-person unit. A child has an identity and a role as the dependent child, and she knows that a parent has the identity of a special caregiver. The child who relies on survival skills, on the other hand, has the identity or role of the boss who takes care of everything. Yet this boss-like identity is not built on strength, knowledge, and capability, for a child is essentially weak. Instead, it is an identity that forces the child to create a semblance of those traits, a false maturity. Because the child is really not fully mature, she must rely on manipulation, charm, or even threats and hostility to survive. This pseudomature identity may fool some adults, including parents, into thinking that the child is secure and competent. In fact such a child feels lost, alone, weak, and afraid, as well as fraudulent.

FOCUS ON YOUR CHILD'S STRENGTHS

If you think that survival skills such as these sound like a description of how a "poorly attached" child behaves, you are correct. But the concept of poor attachment is quite different from the concept of survival skills. Poor attachment assumes that the child failed to do something—attach—or did it poorly. Survival skills focus on the child's strengths and what he has done well.

> *Poor attachment* **assumes that the child has failed to attach; the term** *survival skills* **shifts the focus to what the child has been able to do: survive.**

In the absence of consistent nurturing, a child's survival skills begin to develop right after birth. Every infant starts with the ability to cry, to move about, to eliminate, to sleep, and to suck. These abilities can become survival skills if they are unmediated by nurturing interactions with an adult. Children who develop survival skills become tough, smart, strong, and persistent, starting at just a few months of age. They may express emotions in peculiar ways, such as an overly wide grimace for a smile or a growl to show anger. Nonetheless, they deserve recognition and honor for what they have managed to do under challenging circumstances.

CONNECT BEFORE EXPECTING CHANGE

Children who have come to depend on survival skills need direct instruction in how to live in a family and how to acquire the family skills of communication, cooperation, and sharing. If parents begin this education by acknowledging the child's survival skills and their origins, the child will be more willing to learn the new family behaviors.

Denise, for example, struggled with Demetri, her orphanage-raised child of nearly two years of age, who insisted on grabbing food and running away from the table at meals. By acknowledging to him that his grabbing and hoarding had been a "very good way to survive in the orphanage," Denise got Demetri's attention. Demetri was clearly attracted to his mother's understanding of his past life. Feeling understood at last, he became more willing to listen to her explain the rules of family eating. Denise created a "lesson" in family eating, separate from mealtime. When dinner rolled around, she gave Demetri a chance to practice his new skills.

FAMILY SKILLS AND FAMILY AGE

Learning family skills is a three-part process for your internationally adopted child. First, your child must learn to believe that you are there to offer nurturance and support and are a partner in this life-game. Second, your child must learn to stop using survival skills. Stopping is hard because it requires a great degree of self-control, something internationally adopted children tend to lack. Third, your child must learn new family skills by mirroring the behavior that you model. Non-adopted children have the luxury of beginning directly with the third step. Internationally adopted children have two extra steps, which means both parents and children must devote more time and energy to learning these skills.

Non-adopted children often acquire family skills at specific and predictable ages. This ages-and-stages model makes little or no sense for the child who must set aside survival skills and learn family skills. In this situation many parents find it helpful to use the concept of *family age*, the length of time the child has been a member of the family.

For example, Soon An had to begin her relationship with her new mother and begin learning family skills when she was six months old. By the time she was eight months old chronologically, she had been with her adoptive parents for two months, and so her family age was two months. Soon An did not communicate her hunger to her parents as a typical eight-month-old would, with gradually escalating fussiness followed by calm when she saw Mom getting a bottle or a bowl of cereal. Instead, Soon An went rapidly from silence to screaming, much as would an infant who has not yet figured out the family routine.

Soon An was behaving according to her family age, not her chronological age.

Using the concept of family age puts the task of learning family skills in a new perspective. Most parents rely on this concept during the first year or two after adoption. For a child adopted at one year or more of chronological age, family age is relevant even longer, as with Yi Sheng. His family age and chronological age had the greatest disparity among the children in our First Year Home Group. Yi Sheng was adopted when he was four and a half years old. He began kindergarten when he was six years old, just eighteen months later. His chronological age was appropriate for beginning kindergarten, but his family age was just eighteen months. Yi Sheng had developed family skills equivalent to those of at least an eighteen-month-old child and because he was bright, possibly at a three-year-old level. But we would not expect a child of three to be emotionally and socially ready for kindergarten. Yi Sheng was intelligent and eager to learn, and his parents hoped that his family age would not impact his academic ability. In the area of social and emotional development, however, they realized he would require extra support.

MIXED MATURITIES

In children with a complex background, chronological age and family age diverge, and these children exhibit what we may call *mixed maturities*. A child with mixed maturities bounces among a range of developmental stages, seeming like a five-year-old at one moment and a two-year-old the next. This condition is extremely common among internationally adopted children.

Mixed maturities go along with a lack of resiliency. When a non-adopted child faces a setback, or is tired or hungry or ill, she regresses, but only to a certain point and usually not entirely back to infantile behaviors. For example, a tired two-year-old may want to be carried instead of walking. But when an internationally adopted child meets with a setback, or is even mildly overstimulated, the regression is often profound. The two-year-old reverts to arching and screaming and loses all ability to respond to her parent's soothing.

Children with mixed maturities regress to immature behavior more frequently and more completely. As we have seen (see chapter 2), such children are slower to gain emotional and behavioral control. Understanding this characteristic of development helps parents feel less helpless and more confident that their child's behavior is within a normal range, despite the fact that extra support for emotional containment is still needed.

CHOOSING PARENTING STRATEGIES
APPROPRIATE TO FAMILY AGE

Use family age, not chronological age, to select parenting strategies that match your child's behaviors. Although this often means that you seem to be babying your child, since the behaviors are likely to be typical of a younger chronological age, your responses will help your child recover more rapidly and return to his former level of competence. For example, if eight-month-old Soon An collapses in a fit of screams for food, her mother can remind herself that Soon An's family age is just two months, and this is how two-month-old children behave. Two-month-old babies need to be picked up quickly and soothed with touch and voice, which is what Soon An needs, despite her chronological age. Mothers anticipate the needs of two-month-olds, rather than looking for facial expressions or gestures that communicate hunger, cold, or fatigue. Expecting Soon An to respond to a call across the room of "I'm coming!" would frustrate both mother and child. You will hasten the development of family skills by responding to your child based on family age rather than chronological age.

GETTING ADULT ATTENTION: LEARNING TO HOLD HANDS

All children need to obtain adult attention in order to get the basic necessities of life. Here are some examples of how parents from the First Year Home Group described their child's use of survival skills to capture the attention of adults:

> "I see Mu Ling, at two and a half years old, working to get adult attention when she performs her little dances or gives everyone an extra-wide grin."

> "Demetri is only eighteen months old, but he works the room like an experienced politician, engaging each adult with his dimpled smile. If his goal is to get attention, I think he's incredibly successful."

> "Although Yi Sheng is nearly five years old and seems to understand we are his family, there are times when he walks over to an another family, especially an Asian family with lots of kids, and just stands there, as if he expects to be part of their group. He'll take the hand of a stranger or sit on anyone's lap if it's available."

A child who has been neglected turns to any adult to get attention and care. Such behavior is often called *indiscriminate friendliness*. We now know from research that much of this behavior is the result of a chronically low level of the hormone oxytocin, a socializing biochemical. Typically, the more independent a child is allowed to be publicly, the clingier that child is at home. Some children, however, including many international adoptees, are independent in both locations, treating their parents as interchangeable with other adults.

Parents need to boost their child's oxytocin as much as possible with touch and joyful play. Allowing a child to interact with lots of other adults only reinforces survival skill behavior. When parents see their child seeking attention indiscriminately, they need to intervene quickly, firmly, and kindly. Because this is a survival skill, the child should be informed and educated about her behavior, but not chastised.

For example, Yi Sheng's father needed to be on the lookout for Yi Sheng's wandering when the family was out in public, perhaps noting his son's turning away from the family group as a first step toward wandering off. "Hey, Yi Sheng, I was beginning to miss you!" he could say, taking his son's hand or even picking him up and giving him a hug, using physical connection to release oxytocin. "Let's hold hands while we walk; that's what a father and son do."

Holding hands can be a great way to help a child practice getting adult attention. A useful game called Squeeze Hands goes like this: Walk along holding hands with your child, looking forward. When your child gently squeezes your hand, look at each other, make eye contact, and smile. Then continue walking. Children like this game so much that parents eventually need to set limits, so that the squeezes happen only two or three times in a single block, or in a walk around the house. If your child squeezes too hard, runs away, or engages in other negative behaviors that avoid connection, see chapter 9.

WHINING, TUGGING ON MOM'S LEG, AND OTHER FAMILY SKILLS

The two basic "get attention" skills of young children are tugging at a parent's clothing and whining. I encourage you to teach your child to whine. Whining is one of the earliest ways that an infant or young child communicates, and he knows that he can depend on a parent to respond to it. Other ways to develop connection and pay-attention-to-me skills include encouraging a child to move close to or lean on a parent and to call a parent ("Mama," "Dada") for help. Many parents worry that these methods will teach a child to use "baby" skills rather than age-appropriate behaviors, or that such behaviors

A child reverts to survival skills because he feels he cannot truly depend on the parent to be available.

as whining will turn into bad habits, but it is worth recalling the importance of establishing the most primary forms of connection with an adopted child and of gearing parenting to the child's family age.

A child reverts to survival skills because he feels he cannot truly depend on the parent to be available. Using, or reverting to, survival behaviors is an indication that the child is at that moment feeling alone in the world, and that the belief in his parent's care has vanished. A critical process for connecting with your adopted child is first to recognize explicitly his feelings of aloneness, and then to acknowledge that you are really there and paying attention to his needs, even if he feels you are not and even if you are engaged in other activities. Parenting behavior must reinforce trust from your child's perspective.

CONNECTION WITH NONHUMAN STRUCTURES FOR SURVIVAL

Sometimes children develop survival skills that are shaped by routines or structures in their environment. Goldie was a premature baby who spent her entire pre-adoption life in a hospital and an orphanage. When she was adopted at six months of age, her mother noticed that she played with toys only while lying on her left side. She tucked her left arm underneath herself and handled objects with her free right hand. If Mom sat Goldie up and handed her toys, Goldie again used her right hand only. Mom was concerned.

I asked Mom what she knew about Goldie's life in the orphanage, looking for some clues to her behavior. Mom pulled out a photograph of Goldie in her crib at the orphanage, which showed Goldie lying on her left side facing the wall where the toys hung. She was touching the toys with her right hand.

"That's what Goldie does now!" Mom exclaimed.

Goldie had learned to play with a wall that held toys, not a parent or caregiver. Play was something that seemed to take place only in a lying-down position and only with her right hand. This is a typical example of how routine and structure associated with an activity shape how that activity is pursued even after a child has been home with the adoptive family for months.

Goldie's mother now had to teach her that when she played with *this* mommy, she could use both hands and sit up or even stand. Odd and simple as it seems, Goldie needed to hear from her mother that a mommy is not a wall.

> **Goldie had learned to play with a wall that held toys, not with a parent or caregiver.**

SURVIVAL SKILLS AND OLD ROUTINES

Sometimes parents are upset by their child's behavior, not realizing that it is part of a deeply ingrained routine from the past. When Mu Ling was just over two and a half years old, her mother Laura shared the following story:

"When we brought Mu Ling home, we had a beautiful wooden high chair for her. But every time we put her in the chair she had a bowel movement! It was as if she was producing poop *on cue*, and it happened every single time. Needless to say, we put away the high chair.

"A few weeks later I glanced over some photos of Mu Ling in the orphanage. There was a potty chair that looked almost exactly like our high chair! Mu Ling must have thought our high chair was a toilet. She must have felt confused and ashamed when we got upset with her for doing what *she* thought was the right thing."

When structures and routines, such as Goldie's wall of toys or Mu Ling's high chair, are more consistently present than a caregiver, children learn to rely on these inanimate objects to communicate what is expected of them. If your child has exhibited strange or puzzling behavior, think about what might have shaped that behavior in the past. Then clearly and gently explain the differences between the past and the present to your child. You need to tell her what kinds of behavior you expect and that you are a more reliable source of cues and information than an inanimate object.

SURVIVAL SKILLS FROM FOSTER HOMES

One might assume that survival skills develop solely in institutional settings. But children in foster homes or even in their own birth families may develop skills for survival. Here is an example from a foster home situation: The mother of a two-year-old boy from South America came to see me because she felt the boy rejected her. I watched the mother and son play pleasantly together. When he finally tired, the boy lay down on the floor, facing his mother, and touched her with his feet repeatedly and playfully. His mother ignored this game of footsie, bent over him, and tried to scoop him into her arms. When her son squealed, she abruptly sat back and said, "You see, he doesn't want me!"

I inquired about the foster home where the little boy had been and the mother showed me a picture of three boys, including her son. She explained that there were three children in the home, and that her boy was the middle child. She wondered aloud if, by being in the middle, her son received the least attention.

I agreed with her supposition, and I also pointed out that the youngest child had probably been in the foster mother's lap most of the time. As a result, the middle child had learned to interact with his foster mom while she held another child. This would explain the child's game of playing with Mom with his feet while lying near her. With this new information, Mom realized that her son did relate to her, with his own survival skills of connection. She recognized also that he needed her help to learn about family skills such as lap time.

SURVIVAL SKILLS AND BIRTH FAMILIES

A young child may have learned survival skills in her birth home or foster home, or even in a previous adoptive family. Two boys I know, siblings, were two and four years old when they were adopted from Eastern Europe. Prior to their adoption they had spent a year in an orphanage, but in their earliest years they lived with their maternal grandparents. Not until two years after the adoption did Robert, the older child, reveal what their life had been like with the grandparents.

Robert recalled the grandmother fondly, but she had died shortly after the younger child was born. Robert was two then. The grandfather began drinking heavily and was unable to care for the children. As a result, Robert turned to survival skills to keep himself and his brother alive. He described searching for food, going hungry, changing the baby's diapers, and trying to soothe his brother's hungry, incessant crying. Robert was three years old and the younger sibling a year old before the local social services agency discovered the situation.

Robert entered his new adoptive family with skills for stealing and hoarding food, toileting in random locations, and sleeping on the floor with his brother. When given a room and a bed of his own and shown the toilet, he stared uncomprehendingly. He did not believe he even needed parents, since he had taken care of himself and his sibling since age two.

Robert's "bad" behavior—that is, his survival skills—caused constant difficulties in his family. It was not until he revealed his history that his parents understood the origin of his behavior. Only then could change begin.

GUIDING YOUR CHILD TO LEARN FAMILY SKILLS

Family skills develop slowly for every child, adopted or not. Non-adopted children are likely to pick up these skills intuitively as infants, because they have no survival skills that interfere with the process. Internationally adopted children, however, need parents to explain and teach family skills clearly. Teaching family skills requires a proactive, anticipatory approach to parenting.

Talking to someone about what interests you most is usually the way to get acquainted; it is no different for an internationally adopted child. Survival is your child's primary interest, and talking with him about his survival skills is an excellent way to begin connection. Even if you and your child have lived together for months or years, talking about survival skills your child used in the past is a profound acknowledgment of his complex background and earliest identity. Once you have made this acknowledgment, you need to follow with proactive teaching of family skills to help your child feel a sense of accomplishment in his new family. This requires you to anticipate when your child may need extra guidance or an extra reminder.

For example, before meeting friends, going to the store, or visiting a parent at work, offer anticipatory guidance. "You will meet a lot of new people at Mom's office," you might say, "but I want you to stay near me or Mom. If you need help, take my hand." It is better to overanticipate and have your child say, "I know that!" than to leave him uncertain about what he needs to do. Rejoice when your child tells you he knows his family skills, and plan together to connect through those skills. Say to your child, "You took my hand, just like you said you would!"

Hoarding is another area that requires proactive parenting (see chapter 18).

TEACH YOUR CHILD TO DEPEND ON YOU

Family skills are skills of interdependence between a child and a parent. Interdependence begins with a child feeling safe and confident in a parent's emotional and physical availability. Your internationally adopted child does not initially know that you are available in this way. Therefore, you need to teach, tell, and show by example that you are really and truly available and responsive. If you are able to help your child believe in your responsiveness and availability, she will pick up family skills faster. How do you teach a child that you are responsive?

Teach your child how to get your attention, and then remind her that you are available. Do not wait for her to practice the skill. She is thinking, "Yeah, she says she's available, but I don't believe her." Your actions have to change your child's conviction.

Teach your child to look at your face to see how you are feeling, and tell her that you look at her face to find out her feelings. "Look at me and see what I'm feeling," you might say, and get quite directly into your child's line of sight, even if that means you are nearly nose to nose. Then tell your child, "I'm happy to be with you."

When you leave the room, tell your child where you are going and when you will be back. "I'm going to the kitchen, but Daddy will be here with you. I'll be back when you finish singing 'Old MacDonald.'"

Take your child with you when possible, even if it is just from one room to another. Do not encourage independence, but do encourage connection. "I'm going to the kitchen; let's go together," you might say.

You need to initiate interactions like these for several weeks or even months before you see the signs that your child is developing family skills. When you do see them emerging (see below), continue to encourage them. Praise your child in specific terms. Avoid general phrases like "good boy" or "sweet girl." For example, if your child looks at your face, you can say, "You did a great job *looking at my face* to see how I feel."

SIGNS THAT FAMILY SKILLS ARE DEVELOPING

Child looks at a parent's face to "check in."
Child calms when a parent picks her up.
Child faces a parent when playing or plays close to a parent.
Child hands toys or objects to a parent.
Child seeks a parent's attention by tugging, whining, calling.
Child looks for or follows an absent parent.
Child fusses when a parent leaves her sight.
Child greets a parent with pleasure when parent returns.

EATING AND CONNECTION

For a child raised by parents from birth or from the first month or two of life, eating is all about connection and nurturing. Along with wholesome nutrition, an infant takes in affection, all kinds of communications, early conversations (exchanges of grunts and squeals with Mom or Dad), and a sense of being loved. In addition, research has documented how the process of eating as a young child actually jump-starts the nerves and brain regions responsible for a child's developing self-control, facial expression, ability to focus attention, and conversational skills.

For the majority of internationally adopted children, however, eating has been more of a fight for survival than a warm and cozy connection with another human being. In group settings, such as orphanages, feeding is done on a mass scale. Tens or even hundreds of infants and toddlers must be fed quickly. Typically bottles are propped up for infants, and children as young as three or four months hold their own bottles. Bottles contain liquid gruel and have nipples with large openings so that the gruel flows quickly.

For toddlers, feeding must be accomplished with a minimum of interaction. To hasten feeding, toddlers' heads are tipped back as overcooked soups or gruel are poured down opened throats. Learning to feed oneself and to chew and work the jaw, mouth, and throat muscles are irrelevant. It is not surprising that infants become overly independent with their bottles and think of feeding as a solo activity. Toddlers often fear mealtimes if they have endured forced feeding. Older children hoard and grab food when they can. Eating becomes a fight for survival. In addition, the soft, liquid quality of most institutional food leaves children with underdeveloped mouth muscles, which later affect speech.

PARENTS AS DETECTIVES

Your child's expectations of when and how often to eat are based on routines he experienced with former caregivers. These expectations about food are deeply etched in his mind. You can play detective to figure out what mealtime and the feeding relationship were like for your child prior to adoption. Read the parents' comments below and try to determine how each of the children might have experienced feeding in the past.

> *"Demetri refuses to sit at the table and has tantrums when I try to feed him."*
>
> *"Yi Sheng hoards food and grabs food off the plates of other family members."*
>
> *"Mu Ling eats rapidly and keeps going until all the food is gone from the table."*
>
> *"Sonia refuses food whenever she is upset."*

Eating is basic, of course, to every human being's survival. Therefore it is not surprising that the parent-child connections associated with eating from infancy onward form the foundation of family skills. I encourage you to make use of eating as a crucial time to help your child set aside survival skills and learn and practice family skills.

TEACHING TO CONNECT THROUGH FOOD

When it is time for you to feed your adopted child, you may run into resistance, especially if your child has been force-fed in an orphanage. A child who has had a negative feeding experience may refuse to sit at the table, even on a parent's lap. To counter this kind of behavior, explore food together in a cozy chair or on the kitchen floor, sitting on a big, soft towel, for a "picnic." Often an adopted child never had much of a chance to handle and explore with her senses the food she was fed. Playing with food is important for a child, so offer the opportunity to "finger paint" with chocolate pudding, applesauce, or yogurt. Or build roads with slices of banana. Allow your child to get messy; this helps, too, with Sensory-Motor Integration (see chapter 14).

Putting what we know from research into practice, you need to place your child, turned toward you, on your lap, to get as much body contact as possible. (See chapter 2 for a discussion of touch and oxytocin.) If your child prefers to sit separately, place her to your left. The leftward placement puts your and your child's left eyes in contact, which connects the right sides of your brains (see chapter 2).

Play the Feeding Game: Encourage your child to feed you. Anticipate that she may not at first know how to feed you gently and appropriately, so you might want to demonstrate with a doll. Meanwhile, note how your child offers (or shoves) food toward you, and if necessary describe that behavior as the "old way," the "orphanage way," or whatever description makes sense to your child.

As you play the game, use expressions such as these: "Look, here's a cracker [or piece of cheese]. Can you gently feed Mommy?" "That's right, put it into Mommy's mouth." "Not too fast! I wonder if you had to eat fast at the orphanage." In addition, encourage eye contact (see chapter 2) by saying, "Can I look in your eyes when you give me the food? I think food tastes better when we look at each other." If your child does not want to let you feed her, try this: Hold the food item on your forehead, or between your eyes, and then make a silly sound, blow a "raspberry," or whistle. This is so surprising, your child will look at you and at the food. Getting your child to look at the food and you at the same time is a major accomplishment for a child who has been force-fed in an orphanage or other setting. It is equally important to develop this connection when a child rejects food and nurturing, as Sonia does because she misses her foster mother.

Sitting next to each other during meals, or with your child on your lap, is an important way to build connection. Feeding each other develops the skills of cooperative turn-taking, learning to be gentle instead of rough, and reading each other's facial and verbal cues. A child from an institutional setting may never have learned that a caregiver will stop when the child says, "I've had enough." Through eating games the family skills of trust and communication can be taught and practiced at least three times each day. At first, until your child reaches a family age of at least a year or two, set aside your ideal of the pleasant family dinner with soft conversation and good manners. This will come in time, and sooner rather than later if you address eating and survival skills by keeping family age in mind.

One of my favorite stories from the First Year Home Group is how Yi Sheng learned to chew. He was eating everything in sight, inhaling it without so much as one chew. Spontaneously, or so the story goes, his parents, Kenji and Nina, and their two teenage daughters pointed to their mouths and demonstrated, as one of them put it, "how teeth chew food." The whole family was laughing at each other and encouraging Yi Sheng to chew before swallowing. To demonstrate the technique, Nina perfected a way to pull her lips back while chewing with her front teeth. Yi Sheng mimicked her precisely. Kenji showed his son how to use his fingers to count five "chews" before swallowing. Then Aiko and Rivka, Yi Sheng's sisters, showed him how to take little bites of tofu instead of stuffing the entire rectangle into his mouth. "It wasn't the family dinner I dreamed of," Nina confessed, "but at least Yi Sheng was no longer eating like a ravenous wolf."

TALKING ABOUT THE PAST: NO BLAME

It is not easy for a parent to talk calmly to a child who has just hurled dinner to the floor, or who has grabbed food off Mom's plate or right out of her mouth. So practice this line in the shower, or in front of the mirror as you dress; practice it often so that it will roll off your tongue effortlessly, even in the most daunting situation: "You learned some good survival skills that helped you in [fill in your child's country of origin], but here in our family we do it differently. I'll help you learn family skills."

Resiliency and Reactive Coping Behaviors

HAVE YOU EVER WONDERED how it would feel to be internationally adopted? Perhaps, in fact, you were. If not, you might wonder what it is like to be suddenly immersed in a new life. Join me for a moment of imaginary play. I invite you to picture yourself plucked from your familiar life and "dropped in the middle of nowhere."

You look around you. You are in a remote place in the middle of what seems like nowhere in particular. You have no maps or signs to tell you where you are. Suddenly you are surrounded by strangers, all of whom are overjoyed to see you. These people smile, laugh, and talk loud and fast, and they act as if you can understand them. They touch your hair, your face, and your shoulders, and they hug you repeatedly. You notice they have a peculiar odor. They dress differently from anyone you have ever met. Their language is unintelligible and sounds like gibberish. You have no clue how or why you are here. You have no idea if you will find your way back to your former life.

Before we go further, check to see how you are feeling. Is any part of your body tense? Do any worries pop into your head? How might you feel about these overly friendly strangers?

You feel hands beginning to remove your clothing, and there, in public, these strangers dress you in new garments. Some people appear to be assessing you, sizing you up, looking at your hair and teeth closely and noting any moles or scars on your body. You are given strange food and invited to play unfamiliar games. You are handed a container of strange liquid and encouraged to drink. Everyone continues to laugh and smile and act as though this were a perfectly ordinary and normal situation.

I played this game with the First Year Home Group. Here are some of their responses:

"I'd be scared," said Soon An's mother, Charlotte.

"I'd be mad if they took my clothes," Soon An's father, Joe, added.

Sonia's mother, Carolyn, said, "It would be so confusing to be greeted with such happiness and yet not to understand what was going on."

"I'd get annoyed, with everyone touching me," Mu Ling's mother Meg commented. "I'd run away."

"I might be too scared to run," Mu Ling's other mother, Laura, confessed. "I might pretend to go to sleep so they would leave me alone."

"Is this how we seem to our children when we adopt them?" Yi Sheng's mother, Nina, wondered aloud.

"THE WORLD TURNED UPSIDE DOWN"

Adoption is absolutely the biggest life change a child will ever experience. It is a sudden and complete immersion in a new culture and a new life, with new people. It is the Big Change. One boy of six put it clearly: "The world turned upside down when I was adopted." A nine-year-old girl who had been adopted when she was three years old said, "It was like I walked through a door, and suddenly nothing was ever the same. The door to my past vanished forever. I was trapped. For a long time it was like I was in a dream, but I never woke up. After that, you know that anything can happen."

Upside down. Dreamlike. A door that opens on a new world. A door to the past vanishes forever. Nothing is ever the same. It felt like a dream, but I couldn't wake up. Anything can happen, and did. These are some of the phrases and images that children, as well as adults who once were adoptees, use to describe a magnitude of change most adoptive parents can only imagine.

Your child begins coping even before he is placed in your arms and his familiar caregivers depart. At the moment you receive your child, he walks through a door that then closes forever. Even tiny infants recognize that a life-changing event has occurred. A young child may react by freezing or with anxious activity, or perhaps by going limp or looking stunned. A few children are profoundly grief-stricken. Those who have previously walked through numerous doorways of loss may play, seemingly happy and unaware. No matter how wonderful international adoption is for a parent, it is a surreal and stressful experience for a child.

Evaluating and understanding your child's coping mechanisms, what I call *reactive coping behaviors*, provide you with important information for the present and the future. Reactive coping behaviors that your child uses early on will reappear as responses to stressful events in the future. Recognizing your child's particular coping style is an important guide to understanding him, recognizing when he is stressed, and choosing effective parenting strategies.

COPING BY REVVING UP OR SHUTTING DOWN

Human beings, including infants and children, react to stress in predictable ways. Humans are born with two basic responses to challenging moments in life. One is the fight-or-flight response pattern. Fight-or-flight revs up a person; it involves a high expenditure of energy for a purpose such as running away or engaging in battle. The other response pattern is "playing dead," or appearing to be asleep, which protects a person and conserves energy. Playing dead or shutting down includes the slowing of breathing, heart rate, and digestion and the numbing of feelings and sensations. Sometimes both revving-up and shutting-down responses occur at the same time, or they alternate over a daylong or weeklong or possibly longer period. For example, a man running away from a bear, in the fight-or-flight response, might step on a thorn but not feel the pain, because his senses are shut down and numb.

Internationally adopted young children engage in both revving-up and shutting-down responses. Sometimes, like the man fleeing the bear, a child might engage in both simultaneously. Revving up and shutting down enable a person to cope with stress alone, without relying upon support from anyone else. Reactive coping behaviors are the extensions of basic survival skills. As with the survival skills described in the previous chapter, they are extremely effective for a neglected child, or a child living in an institutional setting, who has experienced the loss of caregivers or other kinds of relational trauma. In a family setting, however, reactive coping behaviors impede relationships and development.

PURPOSES OF REVVING UP AND SHUTTING DOWN

Protection or survival
Rebalancing physiological and emotional states

Revving up and shutting down have a second purpose, too. Both are ways that an overwhelmed, anxious, frightened, or grief-stricken child tries to regain physiological and emotional balance. Revving up acts like an accelerator on a car; shutting down acts like an emergency brake. The result of relying on these two coping mechanisms is a rather jerky, abrupt jolting from one physiological or emotional state to another. It is not unlike riding in a car with a beginning driver.

In the first two months of life, newborn babies shift from sleep to wakefulness, from waking to hunger, and from eating back to sleeping with such jerky jolts. This is because newborns must rely solely on these two coping methods.

Internationally adopted children also begin with the same two basic coping methods. But because they are usually older than a couple of months when they are adopted, they have a slightly wider variety of mechanisms at their disposal. I have identified, using nicknames, five reactive coping patterns (see below); each one is based on either revving up or shutting down. Shutdown patterns are the Warm Rock and the Stunned Rag Doll. The revved-up patterns are the Dizzy Performer and the Royal Boss. The Unwilling Guest tends to swing between shutting down and revving up. Individual children may prefer one or two patterns, but a child may engage in all five.

FIVE REACTIVE COPING PATTERNS

The Warm Rock	Quiet, withdrawn, sleeping
The Stunned Rag Doll	Spacy, frozen, limp
The Dizzy Performer	Active: performing and charming, overly friendly to adults
The Royal Boss	Controlling and demanding; may throw tantrums
The Unwilling Guest	Rejecting and sad; waiting, searching, or calling; or hyper-alert

THE FEELINGS BEHIND COPING PATTERNS

Reactive coping behaviors hide more than they reveal about how a child feels. Parents often misinterpret coping behaviors as maturity and adjustment, or even as attachment to the parent, when in fact a child is feeling upset and alone. What true feelings lie behind these quiet, spacy, active, controlling, or rejecting behavior patterns?

The quiet responses typical of the Warm Rock are often the result of being overwhelmed and overstimulated. The Warm Rock shuts down, numbing feelings and withdrawing into sleep. The child may feel invisible, as if she has vanished, just as her past life has.

The spaciness of the Stunned Rag Doll reflects the child's focus on internal feelings and memories. The spacy stare, sometimes in reaction to a specific trigger such as a familiar sound, odor, or food, may indicate a disconnection from the present, while the child thinks instead about the past. The stare may also be a sign of shock and disorientation. The world and those in it seem unreal, as if the child were watching a movie of life.

FEELINGS THAT LIE BEHIND COPING PATTERNS

Warm Rock	Shuts down to manage overstimulation, feels rejected or inadequate
Stunned Rag Doll	Shuts down to think about the past and be disconnected from the present
Dizzy Performer	Active and revved up, overstimulated, in denial about major life changes
Royal Boss	Controlling, revving, helpless, frightened, and out of control
Unwilling Guest	Rejecting; alternately revving and shutting down with grief, loss, sadness, and anger; waiting to be "found," or searching for lost caregiver

The very active behavior of the Dizzy Performer is often a reaction to overstimulation, a way to cope with anxiety, or a denial that life has changed. Keeping busy is both a response to many new things and a refusal to recognize what feelings those things evoke. The performance is often a way to get adult attention.

The Royal Boss hides feelings of helplessness, weakness, and fear, or of being out of control. These feelings are common among internationally adopted children who were abruptly given to a stranger, as many are. (Of the five children in our group, only Sonia had a chance to become acquainted with her adoptive parents before being "dropped in the middle of nowhere" with them.) As a result, many children experience the adoption process as a kidnapping. The Royal Boss wants to control life's uncertainty.

The Unwilling Guest grieves for lost caregivers and rejects new ones. The rejecting child is angry and feels betrayed and abandoned by former caregivers. She may feel afraid that she did something wrong that caused her abandonment, and she may feel weighted down by guilt. Nevertheless, she searches and calls for the missing caregiver, longing for comfort.

Revving up, suppressing feelings, or grieving is exhausting for a child, and a child who is shut down has no energy to spare. Consequently, coping interferes with every aspect of a child's life. Development slows or even goes into reverse. A stressed child loses previously acquired skills. Both shutting down and revving up disrupt a child's ability to communicate. A withdrawn child has little or no facial expression, few gestures, and limited body language to convey her feelings. A child who is overly active or shut down cannot focus attention on her parents, a new home, or rules and expectations. Such a child may seem deaf to instructions, forgetful of expectations, or even purposely disruptive.

WHAT REACTIVE COPING BEHAVIORS DO

- Reduce the energy available for development and age-appropriate behavior.
- Decrease communication and cooperation with other people.
- Disguise a child's true feelings and needs.
- Increase a child's sense of isolation.

Coping is like treading water; it is hard work but you do not get anywhere fast. When a child is coping, she is not focused on forming a relationship with a new parent and family. A coping child does not reach out, ask for help, or act in cooperative ways. A coping child is just trying to stay afloat.

INDUCEMENT: FEELING YOUR CHILD'S PAIN

When you learn to recognize reactive coping behaviors, you will begin to understand the feelings these behaviors mask. Here is how some of the parents in the First Year Home Group made use of the coping patterns I identified earlier, as a first step toward gaining a sharper understanding of their child's behavior:

"Soon An is definitely the Warm Rock type," Charlotte said. "She's so shut down that I feel rejected. I know from raising our son that I'm a good mom, but if Soon An were my first child, I'd be afraid she didn't like me. I feel inadequate as it is."

"Demetri is the Dizzy Performer type. He's so active and all over the place, it makes me feel completely disorganized and mixed up. I find myself forgetting to fix lunch or give Demetri a bath," Denise confessed.

"Sonia is more of the stunned, spacy Rag Doll. Sometimes she looks like a deer in the headlights and other times she just looks right through me," Carolyn said. "I guess I feel a bit stunned myself about becoming a mom so suddenly. One day we were in Guatemala visiting Sonia's foster mother, and the next day *I* was the mom. I'm having trouble feeling connected with my new role."

"Mu Ling is our family's Royal Boss," Meg commented. "I can't believe that this little girl from half a world away and who speaks no English can turn our family upside down. We go from one power struggle to another. First it's getting up, and then getting dressed; next it's what's for breakfast. It's endless."

"Yi Sheng is definitely our Unwilling Guest. He acts so polite; sometimes I wonder if somebody coached him. He uses perfect table manners, and when he says good night he shakes my hand," Nina, said. "I guess I don't feel like he's really my child yet. I mean, I feel responsible for him, but it's like he's an overnight guest who's waiting to be picked up. It's hard to feel close to someone who wants to leave."

"I feel a bit like a stranger in my own home," Kenji, Yi Sheng's father, admitted. "Yi Sheng makes me see everything differently, through his eyes. I feel like he's an anthropologist studying our strange habits and customs. I guess I'm self-conscious."

As you can see in these comments, a parent's own uncomfortable feelings often mirror the feelings the child is experiencing. Sometimes, without words, a child's behavior makes a parent experience the same feelings that the child has hidden inside. This transference of feelings is called *inducement*. The parent is induced (literally, as in the Latin root of the word, "led") to experience the child's feelings. Even adults engage in inducement. For example, a grumpy woman comes home from a hard day at work and bangs around the house until everyone in her family feels just as grumpy as she does.

Soon An, who felt rejected and unwanted, withdrew into the Warm Rock, thereby creating a parallel feeling of rejection and inadequacy in her mother. Mu Ling, who felt confused, out of control, and helpless and acted like the Royal Boss, induced similar feelings of helplessness in her parent. Demetri, who felt dizzy with the overwhelming stimulation of his new life and so became excessively active, induced dizziness in Denise. Similarly, Sonia and Carolyn both felt disconnected from the present moment and from other people, and Yi Sheng and Nina were mutually distant and self-conscious. Yi Sheng was waiting to return to his familiar world as magically as he left it. Nina was waiting for Yi Sheng to behave like a son to her. Both were waiting for the other to break the ice or for the situation to become more relaxed and normal. The child who feels there is no one to care for him performs and charms every adult but Mom, leaving her feeling alone and unwanted. A child who is angry and frustrated induces feelings of anger in his parents. A child who feels like a guest leaves parents feeling as if they are hosts to a foreign exchange student, albeit a very young one.

PARENTING STRATEGIES THAT *DO NOT* WORK WITH A COPING CHILD

Understanding inducement helps parents avoid going off on the wrong track with a coping child. Here is how some parents in the First Year Home Group described their initial reactions to their coping children:

"I found myself withdrawing from Soon An when she acted like a Warm Rock," Joe said. "I figured she'd eventually reach out to me."

"I tried extra hard to engage Soon An by being playful and silly," Charlotte added. "But nothing Joe or I did really worked. Soon An just retreated further from us."

"When Mu Ling began performing for us, I became her audience," Meg reflected. "When she becomes controlling, I get angry and give her time-outs. But Mu Ling laughs at punishments."

Parents' intuitive responses often fall flat because these parenting strategies fail to address the child's true feelings. Behind a child's reactive coping behaviors is her belief that she must survive alone. The best and most effective parenting approach to coping behaviors is to empathize with and respond to the child's feelings. For example, when Soon An withdraws, Joe and Charlotte need to comment on her behavior and link it to her hidden feelings. This lets Soon An know, not merely by words but also by her parents' tone and body language, that they understand her true concerns. When a child feels understood at this level, she feels connected to the parent.

MIRRORING TO CONNECT WITH A COPING CHILD

Here is a technique that parents may use to connect with a child, involving mirroring activity and mirroring emotion. It is easier with a quiet child than with an active one. I suggested to Meg that she mirror—talk about—Mu Ling's feelings while offering her daughter a chance to mirror Meg's play behavior. This double mirroring would help Mu Ling feel in control of her actions and know that Meg understood her feelings.

Meg got up and went to where Mu Ling was emptying a bucket of small blocks by tossing them one by one over her shoulder. Meg handed her daughter a beanbag, which promptly sailed off into space. Meg retrieved it and put it on her head; she showed Mu Ling the beanbag and offered her another beanbag. Then she launched into her script.

"Mu Ling, look at me. I know everything is new and different. You must feel helpless in this new life, as helpless as those beanbags you toss over your shoulder." Meg tossed a beanbag to demonstrate. "I will help you figure things out. Look at me; see the beanbag on my head? Now you put your beanbag on your head."

The other members of the First Year Home Group held their breath as Meg ran through the routine. Mu Ling looked at her mother and then at her own beanbag. Meg repeated her script. At the end, Mu Ling put the beanbag on her head and grinned. Meg grinned back and the two connected for the first time.

The parents applauded. Then Mu Ling got distracted and scampered off.

"This is so counterintuitive," Nina commented.

"It almost seems like you are rewarding your child by playing with her, instead of insisting she stop throwing blocks around," Meg said.

CONNECTION BEFORE CORRECTION

Meg's point is the most common concern of parents in such situations. The answer lies in one important fact: A coping child is disconnected from a parent. You must establish a connection with your child before a correction (reprimand, consequence, or punishment) can be effective. (If your child is violent, or verbally or physically abusive, or unwilling to connect, see chapter 16.)

Meg mentioned that Mu Ling laughed at an order for a time-out, or at a verbal reprimand for inappropriate behavior. Until Mu Ling felt connected to Meg, until the daughter felt an allegiance to her parent, corrections were likely to evoke laughter, or fingers in the ears followed by the chant of "I can't hear you" or "You can't make me."

You must establish a connection with your child before a correction can be effective.

To move your child effectively beyond reactive coping behaviors, you must first connect with him *and* get him to connect with to you. Here are two specific ways to do this: First, make a comment that links your child's behavior to his feelings. Then engage your child in a back-and-forth game.

Playing the Row, Row, Row Your Boat game with your child is an excellent mirroring activity that requires your child to connect and cooperate. There are two ways to play the game. One way, appropriate for very young children, is to hold your child in your lap and sing the song while rocking forward and backward together. The other way, good for preschool and older children, is to sit on the floor, facing your child with the bottoms of your feet together and holding hands; sing the song, look at each other, and rock together back and forth. You can play this game as often three times a day for a full week when you are first teaching connection. Then invent or find similar games and interactions that continue to reinforce connection and cooperation.

HEALTH AND SAFETY

When health and safety issues arise, parents must step in. It is important to stop a child who engages in dangerous behavior. When such behavior is a form of coping, a parent must "help" a child stop; a simple command does not suffice. In Mu Ling's case, it was too early in the first year of the parent-child relationship for her parents to expect her to obey a verbal command to stop throwing blocks. Her parents needed to help Mu Ling understand the reason for the rule, perhaps by stating, "It's dangerous to throw blocks. In this house the rule is 'No throwing.'"

"I will help you stop," Meg or Laura might add, gently but firmly holding Mu Ling's arm when she swung it back to launch the next block. "You can stop yourself or I can help you. You can keep the blocks if you stop throwing them. If you throw the blocks, I will remove them."

ONE SIP AT A TIME: FROM COPING TO SELF-CONTROL

I described earlier how reactive coping behaviors are like the accelerator or emergency brake of a car, and that a newborn is as jerky in transitions as a new driver. How does a newborn become able to transition smoothly from sleep to wakefulness, from waking to playing, and from playing to feeding? What is the process that develops this type of self-control? Surprisingly, the answer lies in the ordinary interactions of a mother feeding her baby.

Let us follow the development of self-control step by step. A baby cries (revs up) when she gets hungry. Mom comes and picks up the baby (tactile connection), croons softly (auditory connection), and gets the breast or bottle ready. The tactile connection starts the baby's oxytocin flowing and the baby begins to calm. But an equally important change takes place when the baby begins sucking.

Sucking is an early and powerful way that a revving baby shifts gears, so to speak, and calms down. (Even adults use sucking to calm themselves. Think of all the lattes, water bottles, hard candies, and even cigarettes that are purchased each day and eagerly sucked down or sucked on.) Besides the sucking itself, other aspects of feeding soothe the baby, including proteins in the milk that slow the child's heart rate and the warmth of the mother's body, which calms the baby's physical activity.

Sucking activates the vagus nerve in the baby's body. This nerve travels from the brain to the stomach, lungs, and heart as well as the mouth, eyes, and ears. This single nerve acts in many ways as a brake on revving behavior. As a baby begins to suck, the vagus nerve slows her heart and breathing rates to create a calm interval for digestion. Eye contact during eating, too, becomes associated with calming, so that just looking into Mom's eyes, whether the baby is feeding or not, can calm her. The vagus nerve also influences facial expressions and vocalizations. So when a baby learns to modify a revved-up cry to a whine or to a modulated call to Mom, the vagus nerve is operating as a brake on revving.

Newborns and infants less than two or three months old are known for their jerky, or abrupt, transitions from crying to frantically sucking to suddenly falling asleep or waking up. Newborns are either revving up or shutting down because their vagus nerve is not yet fully operational. By four months of age, babies begin to move smoothly from one activity to another. The child's sucking behavior has helped the vagus nerve develop. The continuing refinement of the vagus nerve leads to increasing behavioral, emotional, and social self-control.

This control ultimately results in a child who pays attention, focuses on one thing at a time, engages in conversations, takes turns, and is able to wait.

TURNING BACK THE CLOCK TO BUILD RESILIENCY

Psychological research has shown that resiliency, a child's capacity for emotional balance, builds more slowly in internationally adopted children (see chapter 2). Is there any way to hurry the process along? The answer is yes. Along with building connection and identity, every internationally adopted child can build resiliency when parents use effective strategies. Because resiliency begins with a feeding relationship, it behooves a parent to establish that feeding relationship, regardless of the child's age. The most effective way to activate the vagus nerve is to tap a child's sucking ability. Using a bottle is the easiest way but there are other ways as well. Of course, children of different ages need different strategies, but the basic concept of connection through sucking and eye contact is the same. (In chapter 9 you will learn step by step how to build your child's resiliency.)

The younger the child, the easier it is to rebuild resiliency. If you have an infant who is still taking a bottle and reclining in your arms, you can hold him on your left, look into his eyes, and make silly sounds, sing, or talk to keep his attention on your face. With a toddler (especially one who has been force-fed in an orphanage), you might practice sucking and eye contact at a time other than mealtime, perhaps by incorporating a sippy cup or juice box "reward" into a play session of Row, Row, Row Your Boat. With a child of any age, putting a cracker or piece of cheese on your forehead and requiring eye contact from your child to "earn" the food reward is another method of building the basics of resiliency. Be sure to tell your child what you expect by saying things like "Food tastes better when we look in each other's eyes. Look at me! I'm looking at you."

This type of interaction needs long-term practice, for one major reason: Children with complex backgrounds tend to revert to their old coping behaviors and survival skills. They do not generalize their connection and resiliency behaviors from one day to the next. You will notice that without daily practice for several months, or even, if needed, for the entire first year home, your child's skill in this area is sporadic. The more energy you put into building the basics of resiliency, the better off your child and family will be in the years to come. For children who come to you at one year of age or older, you may need to return to this type of intensive practice every month or so, even after some initial success. When a six-year-old is about to start first grade, he may revert to old coping skills. The minute you see your Warm Rock or Royal Boss reappear, it is time to return to these resiliency games. Your six-year-old may even help you invent new versions, which is all to the good.

COPING BEHAVIORS AND SAYING GOODBYE

At the end of every First Year Home Group session we sing goodbye to each child. This simple routine brings out reactive coping behaviors as if on cue. These children do not associate saying goodbye with pleasant changes. Goodbye can feel overwhelming, and their behavior reflects that.

Watching each child respond to the song reveals clearly how stressful ordinary life can be even after children have been home a month, four or five months, or even an entire year.

"Goodbye, Soon An; goodbye, Soon An; goodbye, Soon An. We'll see you again in one week," we sing.

Soon An's response is to close her eyes and fall asleep, retreating into her Warm Rock persona.

We sing the song to thirteen-month-old Sonia and she stares straight ahead, looking as if she has left her body and flown away. "That's it!" David exclaims. "She has that deer-in-the-headlights look again."

We sing to Demetri, who claps for himself and then twirls around in the circle. He grins crookedly and then bites his lip. He is the Dizzy Performer all over again.

"Me, me!" shouts Mu Ling, the Royal Boss. She joins Demetri in the circle and prances around, singing, "Goom-baii! goom-baii!" trying to fit her mouth around the foreign words.

Only Yi Sheng seems to take in the gravity of the farewell. He takes a small truck and will not let go. It may be a souvenir of this group experience that he cannot trust will come again. Nina reassures him. "We'll come back next week, in seven sleeps," she says, showing the number of days with her fingers and pantomiming sleeping. He looks at her and, after a long, searching gaze, releases the truck into her hands. His face droops and he rubs his eyes with his fist.

We sing, "Goodbye, Yi Sheng; goodbye, Yi Sheng; goodbye, Yi Sheng. We'll see you again in one week." Yi Sheng looks on, unbelieving. One by one, the children begin to stall, grab toys, and twist in Mom or Dad's arms to look back, or run back, into the playroom. None of them wants this safe space, complete with attentive parents, to vanish.

Memories from
a Complex Background

DOES A YOUNG CHILD really have accurate or meaningful early memories?
Can a child recall what happened to her in the time before she could speak? Can
we trust what a young internationally adopted child tells us about the past, since
we have no way to verify the truth? Is it more emotionally disruptive to dig up
events of the past with a young child than to leave those events quietly buried?
These are the kinds of questions parents ask me when I introduce the importance
of early memories. In fact, the only parents ever to leave the First Year Home
Group departed over this very issue.

In this chapter I quote a variety of young children's memories of their adoptions and their lives before they were adopted. All of the quotations are accurate
and all of the stories are true, but to protect the privacy of the children and
families who shared this information I have attributed the stories to the children
of our composite First Year Home Group. First, however, we will hear from two
adult international adoptees about what memory means to them. Next we will
examine what adoptive parents can learn from psychological research on the
importance of children's early memories. Finally, we will hear about the memories of very young internationally adopted children.

MEMORIES THAT VANISH

"What do you regret losing the most?" I asked the waitress.
"My memories," the young woman told me.
The waitress, a poised woman in her mid-thirties, had shared with me that

she was internationally adopted. As a four-year-old she had arrived in the United States from Vietnam, under the auspices of Operation Babylift. I encouraged her to continue.

"When I first arrived I had lots of memories of my life in Vietnam. But no one talked with me about them; no one asked. I guess my new parents didn't really know what to say. Gradually my memories faded until they became dream-like. Finally they disappeared completely. To me, this is my greatest loss."

MEMORY TRACES IN ADULTHOOD

"I know this sounds really strange, especially because I consider myself a mentally healthy person, but sometimes I get this irrational feeling that I'm going to be abandoned," Mary told me.

Mary (not her real name) is in her late twenties and is currently enrolled in a PhD program in communications. She is articulate, self-aware, and confident. A midwestern family adopted Mary from Korea at four months of age. We were talking about her current life when she digressed and shared her fear of abandonment.

"I have a boyfriend and we're planning our future together, but sometimes I find myself afraid. This sometimes occurs around a disagreement and I find I am afraid to argue with my fiancé. I am afraid, and I don't know why, that he will leave me. This feeling makes me feel crazy because I can't relate it to anything, even my adoption." Mary believes that her young age when adopted precludes her having memories or anxiety associated with separation or abandonment, which is why she cannot relate her fear to her adoption.

Mary's fears do not feel like memories. We think of memories as words and images, sequences of events that one can recall at will, what psychologists call *explicit memory*. But Mary's fears are rooted in her *implicit memory*. Implicit memories are often sensory or pictorial, they are unconscious, and they are triggered by events or sensory experiences that are similar to the original situation. Mary's fears of abandonment and her lack of trust in the permanence of a relationship are implicit memories triggered by her current close relationship and her impending marriage commitment.

What Mary described has its source in the way that relational trauma fragments a child's sense of identity. The implicit memories of loss are disconnected from the explicit story line of "what happened to me."

RESEARCH ON EARLY MEMORIES

We can find confirmation in two areas of research that Mary's fears are genuine artifacts, implicit memories, from the first four months of her life. The first area of research concerns the ability of newborns to recognize their own mother's voice from having heard it in utero, and even to recognize familiar stories they heard in the same environment. In 1980 Anthony J. DeCasper and William P. Fifer published research that demonstrated that even infants reared in a group nursery with minimal maternal care still preferred their mother's voice to the voices of other women. This research confirmed that auditory memory is not something that begins when a child is four or five years old.

How does an infant communicate that a voice, song, or story is familiar? Babies are known to suck more vigorously when presented with something familiar and to slow sucking when presented with something new. The infants in this study sucked approximately 24 percent more vigorously when listening to Mom's voice.

Even very young infants instantly have the capacity to distinguish their birth mother from another adult woman. Additional research has shown that two-day-old infants prefer hearing their native language to another language and that newborns have the capacity to recognize their mother's face within hours of birth. With such strong recognition capabilities it is no surprise that even newborns react to losing a familiar caregiver, and that older infants have an equal or greater response.

In 2002 Theodore J. Gaensbauer presented research in which he described the way infants and toddlers react days, months, or even years later to reminders of their early trauma. In all cases Gaensbauer had factual evidence of what had happened to the children he studied, and none of them had been told, in the intervening time, about their early traumatic experiences. Gaensbauer gave examples of how infants just a few weeks old engaged in "remembering" behaviors, and he then showed how older babies, toddlers, and preschoolers signaled, both through play and through words, their memories of traumatic events that occurred long before the verbal stage. Gaensbauer described an infant whose father had abused him repeatedly during the first ten weeks of life. Subsequently the infant was placed in a foster home, where he showed a persistent fear of men. For more than a year after the abuse ended, this child greeted all men with startle reactions, fearful expressions, frozen posture, and hyperventilation. Women never elicited such distressed behavior.

Another example was a two-year-old who used toys and dolls to "describe" the details of a car accident he had experienced at nine months of age. His play clearly portrayed the way in which the car was struck, rolled over, and landed. Another child of sixteen months who had been in an airplane crash was able, nearly a year later at just over two years of age, to provide an extraordinarily detailed and precise description both verbally and through play.

Children as young as infants retain memories of very early events in their lives, and children of any age can show the symptoms of posttraumatic stress years later.

Gaensbauer has documented convincingly that children as young as infants retain memories of very early events in their lives, and also that children of any age can show the symptoms of posttraumatic stress months or years later. Such symptoms include startle responses, difficulty sleeping, fear of reminders of the trauma, tantrums, repetitive play about the trauma, phobias, and loss of trust in others.

Fortunately there is hope that these children can progress beyond their posttraumatic behaviors and memories. According to the work of Alicia Lieberman and others, when parents talk with a child about his experience and from his perspective, the child's symptoms of distress decrease significantly. We can reasonably presume that if Mary, the adult adoptee who feared abandonment, had been talking regularly with her adoptive parents about losing her foster mother and her birth mother, she would now be less likely to confuse her early feelings of abandonment with her relationship with her fiancé.

Let us turn now to some of the memories that internationally adopted infants, toddlers, and young children have shared with their parents.

BLOWING BUBBLES TO REMEMBER

Yi Sheng was lying on his back, using his saliva to blow bubbles. He was five years old and had been with his family for six months.

"I don't know what to do with him when he does this," Nina, his mother, confessed. "I told him it was 'icky,' but he ignored me."

Sometimes a child's behavior is puzzling, annoying, or even repulsive to parents. But it may have some meaning, rooted in the past, for the child. Nina agreed to ask Yi Sheng, "Where did you learn to do that?"

"We all did it," Yi Sheng answered calmly. "My whole family."

"Why?" his mother asked, sidestepping the issue of "my family."

"Because it's fun," he replied. "It's free, and anyone can do it."

"Your first family did this, together?" This was the first time Nina had heard Yi Sheng mention his first family. She was not sure when he had been separated from them, yet he blew bubbles like this from the day she met him. Was he really thinking about his birth family in China?

"So when you blow bubbles like that, are you thinking about your Chinese family?"

"Yes."

"I guess you think about them a lot, because you do that just about every day."

"Didn't you know?"

"I'm glad you told me, not just with the bubbles, but with words. I didn't know until you used words that you were thinking about them so much," Nina admitted to him.

When parents adopt an older child of seven or eight, they recognize that their child has memories of the past. However, even much younger children have memories as well.

"WHY DO PEOPLE HAVE GLOVES?"

Mu Ling hated to have her hair combed or her head touched from the day she arrived as a two-and-a-half-year-old child. A year after she was adopted she developed an obsession about gloves. Every day that winter Mu Ling pointed out people wearing gloves, or "glubs" as she said. "Why do people have glubs?" Mu Ling asked over and over. Somehow her parents' answers were always unsatisfactory.

Finally her mother Meg asked Mu Ling, "Were you ever somewhere that you saw everyone wearing gloves?" Mu Ling's face lit up and she nodded vigorously.

The image of a hospital came to Meg's mind and she envisioned doctors wearing gloves. "People wear gloves in a hospital, where they take care of sick people. Were you sick?" Meg asked her daughter.

Mu Ling nodded vigorously again. "Leaky poopies," she told her mother.

By playing detective Meg began to unearth Mu Ling's memories of being in the hospital with dysentery and having an IV in her head (a typical location for infant IVs in some countries). Suddenly Mu Ling's obsession with gloves, as well as her dislike of having her head touched, made sense.

Laura, her other mother, recalled that Mu Ling seemed to know a great deal about medical instruments. When the doctor examined her in China during the adoption process, she handled the stethoscope knowledgeably and the doctor commented that she must have had some medical care. This puzzled Mu Ling's parents, who had been assured by the orphanage that Mu Ling had never been sick a day in her life.

Meg showed her daughter pictures of different medical instruments and machines in a children's book about going to the hospital. Mu Ling saw the IV and pointed to it, saying, "Mine hang on door."

"Was that when you had leaky poopies?" Meg asked, and Mu Ling confirmed that was true.

Over several weeks of conversation, looking at pictures, and thinking over the memories that Mu Ling shared, her parents were able to put together a story of how Mu Ling had gotten sick with a gastrointestinal infection and had been treated at the hospital for dehydration. This scenario was confirmed by the fact that Mu Ling had tested positive for a highly contagious intestinal bacteria, shigella, when she first came home. She did not have symptoms but she was a carrier of the disease, a condition that could have arisen from having had insufficient antibiotic treatment when she had had "leaky poopies."

ASK THE RIGHT QUESTION AND MEMORIES POP OUT

Soon An was eighteen months old and had been home with her adoptive parents for a year when Charlotte became aware that her daughter had a preference about how she was rocked. Soon An kicked and squirmed when Charlotte rocked her in the rocking chair. After consulting with me by phone, Charlotte asked her daughter, "How did your foster mother rock you?" Soon An responded by pushing and pulling her mother into a kneeling position on the floor, crawling into her arms, and pushing back and forth from side to side. Then Soon An smiled up at Charlotte as if to say, "See? This is the right way to rock me." Although two-thirds of her young life had gone by since she last was rocked in this manner, the memory was still strong.

"AREN'T YOU MY FOSTER MOTHER?"

Joe and Charlotte were also struck by the fact that Soon An formed an immediate and intense bond with an older woman, Polly, who was a close friend of the family and a frequent visitor. After being with Polly for as little as an hour, Soon An rejected Charlotte for days. In addition, after visits from Polly, Soon An refused to eat when Charlotte fed her, and she experienced night terrors from which she could not be awakened. Charlotte was puzzled and worried about how this behavior was jeopardizing her friendship with Polly, not to mention her relationship with her daughter.

Joe observed that Polly had dark hair and eyes and strongly resembled the photo they had of Soon An's foster mother. Polly had a similar haircut, and she wore glasses of a similar style. Could it be that Soon An had somehow mistaken Polly for her own missing foster mother? Her behavior seemed to say yes.

To unravel the difficulty, I encouraged Joe and Charlotte to talk to Soon An about her foster mother, using the photograph. They needed to explain to Soon An that Polly was not her foster mother but did look similar. Charlotte and Joe followed this advice and found themselves drenched in Soon An's anger and grief. The eating, sleeping, and rejection difficulties eased, but in their place Soon An, the Warm Rock (see chapter 5), became deeply in touch with how she felt about losing her foster mother. She began rejecting Polly when she visited. Charlotte had to explain the story to her friend, who then became involved in telling Soon An her story, using the photos Charlotte supplied. "See, I have the same haircut as your first mother, but I'm really a different person."

SILENT RECOGNITION

One day Denise was shopping with her adopted son and stopped at an antique and junk store to browse. Demetri was now four years old, with a family age (see chapter 4) of two and a half years. Denise looked around and noticed Demetri standing silently and holding on to the bars of a white iron crib. He was staring at her with a peculiar look on his face, a look of recognition and discomfort. Denise felt she could almost read his mind, as if words flew from his brain to hers. She asked a question to see if her assumption was correct.

"Is that what your crib looked like at the orphanage?" she asked.

Demetri nodded soberly, more quietly than his typical exuberant style.

"I'm glad you showed it to me," Denise assured her son, and she stood with him, looking at the crib.

Later that day Denise went through her photographs and found that the crib indeed matched pictures of the infant cribs in her son's former orphanage. Demetri had been moved from the infant room at least six months before she picked him up. Thus his memory was at least three years old—from the very beginning of his life.

HAIR ON THE WATER

Sometimes a single behavioral episode seems to point to an early memory, even when the child does not reveal the memory verbally. Such behavior often stands out in a parent's mind as odd and disconnected. That was the case in one instance with Sonia, who was adopted at one year of age. Three years later, she was old enough to have a bath with her slightly older cousin. The two girls were playing happily one evening while Sonia's mom, Carolyn, watched over them.

Suddenly, the cousin decided to demonstrate her new floating abilities and put her face into the water, reaching her arms out and letting her hair spread out on the water. Instantly Sonia began screaming in terror. Carolyn went to pick her up, and Sonia climbed up her mother like a tree, screaming and frightened. The cousin pulled her head out of the water, and gradually Sonia calmed.

Sonia could not or would not say anything about the incident. Nothing like it had happened before or since, yet it seemed to Carolyn to have the eerie feeling of a memory. She wondered if Sonia had seen a person lying in the water face down like that, hair spread out, somewhere in the past. Had her daughter seen a drowned person? Or was it just a sudden reaction to the strange and unexpected appearance of her cousin?

Charlotte decided not to ask Sonia these questions, afraid of creating a recurrence of her daughter's distress. The questions would have offered the child a chance to find words for her intense reaction and its possible source. Although Sonia did not show any other behaviors related to this possible trauma, she might in the future have memories triggered by swim classes or other water-related experiences. It would have been valuable for her and her family to be prepared for such possibilities by talking about the incident. Such a discussion need not be extensive. "You screamed and were terrified of the water when you saw your cousin floating with her hair spread out around her head," Sonia's mother might say. "I wonder: Did you ever see anything like that before?" Most important, the discussion should acknowledge the child's feelings and behavior, because it is critical to make sense of such mysterious or painful pieces in the child's life story. Doing so may help reduce the child's traumatic response to similar events when encountered later in life.

PERSISTENT REPETITIVE BEHAVIORS OR COMMENTS

Few parents are directly told that their child has been physically or sexually abused. Often it is the child's frightened or odd behavior that reveals such a past.

Paul, a boy I know who was adopted from Central America, became "corpselike" and "physically frozen" when approached by his first male teacher, who also happened to be his swimming instructor. Judy, Paul's mother, reported that he refused to go into the pool or even near the man. In answer to Judy's questions about his refusal, Paul explained repeatedly, "I'm afraid of his belly button; he has too much hair there. He's bad. I don't like him." He repeated these comments week after week, although the teacher never actually touched him.

This type of verbal repetition, along with Paul's emotional and physical signs of fear, convinced his parents that their son had experienced something "bad" with a man prior to joining their family. Believing that something serious had happened to Paul was a leap the family was willing to make only after being reassured that a child of five would not and could not make up such an odd set of concerns or play-act such frightened behaviors.

Judy and her husband, Donald, decided to embark on family therapy with Paul to unwrap the memories of what their son eventually began to call "the story of the bad babysitter," a memory that was tied to male teachers, especially those who were bare chested. Having his family's support enabled Paul to incorporate his scary memories into his larger life story and identity. Despite reassurances by agency workers that a child has not been abused, memories like Paul's often surface when the child feels safe enough to reveal them to new parents. Persistently repeated comments, behaviors, or other signs may not offer up an instant interpretation based on what parents know—or think they know—but as Paul's family discovered, they may well be the result of buried memories of important life events.

MIND-READING EXPECTATIONS

One of the notable aspects of a young child's memory is that she expects the parent to share the memory and to know what the behaviors (such as Yi Sheng's bubble blowing) that express that memory, however indirectly, are all about. Most children expect adults to "know everything," including what they are thinking. A child is often surprised to discover that her parents cannot read her mind. Adopted children often assume their parents know that they are thinking about their birth parents, their fears of being sent back to the orphanage or of having been kidnapped, and so on.

A child expects her parents to share her memory and to know what related behaviors are all about.

MEMORY AND IDENTITY

Young children have a lot of sensory memories from the past. Some of these memories are explicit and have clearly delineated ideas and words attached, such as Mu Ling's memory of the gloves, the IV, and the "leaky poopies." Some memories are implicit or bodily memories that are not expressed in words, or even fully conscious, such as Soon An's memory of how her foster mother held and rocked her. Soon An may have experienced Charlotte's rocking as "not right," rather than being fully conscious of what her foster mother did. All such memories must be "translated" from sensory information that the child has into words in the child's new language. These memories can be included when telling the child's story to help him build an identity based on felt experiences. For example, when Charlotte talked about Soon An's first mother, she always mentioned how First Mama rocked Soon An. In this way identity and physical memory become intertwined for a child. Once Mu Ling's mothers learned about the "leaky poopies," they often commented when they changed Mu Ling's diapers, "No leaky poops today! Those leaky poopies were in China." Again, the reminder and sequencing of the current events and the past with physical sensations and memories help a child to maintain a continuous sense of self since babyhood.

Autobiographical memories are at the core of a child's identity. A child needs to have access to these memories in order to develop a sturdy self-concept that includes the past, present, and future. Memories such as these may be the only connection a child has with the past, especially when there is little or no information about birth parents. Your child needs your help in gaining access to his memories, and that often means you have to interpret, decode, and ask pointed questions about memories that emerge only in fragmentary and indirect ways. Once you have done this together, you can make the memories part of your child's life story as it is reflected upon daily and told for many years to come.

Part II Key Parenting Strategies

Providing a Framework for Fragmented Memories

IN A FAMILY with an internationally adopted child of any age, parent and child together must learn to tell a coherent story of the child's life, a story that resonates with and captures as accurately as possible the child's experience. I tell the parents with whom I work that this is the most important parenting strategy they can pursue, for three reasons. First, researchers have demonstrated that telling a coherent life story reduces a child's out-of-control posttraumatic behaviors. Second, a coherent story mends a child's shattered identity. Third, a child's story is the most powerful means of building connection between parent and child.

THE JIGSAW PUZZLE MEMORY

Among adoptive parents as well as among professionals, there is a school of thought that says parents must not put ideas about the past into a child's head. Rather, parents should wait for a child to ask about adoption, or let the child come up with explanations for why she was adopted. I liken this approach to the challenge of doing a thousand-piece jigsaw puzzle without a picture for guidance. Parents who follow this strategy often comment that their child "remembers nothing" and "isn't interested" in asking or hearing about adoption.

An adopted child's fragmented memories, full of sensations and feelings from the past, are like the thousand pieces of such a puzzle. When parents provide a basic structure for organizing the pieces, they help a child put the puzzle together. A parent's job is to help a child make sense of the world. For example, when a bully is mean to our child, we help her understand what happened. We talk about emotions she is likely to have, such as hurt feelings, anger, or sadness. When we do this we are not putting ideas into her head; if we are on the wrong track the child is likely to tell us so: "I don't feel sad; I want to hit him back." We are not living in an age when children are "seen and not heard." We constantly hear our children's ideas and feelings, and we need to attend to and trust their responses to our suggestions. A blank look means you are off track. A smile or nod means you have hit the nail on the head. One child I know says "Ding-ding-ding," like a game-show bell, when Mom or Dad correctly intuits her feelings about adoption.

WHAT HAPPENED TO ME?

Early-childhood professionals in many fields recognize the immense importance of speaking honestly to a child about challenging topics. Alicia Lieberman has written, "Children profit from the parents' ability to tell a story of what happened, to speak to the child's fear of loss, and to reassure the child that the parent 'is here to stay.'" Fred Rogers made the point succinctly. "What is mentionable is manageable," he wrote. Working with your child so that he can tell his own story makes the story "mentionable" and makes "manageable" the feelings associated with the story. There is no better time than the moment you meet your child to begin telling him about what just happened. Reflect on your child's behavior and the feelings associated with the behavior using the five coping skills (see chapter 5). For example, when meeting your child for the first time, or during the subsequent hours and days, you can comment, "It's easier to sleep [or keep busy] than to look at a strange, new face. I bet when you have that stunned look on your face, you are wondering where all your familiar caregivers and the other children went."

THE THREE-PHOTO STORY

Once you are settled at home, or any time thereafter, the simplest way to tell your child's story is with a sequence of three photographs. The first photo is of your child before adoption. The second photo is of the "handover," showing you receiving your child from the orphanage caregiver or director, or from foster parents. The third is a photo of your child with her present family. These three photos pasted in sequence provide the context for answering what I call the Four

Questions (see the next section of this chapter). If your earliest "photo" is a video, you can transfer a single frame to a photo format. If you do not have a handover photo, create one by making a collage that combines your child, a caregiver, and yourself into a single picture. A pencil sketch with stick figures is better than nothing; you just want your child to see whom you are talking about.

Photocopy each of the pictures and size (or resize) them equally. For example, each photo might be three inches wide by five inches tall. Together the three pictures make a nine-by-five-inch unit. Then place the three photos together in the copy machine to create a single sheet.

The first photograph, ideally the earliest one you have of your child, opens the door to the past. "First you lived with [birth parent or foster parent or other caregiver's name] in [name of country]." The second photo explains the Big Change, the handover: "This picture was taken when you joined our family." Of the third photo you might say, "Now we are a family: parent and child."

Young children will need your help with putting together this simple set of pictures, but they will benefit from helping you. Children of four years and older may want to choose specific photos or additional items other than photos. One child I know wanted to include her green card in a collage that represented her transition from Korean national to American citizen. Another child wanted to include a picture of Guatemala's national symbol, the quetzal.

Once you have the three photographs in sequence on a single sheet, make at least ten copies of it, because some copies may be lost, hidden, or destroyed as your child works through her feelings about the past. You do not need color photos or photocopies, but you can certainly use color if you wish. Laminate some sheets to protect them. Leave others in paper form, but be prepared for them to be ripped apart, hidden, or chewed upon. Place the copies in your home where your child can see and reach them. One might be placed on a lower part of the refrigerator door, for example, or on your child's bedside table. Laminated versions of the Three-Photo Story should be small enough for your child to hold in her hand, and also small enough to keep in a backpack or to tuck next to a car seat. The Three-Photo Story is an adopted child's special talisman.

Even when you are not present to tell your child her story, she can look at the photos and recall what happened. The photo story provides a reality check for the child's feelings as well as her memories, even those she has not yet found the means to express verbally.

If you are reading this before you meet your child, ask for the earliest photos available. Have a photo taken of the moment you receive your child from whoever presents her to you, or photograph a reenactment. If you are reading this book after returning home, start putting these three photos together as soon as you can.

What can you expect when you use the Three-Photo Story? When a child hears her own story, she calms and is able to focus attention. If you are not there, just looking at the photo story can help a child organize her feelings and actions. Sometimes focusing on the Three-Photo Story becomes the occasion for a pre-verbal child to act out specific feelings. For example, Soon An at one year of age repeatedly hid her Three-Photo Story among her stuffed animals. Sonia at eighteen months tore several of her unlaminated stories apart and chewed up the handover pictures in each case. Mu Ling threw several story collages in the trash, and Yi Sheng expressed his feelings about what happened by stomping on his photos and yelling, "Bad!" Providing a focus for your child's upset, negative feelings is an important step away from randomly directed negative behaviors. The story photos help a child make sense of her coping or survival behaviors, and they provide a context for as yet unshared memories.

When a parent engages with a child who is reacting to her photo story, the child's life becomes the hub for connection with her family and a part of the foundation for her developing identity and resiliency.

USING THE THREE-PHOTO STORY TO ANSWER THE FOUR QUESTIONS

Young children who have been adopted, I have found, have four vital questions to which they need simple, concrete answers. These questions and their answers will guide much of what you say to your child about his experiences. You are likely to find, however, that there are no perfect answers. Your child will ask again and again to hear the questions and answers, so if you goof up one or two times, you will have many opportunities to get it right. Think of it as a process that is at least eighteen years long.

Question 1: What Happened to Me?

Answer: Tell your child that she has gone through a big change. You might say, "First you lived in [country name, birth home, and foster home or orphanage], and then you came to live here with me. This was a very big change." You can spread your hands out wide to show how all-encompassing the change was. To explain further, you can describe how you are different from former caregivers, in terms of appearance—eyes, hair, age, odor, and so on—as well as language and culture. You can say that everything now is new and different. Using the child's native language for terms such as *big, change, new,* and *different* can be helpful. The term *Big Change* is more concrete and meaningful to a child than the abstract word *adoption*.

Use the Three-Photo Story to summarize your explanation visually. Point to the first photo of your child when you say, "First you lived in [name of country]." Point to the second photo when you acknowledge that "[name of caregiver, or word for the caregiver in the child's first language] gave you to me, to be my child." Point to the third photo when you say, "Then you came to live with me. And you will live with me until you are an old lady [man] just like Grandma [Grandpa]!"

Question 2: Who Will Take Care of Me Now?

Answer: "I will take care of you all day and all night," you might say, "every single day." Point to yourself and pantomime sleeping and waking. You may want to make an additional series of photos to show how you take care of your child. Again, photos or drawings make your words more real and memorable to your child.

Question 3: Did I Make the Big Change Happen?

Answer: Tell your child emphatically, "You did *not* make the Big Change happen. Grownups made it happen." This seemingly simple concept is virtually impossible for young children to grasp. To help your child understand, point out other infants or toddlers and ask, "Could that baby make a mommy leave?" If your child says yes, ask how. Help your child conduct a reality test about the limited power of young children. This will help him grasp that the Big Change could not possibly have been caused by his own actions or choices.

At this juncture you might want to have your child look at the two early photos in the photo story while you ask, "Were you big enough when this picture was taken to change what was happening to you?"

Question 4: Will Everything Change Again, and Will I Lose You, Too?

Answer: "I don't think there will be any more big changes," you can say, "but we both know nothing is certain. I will let you know if another big change is coming, so that you won't be surprised. I made a plan that if anything happens to me, [name] will take care of you. But I hope and believe that you and I will be together while you grow up until you are at least as old as I am. I think we will be two old people together one day." For a child more than three or four years old, who lives in a two-parent family, you eventually want to add, "If anything happens to me, your [other parent] will take care of you." By age six or seven many children ask what will happen if both parents die, so be prepared to explain your guardianship plans.

EARNING YOUR CHILD'S TRUST

Let your child know you are smart enough to understand that "anything can happen." Your child, no matter how young, already knows this from experience. If you try to avoid this reality, she will know immediately that you are lying.

How can your child trust you if you are so naive as to believe that nothing bad can happen? How can a child trust you if you lie? The truth is more reassuring than a "sweet answer." For this reason I do not encourage parents to use the phrase *forever family*, which some adoption professionals and adoptive parents favor. Nothing is forever, and your child knows that.

Forever family is also an abstract notion for a child. Young children do not grasp *forever* as an unlimited time. This is why describing how aged your child will be ("old like me," "old like Grandma") is more effective. Instead of "forever family," you can say "second family," "United States family," "Canadian family," or another similar phrase.

WHEN THE FOUR QUESTIONS REMAIN UNANSWERED

A child who needs answers to the Four Questions and has not received them becomes anxious about the future, regardless of how young he may be. Infants who do not hear an explanation expect the worst—another handover at any moment. These worries cause the infant, toddler, or preschooler to be hyper-alert, to scan the room, to be unable to soothe and interact playfully with parents, or to be unable even to sleep through the night.

Many parents do not realize that even the youngest child worries about "what will happen next." Toddlers sometimes enter my office and behave like Tigger, bouncing all over while Mom or Dad wonders aloud if the child is "hyperactive." When I ask parents what they have told their child about adoption and the past, they often say to me, "My child is too young to understand what happened," or "My child has forgotten about it," or "She isn't really interested." Parents cannot be faulted; they do not know how to talk about this with very young children.

An infant experiences his fear in physical terms: Who will feed me? Will that person continue to bring me food? Parents of a child less than a year old can talk to him at feeding time, saying, "You know that someone else used to feed you in [child's country or name of orphanage] and change your diapers. Now I am your Mama [Papa] and I will feed you and diaper you every day. There will be no other grownups taking care of you like before. Family is different." Avoid including even regular caregivers, as this blurs the boundaries between parents and other adults. When an infant hears words like these, which refer to his simple bodily needs, with a prop, such as a bottle, for illustration, he quickly grasps the meaning. Adoptive parents with whom I work often do not believe this and dismiss the smile, the chortle, or the outstretched hand that is the infant's form of communication. I can assure you that these are not random acts.

Let us use the bouncy, "hyperactive" toddler to illustrate what hearing his own story can do for a child. In my office I pull out my dolls and begin telling the child's story from his viewpoint. "You were a little baby in [country name] and this lady took care of you," I say. "You called her [name]; then one day some strangers came and took you with them, and you never saw your first caregiver anymore." Then I retell the story in more detail, this time including answers to the Four Questions.

The parents, I find, often listen to the story as if they have never heard it before. The story from the child's viewpoint is new to them. Parents watch as their previously hyper-alert infant focuses his calm attention on the dolls, or as a sleeping child rouses to watch. The toddler stops bouncing off the walls and comes over to listen. Telling the child's own story, from the child's viewpoint, creates a calm, alert state, what psychologists call a *regulated state*, in both children and adults. Often the child turns to the adoptive parent and acknowledges the parent's presence with a gesture, smile, or touch. When the child knows a parent understands his story, he reaches out and connects. The child begins to trust that the parent "knows what happened to me in the past and what is going on now."

When parents fail to make sense of the child's experience, the child becomes more agitated or withdrawn, falling repeatedly into a *disregulated state*, alternating between revving and shutting down. The child becomes less interested in interacting with parents and blocked in his development. A hyperactive or withdrawn child has trouble listening and making sense of directions. Such a child has trouble with memory, physical coordination, and interacting socially with others. Without being able to listen, pay attention, and remember, even learning to put shoes in the closet becomes a major challenge. This child can easily become misidentified as learning disabled, hyperactive, or depressed.

"What is mentionable is manageable."

Fred Rogers

MOST ADOPTION STORIES TELL
THE PARENTS' SIDE OF THE STORY

If you tell the adoption story from your point of view as the parent, you will have a hard time building a connection with your child. She will not achieve a calm and focused regulated state within which she can come to grips with her experience. If, for example, you say, "We wanted a little girl to be our own daughter, and we looked for you and found you in Guatemala," your child hears you saying that her own story is not as important as yours. Most adoption books marketed for children tell the story from the parents' viewpoint, not the child's. These **A child learns to parrot the adoption story from a parent's point of view.** books satisfy adults but frustrate the child. They suggest to a child that her feelings should not be revealed or discussed, especially negative feelings. However, children do grasp that the story is important to parents and quickly learn to "parrot" it perfectly, but without genuine emotion.

PARENTS FEAR TELLING THEIR CHILD'S ADOPTION STORY

Some parents are afraid to tell their child's story, to show a photo of the foster mother or the orphanage staff to their child, or to watch a video of them receiving their child or visiting the foster family. These parents fear that the images or discussions will cause their child to be more upset. "I can't say the *o* word," one mother told me. She and I then practiced whispering the word *orphanage* until she could say it comfortably.

These feelings are understandable. Your child's past was and is a painful reality. Until you are comfortable with the realities of your child's past, you cannot talk meaningfully to him.

Refusing to talk about the past with your child creates an unnecessary divide between the two of you. Bringing about this divide creates more problems than it solves. Mostly these problems are the parents' own difficult feelings: jealousy of a foster mother, fear of not being a good enough parent, insecurity about claiming the child as one's real son or daughter. If you struggle with these feelings, get help. Usually it does not take long to untangle painful feelings and to move on and talk comfortably with your child.

Your child has already experienced all alone the upsetting feelings of separation and loss. Recalling those past situations does bring upset, but you can help your child manage these feelings because now he is no longer alone.

Remembering loss with someone changes the memory. From then on, the child (and you) will remember the loss as shared, not as experienced alone. The experience of shared loss is the healing balm of a relationship.

Many parents point to their child's enormous success in language and cognitive development and tell me that it was all accomplished without ever having had to tell the child's story. This omission silently puts pressure on a child to "move on" or "get over it," to think about anything other than adoption and loss. These parents tell me they want their child to "be normal." They quote the old adage "Least said, soonest mended." This approach forces a child to continue relying on survival and coping behaviors that mask true feelings. Often such a child engages in repeating and reflecting the very feelings he attributes to those who abandoned or left him. For example, one boy of eight was described by his mother as "incredibly well adjusted"—he "just doesn't think about his adoption," she told me. But the same boy told me, "They [his birth parents and other adults] didn't care about me and I don't care about them. I won't think about them."

MEMORY TRIGGERS AND ANNIVERSARY REACTIONS

Scars from trauma often emerge in the form of an intense emotional upset or, as one mother put it, "an emotional storm." Recognizing what triggers such storms can help parents learn more about their child's past. Mu Ling's parents noticed that she became distraught at the sight and odor of cardboard boxes. She consistently reacted with hysterical crying even when she spotted a box at a distance. Her parents naturally wondered if Mu Ling had had some frightening experience with a cardboard box. They wrote to the orphanage for details of how she was found and were told that Mu Ling indeed had been found in a box. We can well imagine the emotional connection Mu Ling made as a tiny infant to being alone and seeing and smelling the cardboard container in which she was left. Her parents could now help her make sense of her feelings by giving them a context.

Watching for and understanding *memory triggers* is a unique part of parenting an internationally adopted child. Figuring out the source of a memory trigger requires some detective work, predicated on the parent's belief in the implicit memories of infants and young children and a willingness to honor those early experiences as real.

Sometimes the memory trigger is an anniversary of some sort. The first anniversary trigger I encountered was with a non-adopted adult, a thirty-five-year-old woman whom I was seeing because her depression was interfering with her parenting. The client informed me that "May is the worst month of the year" for her, but she did not know why. On a hunch I asked her to inquire of her parents what, if anything, might have happened in May during her early childhood. The woman returned the next week with information that stunned both of us.

My client's father told her that her mother had suffered a complete nervous breakdown not long after giving birth to her daughter. The mother was hospitalized, and the father took his four-month-old daughter to stay with her grandparents more than a thousand miles away. The month was May, and though my client had been an infant at the time, the month still had meaning for her as an adult.

Anniversary reactions are emotional and physiological upsets that commemorate a painful event. They often occur yearly, but they may take place as often as weekly. Internationally adopted children frequently have anniversary reactions. Carolyn and David, for example, were stymied by Sonia's refusal to leave the house on Wednesdays. Every week it was a struggle to get her off to daycare on that particular day. "It doesn't make sense," David said. "Monday is the first day after a weekend, and Mondays are no problem. Tuesdays and Thursdays and Fridays are fine, too. On Wednesday Sonia throws unbelievable tantrums and cries like she'll never see us again."

Wednesday certainly had some importance to Sonia. When David and Carolyn learned about anniversary reactions, they checked their records and discovered that Wednesday was the day they left Guatemala with Sonia, who was one year old at the time. Although they found it hard to believe, this was the only connection or explanation they could find.

Some children have a monthly reaction, especially during their first year in their new home, on or around the date they were separated from their birth mother, or were brought to the orphanage, or left the foster home or orphanage with their new family. Adoption Day is often just a day or two apart from the day a child left her birth country, and the two events blend together into one Big Change.

How a person's mind and body keep track of anniversaries of trauma on a weekly or yearly schedule is not completely understood. (See "The Body Keeps Score" by B. A. van der Kolk for a summary of research on trauma and memory.) But anniversary reactions are an accepted phenomenon among clinicians and researchers who study trauma. An anniversary reaction provides an opportunity to reflect on or mourn losses, changes, and traumatic events.

PREPARING FOR ANNIVERSARY REACTIONS
AND KNOWN TRIGGERS

Adopted children are reminded of their past on their own and others' birthdays, on the Mother's Day and Father's Day holidays, and of course on the anniversary of their adoption. Any and all of these occasions may be preceded by emotional storms and coping behaviors (see chapter 5). What might your child be thinking on his own birthday, or the birthday of a sibling or parent? One child I know said to his mother, "You have your birth mother with you and you are old. I'm little, and I don't." Other children express feelings of loss by worrying that "my birth mother doesn't know it's my birthday" and "everyone has forgotten about me." These comments reflect a child's fear of being unlovable.

Most parents are frustrated, if not furious, when a child is cranky and negative on Mother's Day or Father's Day, let alone during a birthday celebration. Major disconnections occur between parent and child when the adult is unaware of the child's anniversary reactions. On Mother's Day, for example, a four-year-old child may be thinking not about his adoptive mother but about his birth mother, and he may be feeling sad, angry, or rejected. A two-year-old child, or even an infant, may sense that something, or someone, is missing and may feel the letdown of having been rejected. Just as the child is feeling especially and truly unlovable, he is expected to show loving and happy feelings toward a different mother. Usually the mother who is present gets the full blast of the emotional storm as the family attempts to enjoy a lovely holiday.

Some parents have their own grief issues connected with birthdays and holidays. Infertility makes a child's birthday in particular a double-edged sword. The illness or death of a parent's parent, or a dysfunctional relationship between a parent and his or her own parent, may cloud the day as well. These factors can interfere with a parent's compassionate focus on the child.

Contrary to some people's belief, preparing for anniversary reactions does not make those reactions worse. In fact, the best thing to do is to mark your calendar the *week before* every anniversary or birthday. Do not forget to mark the days on which you met your child, left the child's birth country, and arrived home. If you know the days your child separated from his birth parents, moved from a foster home to the orphanage, or underwent similar transitions, note those as well.

As you prepare, focus on a plan to help your child manage strong feelings. Reduce social expectations of your child, and keep stimulation lower than normal. Some families make these anniversaries days just to stay home and "chill."

Some children may want to eat their favorite comfort food or see a special friend. The important thing is to minimize stress and anxiety so that your child can feel in control emotionally and behaviorally as much as possible.

Of course, many parents want to celebrate Adoption Day with a big family extravaganza. Parents view Adoption Day as wonderful, but your child may look back on this day as the day strangers turned his life upside down. I have heard the term *Gotcha Day*, which I think is ill advised, because "gotcha" focuses on the parents' feelings, not the child's. If you sidestep your child's feelings, your child is likely to hide his genuine feelings behind coping behaviors and fall prey to an emotional storm before or after the big event.

A week to a few days before the anniversary, tell your child his story using the Three-Photo Story and go over the answers to the Four Questions. Leave space in your conversations to allow your child time to get in touch with his feelings. Talk about and play about how your child feels about these events, even if the feelings are not completely happy. Draw some big faces, each with a different expression—sad, scared, surprised, happy, tired, hungry—and talk about when your child may have had these feelings in the past. Some children may want to display these drawings; others may choose to rip them up, throw them away, or hide them. Any of these choices is acceptable. These activities, from drawing to ripping, enable your child to express his strong feelings appropriately and in this way defuse the emotional storms. Then he will be ready to celebrate the happy aspects of anniversaries and birthdays.

MOTHER'S DAY AND FATHER'S DAY

These two days in particular need some special comment. Parents who set aside the night before each of these holidays for birth parents find that their children are much more positive celebrating the next day, when the adoptive parents are the focus. One mother I know decided to light a candle for her child's birth mother. Another mother decided to light one candle for her child's birth mother and another candle for the foster mother. In Yi Sheng's family everyone lit a candle for an adult who had nurtured him or her but was no longer part of the person's life. Nina, Yi Sheng's mother, mentioned that her second-grade teacher was a very important nurturing influence in her life, but that after elementary school they drifted apart. The night before Mother's Day, Nina lit a candle for her teacher and a candle each for Yi Sheng's foster mother and his birth mother. On the night before Father's Day Kenji, Yi Sheng's father, lit a candle for his soccer coach, who had been like a second father but now lived in another state. Kenji also helped Yi Sheng light candles for his birth father and foster father, and Nina lit a candle for an uncle who was an important support in her life.

When your child gets older, starting at four or five years of age, she can dictate a short note to the birth parent or draw a picture. Place the note or picture in a special box that is for similar communications in the future. Yi Sheng wanted to "burn paper" to send messages to his family. Somewhere in his short life, he had learned of this Chinese tradition of communicating with and supporting departed ancestral spirits. Nina and Kenji incorporated this tradition into their celebrations of birthdays and other holidays. Finding out about your child's cultural heritage and how communication with the "dead" is arranged may be a way to help your child feel connected with her birth parents.

Internationally adopted children feel less out of the ordinary, and less as if they are in a spotlight, for having a missing set of parents when, on the night before Mother's Day or Father's Day, every member of the family honors special people who are no longer present.

TRANSITIONS

Beyond holidays, internationally adopted children typically experience a strong response to other transitions and life changes, such as the last day of school or of daycare, the last day of summer, the beginning of a school term, or the beginning of summer camp. Transitions are changes, and all changes evoke feelings connected with the Big Change, the adoption handover and the time the child's life was turned upside down. Approach these days much as you would Adoption Day and other holidays. Keep stress and stimulation to a minimum. Some children just need an R & R Day, a day of rest and relaxation.

Transitions, anniversaries, and holidays are important times to retell your child's story and help him begin to tell it in his own words. However, adopted children think about their stories every single day, which you may observe when you see how frequently your child looks at his Three-Photo Story. Talking about the continuity of your child's life every day in some small fashion is a worthy parenting goal. Remember, helping your child tell his story is a fundamental strategy for building his connection with you. It is a critical factor in mending your child's fragmented and complex sense of identity. Finally, it helps your child use his conscious, rational brain to control the stress-shaped brain (see chapter 2) and develop self-control of emotions and behaviors. Telling your child's story, from his perspective, is at the core of successfully parenting every internationally adopted child.

The Roots of Identity

We Are Alike, We Are Different

THE WORDS OF PARENTS, spoken to a child or about a child, are a child's first mirror. A child's sense of identity begins when a parent calls a child by name. Identity grows as Mom, Dad, and others comment, "What a cute little baby!" "What lovely dark eyes!" "She's so active!"

Often the first word a child hears from a parent is the child's name, and the name is repeated more frequently to or around the child than any other word. Bill Cosby, the comedian, commented on this phenomenon when he described how for years he believed his name was "Bill-Damn-it," because that was how his father addressed him. A child's name, and other words used frequently in association with that name, are the earliest ways a child knows who she is.

Researchers have demonstrated that by four and a half months of age a child can pick her first name out of a stream of words and shows clear signs of identifying with the name. In 2000 the Parliament of New South Wales, Australia, revised the country's adoption laws and made it illegal to change the first names of children who were either noncitizens of any age or citizens over six months of age. "Adoption law . . . must assist a child," the Parliament wrote, "to preserve their [sic] identity, including their cultural heritage. The preservation of a child's name is important to their identity."

NAMING AND IDENTITY: THE BEGINNING OF A COHERENT STORY

Adoptive parents have strong feelings about, and reasons for, renaming their child. Many feel that bestowing a name is an immediate way to claim the child.

Choosing a name can make the pending adoption feel more real to the parents and make them feel more "parentlike." But abandoning the child's former name also jettisons a part of the child's past. Identity is a challenging issue for internationally adopted children. Changing a child's name sends a powerful message to the child and to others about the child's identity: It suggests the child's past should vanish, just as the child's original name has.

REASONS TO KEEP A CHILD'S ORIGINAL NAME

1. The child recognizes and identifies with the name by four months of age.
2. A name is the first way people identify themselves, from infancy onward.
3. The name provides a link to the past.
4. The name may have been given by birth parents.
5. The name is linked to a child's ethnic or national origins.
6. A change of name is confusing for young children.
7. A change of name suggests a parental rejection of country of origin or ethnic background.
8. Parents want to keep the child's past and present life connected.

"My mother says the name Demetri sounds too Russian," Denise, who is Demetri's adoptive mother, commented. "She thinks it will remind him of the orphanage."

Many parents feel uncomfortable with keeping a child's former name, believing he does not want to be reminded of the past. If you are uncomfortable being reminded of your child's past, ask yourself how you will be able to help your child accept and integrate his past into his identity. The issue of the past is always on the table, always present, in the adoptee's mind. Changing the child's name makes life easier for a parent, but only temporarily.

If you have already changed your child's name, turn this decision into a positive opportunity for talking with your child about his past. When you tell the Three-Photo Story (see chapter 7), use your child's original name and link it to his new name. Explaining the name change is a critical part of supporting your child's development of a healthy identity. For an infant or toddler, a simple statement is sufficient. "In [birth country] you were called Maria. That's what your foster mother called you. But we picked a new name for you: Sonia. Maria was your baby name, and Sonia is your big girl name."

Some children who have difficulty integrating their identities use different names to represent compartmentalized feelings. An example of how identity shatters after trauma and names become involved emerged in the way one four-year-old used his Chinese, English, and Hebrew names. "I'm An Li when I'm angry," he told his mother and me, "and when I am with my friends at school I'm Alex. Ari, my Hebrew name, is who I am when I'm sad." Parents can help a child like An Li–Alex–Ari integrate his sense of self by touching base with all three "parts" and encouraging the parts to share the same feelings.

Many cultures give more than one name to a child. In China an infant is given a "milk name" to ward off evil spirits. Later the child is given a "school name" and also receives a private family nickname. Having two names is not the issue. It is the loss or rejection of the original name that leads to identity concerns. It is important that your child be able to hold on to the past by holding on to his original name, even a name provided by the orphanage.

PHYSICAL APPEARANCE AND IDENTITY

Physical appearance is another important early element of identity. The identity of a child who is born into or grows up in a family that shares a strong resemblance derives in part from shared physical traits. "Oh, he's one of the Joneses; look at all his freckles!" you might hear. Such a comment helps a child identify with the family: "Hey, I'm one of the Joneses!" Similarly, a child who grows up in a homogeneous racial environment has a sense of belonging because she looks like everyone around her. A child concludes that "we all look similar, so we all belong together." This is a basic identification connection, which all children seek. Researchers think that this perception of the division of the world into "the familiar" and "the other" is an important component of human survival instincts.

Your challenge as a parent of an internationally adopted child is to create a sense of identity and connection by *inclusion*, not by *exclusion*. The key is making your child believe that differences do not undermine either her identity or her connection to the family.

What your child needs to hear: "We are different in some ways, we are the same in other ways, but we are always a family."

Step 1 in building identity is for parent and child together to acknowledge and explore the differences between them. This includes physical differences and such ordinary things as preferences for foods, games, or colors. Step 2 is to look for and be aware of similarities between a parent and child, including physical features, interests, food preferences, and the like. Step 3 is an overarching statement that asserts the deep and basic connection between parent and child: "We are different in some ways, we are the same in other ways, but we are always a family."

EXPLORING PHYSICAL SIMILARITIES AND DIFFERENCES

A child as young as four months is avidly focused on a parent's face. Talking about facial features is a good way to begin conversing with your child about physical similarities and differences. Children of all ages are interested in faces, so this type of activity is not age limited.

Looking in a mirror together is an excellent way to get started. Point out the same features on your face and on your child's face. Let your child help. Once you have looked in the mirror, try gently touching each other's faces. When your child is familiar with the similarities, you can point out differences. "Baby's eyes are brown," you might say, "and Mommy's eyes are blue." You can then add a third concept, that *differences do not separate*, that they do not create a disconnection between two people, soon after your child grasps the idea of *different*.

The exploration of *same* and *different* can extend to physical movements and activities. Point out that "Mommy walks, and Baby walks, too." Or, to show a difference, say, "Mommy walks, but Baby runs." Remind your child that "even when Mommy and Baby are different, they still love each other; they are still a family."

Learning that difference is not equivalent to separation or disconnection between people is a critical piece of identity work during your adopted child's development. This concept will grow in importance as your child gets older, when you begin to have differences of opinion and different notions of what you each want. In the early years these differences are the context in which you set limits ("Baby wants cookies and Mommy doesn't want Baby to eat cookies; Mommy says no"). Later, when, for example, you and your teenager disagree about values and beliefs, the concept that *connection exists despite differences* becomes increasingly important.

EXPLORING SIMILARITIES AND DIFFERENCES IN THE FAMILY

You do not need to look alike racially or share the same ethnicity to develop a family identity or a parent-child identity. Families have their own identity that develops from the contributions of all the members. There are simple ways to express or symbolize this family identity to your child. For example, mother-daughter outfits, or father-son hats, never go out of style. Such fashion statements make the point that "we go together." Of course, you do not have to stick with gender stereotypes. Girls might want a baseball hat like Mom has or an apron like Dad, the family chef, has; little boys might love a ski hat or carpenter's belt that looks just like the one Mom has. Wearing similar clothes, colors, hair ornaments, or accessories is a great way to help an internationally adopted child identify with the new family or parent despite differences in racial or ethnic background.

SOME FAMILY RESEMBLANCE EXAMPLES

Family's favorite expression: "Oh, boy!" or "Wowie!"
The hat family
The loud family
The family with red belts
The mother-and-son matching cowboy boots family
The red socks (or Red Sox) family

You will thrill at your child's delight when a complete stranger comments, "Oh, you are both wearing red socks!" Then you can reply, "Of course, because we are mother and daughter." This is the kind of experience that reinforces a child's feeling of a special seamless connection of family, a connection that other people immediately recognize.

MU LING: DIFFERENT EYES

Mu Ling, when she was almost three years old, one day pointed to her mother's blue eyes and then at her own dark brown eyes, and then she frowned. Meg wondered if Mu Ling was developing a negative self-image.

Children as young as two can demonstrate that they recognize the difference between round Caucasian eyes and almond-shaped Asian eyes, and researchers have shown that babies less than one year old perceive such differences. They do not yet know about racism, but they do know about similarity and difference. Mu Ling did not have the words to let Meg know that Meg's eyes looked different from her own eyes and those of her former caregivers. Mu Ling needed vocabulary and concepts to explain her observation.

You should acknowledge differences when your child notes them, or begin when your child is between two and three years old. Dolls or other play characters with different racial and ethnic features can help your child understand physical differences. They can also help your child feel less "on the spot," less self-conscious. Talking about differences is part of being in tune with your child's observations. Providing your child with descriptive language about shapes, colors, and sizes, and about the concepts of *same* and *different*, will deepen the connection between the two of you.

TERMS OF BEAUTY AND ENDEARMENT

Each culture has terms, both concrete and metaphorical, for describing such qualities as beauty or cuteness. To Chinese people, for example, "almond-shaped" eyes, a "moon face," and small hands and feet are signs of beauty. Spanish speakers may refer to a child as "my soul" or "my heaven."

Identifying the specific affectionate terms or phrases of beauty appropriate to your child will take a little research and perhaps a bit of gumption. An easy approach is to ask the wait staff at an ethnic restaurant what compliments are given to children in their native country. Write down the answers using phonetic lettering, and practice with your "teachers" to make sure you are saying the words correctly. Another source is the love poetry of your child's country, either in the original if you know the language or in translation, in which you can seek recurring phrases of praise or beauty.

SPECIFIC PRAISE AND THE FEAR OF BEING UNLOVABLE

Internationally adopted children often struggle with the belief that they are responsible for their own abandonment. When a child fears that he is unlovable, and that this was the cause of his abandonment, he may interpret his mistakes or his parents' criticisms as confirmation of his negative self-image. This feeling can contribute to a loss of resiliency in the face of criticism. As children reach school age, their struggles with this identity issue frequently emerge as perfectionism.

Specific praise can give such a child a reality check. "I'm careful, neat, and thorough. I guess I can't be all bad!" the child may reason. Psychologists who study children have found that a child with a more complex and well-defined self-image is less likely to be emotionally devastated by criticism than a child who has a generalized sense of identity. Thinking hard to come up with specific words of praise is a positive contribution you can make daily to your child's sense of self. What you tell your child about himself piles up on the positive side of the balance. Your child will ultimately use these specific descriptions to combat his fears that he is or was unlovable and deserved to be thrown away.

CULTURAL AND ETHNIC IDENTITY FOR YOUNG CHILDREN

Many parents of internationally adopted children are rightfully concerned about how to integrate the ethnic and cultural heritage of their children into the family. The best way to do this is to focus on the tangible and ordinary world of home and neighborhood. Toddlers, preschoolers, and kindergartners need concrete experiences to develop their cultural and ethnic identity.

Culture for young children and even those of school age begins in the kitchen. One of the best ways to start the day is by having a familiar food. A Russian breakfast might consist of blintzes, which are thin pancakes filled with cheese, and eggs. Russians live on soups of all kinds, especially those that include barley. A Chinese breakfast begins with a rice porridge such as *congee* or *jook* and a fried "doughnut." Korean children have rice or porridge with *kimchi* or with flat sheets of seaweed. In Guatemala breakfast might be corn tortillas and eggs along with leftover chicken or meatball soup.

Serving ethnic food is a tangible experience of culture for your child. Obtain an ethnic cookbook, or find recipes from your child's homeland on the Web. If you feel that you cannot cook ethnic meals, find a restaurant and get takeout.

You may need to shop in neighborhoods other than your own to find ethnic foods and spices. If you have the appropriate ethnic neighborhood in your city or town, try to visit and shop there weekly. Find a grocery store with a friendly clerk who can direct you around the store, suggest recipes, or point out special treats from your child's country of origin. Bring your child along on these shopping excursions.

Find a restaurant you like, too, and eat there regularly with your child so that the wait staff gets to know your family. These workers, typically immigrants, first-generation Americans, like your child, are invaluable resources for you. Each one of them misses a homeland that you need to know about. They have a deep need to talk about and share their culture, and you can benefit by listening.

You may also be able to locate a gift store that sells holiday items from your child's country, or one that sells clothing, artwork, baskets, pottery, toys, or decorative items to hang on the wall. The shopkeeper in one of these stores is another resource from whom you can learn about customs, language, phrases, holidays, and toys.

Adopt this neighborhood as your second home. Read its local paper and keep it on your coffee table. Find out what issues affect the people from your child's homeland. You can also keep track of events in this community by reading the posters in the neighborhood. Be sure to attend local events such as parades, performances, and theater.

I recommend that you plan on a field trip to the ethnic neighborhood once a week, or at least twice a month, during the preschool years. These trips will provide your child with a comfortable familiarity, a foundation for returning when she is in elementary school and becomes more shy with strangers. Over the years the shopkeeper will see your child grow up and will be an ally in the community. This community connection will help you find resources when your child decides to take an ethnic dance class or learn to play a musical instrument from his homeland. The storekeeper, waitress, and grocer who know your child, and whom your child knows in return, will be important personages when your child is a teenager and feels awkward growing into an adult who looks quite different from Mom or Dad. Regardless of your child's age, going back to the neighborhood offers instant visual connections: "Hey, Mom, I look like these people!" Finally, these visits are opportunities to find foods, recipes, and household items that can be integrated into your family's meal planning and home life.

PRESCHOOL IDENTITY CHALLENGES

Preschool is usually the first place that an adopted child encounters questions and challenges about who he is, where he comes from, and why he and his parents "don't match." Six months after joining his family, five-year-old Yi Sheng began a year of preschool. As part of a family curriculum unit, Yi Sheng's preschool teacher asked the children to tell about their families. Yi Sheng came home silent and withdrawn. When his father asked him what was wrong, Yi Sheng explained that he knew nothing about his family, not even what part of China they came from. "Who am I?" he asked his father. "I have nothing to say. I won't go to school anymore."

It took weeks of patient work with Yi Sheng to put together some information that satisfied him. The family looked at maps and photographs, and they took out Yi Sheng's adoption papers and his Chinese passport and photo. Nina, his mother, checked out ten library books for children about China. She tried to read one with Yi Sheng but he threw a tantrum. It was clear he could not or would not sit and learn facts about China. After this "emotional storm," Yi Sheng asked his parents if he should simply talk about his American family. Finally, he decided he would tell the class he had two families, from two countries, and that he liked two types of food. He said he did not want to talk about being adopted. That was too private.

The big day arrived and Mom and Dad were invited to come for the presentation. Yi Sheng stood up in front of his class and said, "I am Chinese, because I come from China. I like Chinese food like pot stickers and noodles. I am American, too. I like pizza and French fries. I have two families and two countries." He proudly sat down.

The teacher wondered why the family said this was such a big deal for their son, for he seemed so poised and clear. She commented, "You did a fine job, Yi Sheng. You see? There was no need to worry so much."

There is no way that anyone but Yi Sheng and his parents could know that this brief and seemingly simple report was the result of so much heart-wrenching, soul-searching work. For Yi Sheng, who had explicit memories of his pre-adoption life, this preschool assignment was overwhelming.

Soon An, adopted at six months of age, reacted quite differently to the same assignment when she was four years old. She was delighted to talk about being "'dopted from Korea." For a child like her, with implicit memories only, such assignments generally are not emotionally difficult; it is not until seven, eight, or nine years of age that they create problems for the child.

These two examples represent two ends of the continuum of what identity work is like. For every internationally adopted child, constructing an integrated identity out of complex pieces requires extra work, extra sensitivity, and extra support.

Connection Activities and Games

LET US RETURN NOW TO THE FIRST YEAR Home Group (see chapter 1 for an introduction to the Group) and look at how the five children are doing in terms of connecting to their new parents. Each child now has a family age of two months, and the Group has met weekly over the past month. As we watch the children, we see how their connection to their parents has changed since the first week of the Group.

Soon An is now eight months old. She is on the floor, lying on her tummy and trying to scoot toward a toy.

Sonia, fourteen months old, is toddling around the room picking up toys. She scoops up a toy, takes a few steps, and puts the toy down. She repeats this over and over as she tours the room.

Demetri is twenty months old. He is across the room from his mother, busily unloading large beanbags from a wagon. After he empties the wagon he climbs in and then falls out, tipping the wagon over and banging his head. His back is toward Denise and he does not turn around, even when she calls his name.

Mu Ling is nearly three years old. She is dumping dolls out of a basket and then throwing them toward the basket, scattering them across the floor. Like Demetri, she is across the room from her parents, with her back turned to them.

Yi Sheng has hidden himself behind a large, overstuffed blue chair.

All of the children, with the exception of Soon An, who is not yet mobile, seem to be exploring the room and investigating the toys. In the process each child has put some distance between himself or herself and his or her parents. Despite the toys and the appearance of play, the children's behavior is not fully playful. Instead it literally reflects each child's difficulty with keeping things connected and under control. Sonia can hold on to a toy for no more than a few steps. Demetri empties the wagon and then falls out of it himself; nothing and no one can hold him, and he gets a bump in the bargain. Mu Ling scatters the dolls even as she tries to replace them in their basket. Yi Sheng has distanced and hidden himself not only from his parents but also from everyone else in the Group. Dropping things, emptying containers, falling out of wagons or off chairs, the inability to keep a block tower together or even to try to build one with available materials—all are play-signs of feeling lost. These types of play behaviors are typical of how children "talk" about their feelings of being alone, disconnected, and out of control. The repetitive nature of these activities over days or even months speaks to how "stuck" a child is emotionally.

CONNECTION AND CONTAINMENT

Children at similar chronological ages but who do not have complex backgrounds filled with separations typically engage in a more connected kind of play. Such a child picks up a block or toy and brings it to Mom, making a connection. The child repeats the activity often, confirming the connection. Children who feel connected represent their feelings in the way they arrange their toys. Blocks are stacked; train tracks or pillows are laid end to end. Dolls interact. A box of dolls that is emptied is refilled, showing the coming back together after a separation. When non-adopted children start learning how to master separation from their parents, such as when they begin daycare or preschool, their play resembles the play of the internationally adopted children described above. Within a few days or weeks, however, non-adopted children resume their connected style of play.

A sense of connection for all children begins in the nine months prior to birth. During this time the baby is connected to the mother with an umbilical cord and contained by the walls of her womb. The mother and child together inhabit what I call a Magic Circle. For some children this special sense of proximity and connection continues after birth, as a baby spends hours and days in a parent's lap or arms. The Magic Circle continues throughout the early childhood years of non-adopted children.

For children who are adopted, however, the Magic Circle is broken at the point when the birth mother and her child are permanently separated. In some cases this happens at birth, in others at a few months of age, and in others when the child is older. Occasionally a birth mother repeatedly visits her child after the separation but before adoption. This is what happened to Mu Ling, who lived in an orphanage but saw her birth mother every day when she came to work. A single separation is traumatic enough; multiple separations, such as Mu Ling's, are even more so.

THE MAGIC CIRCLE . . .

- is a fueling station for Parent Juice, to strengthen connection and soothe pain.
- protects a child from overstimulation, from exploring the world too fast.
- protects a child from the physical dangers of unsupervised exploration.
- provides an organizing center to the child's world.

Louise Kaplan, a noted author of books on infancy, babyhood, and toddlerhood, describes the first year of a child's life as "a time of Oneness" between parent and child. D. W. Winnicott, a child psychoanalyst and writer, has described how a parent provides a "holding environment" for the child. This sense of being held is not merely about physical security for the child but also about emotional security as well.

Vasopressin is a biochemical in the body that causes a child to stay close to a parent. Researchers have found that a child with low vasopressin levels engages in exploratory behavior and fails to stay close to a parent. It is known that internationally adopted children have a consistently lower than normal level of vasopressin, continuing as long as three years after their adoption. Therefore, adoptive parents who wait for their child to learn "automatically" to stay close to them may be in for a long wait. Instead, these parents have to be proactive and teach their child the family skill of *staying close.*

Children need to stay close to parents because parents meet a child's needs for survival: food, warmth, and shelter. In addition, proximity to parents is necessary in order for a child to learn from and communicate with a parent.

FUELING, AND REFUELING, WITH "PARENT JUICE"

What does this kind of containment or holding, this oneness, accomplish? Holding and other close interactions between parent and child stimulate the chemicals that both encourage and reinforce connection. The connection process also releases chemicals in the child that soothe sensations of physical and emotional pain. Holding, touching, playing with, and interacting with a child is the way a parent "fills up" the child with what I call Parent Juice. Researchers have shown that when a child is "filled up" by a parent prior to a separation, that child is more resilient and manages the emotional pain of separation with less difficulty.

Research shows that when a child is "filled up with Parent Juice" by close contact prior to a separation, the child is more resilient and the emotional pain of separation is less severe.

When you reach out to your child, you are providing her with Parent Juice. You can deliver Parent Juice only if you and your child are close together and mutually interacting, not when you are talking to your child from across the room. Even teens need a physical connection such as a hug or a hand squeeze from parents—at an unobtrusive moment, of course. Forming and re-forming the Magic Circle and regularly delivering Parent Juice are ways that you can overcome your internationally adopted child's difficulties with staying close to you and interacting frequently with you.

BUILDING THE MAGIC CIRCLE

When internationally adopted children first arrive, they cannot feel or see the Magic Circle of your love and care. Parents must teach a child how the Magic Circle operates, using activities to make it real.

I recommend three simple activities for teaching a young child about the Magic Circle. You can try them in any order. I describe them here in the context of the First Year Home Group, but you will find them easy to re-create at home.

MAGIC CIRCLE PARENTING ACTIVITIES

1. The Visible Magic Circle
2. Parent-on-a-Leash (or the Extended Umbilical Cord)
3. The Slinky Connection

The Visible Magic Circle

Soon An, eight months old, is lying on the floor near her mother. I hand Charlotte a ten-foot-long ribbon and ask her to create a circle with it on the floor. Both Soon An and her mother must be inside the circle.

Soon An can look at the ribbon and see that she and her mother are together within it. This is something a child as young as three or four months can observe. Charlotte uses both gestures and words to communicate what Soon An observes. "This ribbon," says Charlotte as she touches it, "holds us *together*." She gestures around the circle and continues, "We are *together* inside the circle." (For a child who is not yet mobile this small circle is sufficient; later in this chapter I describe using a larger circle for a child who is crawling or walking.)

Parent-on-a-Leash (or the External Umbilical Cord)

Mu Ling, almost three, is too active to want to stay in a circle made of ribbon. Parent-on-a-Leash is the ideal activity for an active toddler like her. Meg ties one end of the ten-foot-long ribbon to her own wrist and gives the other end to Mu Ling. Now Mu Ling moves away from her mother, but she discovers that her mother is connected to her! It takes only a few moments for Mu Ling to recognize the possibilities of this setup.

Safety note:

Careful supervision is needed when using ribbons, ropes, Slinkies, and other toys that could become wrapped around a child's neck.

Mu Ling walks backward, holding her end of the ribbon and watching her mother. When the ribbon becomes taut, Mu Ling tugs at it and observes how Meg moves toward her. Mu Ling grins and pulls the ribbon again. Without any requests, demands, or instructions from her mother, Mu Ling is suddenly deeply engaged in connecting with Mom.

Demetri observes what is happening. He gets his own ribbon, walks up to Denise, and motions that she should tie it to *his* wrist. Denise does so, and then she ties the other end to her own wrist. As Mu Ling did, Demetri begins experimenting with this new relationship. He turns and runs away from his mother, once they are tied together. When he reaches the full extent of the ribbon, he is stopped by the connection to his mother and tumbles to the ground. He jumps up and runs in a different direction and experiences the same thing. Despite his falls, Demetri seems to love the fact that he is contained by the connection.

Slinky Games for "Away" and "Back"

A Slinky is a toy that even a six-month-old child can manipulate. It is the perfect toy to use for talking with young children about the concepts of *going away* and *back together*. When I work with young children I simplify these concepts to *away* and *back*.

Yi Sheng, who has been hiding behind a chair, now peers out at the Group.

He watches Demetri and Mu Ling experiment with being tied to their parents. I give Yi Sheng's parents a Slinky to share and suggest that they play Away and Back, with each parent operating one end of the Slinky.

Yi Sheng is drawn to his parents and the game. He reaches out for the Slinky and begins experimenting with how it works. Each of his parents picks up a new Slinky and begins playing individually. As they pull the ends apart they say, "Away," and as they push the ends together they say, "Back together." After exploring his own Slinky further, Yi Sheng wants to take his mother's toy. She gives her son one end, but to create connection she continues to hold the other end. Now Yi Sheng and his mother play the Away and Back Game together. Yi Sheng begins to wave his end of the Slinky, and he looks at his mother and smiles. Connection between the Unwilling Guest (see chapter 5) and his mother is under way.

FROM COPING TO CONNECTION

As a child begins interacting with his parents within the Magic Circle, he begins to set aside his reactive coping behaviors and his play about separation. The purpose of reactive coping behaviors (described more fully in chapter 5), to manage stress by oneself, is no longer an issue. By connecting with a parent, the child gets a dose of Parent Juice and in this way receives support for staying emotionally and behaviorally calm.

These parenting strategies are aimed at teaching a child's brain to build new pathways that counterbalance the stress-shaped brain's reactions. Connection builds resiliency and family skills simultaneously. Each of the three activities just described encourages a set of basic family skills. Each child is learning how to recognize and stay close to a parent, how to focus and share attention, how to engage in face-to-face interaction, and how to play interactively with another person.

FAMILY SKILLS THAT ARE BUILT THROUGH MAGIC CIRCLE ACTIVITIES

1. Interacting face to face with a parent
2. Recognizing a parent
3. Staying close to a parent
4. Focusing attention on, and sharing attention with, a parent
5. Playing interactively with, and sharing joy with, a parent

---

MORE MAGIC CIRCLE GAMES AND ACTIVITIES

Many parents are convinced that once connection play begins, they are off the hook for additional work in this department. Nothing could be further from the truth. Internationally adopted children have a deeply etched belief that they are alone in the world. Under any degree of stress they quickly and easily revert to their solo coping behaviors. Building family skills takes time and practice. You need to have several activities at the ready to teach and reinforce connection with your child on a daily basis. These activities are as important as having a routine for brushing teeth or getting ready for bed. Look at these activities not as chores but as sources of joyful and happy connection, things that you and your child can look forward to doing and *want* to do together.

The Magic Circle Game

Use a longer ribbon or rope, about thirty feet, to create a circle on the floor, larger than the one in the Visible Magic Circle activity, in which you and your child can sit and play together, or play apart but nearby. This tactile, visual boundary creates a shared space for you and your child. Explain to your child that she must stay with you in the circle. She may leave to get a toy, but you expect her to return to the circle. If she does not, you will go to her and playfully bring her back. This is an opportunity to let your child know how important she is to you and how much you enjoy spending time *together*. A child who is old enough to move about needs to experience *simultaneously* being close to a parent *and* playing "independently."

At first a child will test the single, simple rule—Do not leave the circle—if only because of the habit of being on her own. Some children are hesitant or uncomfortable when physically close to a parent. Therefore, make the circle quite large to begin with, between eight and ten feet in diameter. As your child learns to play the game, you can reduce the size of the circle.

Birth children who play this game at first sit or play close to their parents, often facing them, and then they gradually move farther and farther away, periodically checking in. Internationally adopted children begin playing far from their parents, without checking back. Then they slowly move closer and gradually begin to face their parents. After this approaching period these children may begin to play again at a distance, but this time they are likely to check back if taught to do so by a proactive parent.

Parents observe that Magic Circle games help their child to remain focused and calm. Gradually a child learns to prefer the circle to the "outside world."

FAMILY SKILLS OF PROXIMITY

1. Facing parent while playing
2. Playing nearby parent
3. Engaging parent in play
4. Checking back with parent after moving away

Circle Games and Ring around the Rosy

This game requires that your child be old enough to stand up and walk on his own. Stand together inside the ribbon that forms a circle on the floor. Make sure that the ends are tied together securely. Face your child as you each pick up the ribbon, holding it behind your back. Then back away until you and your child are pulling the ribbon tight and you can feel the connection between you. You might play a walking game, moving in a circle as you hold the ribbon, pulling outward to keep the tension up. You can sing a song like "Ring around the Rosy" or "Sally Go 'round the Sun" during the walking part. When you "fall down," your child will feel the release from the circle and the lack of contact. This activity is a step beyond the away-and-back Slinky Game. Your child is developing a sense of connection, and of interdependence, that is uniquely different from the "I'm on my own" type of interdependence that most internationally adopted children develop. Both games will help your child get the feel of interdependence with a parent, whether when close by or at a distance.

This chapter describes very simple games suitable for young children. But it is also a model for how parents can build connection with their child at any age. Parents from the First Year Home Group report that their children will pull out a Slinky even as preteens or teenagers when they feel that the Magic Circle has been stretched too far or broken. So keep the Slinky and ribbon available even as your child grows up.

Eye Contact and
Face-to-Face Interaction

THE PREVIOUS CHAPTERS EXPLORED THE ROOTS of connection, following the stages of connection from infancy into early childhood. In the last chapter I introduced the concept of the external umbilical cord, with suggestions about how you can use ribbons to make the Magic Circle concept real for your child. In this chapter we move on to the next stage, face-to-face interaction and eye contact. Although such contact begins when an infant is first fed, your internationally adopted child may have had minimal contact of this kind during infancy, and in any case it was likely to have been with another caregiver. You need to teach your child the skills of eye contact and face-to-face interaction.

STRATEGIES TO TEACH AND MAINTAIN EYE CONTACT

Eye contact is a skill embedded in the process of feeding a baby. For a child raised by birth parents, face-to-face interactions occur so naturally that few parents realize how many hours of practice actually take place. In the first two weeks newborns eat every two hours for approximately twenty minutes each time. Feeding creates a physical interaction that brings infants and parents together face to face. At birth babies have a focal length of about twelve to eighteen inches, the distance between the baby and the parent's face when feeding, and they also have the innate ability to recognize and respond to faces, particularly eyes. With twelve feedings a day, a baby gets a

An infant gets approximately four hours of eye contact practice each day, spread out over about twelve feedings.

minimum of four hours of eye contact daily. In a week the baby has nearly thirty hours of practice.

In their first two months together, an infant and parent practice eye contact for approximately two hundred hours. Parents of an internationally adopted child need to replicate this level of eye contact and face-to-face interaction in order to retrace these early connection steps. Here are three strategies you can follow, beginning with what I believe is the best method—rewarding eye contact and face-to-face interactions with food.

Strategy 1: Use Food to Make Eye Contact and Establish Connection

Make your eyes stand out for your child. One mother I know used washable markers to draw a butterfly on her temples. Another mom put a beauty mark in the same place. Some parents simply point to their eyes.

Next, tell your child what you expect of her. Tell her that each time you speak to her, or she speaks to you, she needs to look in your eyes. Show your child a picture of a parent and child looking at each other to clarify your expectation.

Finally, tell your child that when she makes eye contact with you she will earn a treat. Some parents find that the child looks at the parent's face, but not into the parent's eyes. Tell your child, "Everything tastes better when we look in each other's eyes." This is truer than you might at first think, because eye contact helps release Parent Juice (see chapter 9), which in turn makes the child feel good and experience the food as tastier.

When you begin to work on this strategy, your child is unlikely to look directly at you. You need to get right "in her face" and make the eye contact, pointing to your eyes and her eyes. Tell her how much you want to see her face, look in her eyes, and send her love. Although this is a serious game, your emotional level needs to be upbeat and positive, conveying a sense of joy in connecting. Your joy is infectious and will eventually draw your child into the game.

This is not the time to worry about using food as a reward, which you may be hesitant to do. Eating is the way infants first learn to look at their parents. Eating problems develop when a child uses food alone to nurture herself in place of a missing connection with a parent. The strategy I describe here initially uses food to create a connection, but with the understanding that a genuine connection will eventually be experienced without food. (The next chapter focuses on how interacting playfully and sharing emotions replace food as motivations for connection.) In the beginning, food is the most appropriate and strongest reinforcer you have at your disposal to build the family skill of eye contact.

Strategy 2: Mirroring Games

Babies love to play silly games, many of which help develop face-to-face interaction. Babies blow "raspberries," coo, make funny noises, and cover their eyes. Parents respond by mirroring their baby's behavior. Mirroring is an essential family skill that builds connection.

No matter what age your child is, from infant to teenage, making faces at each other is always an amusing game. When you are getting started building connection with your adopted baby, play a mirroring game at least three times a day. Most children love to have the same game repeated over and over, making it predictable and therefore safe. A child with a complex background does not enjoy surprises, so be repetitive and hold back on the spontaneity. Rather than changing the game yourself, let your child lead the way in introducing new twists. Then mirror your child.

Mirroring is the way that one person lets the other person know that "hey, I understand you and what you are doing or saying." Mirroring is a way you can let your child know that you understand him.

Strategy 3: Baby-in-Control Games

Young children from complex backgrounds are confused about just how much control they have over their lives. Sometimes children feel completely helpless (the Warm Rock, the Stunned Rag Doll, or the Unwilling Guest), whereas others act as if they are king of the world (the Royal Boss or the Dizzy Performer). Sometimes they go from one extreme to the other.

Baby-in-Control games are especially useful for children who tend to fall at the helpless end of the spectrum. Parents need to help such a child learn what she can control. For example, if a child looks in Mom's eyes, she can earn a treat. This sequence teaches a child about her power to make things happen, and about cause and effect generally.

In the game of Pop Cheeks, Baby gets to make Dad's puffed-up cheeks deflate with a "pop." Young children love to make something happen, to be in control, and to anticipate the popping sound. Anticipation itself is a form of mental control. When we know in advance what will happen we feel in control, as opposed to not knowing and being surprised.

Funny Sounds/Funny Faces is a game similar to Pop Cheeks, but it involves more facial features. A different funny sound is associated with each feature. For example, Mom pushes on her nose and says, in a deep voice, "Honk!" Then she encourages Baby to try pushing Mom's nose gently, and when Baby does so, Mom gives her distinctive "Honk!" Next, Mom demonstrates that gently pulling her left ear causes her tongue to pop out of her mouth and point to the left; pulling the right ear moves the tongue the opposite way. Pressing Mom's forehead elicits a whistle. Soon Baby and Mom are face to face with Baby pushing or pulling gently at Mom's different facial features. Encourage your baby to look in your eyes just before she presses a new "button." Not only does this pause evoke a sense of anticipation, it can also teach cause and effect. The longer the look, the louder the sound Mom makes, increasing the laughter you share.

Strategy 4: Peekaboo Games

Many children initiate Peekaboo games as they learn about *away* and *back. Away* is the hidden place, and a child who wants to be in control (such as the Royal Boss) enjoys going away and hiding. A child who is frightened of separation (such as the Stunned Rag Doll) avoids hiding. For internationally adopted children, Peekaboo is a way to transform coping behaviors into family skills. Peekaboo is one way a child can begin moving away from a parent, while still being able to check in for refueling with Parent Juice. When the child peeps out from behind his hands and sees Daddy, the excited giggle or wide grin is the result of a jolt of Parent Juice.

Peekaboo is an important game that engages a range of family skills, including eye contact, the interactive release of Parent Juice, and tolerance of physical separation and reunion, all with their associated emotions. Children of any age can benefit from playing Peekaboo games; more mature versions for older children include Hide and Seek or Chase Me games.

GENERALIZING EYE CONTACT TO EVERY SITUATION

Demetri's mother felt that her son made surprisingly good eye contact, given that he had spent his early life in an institution. "When I change his diaper he looks right at me and smiles," Denise reported. Denise admitted, however, that at most other times, such as mealtime, play time, or taking a walk, Demetri rarely looked at her face, much less in her eyes. In the orphanage, it seems, Demetri learned to associate eye contact with one specific situation and time: diaper change. Demetri has learned to make eye contact as part of a routine, but not in response to an individual person's interaction with him.

As the parent of an internationally adopted child, you need to teach your child to make eye contact in every situation that occurs in her life, so that it becomes a generalized skill not limited to specific routines. Tell your child that eye contact and looking at each other should happen day and night, at mealtime, bedtime, and play time, and at dressing, bath, and toileting times as well. You need to name the times and situations to make this point clear. Merely saying, "We need to look at each other no matter what we are doing" is too vague.

KEEP SHORT-TERM EXPECTATIONS LOW

Family age is important as you evaluate your child's progress with eye contact. You can even think of eye contact age, using the date you start developing this family skill as "birth" and counting forward. Do not expect long eye-to-eye gazes immediately. At first children will spend just a few seconds looking in your eyes.

When you begin, count the number of seconds your child gazes into your eyes, using the "one-one thousand, two-one thousand" method of counting out the seconds. Most parents find that internationally adopted children initially look in their eyes for about one to three seconds. Practice with your child to try to double, by the end of the first week, the amount of time he looks in your eyes. This is still a relatively short period of time. Your goal is to work toward a gaze that lasts for a minute or more, coupled with a child's increasingly happy or joyful feelings. This will take weeks and perhaps months. Eye contact is a challenging skill that develops slowly. Be patient, with low short-term expectations and high long-term goals.

LOOKING AWAY TO TAKE A BREAK

A child who is learning to make eye contact must also learn how to break it. Breaking eye contact, or taking a break from face-to-face interaction generally, is a basic way infants and young children exert control over the feelings generated by connection. Eye contact is stimulating. It releases Parent Juice (see chapter 9), a substance your child may at first experience as unfamiliar and therefore uncomfortable. Even a few seconds of eye contact will feel overwhelming, as if you are invading the child's personal space. Your child will look away and break the connection in order to control her feelings. The ability to look away is a family skill and an important early step in the beginning of self-control, behaviorally and emotionally.

Looking-away skills have been linked to the ability of older children to control their emotions. Researchers have shown that looking away from a scary movie is more common among school-age children with good emotional and behavioral control than among children with poor self-control. Children with poor emotional control continue to stare at the screen, despite their uncomfortable feelings.

 You can use the following strategy to help your child learn looking-away skills after having learned to make eye contact. First, when your child looks away from you, acknowledge her self-control by saying something like "Looking at each other is exciting, or maybe a bit uncomfortable or intense. I'm glad to see that you know when you need to look away and take a break!" Praise your child for this form of self-control. Then encourage her to look back at you by engaging in a familiar attention-getting device, such as sticking out your tongue or saying an exaggerated "Hi, honey!" to make the face-to-face experience predictable and fun.

> **"A mother's most effective technique in maintaining an interaction seems to be a sensitivity to her infant's capacity for attention and need for withdrawal—partial or complete—after a period of attending to her."**
>
> T. Berry Brazelton and Bertrand G. Cramer, *The Earliest Relationship* (1991)

THREE STEPS FOR GOOD EYE CONTACT

Your ultimate goal is to develop a three-step eye contact routine. First, you and your child lock gazes; second, your child looks away and takes a break; and third, your child looks back to you. Think of the three steps as establishing connection by means of eye contact, then allowing your child to look away in order to disengage and calm himself, and finally encouraging a reengagement and reconnection.

THREE-STEP EYE CONTACT ROUTINE

1. Child is encouraged to engage in a mutual gaze with parent.
2. Child disengages; parent waits.
3. Before child disconnects entirely, parent encourages child to reengage.

 The goal of eye contact practice is for Parent Juice to be released so quickly that the gaze can be brief. Researchers have discovered that once a child learns to connect in this way, it may take only ten seconds for him to experience the release of Parent Juice.

FACIAL INDICATORS OF ENGAGEMENT AND DISENGAGEMENT

Facial expressions that signal engagement are raised eyebrows; widely opened eyes; a round, open mouth; and, of course, a smile. You can teach your child to look at your face to see what you do when you are engaging or disengaging. Then, using a mirror, help your child learn to make the facial expressions that signal what she wants. Disengagement begins with a child turning eyes, head, or body away from the stimulating experience. These behaviors signal that a child "has had enough," even if the interaction was good. Making grimaces, sticking out a tongue, squinting eyes, wrinkling the forehead, frowning, and wrinkling the nose and pushing lips out may also indicate disengagement—or the child's dislike of the preceding engagement. Such dislike may stem from overstimulation, even of the nicest sort. Watch for these subtle and overt signs and respond to them by allowing your child to disengage, rather than demanding that she always remain engaged. Intrusive or overly demanding parenting can create distance when a parent's intent is exactly the opposite.

> **"In sustained mutual gaze transactions, the mother's facial expression stimulates and amplifies positive affect in the infant . . . The gleam in the mother's eye thus triggers dilation of the infant's pupils, [which indicates] brain activation."**
>
> Allan N. Schore,
> *Affect Regulation and the Origin of the Self* (1994)

Many parents find themselves overeager to pursue engagement because they feel their child has not made enough eye contact. Although I hope I have made clear in this chapter that it is important to encourage eye contact and engagement, too much eagerness or hurry on your part will feel intrusive to your child, and she will continue to disengage. Remember to give your child plenty of chances to "recover" from the stimulating experience of face-to-face interaction, and then look for signs that she is ready to reengage. Signs of wanting to engage or reengage are often indirect. For example, a child may walk up to a parent and then turn around and begin to walk away. Or a child will offer a toy and then take it back. Some children back up into their parents, so they do not actually face the adult. Other children look past the parent's face. It is helpful to work on eye contact within the Magic Circle formed by a rope or ribbon (see chapter 9) so that there is a "container" for the child even when she disengages.

Discovering and creating a *rhythm* of engagement and disengagement is a core ingredient of learning how to be in sync with your child. And your *emotional sensitivity* to when your child is engaging and disengaging is central to your being in tune with your child.

Joyful Play, Language, and Connection

FOOD IS THE INITIAL MEDIUM through which a child and parent connect face to face. At each intense connection established through food and feeding, the child experiences a jolt of Parent Juice. As a result, happiness, joy, excitement, and pleasure become associated with the parent-child relationship. How long can this take? Anywhere from six months to a year or more, depending on your child's age at adoption and age when you begin working on this basic family skill. After this level of connection is firmly established, the relationship must move beyond food. This transition occurs as play begins to substitute for food in parent-child interactions. Play, with the face-to-face eye contact it inspires, becomes the dominant means of releasing Parent Juice as a child grows older.

Of course, even if you are past the first year home it is still appropriate to use food initially to build and strengthen your child's connection to you. In addition, there will be times when stress creates a disconnection between you and your child. At these times you may want to turn again to connections rooted in food to reestablish your overall connection with your child quickly and powerfully. Offer a juice box or a bag of dry cereal to your upset child in order to soothe and reconnect.

Maturation of the Parent-Child Connection

Food and Eye Contact →
Play → Mirroring →
Facial Exploration and Expression → Gesture and Language

As play between a parent and child develops, so, too, does communication between them. Facial expressions, gestures, and words combine to strengthen the parent-child connection. The exhilarating feeling of a jolt of Parent Juice from food or play now becomes linked to words and gestures. A hug, or the words "I love you," can release Parent Juice but only when all the related family skills are in place. In this chapter I provide parenting strategies that you can use to build connections between you and your child through play and language.

JOYFUL PLAY AND PARENT-RECOGNITION BEHAVIOR

As a child learns to feel comfortable playing with his parents, he is apt to become more inquisitive about his parent's body. Demetri, for example, had never spent much time in any adult's lap, and because he was an active walker at nearly two years of age, he was unlikely to sit quietly in his mother's lap and get acquainted with her facial features. Playing the games described below will help a child become at ease with and curious about a parent's body.

For example, while playing the Beanbag Game, Demetri realized that he could move physically closer to his mother and touch her head, face, and shoulders. As a result, he began using his hands to explore his mother's face and increase his familiarity with her. This is why I introduce the Beanbag Game before teaching a child to explore a parent's face. Although a non-adopted child might do this at four through nine months of chronological age, this parent exploration takes place at a later age for internationally adopted children. Family age is a better guide than chronological age for understanding why an older adopted child is suddenly pulling at Dad's nose, tweaking off Mom's glasses, or pulling her hair.

Strategy 1: The Beanbag Game—A Model for Play

The Beanbag Game is a great way to begin shifting eye contact from food-based interactions to play-based interactions. Sit on the floor in front of your child and put a small, hand-sized beanbag on top of your head. If your child is interested, hand a second beanbag to her and suggest that she mirror what you do, perhaps simply by saying, "Act like me." Then sing, to the tune of "Put Your Finger in the Air," and act out this song:

> *Put your beanbag on your head, on your head.*
> *Put your beanbag on your head, on your head.*
> *Put your beanbag on your head, and drop it on the floor.*
> *Put your beanbag on your head and—[pause] drop it on the floor.*

The pause in the last line gives your child an opportunity to drop the bean-bag before singing about doing so. This pause of anticipation helps a child with self-control and briefly focuses her attention on the concept of cause and effect—nodding her head causes the beanbag to fall.

Continue to play the game, as you and your child face each other, for as long as she remains interested. Let the joy of the game build in your child. As your child laughs louder, mirror her enjoyment. This back-and-forth interaction is a significant means of releasing Parent Juice through connection. When your child reaches the maximum amount of joy she can tolerate without emotional or physical collapse, it is time to disengage briefly. During this decrease in excitement your child can recoup her emotional and physical balance. Then she will be ready to engage and connect again. Over time your child will learn to stay balanced, even with increasingly high levels of excitement.

FAMILY SKILLS LEARNED FROM PLAYING THE BEANBAG GAME

A child learns to:

1. Be comfortable with longer periods of face-to-face interaction.
2. Associate eye contact and release of Parent Juice with happy play.
3. Increase mirroring of the parent's activities and feelings.
4. Increase control of her own behavior by mirroring the parent's self-control.
5. Increase self-control as joy and excitement build.
6. Practice the cycle of engagement, disengagement, and reengagement.

A parent learns to:

1. Modulate stimulation or excitement to help the child develop behavioral control.
2. Allow the child to disengage when overstimulated or overexcited.
3. Mirror the child's expressions of emotion, such as through smiles, giggles, and laughs.
4. Mirror the level of intensity of the child's emotions.
5. Stay in sync with the child's rhythm of engagement, disengagement, and reengagement.
6. Increase excitement slowly and in small increments, to help the child tolerate strong feelings of joy.

The Beanbag Game has many benefits. Learning to balance and drop the beanbags at the right time, for example, develops behavioral control in young children. After all, if your child laughs too hard or falls over on the floor, she will not be able to balance the beanbag successfully. If you use your child's balance as a guide to modify your own level of playfulness, you will automatically help your child to modify her own level of play. Your self-control provides a model for your child. In this way your child learns to manage emotions and behavior simultaneously. The box on page 113 offers a more complete list of what the game accomplishes.

Variations of the game include putting the beanbag on other parts of the body, such as an arm, and dropping it from there. Another variation is to put the beanbag on a block or plastic plate and drop it off the block or plate. These are additional ways to build your child's ability to balance physically and emotionally at the same time, and thereby to practice resiliency. Note that since most internationally adopted children like things to be predictable, under easy mental control, your child may merely want to repeat the original game for a long time.

Once you understand the way the Beanbag Game promotes family skills, you can apply its principles and the accompanying parenting strategies to all kinds of games and play. Tossing or rolling a ball back and forth is, of course, a favorite activity for young children. You might encourage family skills not only by requiring that you and your child face each other as you play this game, but also by adding a rule that a player must look into the eyes of the other player before rolling the ball. This can be expanded to include mirroring: The person with the ball makes a face and the other player must mirror that expression.

Building family skill practice into daily activities and play is a proactive type of parenting, meaning that you teach, practice, and reinforce specific skills. Joyful play, extended eye contact, and emotional and physical balance are some of the skills used in the Beanbag Game. Like a good schoolteacher, parents can consciously watch for a teachable moment in which to nurture and extend these skills through interactive play as well as daily activities with their child.

Strategy 2: Guided Facial Exploration

This activity involves two steps or skills. In the first you teach your child how to touch gently, not roughly. Next you give your child permission to touch your face, while you talk about and touch features on your own and your child's face.

Like most adopted children, your child will want to explore your face and body many times, to become familiar with you on a sensory and intimate level.

Set limits about roughness, and about touching private parts or other off-limits areas (up the nostril, for example, or into an ear). This will serve as a model for how your child will allow others to touch him. Remember that in the past your child may have had little or no control over how he was touched. Children who have experienced abuse have a particularly hard time setting and accepting physical boundaries between people; they may be overly sensitive (or surprisingly insensitive) about their personal space, or they may be insensitive to the personal space of others.

At one session of the First Year Home Group, I helped the parents encourage their children to try guided facial exploration. Yi Sheng, now almost five years old, reached out and touched his father's glasses. Kenji removed the glasses and let Yi Sheng touch his eyebrows and nose. Kenji began to teach Yi Sheng the concept of *gentle*, as his son grabbed at his father's nose.

Meanwhile, Mu Ling, almost three years old, compared her two mothers, pointing to their eyes. Meg has brown eyes and Laura has blue eyes. Mu Ling, seeming to recognize this, pointed to her own eyes with a questioning look. Meg spotted a mirror on the wall and lifted Mu Ling up to see herself. Mu Ling laughed when she saw her mom with her in the mirror. She was more willing at this stage to smile at her mother's reflection than at her mother directly. This is not uncommon among adopted children, and a mirror is a good place to initiate eye contact with a child who is reluctant to make direct eye contact.

Sonia, at fourteen months, was standing in her father's lap and smelling his neck. She tried biting it and got a quick "No" from David. Soon An, eight months old, lifted and waved her hands toward Charlotte, who pointed first to her own nose and eyes and then to her daughter's features. As they explored their parents' faces, each child became more engaged and used touch, vision, smell, and taste to explore this special person more fully and intimately.

"I'm surprised Yi Sheng is as fascinated with this game as the younger children are," Kenji commented. But as we have seen, children who are relatively old chronologically but still young in terms of family age find games and activities such as these to be irresistible, because they meet the child's need to engage in interpersonal play and to connect with a parent.

Strategy 3: Teach a Child to Recognize Basic Emotional and Physical Feelings
Internationally adopted children need to be taught explicitly to recognize basic feelings, both in their own selves and in others' facial expressions. The four feelings you may want to begin with are *happy, sad, angry,* and *scared.* With a

nonverbal child you need to use these feeling words repeatedly and in a variety of appropriate contexts. As your child begins to speak, you will need to teach her to use these words.

Look for situations in which your child appears to have or should have one of these feelings, and then link her behavior to the feeling word. You might say, for example, "You are smiling as you eat the apple; your face looks happy." If your child appears fearful, you could say, "Your shoulders are up around your ears and your face looks scared." A child often has no name for emotional feelings, and even physical ones; this is even more true of internationally adopted children who are learning a new language and who have been in environments in which there was little opportunity for the expression of feelings.

The familiar preschool song "If You're Happy and You Know It Clap Your Hands" is a good introduction to the four basic emotions and a way to connect those emotions to appropriate situations. Each feeling is paired with a facial expression or gesture, and children practice these pairs during the song. See the next page for the song's verses, with some suggested personalized variations. Do not hesitate to have your child choose what gesture or movement shows a particular emotion, or to make up your own variations. In the First Year Home Group I once asked the parents how they knew if their child was happy. Each parent identified a sound or movement that his or her child made when happy, and each was able to imitate it to share with the Group. When the children heard and saw their own signs of happiness, they looked delighted and imitated their parents in turn—an excellent indication that they were following the adult conversation. When we sing the song in our Group, we incorporate each child's sounds and gestures into the song to personalize it. For example, the main sound one child makes to express happiness is an open-mouthed rising "Ahhhh!" For him we sing "say, 'Ahhhh!'" instead of "clap your hands."

The Group sings the final verse, the one that focuses on "sad," in a different way. Children with complex backgrounds have a difficult time with this emotion because of their many separations and losses. For this reason I have altered the last verse; it is about feeling sad in the first line, but then it goes right back to happy for the final three lines. An entire verse about sadness would be overwhelming; a child might shut down or resort to a fight-or-flight response such as leaving the circle or throwing toys. Mentioning *sad* only once helps a child "put a toe into the sad pool" and then regain emotional balance by withdrawing it.

IF YOU'RE HAPPY AND YOU KNOW IT, CLAP YOUR HANDS

If you're happy and you know it, clap your hands
   [or "say, 'Ahhhh!'" or another child's individual variant],
If you're happy and you know it, clap your hands,
If you're happy and you know it, then your face will surely show it,
If you're happy and you know it, clap your hands.

If you're angry and you know it, shake your fist
   [or "stamp your feet," "make a frown," or other action],
If you're angry and you know it, shake your fist,
If you're angry and you know it, then your face will surely show it,
If you're angry and you know it, shake your fist.

If you're scared and you know it, call your mom—Mama!
   [or "call your dad—Daddy!" "get a hug," and so on]
If you're scared and you know it, call your mom—Mama!
If you're scared and you know it, then your face will surely show it,
If you're scared and you know it, call your mom—Mama!

If you're sad and you know it, you can cry
   [or "wipe your eyes" or another variant],
If you're happy and you know it, you can smile,
If you're happy and you know it, then your face will surely show it,
If you're happy you know it, you can smile.

SADNESS AND GOODBYES

Sadness is a difficult emotion for nearly all internationally adopted children.
Hearing the word *sad* and seeing the facial expressions of sadness trigger a major
shift in the children's behavior. Some shut down and assume a blank expression;
others get up from a group and walk away. Most children are reluctant to look
at a parent's sad face or imitate a sad expression. We see similar behavior when
it is time to sing the "Goodbye Song" at the end of each First Year Home Group
session. Goodbye is even more specific than sadness, and it has been said too
many times to and by internationally adopted children. The word makes them
fidget, kick, and hide their faces. They might struggle to maintain a crooked

smile, bite a lip, or even throw things. Some children react to goodbye by hoarding, or by holding on to a toy as a keepsake from their time in the Group.

Proactive parents need to help children learn to tolerate the uncomfortable feelings of sadness and goodbye, if only to prepare for separations at daycare or preschool. Some practice opportunities include singing the "Goodbye Song" at the end of any group gathering; singing or saying goodbye or good night to stuffed animals, pets, and people at bedtime; and having a goodbye routine when a parent leaves the house. A routine may be a kiss on both cheeks, a special wave, or sharing the sign for "I love you" (thumb and first and pinky fingers extended) in American Sign Language (ASL). Charlotte kissed Soon An on both cheeks and then blew her a kiss from the door when she left her with Joe, even to go into another room. Demetri, at a year and a half, learned to make the "I love you" sign, and he and his mother both made the sign and touched their extended fingers together in a special goodbye gesture. It takes no more than two or three times for even the youngest child to associate these actions with separation. Engaging in a special goodbye ritual with a parent gives a child a sense of control and connection, which in turn helps the child tolerate the sadness of separation.

EMOTIONAL MIX-UPS

Many adults assume that the capacity to recognize feelings, whether one's own or another person's, as distinct from one another is innate and simple. In fact, this is a learned skill, and a particularly challenging one for a child with a complex background. Children need to be taught how to make such distinctions, yet adults either do not take the time to do this, or they assume a child will intuitively pick up such information. As a result, many children reach school age still uncertain about how to recognize and sort their own feelings. Frequently children, for example, confuse hunger with feeling scared or angry.

For this reason many parents find it helpful to teach an infant, a toddler, or even an older child to differentiate among basic physical sensations, including hungry, full, tired, awake and alert, and the feeling of fullness that indicates a need to use the toilet. Even a child who appears to know the differences can benefit from a review and from practice in using the appropriate feeling and physical-sensation words. Sometimes parents discover strange misunderstandings. For example, when Sonia was five years old, four years after her adoption, she revealed that she thought *mad* and *sad* were the same feeling because, as she explained, they "sounded" the same in English, to her ears. Taking a more proactive role in teaching feelings can prevent such confusion or uncover it more quickly. Teach your child about feelings as carefully as you would teach the alphabet or colors. All of these skills give your child a better start in life.

Some Basic Body Sensations to Teach a Young Child

Hot and cold

Hungry and full

Tired or alert and awake

Anxious ("butterflies in the stomach")

Full bladder or bowel

Strategy 4: Teach a Child to Watch a Parent's Facial Expression

An infant who has a consistent caregiver or parent learns to look at that adult's face to determine how the adult feels. The child is especially likely to do so when something new occurs—a stranger enters the room, a chair topples over, or the dinner burns. When a child feels connected to a parent, he looks to the adult for guidance on how to react.

When a child feels connected to a parent, he looks to the adult for guidance on how to react to new or challenging situations.

Facial expressions are a primary way that children learn about appropriate feelings, and a way that parents and children communicate in general. You will find it helpful to remind your child to watch your face, especially in new situations. For example, Nina asked Yi Sheng to "read my face" when they first met his preschool teacher. "Look at my face to see how I feel when I meet your teacher," she told him. "See if I look happy, sad, angry, or scared. And I will look at your face to see how you feel."

"I'm scared," Yi Sheng announced immediately. "Will I sleep at school?"

Opening a conversation about watching Mom's facial expressions naturally leads to discussions of feelings. Some of them, like Yi Sheng's concerns about where he will sleep at night, will be unexpected, yet very important. Yi Sheng's comment reveals a typical misconception of older adoptees about schools: Children from a complex background may anticipate that a school is another type of orphanage.

Strategy 5: Help Your Child Recognize Different Relationships

In order for a child to understand the connection with her parents, she must have a sense that this relationship is different from all others. To understand what a parent *is*, a child needs to know what a parent is *not*. Parents need to teach their child about different relationships, such as friend, stranger, or occasional caregiver, in order to help her grasp the meaning of *parent*.

Define first in your own mind how you categorize the types of relationships in your family's social universe. When I work with parents of international adoptees I often suggest five levels of relationship: parents and immediate family, extended family, friends, acquaintances, and strangers. If you prefer, you can simplify this scheme to three levels: family, friends, and strangers. Next, define how you would like your child to respond to and treat people in the various categories, perhaps by making a two-column chart like the one shown here. Then instruct your child how to behave as you come in contact with persons from each category. Understanding different relationships will help your child grasp the unique and special nature of the parent-child relationship.

ALIGNING TYPE OF RELATIONSHIP WITH BEHAVIOR

Parents and siblings	Hugging and kissing; sitting on lap
Extended family	Blowing kisses; sitting close but not on lap
Friends	Shaking hands; sitting nearby
Acquaintances	Waving, but not touching
Strangers	Nodding; keeping near parents; not touching

LEARNING TO SPEAK A NEW LANGUAGE

Every internationally adopted child learns a second (or third) language after adoption. Communicating with words in the child's new language is an enormous step in building a parent-child connection. There is a widespread belief among parents that only very young children can learn a new language quickly, and that learning a second language is not a problem if a child starts before five years of age. These assumptions have not been proved by researchers. What we do know, based on research by Patricia Kuhl at the University of Washington, is that by six months of age a child is already primed to hear certain sounds and expect certain structures of speech based on what he has heard in his environment.

Although many children *seem* to catch on to a new language quickly, they often use social context to make sense of the words.

Social language is quite different from school or academic language. I remember becoming confused by the word *restroom* as a kindergartner. Why would anyone need to rest at school? I wondered about that and, by the way, where were the toilets? Not only do teachers introduce new vocabulary, but in many cases a child struggles with the fact that there is no social or practical context for the new words. Instead of activities and demonstrations, many classrooms are centered around paper-and-pencil work with new signs, symbols, letters, and expectations. For example, following the direction to "put your name on your paper in the upper left-hand corner" contains several abstract concepts that seem obvious to adults but not to a child from halfway across the world. Parents may want to anticipate some of these new words and concepts. You and your child will likely stumble over academic language surprises together for many years.

Context-based social language is relatively easy for all children to learn. On average, two years are required for an adopted child to learn social English, if in fact the child already has a solid foundation in his first language. However, most internationally adopted children have a less than adequate first-language foundation. Moreover, academic language proficiency, achieving what some specialists call Cognitive Academic Language Proficiency, takes five to seven years under the most favorable conditions. To understand your adopted child's challenges in this area, it helps to take family age into consideration. Yi Sheng was nearly five years old when he was adopted. He would learn social English by the time he was seven years old. But he would not begin to be proficient in academic English until he was at least ten years old. Based on his family age, Yi Sheng was right on target in terms of learning language. But chronologically and academically he was delayed. At ten years old he will have struggled with five years of academic language at school and may have fallen behind. Most adoption professionals recommend that parents get language support and tutoring for their child as quickly as possible, particularly if the child is more than a year old at adoption. There is just too much time lost if a child must catch up on his own . (See the Appendix for specific strategies.)

MORE CHANNELS OF COMMUNICATION MEAN MORE CONNECTION

To build connection with your child, and to hasten her developing communication skills, you need to do more than merely "talk a lot" with her. Communication also includes facial expressions, hand and body gestures, tone of voice, and pantomime. Each of these can be considered a different channel of communication, sometimes simultaneous with spoken language and sometimes separate. Each channel can be exaggerated to facilitate communication when parent and child do not share a common verbal language. In addition, teaching your child a basic vocabulary in American Sign Language is extremely helpful in promoting language development.

Using American Sign Language is an excellent way for a young, preverbal child to begin learning language. It promotes parent-child connection regardless of the child's age.

When a parent and child communicate through sign language, the connection between them is strengthened even before the child can speak or acquire a second spoken language. In addition, the child learns words and concepts that can later be translated into spoken language.

Preverbal children become frustrated when they lack the right words to express their thoughts and desires, and this frustration undermines their relationship with a parent. However, by using American Sign Language, or just any agreed-upon set of gestures and meanings, your child can feel connected to you and competent to make herself understood. There are many books and websites from which you can learn the basics of ASL.

SHOULD AN ADOPTED CHILD MAINTAIN A NATIVE LANGUAGE?

Some parents try to help an internationally adopted child maintain and develop his first language. A parent may hire a nanny who speaks the child's native language, for example. If the parents are not fluent in the child's first language, however, this situation can confuse the child. If he is able to communicate more fully with the nanny, his connection to his parents may be jeopardized.

A shared form of communication with a parent, such as sign language or the language spoken in the parents' home, is preferable to trying to have a child maintain his native language, especially if no one in the home speaks it fluently.

Because connection is such an important component of development, I always advise parents to place their highest priority on helping their child learn a language that he will share fully with the parents. This does not preclude having the child continue to learn his native language. But a child has to put a great deal of time and energy into learning the language that is regularly spoken in his new home and in school if he is old enough; parents should be careful when making the decision to have the child work on his first language as well.

PATTERNS OF LEARNING A SECOND LANGUAGE

Several common phases occur as a child learns a second language. These are normal and predictable, but they can cause some frustration for parent and child. The first phase is *language loss*, when use of the first language ceases, as it does rather abruptly for most internationally adopted children. Language loss affects how competent the child appears to herself and to others. This is often a period of high frustration for the child. Having a shared set of ASL signs with which to communicate helps parent and child manage this challenging period together.

A second phase is a *silent period*, during which a child uses neither her native language nor her second language. During this period a child may be shut down, or listening but not speaking. Estimates vary, but most researchers believe this silent period lasts between three and six months. If a child continues to have a severe emotional impact from the Big Change—the adoption—or from other previous losses, this silent period may last even longer. Again, using signs to communicate with a child during this period allows the parent-child relationship to continue to develop, rather than grinding to a halt just as it is beginning.

The third and last phase is the *emergence of the new language*, which, as you will discover, eventually does happen. During all three of these phases, which can last for years, a child's language use may exhibit what is called *interference*, which means that the first language interferes with, or partially shapes, the second language. For example, Yi Sheng often used the phrase "Is it good or not good?" The Chinese equivalent of this phrase is used as a greeting, akin to "How are you?" or, literally, "Are things good or not good with you?" or in conversational interactions about food—"Is the soup good or not good?"—among many other uses and contexts. In a similar vein, grammatical constructions from Spanish seeped into Sonia's English two or three years after her adoption. Sonia used the Spanish-like construction "I have four years" instead of the English construction "I am four years old." She said, "I have heat," or "I have hot," instead of "I am hot." Asian languages use specific number words instead of plurals and have no pronouns, so a child might say, "Two ball dropped," instead of "I dropped them." Such subtle differences seep into a child's spoken or written language. For this reason, understanding some basics about the structure of your child's native language may be more valuable than actually learning the language. Knowing the structure, you can spot the interference. When you detect an error that you believe stems from language interference, gently explain to your child that "in [native language] saying it *that way* would be correct! In English we say it a bit differently: [then say the example]. I'll help you remember."

Interference can be a powerful experience. One child I know, who was adopted from China at six months of age, began making puzzling vocalizations when she was twenty months old. She was just beginning to speak, but her parents did not recognize the sounds as English or proto-English. A native speaker in a Chinese restaurant recognized the little girl's "baby Chinese" and alerted the mother. Although this child had not heard Chinese in over a year, she began to speak by using Chinese words.

COMMON PHASES OF SECOND-LANGUAGE LEARNING

1. Loss of first language
2. Silent period
3. Emergence of second language, but with interference from first language

SHOULD YOU LEARN YOUR CHILD'S NATIVE LANGUAGE?

A parent's attempts to use an adopted child's native language provide plenty of entertainment for the child. Demetri giggled when Denise tried to say, "You are my son" in Russian. When Meg said, "I am your mother" in Chinese, Mu Ling laughed and said, "Bad. You talk bad Chinese." However, if you have the time and motivation, learning even a few phrases or words in your child's native language can be a valuable way of communicating and connecting with him.

The parent-child connection is strengthened when a parent can explain to a child why she makes certain mistakes repeatedly. For example, Nina was able to tell Yi Sheng that his repeated question "Is it good or not good?" was actually an English version of a common Chinese phrase, but that it was not a common expression among English speakers. She also explained that his difficulty with plurals and pronouns was a typical mistake of all Chinese speakers learning English. This information helped Yi Sheng feel close to his mother, who understood and explained his difficulties to him. It also helped him shape his identity. Yi Sheng from an early age understood that he was an immigrant who had immigrant concerns and difficulties, in this case with language.

Although Yi Sheng by age ten was a fluent English speaker, he retained his empathy for and understanding of what it was like to come to a new land and learn a new language. For many years his favorite book was *I Hate English!* by Ellen Levine, which is about a twelve-year-old girl from Hong Kong who did not want to give up her first language.

If a child associates his native language with unpleasant events or life changes, he may be eager to leave his original language behind. This was true of Yi Sheng. He associated Mandarin Chinese with the orphanage and refused to participate in the preschool Mandarin classes in which his parents enrolled him. If you are considering such classes, let your child's own emotional reaction, not what other parents do, be your guide. There are many other ways for your child to connect with his birth culture. Note, too, that many internationally adopted children decide to relearn their native language as young adults, when it has more meaning for them.

MISDIAGNOSIS OF, OR FAILURE TO IDENTIFY, LANGUAGE PROBLEMS

Most internationally adopted children have what is called *subtractive bilingualism,* which means that their first language is being subtracted or lost in favor of their second language. It is common for children with subtractive bilingualism to be mistakenly diagnosed with general learning disabilities, rather than specific second-language-learning issues. These children may be placed incorrectly in special-education classes or given inappropriate therapies. Such misdiagnoses occur because educators and teachers may not know or realize that English is a child's second language. Typically the teacher assumes that English is the first language of a child when the adoptive parents are native English speakers and the child is a competent, unaccented English speaker in social situations. This predicament calls for a parent to be watchful and to advocate actively for a child to receive academic help in language.

It is common for internationally adopted children to be mistakenly diagnosed with learning disabilities rather than second-language-learning issues.

Soon An, for example, was diagnosed with learning disabilities when she was having some language difficulties in the second grade. In the first six months of Soon An's life her brain had been "wired" for Korean, and that early experience made academic English a challenge. Fortunately, Charlotte and Joe intervened and consulted a language specialist, who determined that their daughter's difficulties were linguistic and specific, not neurological and general.

CHILD-CARE PROVIDERS AND LANGUAGE ACQUISITION

Many of the caregivers in daycare centers are immigrants themselves, with partial or even minimal skills in English. They speak with accents, overuse routine or "canned" phrases, and have their own second-language difficulties. Even non-adopted children in such situations pick up combination languages such as "Spanglish," or even a caregiver's native language. My own non-adopted son at age two began speaking Swedish, which he learned from a nanny who was with him only three days a week. Situations like these present extra challenges for a child who is still learning the nuances of a new language. To avoid these problems, consider hiring a college student as a nanny, especially one who already knows sign language or is willing to learn. If your child will go to daycare, look for a center that is staffed with competent English speakers.

WHEN AND WHERE TO ASK FOR HELP

Both adoption professionals and parents who waited to see if early language problems would work themselves out without professional guidance recommend seeking early language intervention. Remember, your child does not need to be speaking in order to benefit from speech and language help. Note that many adopted children who spent time in institutions may not have developed their mouth muscles by chewing food and properly sucking liquids of different consistencies, since most institutional food is cooked until it is soft. Speech and language professionals also work with children who have difficulties with chewing, swallowing, and drinking that are related to underdevelopment of the mouth and throat, because such difficulties often affect speech production.

If you have questions or concerns, look for a speech and language therapist who specializes in working with internationally adopted children or in English as a second language (ESL). Ask for referrals from the early (birth to three) intervention programs in your school district, a local children's hospital, your adoption agency, or local adoption support groups. The Appendix provides several suggestions to help you teach your child your language.

Sleep, Connection, and Separation

SLEEP IS AN EMOTIONALLY CHARGED ISSUE for everyone. Pediatricians, grandparents, friends, and neighbors, not to mention the lady at the supermarket, will tell you they have the "right" answer. Many families are told that they are "spoiling" their children by rocking them to sleep, letting their children sleep with them, or responding to their cries at night. On top of the sleep deprivation that parents experience, the implication that they are poor parents is devastating.

UNDERSTANDING SLEEP PROBLEMS

Sleep disruption is one of the first signs that a child has experienced stress or trauma. It is to be expected, therefore, that internationally adopted children have sleep disruptions and difficulty falling and staying asleep, not only through childhood but into adolescence. In addition, internationally adopted children follow a different pattern of learning to sleep through the night than do non-adopted children.

Sleep disruption is a primary indication of stress or trauma in children.

There are four types of childhood sleep problems. The first three are difficulty falling asleep, difficulty staying asleep, and waking up excessively agitated or cranky. The fourth, which may not at first appear to be a problem, is going to sleep in a dark room without complaint and waiting silently until a parent returns in the morning.

I will begin with the fourth problem, because it is often the first sleep problem parents encounter and because parents often do not recognize it as problematic.

The child who goes to sleep without complaint is often mistakenly considered "mature," when in fact she is engaging in coping behavior (see chapter 5).

THE "PERFECT SLEEPER"

A child who regularly goes to sleep in a dark room, alone and without complaint, has learned to manage alone and does not have a sense of connection to his parent. A child who has spent time in an orphanage, like Yi Sheng, almost always behaves this way. Going to sleep in this solitary manner is virtually unheard of in Western cultures among children between eight months and ten years old who are connected to their parents. The children's protests, their discomfort with separation for the night, are a sign of their sense of connection. Often children who fall asleep alone and without protest remain silent in their beds the next morning until a parent comes into the room. This behavior is a powerful clue to the type of care the child received prior to adoption, regardless of what the official papers might say.

A child from the age of seven months through six or seven years of age who is connected to a parent does not want to separate from Mom or Dad, even to fall asleep. Such a child whines, stalls, and asks for endless drinks of water or "just one more book." Each of these tactics is designed to maintain connection with the parent. By six or more years of age, most children have found a way to soothe themselves to sleep with music or reading, not to mention strong encouragement by their parents. The "perfect sleeper," on the other hand, has no connection with caregivers to maintain. This fact is important; parents who consider the "perfect sleeper" to be perfect deny the disconnection inherent in his sleep behavior. This denial in turn confirms the child's belief that he is alone in the world, especially at night, and it prevents parent and child from working on family skills for sleep and connection.

Later in this chapter I describe how to teach the "perfect sleeper" the family skills of sleep, including how to call parents for help.

THE CHILD WHO WILL NOT FALL ASLEEP

There are three possible reasons a child cannot or will not fall asleep. First, the child may be accustomed to sleeping with others, either adults or children. This is especially common among internationally adopted children who in a prior foster care setting slept with parents or siblings. Children from Asian orphanages often share beds or cribs, and many beds are grouped in one room. Thus, for many adopted children, co-sleeping in some fashion is the norm. Second, the child may be relying on coping behaviors to calm down and, because these do not work well, remains revved up for hours into the night until the need to shut down causes her to fall asleep abruptly. Third, the child may be anxious about separating from a parent and therefore cannot relax and fall asleep.

Sonia spent the first year of her life in a foster home with several other children where the adults and children slept together in one large room. This was what Sonia was accustomed to do. When she was adopted, at one year of age, and was put into her own room alone in her crib, she was terrified and confused. She screamed and cried. One night she vomited when her parents tried the "cry it out" method. Sonia was missing her connection to her first family but did not have the language to explain her plight. Her parents had to use her behavior as a clue to her past sleep experiences.

Demetri also would not fall asleep in his new home. When Denise put him to bed, he played with toys in his crib alone late into the night until he abruptly toppled over into a deep sleep. This behavior is typical of the Dizzy Performer (see chapter 5) who is excessively active and busy and then, out of total exhaustion, suddenly falls asleep. Demetri felt alone and was not yet connected to Denise, and so he relied on his coping behaviors to manage both his play and his sleep.

As Sonia and Demetri became more connected to their respective parents, each developed a similar difficulty with going to sleep. Both children began to demand that a parent stay in the room. They wanted their parents to sit by the bed, hold their hands, and eventually cuddle them until sleep took over. In short, they began to behave more like children who were connected to their parents.

Sleep is a reflection of how connected or disconnected a child is from his parents. Initially the child's disconnection from parents means that he does not look to them for soothing prior to falling asleep. As the relationship between the child and the parent develops, the sleep difficulties change. Demetri's and Sonia's parents felt that their child's sleep problems were worse, but in fact their behavior demonstrated that the parent-child connections were getting stronger. A child's anxiety about separation at bedtime is a positive sign of connection.

> **A child's anxiety about separation at bedtime is a positive sign of connection.**

A CHILD WHO CANNOT STAY ASLEEP

There are four reasons why internationally adopted children have trouble staying asleep. First, the child may have become wet or hungry and cannot fall back to sleep without receiving care. Second, the child may have had a bad dream and then awakened, unable to soothe herself back to sleep. Third, the child may have experienced a night terror, which is essentially a bad dream from which the child is unable to awaken, despite her wide-open eyes. Fourth, a child may awaken and lie awake worrying about the difficulties of the days before and the days ahead. As most adults know, the middle of the night is when worries and fears find their way into consciousness and are magnified. This is the time when a child with a complex background has time to reflect on what has happened to her, and the worries build.

REASONS A CHILD CANNOT FALL BACK TO SLEEP

- The child needs care, because of hunger, wetness, or excessive cold or heat.
- The child has a bad dream and cannot calm down.
- The child has a night terror.
- The child is scared or anxious.

If a child needs care, it is important to teach her to call for her parents to come and help. Most adopted children who come from orphanages are afraid to do this, for they either fear punishment, or believe no one is there to help. Parents need to teach such a child how to "ask for help," for a diaper change or a bottle. Asking for help is an important family skill.

If a child has a bad dream, a parent needs to help out, to quiet and calm the child, but also to build a connection based on providing soothing care. Bad dreams usually begin at eighteen months but can begin earlier, and they usually (but not always) end somewhere between seven and nine years of age. Your child does not produce bad dreams to manipulate you; frequent scary dreams are a sign that your child is struggling with fears or anxiety.

Internationally adopted children awaken frequently both from nightmares and from night terrors. Nightmares are scary dreams from which a child clearly awakens and is able to recognize the people around her. After a nightmare a child can be gradually comforted by parents. Night terrors are more intense episodes in which a child begins to cry and scream but cannot be awakened. A child often strikes out at the parent, pushes the parent away, or kicks wildly. As a result, night terrors are frightening experi-

Experts' advice: Do not try to awaken a child during a night terror.

ences for the parent as well as the child. The consensus of experts is that parents should refrain from trying to wake a child having a night terror and instead simply keep the child safe.

Night terrors, nightmares, and bad dreams can arise from present or past fears that are often not expressed during the day. Demetri, for example, was a happy twenty-seven-month-old toddler absolutely every day, according to his mother. But suddenly at this age, about nine months after he was adopted, he began having night terrors. Denise traced his sudden sleep change to an evening on which she had put him to bed before the babysitter came. When Demetri woke up around nine thirty at night and saw a stranger in place of his mother, he was both terrified and inconsolable.

Demetri had by nine months of family age become more connected to his mother, and he expected her to be there if he awakened at night. When he was surprised by the babysitter and could not find his mother, his whole sense of the safe connection was shattered. His fear of losing Mom in the present was hidden during the day but expressed in night terrors. Although Denise explained to Demetri what had happened, she had to work extra hard to rebuild his trust. He became excessively clingy, constantly asking the question "Mama going?" Denise learned how important honesty and openness about separation are for a child from a complex background. In fact, even non-adopted children react as Demetri did when a parent sneaks out without telling them. The bottom line is: Always tell your child when you will be away, and never, ever sneak out and leave your child, even with a familiar babysitter.

> *Always* **tell your child when you will be away.** *Never* **sneak out without telling your child you will be gone.**

The fourth reason a child fails to fall back to sleep is anxiety. Anxiety develops over what to adults may seem like ordinary life events or changes, such as changes in the child's or the parent's daily routines. For example, children often have sleep difficulties when a parent who has been the primary caregiver returns to work. Similarly, sleep problems arise before, during, or after a vacation, or when a child starts at a new daycare or school. When changes in routine occur, it is ideal to talk about them in advance in order to give the child a chance to process what is going to happen and to express feelings connected with the change. Expressing feelings in advance of an event is hard, both for very young children and for those who are not at ease expressing sad, mad, frustrated, or helpless feelings. Parents can use puppets, dolls, or drawings to help a shy or reticent child to move in an expressive direction, if not actually use the puppets or drawings to express feelings more directly.

When Nina began to do volunteer work once a week, six-year-old Yi Sheng began to wake up at night. "I don't see you in the day!" he complained to his mother. Although it was just a once-a-week job, Yi Sheng experienced this "loss" deeply, and it reverberated with his earlier losses of caregivers. Nina encouraged Yi Sheng to join her in a puppet play about a little boy whose mother returns to work. This helped reduce her son's nighttime anxiety.

A WORD ABOUT THE FAMILY BED AND CO-SLEEPING

The concept of independent sleep is an idea that some cultures favor but not all cultures follow. In fact, most families around the world sleep together in a "family bed" or in close proximity, in the same room, including families in some sophisticated First World countries such as Sweden. Swedes believe that closeness between parent and child is healthy, and children go back and forth between their parents' bed, an extra bed in their parents' room, and their own bed often, all the way into their early teen years.

In families where the primary caregiver (usually Mom) works away from home, a child is likely to want to sleep near that parent because they have missed time together during the day. Children stay up late to be with working parents as well. This is a common phenomenon even among non-adopted children.

There is no one *right* way to sleep. Parents need to find a way to help their child and themselves get enough sleep. I encourage adoptive parents to be creative and open-minded about sleeping arrangements. The family bed does not work if a child thrashes around at night or if one parent is an exceptionally light sleeper. Placing a small mattress or a child-size futon in the parents' room can be a solution. Some parents put a child's foam mattress on the floor of the child's room and a sleeping bag on the floor beside the parents' bed. That way the child can go back and forth as needed. Other parents put a comfortable foam mattress on the floor of their child's room in case a parent needs to sleep there.

Many parents worry that whatever sleeping arrangement they try will be "forever." Not to worry: Like all other aspects of development, sleep goes through stages. We do not worry that infants will suck on bottles when they get to high school or that the diaper stage will last through junior high school. In the same spirit you should not worry that a child will sleep in your room or bed

Sleep goes through developmental stages. A child eventually will want to sleep in his own bed.

forever. Do what is best for your child's development of connection with you in the present. The future will involve changes, but that, too, is part of growing up.

Many parents in the United States and the United Kingdom worry that having a child sleep in the same room compromises their privacy. This is undeniably true. However, parents can be creative about times for intimacy, just as they must be creative about managing other changes in life after children arrive. Adult sex life after a child joins the family is a normal issue for *all* new parents.

FAMILY SKILLS FOR SLEEP DEVELOPMENT

I have identified five family skills that center on sleep development. All of them, though in different ways, focus on developing a child's tolerance for separation from a parent.

The first family skill for a child to learn is understanding emotionally as well as cognitively that she is not alone at night. A child who has acquired this family skill calls for her parents at night rather than remaining silent.

The second family skill is falling asleep with a parent nearby or while being held by a parent. A child learns to substitute the parent's soothing for her own coping behaviors and thereby is better able to relax and fall asleep.

The third family skill is self-soothing in bed and falling asleep without having a parent present. Often a child uses a cuddly object or special blanket as a substitute for a parent's touch.

FIVE FAMILY SKILLS FOR SLEEP DEVELOPMENT

1. Child calls for parent at night and recognizes that she is not alone.
2. Child learns to rely on parent's touch or presence to calm and fall asleep.
3. Child uses self-soothing behaviors and a cuddly object to fall asleep without a parent present.
4. Child self-soothes in strange bed with parent present.
5. Child self-soothes in strange bed without parent present.

The fourth family skill for sleep development is falling asleep in unfamiliar locations *with* a parent present. An example of this would be when a family goes on vacation and stays at a hotel, where the child must sleep in an unfamiliar bed but in the same room as a parent. Finally, the fifth skill is being able to sleep apart from a parent in an unfamiliar location, such as when a child stays overnight at a friend's house.

The following are some specific strategies that will help you teach your adopted child these family skills.

PLAN A BEDTIME ROUTINE

First you need to establish a bedtime routine and a reasonable bedtime. Most young children go to sleep between seven and nine at night, depending on their nap schedules. A good bedtime routine is a fifteen- to thirty-minute set of activities that prepare your child for sleep. The purpose of a routine is to help your child anticipate the steps toward separation and ultimately the separation (into sleep) itself. Anticipation helps a child feel in control: "I know what will happen next!" Being in control helps a child relax, despite the impending separation. Thus it is important, to the extent possible, to follow the same order in your bedtime routine. This enables your child to know or predict what will happen next, and therefore to feel calm and in control.

A sleep routine should not include too many activities. A few are mandatory, such as putting on pajamas, physical contact through rocking or sitting together, and a final hug and kiss to tuck the child into bed.

TALKING ABOUT SEPARATION AT BEDTIME

Bedtime in general and falling asleep in particular are points of separation between parent and child. Even non-adopted children need extra support and help with separation issues at bedtime. A child with a complex background has been deeply sensitized to separations. Not mentioning separation explicitly at bedtime creates a disconnection between child and parent. Talking about separation, on the other hand, helps build and maintain connection. Equally important, acknowledging your child's feelings will help him manage those feelings. Use a Slinky toy to talk about separation at bedtime, showing "away," which is going to sleep, and "back," which is when you and your child reunite in the morning. The Slinky is a powerful tool because when it is stretched out to indicate "away," the two ends are still connected. Point this out to your child. This is a reassuring message that reinforces the first family skill of sleep: understanding that a parent is available all night.

Your child can play with the Slinky to "talk" about his feelings about separation. For example, a child who keeps dropping one end of the toy is "talking" about disconnection. Parents can be in tune with how that feels to a child and can put the feelings into words. "You are telling me it's hard to stay connected," you might say. "Maybe you are afraid I won't come when you call. But I will. We will stay connected even through the night."

Some children play in such a way that the Slinky becomes tangled. This play "talks" about a child's complex background and how tangled up or fragmented the connections have become. This is an excellent lead-in to looking at your child's Three-Photo Story (see chapter 7). The Three-Photo Story helps a child put past separations in sequential order. The photos give names to these separation events and provide a context in which the child can express the two most common feelings associated with separation: anger and sadness. All these feelings and thoughts are evoked at bedtime when a child must part from a parent for the night.

Some parents worry that looking at the photos before bed will cause the child to have bad dreams. In fact, parents who use this tool find that the reverse is true. After looking at the photos and hearing his story, the child relaxes and falls to sleep easily and quickly. If your child when awake does not consciously process his feelings about past separations, and the current separation at bedtime, he will process those feelings in dreams during sleep. Make the Three-Photo Story part of the bedtime routine for several nights, and then use it as often as your child requests it. If bad dreams or night terrors return, bring back the Three-Photo Story, and also talk about anxiety issues from recent days. This kind of bedtime conversation is as important as a good-night kiss; it reassures your child that you are hopeful and confident that there will be no more surprises, no more permanent separations.

> **By using the Slinky and talking about the Three-Photo Story together, you reinforce your presence and help your child feel safe and connected with you.**

FAMILY SLEEP SKILL 1:
TEACHING YOUR CHILD TO CALL FOR YOU AT NIGHT

The first step in helping a child move from reactive coping behaviors (see chapter 5) to family sleep skills is to teach her to call for a parent at night. Although many children do this without being taught, internationally adopted children often need help with this skill. An easy way to explain this idea to a child during the day is to play a game in which the child pretends to sleep in her bed or crib. When the parent is out of sight in the hall or another room, the child can call for the parent. "Call me," you can say to your child. "Say, 'Mama!' [or 'Daddy!']"

Some adopted children who have come from an orphanage setting will think this is the most ridiculous or pointless game in the world. These children may have had no one to call, or they may have had negative experiences with nighttime caregivers, and therefore are nervous about trusting what you tell them. Play the game often, until your child knows what to do and believes in its efficacy. Then try out this routine at bedtime.

Tell your child that during the night you come in and check on her, pull up the covers, and make sure she is safe. Many adopted children have never had this happen in the past. If they are asleep, they may not notice that you do come in; and if they wake, they may not understand that you are there to keep them safe. Some adopted children may have been abused at night and therefore may shut down or be too terrified to look at you when you make your nightly check-in. Until you talk openly about what you do at night, you may not learn from your child about his prior nighttime experiences with caregivers.

You can be sure that young children who have come from an orphanage were left in bed, either occasionally or often, with wet and dirty diapers.

Family skills build a new set of expectations about caregivers. These new expectations grow alongside old expectations formed prior to adoption. The old expectations never completely fade away.

Your child may therefore be reluctant to tell you if she needs help in this regard. She may fear a scolding or a negative reaction from you based on her previous experiences. It is important that you talk calmly and reassuringly about a child's needs to "go potty" at night or to have a diaper changed. Let your child know you will help in a timely manner and will not be angry at her. This topic is worth revisiting when your child begins to use the toilet on her own, for she may be afraid to get up in the night to do so, perhaps because she remembers bad experiences from the past.

To help put the family skill of calling for parents at night in perspective, consider your child's family age. During the first six months of life, infants "call" parents to feed them every two to four hours around the clock. This is a lot of practice for this family skill. A child needs to have this skill taught as soon as possible; then it must be continually reinforced. In terms of family age, your child should be learning, practicing, and using this family skill nightly in the first year home. This lengthy reinforcement time is needed because of the child's complex background and preconceived beliefs about caregivers. You are building a new set of expectations alongside the old ones, but the old ones will never completely fade away.

FAMILY SLEEP SKILL 2:
TEACHING YOUR CHILD TO RELAX WITH YOU AND FALL ASLEEP

As part of your bedtime routine you may already include a period of rocking or sitting together and singing. Singing releases in both the singer and the listener the "feel-good" hormones and other body chemicals that support connection. If you cannot sing or do not wish to sing, pick a music tape or CD and a favorite short song to which you and your child will routinely listen at bedtime. Researchers have shown that an association between a specific piece of music and falling asleep can be developed with practice and can help relaxation to occur.

Singing and rocking create a womb-like experience for a parent and child.

If your child is initially uncomfortable being held or finds holding too stimulating, sit separately. Over time, gradually move closer to him while the music plays or you sing to-gether, until your child becomes comfortable being physically close, and even-tually being held, before falling asleep. Your objective is to help your child find comfort in your physical presence. This bedtime closeness essentially creates a womb-like connection between the two of you, helping your child feel that you, the parent, are holding him not just physically but also emotionally. In the womb a baby feels Mother's motion as she walks and moves and hears Mom's voice. Sitting or rocking together simulates this experience, and singing adds another sensory channel to it.

Do not be discouraged by how long it takes for your child to be comfortable with, and eventually to look forward to, this kind of routine. Even when an ad-opted child has spent time with a foster family or birth family, he will not im-mediately snuggle into your arms. If that appears to happen quickly, be a bit cautious. Often a child who gets too close too fast finds other ways at other times to push parents away.

FAMILY SLEEP SKILL 3:
TEACHING YOUR CHILD TO SELF-SOOTHE WITH A CUDDLY OBJECT

It may take as long as nine months for a toddler or preschool child to begin relying securely on a parent for soothing at bedtime. When you begin to see this happening, it is time to prepare for the next milestone.

If your child has a special cuddly toy or favorite blanket, make sure that this object is present every time you snuggle with her, and especially when you look at and talk about the Three-Photo Story. A toy or small blanket is preferable because it is easily transportable, but your child may have other ideas. Stick with what she prefers or has chosen for comfort.

If your child has difficulty choosing or sticking with a cuddly object, you can help her settle on one. You might choose one of your own undershirts or exercise tops that you are willing to relinquish, making sure that it carries your scent. Offer it to your child as a cuddly object, specifically demonstrating how the shirt "smells like me." Tell your child that when you cannot be with her, the shirt will take your place.

Comfort objects are extremely important for the development of a child's connection with a parent. The child psychiatrist D. W. Winnicott was the first to introduce the concept of *transitional objects*, special objects that substitute for a parent. These cuddly things help a child make the transition to self-soothing, helping her recall the parent. Comfort cuddlies that smell like Mom or Dad are especially treasured because smell evokes memory so powerfully. This is why it is important not to wash a special blanket very frequently. Note that the loss of a cuddly object can be a major traumatic event, so buy a duplicate or be extra careful with the first one.

A child from a complex background has a hard time holding on to a cuddly object. This reflects her difficulty with believing in the connection between parent and child.

When you keep the cuddly object with you and your child during the cuddle at bedtime, the object becomes a symbol of your connection. Eventually the child will be able to use it when you are not available. Preparing for this moment does not, of course, have to be limited to bedtime. When Denise began holding Demetri, he held on to his special bunny. He slept with his bunny. When Denise had to go to work, Demetri brought his bunny to daycare, and when Denise hired a sitter for the evening, the bunny was Demetri's constant companion. When Demetri was away from his mother, however, he had a hard time holding on to his bunny unless his caregivers reminded him to do so. Difficulty with hanging on to a cuddly object, which is a symbol of a child's connection with a parent, is typical of internationally adopted children. Demetri and his mother had a connection, but it was easily and frequently broken; similarly, his cuddly was often lost. Internationally adopted children need to be told frequently that Mom or Dad will return, and that the parent is thinking of the child even when they are apart. When a child asks her parent to find the lost cuddly object, it is her way of asking the parent to help reconnect with her and soothe her feelings of loss.

WHEN CAN YOUR CHILD FALL ASLEEP IN HIS OWN ROOM?

Many parents are eager for their child to fall asleep on his own, so that they can have some adult time getting work done or relaxing. Several family skills must be in place before a child is ready for this level of separation. First, your child should be able to call for you, or indicate that he wants you to stay, when you leave the room. Next, your child should have chosen, and become comfortable with, a special cuddly object. In addition, there should be a minimal amount of stress in the family, and no significant changes or new routines, when you make this transition. Finally, your child should be comfortable sleeping in the bed in which he will be left.

Helping a child learn to self-soothe and fall asleep without Mom or Dad present takes preparation, as the itemization above suggests. You also need to prepare your child for what you expect him to do when you leave. Here are several strategies you can use to facilitate the process.

Strategy 1: The Basic Separation

The five items in the list below are instructions you can give to your child as she prepares to fall asleep without you present. Share this information with her at the beginning of your bedtime routine, go through your routine, and share the information again.

1. "Tonight you are going to fall asleep after I leave the room."
2. "Your teddy bear [or other cuddly object] will be with you. If you miss me, hug your bear."
3. "I want you to go to sleep, and if you wake up in the night, I want you to go back to sleep."
4. "You know that if you really need me, I'll come."
5. "But if you just wake up, go back to sleep."

Complete your bedtime routine with a warm hug and then leave the room.

Your child may cry and call for you. Without entering the room (which is a tease, suggesting that you might stay after all), call to your child and tell her, "Go to sleep. I'm close by. But now it's time for you to go to sleep. You can do it." Your tone of voice *must* convey that you are confident that your child can do this and that you are serious about this limit. If you say in an empathetic voice, "Oh, honey, it's sooooo hard, I *hope* you can do it," your child will know you are not serious and can be manipulated back into the room. Furthermore, your child will suspect that you do not truly believe she is able to fall asleep alone. It is easy to let your own empathy undermine the confidence you want to build in your child.

Many parents who struggle with separation issues from their own childhoods find bedtime good nights an excruciatingly painful process. If you feel that way you have three options. One is to ask your partner, assuming you have one, to take over this particular parenting challenge. Two is to get earplugs, and three is to go into another room after delivering the message and turn on the radio so loud that you cannot hear your child. Of course, you *will* sneak back to listen every five minutes, to make sure your child is still alive. (She will be.)

Listen carefully to your child's crying over five-minute periods. Initially the crying will escalate, getting louder and more intense; your child hopes to draw you back in. When your child realizes that you mean what you say, the crying changes, diminishing in volume and frequency. You are looking forward to hiccupping sobs and small whimpering sounds that say, "I guess Mom [Dad] was right, it is time to go to sleep." Each successive night should bring shorter periods of crying and calling.

After your child becomes comfortable falling asleep alone, there may still be setbacks. Setbacks are common when a child is sick or is exceptionally revved up or anxious, or if something has changed in the family, such as a parent traveling more frequently or going back to work, or an older sibling leaving home for college or summer camp. Take a couple of steps back, knowing that once the disruption is past, your child will be able to resume her former family skills for sleep.

Of course, not all children respond like a textbook case to this basic separation strategy. If your child has difficulty, signaled perhaps by crying for more than fifteen to twenty minutes the first couple of nights, make sure all the prerequisite family sleep skills are solidly in place. Consider your child's temperament, too. Is she especially persistent and stubborn? Is she able to calm down in other types of situations, or does she begin to rev up, cry, and throw tantrums, seemingly unable to stop? Strategies 2 and 3, which follow, should help you if your child is especially stubborn or prone to revving up. Finally, consider your own background and how easy or hard separations are for you. Are you worried you may be harming your child in some way by allowing her to cry? Examine your own fears; if that does not work for you, then it is time to find a good counselor or therapist who can help you resolve your own anxiety over separation.

Strategy 2: Setting Firm Limits

Some children are persistently unable to self-soothe enough to tolerate a bedtime separation. If this is true of your child, you need to set firm limits and hold your child to those limits, but you also need to be sure that the limits are *within your child's capability*. I have sketched out three typical problems and solutions below.

Some children are persistent criers. Others throw toys out of their crib, deliberately mess up their rooms, or engage in other angry and annoying behaviors. Still other children, especially toddlers and preschoolers, repeatedly come out of the bedroom asking for another story, another drink, and so on. Recognize, first, that these behaviors signal connection—your child expects you to be there or to come to him. You have succeeded in building a good parent-child connection.

Children from complex backgrounds, however, often have difficulty calming down (unless they shut down completely) when a parent is not present. Limits are a way to provide a child with a sense of security. They act like the walls of a house, defining what will happen and where. When a parent sets a limit and sticks to it, the parent's consistency feels predictable and therefore safe to the child. This is why a child tests the limits, to make sure the parent is consistent and trustworthy.

A persistent crier needs to hear from a parent in a firm but kind tone that he is welcome to cry for as long as he wishes, but that the parent believes that he can calm down and fall asleep. "I think you *can* do this," you might say. "You can slow your crying and fall asleep. I'll be right here in the living room."

A child who gets angry and throws toys out of the crib or trashes his room will have to help pick up those toys in the morning. Say to your child, "I know you are angry that I'm not with you. You can calm down and go to sleep now. In the morning we'll be together and you can pick up your toys." Reminding a child of the reunion that will take place in the morning is a positive image that will help him calm down.

A child who keeps showing up in the living room needs to be walked firmly back to bed with a minimum of conversation. Often this type of child is chatty, hoping to engage the parent and make Mom or Dad forget the limit. To such a child you can briefly say, as you walk him back to the bedroom, "You belong in bed. No talking. You can do it. See you in the morning."

Strategy 3: Separation with the Revving, Anxious Child

Some adopted children respond very intensely to separation and engage in hysterical crying, gagging, vomiting, holding of breath, head banging, or other dangerous behavior. Parents may find these behaviors manipulative or overly dramatic and may try to dismiss them. These behaviors often induce in parents the very feelings that their child has; they feel controlled, manipulated, and out of control with anger. Recognizing the potential for this kind of inducement can help you approach these behaviors with an effective strategy, rather than your own outburst.

Extreme behaviors are generally signs not that the child is trying to manipulate you but rather that she has negative physiological as well as emotional responses to separation. The physiological effects of separation can occur in many areas, including digestion (stomachaches, vomiting, or diarrhea), temperature regulation (sweating or shivering), control of vocalization (extreme crying or screaming), and the loss of control over behavior (tantrums, throwing, biting, and the like).

Extreme behaviors are the way a child asks for a more gradual separation process. Children are at their worst when they need a parent most.

Extreme behaviors are the way a child reveals that she needs a more gradual separation process. A child who has gone to the extreme emotional edge needs a parent to repair the parent-child connection. Repair must always include explaining to the child that the parent was not separating at bedtime out of anger or cruelty. Rather, the parent believed that the child could handle the separation but realizes he or she "moved too fast" for the child. This type of explanation does not back off entirely from the ultimate goal: a child falling asleep in her own bed without a parent hovering nearby. Repair postpones the goal, but it restores the connection between parent and child.

It requires extreme patience on a parent's part to work with a child who is desperately afraid of separating into sleep. Here are the specific steps I recommend to the adoptive parents with whom I work. First, equip yourself with a comfortable chair, a small reading light, and something to occupy your attention, such as a book or magazine, a crossword puzzle, or a knitting project. Second, obtain a comfortable mattress or foam pad to leave in your child's room as your temporary bed.

Next, reassure your child that you will stay near her or hold her until she falls asleep, just as you used to do. However, tell your child that the new rule is that you will stay *only if she closes her eyes and looks as if she is asleep.* This is vital, for a child over eighteen months of age can keep herself awake for hours, virtually pinning a parent to her side.

With eyes closed and body still, a tired child will naturally fall asleep. Do not leap out of your chair too quickly, for your child may be only lightly asleep and might awaken. Instead, watch and listen for her breathing to change to a slower, deeper rhythm, which will signal that she is actually asleep. Give her about five minutes to fall deeply asleep before leaving.

During the first week, put your chair next to your child's bed and sit there reading, knitting, or meditating until your child falls asleep. The following week, move your chair a bit closer to the door of the child's room, moving an increment closer every second day. Your goal is to develop your child's tolerance for distance between you and her as she becomes drowsy. Continue to remind your child that you will stay in the room only if she closes her eyes and "looks like" she is asleep.

To make this strategy genuinely effective, a parent also needs to help alleviate a child's fears in the middle of the night. Just checking in is not enough; very anxious children wake up repeatedly. To reduce anxiety, the child needs to find the parent present each time she awakens. Therefore, the first time your anxious child awakens in the night, go in and reassure her and then spend the rest of that night sleeping in her room on that comfortable mattress you have.

Each time your child awakens at night and finds you sleeping nearby, in sight, she will be able to fall back to sleep quickly, reassured that you are close. Over several nights or a week, the child's nighttime anxiety will diminish and she will eventually wake less often. Finally, your child will sleep through the night. This is the indication that her anxiety has decreased. But if you leave immediately, your child is likely to wake up, see that you are gone, and thereafter start waking up often to check on you. Be patient: After three or four nights of uninterrupted sleep, you can resume sleeping in your own bed. However, a disruption in home life, such as a parent traveling or the child starting at a new school, may set your child back. If this happens, begin using Strategy 3 anew to help your child through this setback.

NIGHTTIME SEPARATION FROM THE VERY ANXIOUS CHILD

1. At bedtime, sit near your child, moving your chair closer to the door once every couple of nights.
2. Your child must "look asleep," with eyes closed and body still, to keep you present.
3. Do not leave your chair until your child is fully, deeply asleep.
4. If your child awakens in the night, go in and spend the rest of the night in her room on a mattress, until she is able to sleep through the night.

Each time your child expects you to leave or finds you "missing," her anxiety is triggered. For separation-sensitive children, calming after an episode of intense anxiety is quite difficult. Although you should not be surprised if there are setbacks and restarts, the steps I have provided will, if you are patient, pay dividends.

FAMILY SLEEP SKILLS 4 AND 5:
TEACHING YOUR CHILD TO SELF-SOOTHE
IN AN UNFAMILIAR BED

When your family goes on vacation or stays overnight at Grandma's house, your child will have to sleep in an unfamiliar bed. This newness triggers separation anxiety and may cause family sleep skills to regress or fall apart.

Learning to sleep in an unfamiliar bed, even with a parent present, is the next step in family sleep skills. Prepare your child ahead of time, making sure his special cuddly object, and perhaps also his familiar pillow or blankets, come along. Be sure to follow the same bedtime routine you follow at home. Talk openly with your child about separation from home and how that makes him—and you—feel. If while you are away from home you are not sleeping in the same room with your child, you may need to sit near him as he falls asleep, at least for the first night, even if you are already past this hurdle at home.

As your child grows older, he will be invited for overnights at the homes of friends. Sometimes even elementary schools have an overnight trip for older children. These ordinary events can present a big challenge for an adopted child from a complex background. First, talk over the situation with your child. There is no requirement to do sleepovers; a child can choose to say no. Second, take steps that will help your child feel in control of the situation. Some parents begin with overnights with friends at the child's house; other parents create overnights with the child and siblings sleeping in the living room or, in summer, outside in a backyard tent. Arrange with a parent of your child's friend for the children to have an "almost overnight" at the friend's house; your child will take his pajamas and blanket there but will get picked up and brought home at, say, eleven o'clock. School trips need to be discussed and planned for as well. Although your instinct may be to offer up nothing but confidence and reassurance in advance of such a trip—"I'm sure you'll be able to sleep just fine"—I have found that discussing with a child the real possibility that he will have a hard time sleeping, if only temporarily, makes the reality less scary when it happens. "Oh, Mom told me this would happen," a child says as he lies awake. This more realistic kind of reassurance is often enough to help a child relax and fall asleep naturally.

PREPARE FOR SETBACKS

There are times when every internationally adopted child experiences extra stress or a trauma-trigger that reminds her of some early challenge in life. During these times children and adolescents regress and may lose their sleep capabilities. They need extra support going to sleep. Older children need parents to sit in their rooms, give them a back rub, or offer them one of the parent's own pillows (with the parent's scent); they may even ask to sleep in the parent's room or bed.

These methods of offering extra support should be accompanied by conversation that helps the child link the sleep challenges with the real-life events that are causing stress, or with the parts of the child's life story that created the present separation anxiety. Talking about separation, the child's complex background, and connection with a parent are vital components of helping a child develop the family skills of sleep.

Teaching Your Child
to Self-Soothe and Self-Calm

"AFTER YI SHENG HAS BEEN PLAYING ALONE for a long time," Nina said to me of her nearly five-year-old son, "I often find him sucking on his arm, his fingers, or any piece of cloth close at hand, like his collar or sleeve, as he plays or stares into space. He's too old to be sucking on his fingers! What's going on with him?"

THE CHILD WHO EXPECTS NEGLECT

Yi Sheng experienced neglect in the orphanage, and he expected the same in his adoptive home, where he had now been for just a few months. After playing for a while, Yi Sheng might have been frustrated, bored, or tired. Emotionally he was depleted and turned to sucking to soothe himself. Yi Sheng sucked on everything—his fingers, an arm, his clothing—much as an infant would, despite being almost five years of age. Sucking had become a survival skill for him. Yi Sheng's ability to soothe himself might be identified as a form of maturity, but it was really falsely mature or pseudomature behavior.

Checking in with a parent is the family skill a child needs to receive soothing and comfort. "I saw Sonia checking in with her foster mother in Guatemala," David commented, "and I noticed that since we've become a family, Sonia, who's now nearly a year and a half, is somewhat erratic and ambivalent about this type of behavior. Sometimes she checks in and other times she doesn't. And I've also noticed a certain ambivalence when she does check in. For example, last night she had been banging two blocks together for a while and then she toddled over to me, presumably to check in. But she turned her back on me, just as I was about to embrace her. It seems like she lost the family skill of checking in that she had in Guatemala."

Some children in the First Year Home Group, like Yi Sheng, Demetri, and Mu Ling, expected neglect because that was their primary experience in an orphanage before adoption. They did not check in as a means of soothing or calming themselves. Instead, they relied on solo means of self-soothing or on the survival skill of shutting down. Other children in the Group, like Sonia and Soon An, may have gained family skills such as checking in with a foster family, but these skills were disrupted or lost at the point of adoption. The ambivalent behavior demonstrated by Sonia, of turning away from or backing into a parent, is typical of children who are uncertain about trusting their new parent or caregiver. They are not sure whether to expect neglect or care.

ODD SELF-SOOTHING BEHAVIORS

When a child expects neglect, he must find ways to manage feelings of anxiety, fatigue, fear, or loneliness. Sucking is a common and easily recognizable self-soothing behavior. Other soothing behaviors appear odd or potentially harmful. Repetitive hair twisting, pulling hair out strand by strand, nail biting, touching one's own private parts, compulsive nose picking, head banging, repeated twisting or tensing of muscles, grimacing, and tics and tic-like behaviors are all forms of self-soothing and tension relief. Not surprisingly, parents find these behaviors, which psychologists call *stereotypies*, disturbing. Stereotypies are common among developmentally delayed and autistic children. Experience in an institution, such as an orphanage, or neglect (even in home settings) can cause stereotypies in children who are neither autistic nor inherently developmentally delayed. Many internationally adopted children have stereotypies.

Painful habits or behaviors such as head banging, nail biting, hair twisting or hair pulling, and the like cause the release of small amounts of endorphins, which are painkilling chemicals naturally produced by the human body. Because the same nerve pathways carry physical pain and emotional pain, the release of endorphins enables a child to manage the emotional pain of frustration, stress, loneliness, or anxiety. A single painful behavior releases only a small amount of endorphins, so the action must be repeated to continue the soothing flow of biochemicals.

If you have seen such behaviors in your child, you have probably found them upsetting. It is important, however, that you remain calm. An angry or upset reaction may cause a child to continue and even intensify the activity, if only to get a parent to continue providing attention, albeit of the negative kind. Focusing on a parent's reactions is, for the child, a further distraction from his own feelings.

PARENTING THE SELF-SOOTHING CHILD
WHO USES SURVIVAL SKILLS

Typically a parent orders a child to stop the inappropriate behavior: "Stop banging your head!" "Stop that rocking!" Orders, punishment, ridicule, or similar parenting strategies rarely stop self-soothing behaviors. Instead, view your child's behavior as a call to you for help.

The best intervention for all repetitive self-soothing behaviors, whether painful or not, is to acknowledge verbally the feelings that cause the behavior. Assume that your child will understand your tone of concern if not your precise words. "You must be so lonely and frustrated," Carolyn might tell Sonia. "Everything is hard since you came to Norteamérica." Speak honestly about your child's survival skill (see chapter 4) and its origin. Make no pretense that the Big Change, the international adoption, was easy. Offering assurance that "everything's all right now" makes you a liar in your child's eyes. Acknowledging the child's genuine emotional experience is often enough to reduce her painful feelings and, in turn, to reduce her self-soothing behavior.

Second, offer yourself for physical comfort to your child. Say something like "I can hold you, or hold your hand, while you feel sad."

Third, invite your child to drink or suck on something for comfort along with your physical touch: "Sit in my lap and have a bottle of water or a juice box," or "Let's play the Look-in-My-Eyes Game while you drink your juice." Play soothing music or sing to your child; rock together in a rocking chair. Listening to music releases dopamine, which is a naturally soothing body chemical.

What is most important is using your physical and emotional connection to soothe your child. In this way she incorporates the relationship with you into her process of calming, building family-based skills for handling bumps in the road of life.

Fourth, help your child connect her physical experiences to sensations and emotions and to the words that describe them. "Demetri doesn't use any self-soothing when he runs into a chair or a wall. He just keeps on going. I always tell him, 'That was an owie,' and my friends say this is spoiling him," Denise says to the other parents in the Group.

Far from spoiling her son, Denise is on the right track to help Demetri develop family skills. Some children shut off their feelings of pain because there has been no one to offer them comfort. Demetri, at twenty months of age and with only two months of family age, needed Denise to help him feel his own bodily reactions to pain and pleasure. In such a situation, without overdoing the "owie," let your child know that you are aware of her bump, and, as obvious as it may seem, tell her explicitly that most people say "Ouch!" and stop to soothe a hurt. Offering to kiss the "owie" is a good way to help your child learn to be in touch with her body and accept your soothing. In addition, your touch releases a feel-good chemical in your child that further increases connection.

THE DANGERS OF SHUTDOWN FROM "HOLDING" AND OTHER COERCIVE TECHNIQUES

Some parents feel they must control their child's painful, revving, or out-of-control behavior at any cost. A few have turned to a technique called "holding time" or to related methods that essentially coerce or force a child to become calm.

Holding Time, the primary and evangelical book on this "technique," instructs parents to hold their child tightly at any time the parent judges the child to be extremely upset or emotionally out of control. The parent is instructed to immobilize the child physically until he enters a "blissful state."

Other coercive techniques to subdue a child may include tickling; physical or verbal prodding; forced "rebirthing" (in which the child is made to reenact his own birth under the direction of a "therapist"); physical intimidation, such as a large adult using his or her physical presence to imply harm will come to the child; or isolating the child without access to food, drink, or toileting opportunities until he complies with the "response" demanded by the adult.

Stress beyond what any child can handle— which is not always the same level of stress that a parent thinks the child should be able to manage— can induce shutdown. Extreme shutdown reactions include a precipitous drop in heart and respiration rates, which can cause a loss of consciousness and of control of body functions. This event is called a

There has been no peer-reviewed research on so-called holding therapies. This is one of several reasons that conscientious and professional therapists never use or recommend such procedures, which risk creating extreme emotional and physiological shutdown in children. At least one child death has been reported as a result of such "therapy."

vasovagal episode. In simple language this means the person faints because of falling blood pressure and slowing heart and respiration rates. The person may lose bladder or bowel control in the process. This is a very real danger with any type of "therapy" or "discipline" that coerces a child with enough force to cause shutdown. Holding or other coercive tactics may result in physiological shutdown to the point of death, particularly in a child who has been abused or neglected or has experienced relational trauma.

Abused and neglected children are more vulnerable to shutdown. Because parents of internationally adopted children usually have no certainty about whether their child experienced abuse and, if so, what kind, they need to be especially careful. I raise this issue because some parents look to coercive "holding" as an approach to solving attachment problems, or behavior problems in general, without realizing the possible consequences. The long-term results of such coercive treatment include humiliation and shame (at losing control, including of bowel and bladder) and intense rage. These feelings do not encourage a child to trust or connect with the parent.

HANDLING THE DIFFICULT TIMES—ALONE

Every internationally adopted child, including your own, has had to face life alone at an early age after losing one or more caregivers. As a result, your child has learned to handle life's difficulties without adult support. After such experiences even ordinary life events can feel overwhelming, largely because of the effects of a stress-shaped brain (see chapter 2).

Here are some examples of stress responses—revving up and shutting down—from the First Year Home Group:

"Soon An sucks on her lower lip for long periods of time," Charlotte says of her eight-month-old daughter, "and now I'm wondering if she feels alone, without her foster mother, and is comforting herself." Children find ways to self-soothe. Sometimes they are calming themselves after revving up, and at other times they are forcing themselves to be alert rather than shutting down.

"Sonia is just fourteen months old and she has begun to bang her head on the floor when she's frustrated. She doesn't call for me or ask for help the way she asked for help from her foster mom, and even when she got to know me in Guatemala, when she was much younger. I've been puzzled, but if she feels alone, maybe she is using survival skills to manage her frustration," Carolyn thought aloud. Whereas many children bring survival skills with them from their past, others, like Sonia, develop new survival skills when they feel as if they are alone with strangers in their new family. Sonia's behavior is less mature, more survival-oriented in her new family than it was in her foster home. This can be confusing for adoptive parents who believe a former foster child would have few if any adjustment problems to family life. But such behavior is not uncommon among adopted children who come from nurturing foster homes and are acutely aware of their losses.

"Demetri plays until he falls over in a dead sleep," Denise adds. "There's no slowing down for him."

"Soon An is happy to sleep all the time, but then she starts screaming, seemingly out of the blue, and there's no stopping her," Charlotte comments. "I don't think she knows how to relax. She has an intense personality."

Both Demetri and Soon An show, though in different ways, a lack of behavioral and emotional control. We know that this is an area that is challenging from Adoption Day through the end of the teen years. Parents need to begin to work on developing such control as soon as possible.

THE DEVELOPMENT OF SELF-SOOTHING AND SELF-CONTROL

A child's stress response is modified by a braking system governed by the vagus nerve. I will explain briefly how this system develops, because I think it is a fascinating component of how humans work and useful for adoptive parents to know, as a background to much of what their parenting work is all about.

My favorite metaphor for the braking system that provides self-control is the automobile, with its accelerator, foot brake, and emergency brake. Imagine for a moment that your child is a car with two of these three controls operating: the accelerator, for revving, and the emergency brake, for shutting down abruptly. When your child revs, puts the "pedal to the metal," his fight-or-flight response is fully engaged; his heart and respiration rates increase, and his digestion slows. He feels neither hungry nor sleepy. When Demetri or Mu Ling play without seeming to tire, they are accelerating, or revving.

Shutting-down behavior is like applying the emergency brake. When the emergency brake is applied in a car, it not only stops but often stalls completely. This is what happens when Demetri shuts down in the midst of play and falls abruptly asleep. Stalling is the equivalent of physiological shutdown. For example, when eight-month-old Soon An withdraws, she slows down her sympathetic nervous system, including heart and breathing rates, effectively putting on her emergency brake. When she realizes she needs something, such as food, she releases the brake and accelerates, shifting suddenly into loud, frantic screams, revving for food or attention.

Such jerky behaviors, with little or no modulation from one emotion to another and abrupt transitions from sleep to screaming, or from playing to sleep, are the result of an "on or off" method of controlling energy. Having only an accelerator and an emergency brake for self-control causes a child to have difficulty lowering his loud voice, or expressing the beginning feelings of hunger or the gradual onset of fatigue. Under such conditions connection with others, focusing attention, and learning new things can be difficult, if not impossible.

What is missing in such a child is a "foot brake." This marvelous addition enables the driver of a car to control acceleration and deceleration in a modulated manner. Humans have such a foot brake; it is the vagus nerve, which runs from the brain to many parts of the body, including the face, heart, lungs, and stomach. Interaction between infant and mother or father teaches the infant to manipulate the foot brake smoothly and thereby control his behavior and emotions. But many internationally adopted children do not have the opportunity to undergo this kind of interaction and training as infants.

This foot brake is such an important developmental nexus that I consider it one of the central themes of this book. The reason is that the behavioral and emotional foot brake provided by the vagus nerve not only modulates behavior; it gives a child the ability to pay attention in a calm, alert way and thereby to acquire information and learn. Learning can take place only when a child is able to pay attention. Learning is difficult, if not impossible, when a child is shut down or revving up. If a child lacks or has a poorly developed foot brake, he is almost certain to have problems with attention, learning, and behavior. Thus, developing your child's foot brake is one of the most important things you can do to benefit his future.

A working "foot brake" enables your child to control his attention, emotions, and behavior. Helping your child develop a foot brake is one of the most important things you can do to benefit his future.

THE DEVELOPMENT OF THE "FOOT BRAKE"

How does the "foot brake" system develop? The psychologist Stephen Porges has identified four main avenues for stimulating the nerves that bring the foot brake system, which he calls the polyvagal system, into play. The first is *sucking*. We know that infants suck their thumbs in utero, and sucking is considered the first and primary means of self-soothing. Nursing or using a bottle or pacifier provides the same stimulus. The second avenue is *listening* to the human voice, particularly a human voice that is directed at the child. Third is the child's own *vocalizing*, to make sounds, to respond to the vocalization of others, and to sing to herself. The fourth is the child's developing capacity for perceiving in others, and then making her own *facial expressions* that convey emotions.

All four of these stimuli are embedded in the feeding experience of infants. When a mother nurses or feeds her child, she talks or sings while her child sucks, gurgles, and gazes at Mom's expressions of love. Frequent feeding every two to four hours in the first months of life stimulates the four avenues of regulation repeatedly, every day and through the night, integrating these behaviors tightly.

THE FOUR BASIC MEANS OF ACTIVATING THE FOOT BRAKE

1. Sucking
2. Listening
3. Vocalizing, singing, or speaking
4. Observing and making facial expressions

THE FOOT BRAKE IN CHILDREN WITH COMPLEX BACKGROUNDS

Internationally adopted babies and toddlers have experienced repeated disruption in their feeding and care routines, in contrast to a birth child or a child adopted at birth. Many of these adopted children learned to feed themselves at an early age, and therefore missed out on early opportunities for stimulation of the vagus nerve during interactions with their mothers. Such children, especially those who have undergone many caregiver changes, need extra attention to help activate this foot brake. Children who rely on survival skills (see chapter 2) do not use, or may not even have developed, this mechanism. Do not wait to see if your child develops these skills; begin practicing them the first weeks and months after becoming a family. Perhaps you have been home for more than a year and recognize that your child is still using survival skills and coping behaviors. Just introduce, and begin regular practice of, the strategies in the remainder of this chapter, in order to replace those survival skills with family skills that engage the polyvagal system.

THE ROOTS OF CO-REGULATED
SELF-SOOTHING AND SELF-CALMING

Let us now look at some strategies that teach family skills such as the expectation of care and that help bring survival-based self-soothing behaviors, including stereotypies (see page 147), to an end. Be sure to apply these suggestions consistently and give the process as much time as it needs. Be patient, because learning family skills takes time. Your consistent interventions will at first coexist with, and ultimately replace, your child's survival-based self-soothing behaviors.

Our concern for the moment is more with *how* a child soothes himself than with whether he does so. Does he do so alone, with survival skills or stereotypies, or does he do so by interacting with a parent through eye contact, touch, and a succession of age-appropriate soothing behaviors? The latter start with sucking and extend with age into a range of family skills, such as using a cuddly stuffed animal, calling for a parent, or asking for a hug.

Research on parent-child interactions has taught us a great deal about how parents and infants work together. Researchers call such interactive behaviors *co-regulating*, because they are a joint effort, a "dance" of sorts, between parent and child. Co-regulating begins when a child is fed by a parent who consistently connects emotionally and physically with the child during the feeding process. Co-regulation develops as a child learns to associate the parent's expressive face, voice, and eyes with the relaxation of sucking and a full belly. These interactive soothing experiences gradually become linked to experiences beyond feeding, such as a cuddly object or a parent's smile or singing or voice.

To soothe or calm your child, position him on your left side and make sure his left eye and ear are focused on your face and words.

Eventually the child internalizes these comforting experiences, so that even in the absence of the parent the child can imagine being held by the parent, or otherwise think of the parent in order to feel soothed. Let us look at some of the details of what we know about how co-regulation develops in young children.

First, holding your child on your left side is important because this position puts your left eye and your child's left eye in contact with each other. The left eye connects to the right side of the brain, which is the dominant side in the first three years of life. This side generates soothing and calming behavior in part by releasing oxytocin, dopamine, and other soothing chemicals in response to face-to-face interactions. The right side processes visual information, both facial expressions and other kinds of social and emotional information. Porges has shown that the right side of the brain also controls both the revving behaviors and the shutting-down behaviors of a child's nervous system. A calm parent's face is fed directly into the right side of the baby's brain and produces these calming effects. This is literally brain-to-brain interactive soothing.

British researchers Victoria Bourne and Brenda Todd write, "Research has indicated that seventy to eighty-five percent of women and girls show a bias to hold infants to the left side of their body." Bourne and Todd believe this tendency has evolved to support the development of the infant's right brain. Left-sided holding, as we have seen, is vital to soothing and calming a baby, directing the flow of facial and voice information to the child's left eye and ear. When I work with parents, I often suggest that they shift their child to the left side. This is especially important for a child who may not have been held frequently as an infant or was held by a succession of caregivers.

WHAT THE RIGHT SIDE OF THE BRAIN DOES TO HELP SOOTHE AND CALM

Releases oxytocin, opioids, and endorphins in response to face-to-face behavior

Processes information from others' facial expressions

Processes social, emotional, and visual information

Dominates development during the first three years of life

Directs calming behaviors

Second, a young child's sucking activates the vagus nerve, which in turn regulates the child's breathing into a smooth, slow pattern of inhaling and exhaling and slows the child's heart rate. Sucking thereby activates the foot brake, soothing the child. When a child is anxious and revving up, the foot brake is off and he eats less, yet his heart and breathing rates and his activity level are high. With the foot brake on, the child can slow heart, breathing, and activity to focus attention and eat and digest food.

Third, when a child associates sucking with a parent's voice, eye contact, and general presence, and eventually with a cuddly object, a foundation is laid for new soothing possibilities that do not rely on sucking. Infants suck on bottles and thumbs, preschoolers hang on to their favorite blankets or stuffed toys, and older children wear a favorite shirt day in and day out. As adults we serve our mother's best chicken recipe and wear our favorite soft coat to soothe and calm.

PARENTING STRATEGIES TO BUILD
CO-REGULATED SOOTHING AND CALMING

The parents with whom I work use the following five approaches to get the foot brake system going in their children: limiting stimulation, sucking and breathing routines, listening to music, singing, and movement and music. These strategies may be used with very young children, or with older children—including many internationally adopted children—whose systems must be repaired or built from scratch. Keep in mind the concept of family age as you begin to work on these soothing and calming strategies. Your child may be a year to two years old or older chronologically but with, say, just six months of family age and little or no experience with the foot brake. Set your immediate expectations low and your long-term hopes high if your child has mixed maturities (see chapter 4).

Strategy 1: Limiting Stimulation

It is easy to overlook how stimulating our families' lives are for our internationally adopted children. It is difficult to be relaxed and calm when the world around you is overstimulating. In order for an adopted child to develop and use her foot brake capacities, she needs a low-stimulation environment.

Each time a child is stimulated by attending a party, a playgroup, or a swimming class, or goes on vacation and visits several different places in a week's time, she is prone to reverting to coping behaviors. When I work with adoptive parents, I often tell them that they need to curb these experiences more than they might otherwise do with a birth child, especially during their adopted child's first year or so in the family.

"Does this mean we have to limit our lifestyle severely? Cancel vacations and drop out of playgroups?" they often ask. You can be realistic: You do not need to go into seclusion for a year in order to nurture your child's foot brake. But if you find that your child is not learning regulation after you have tried the other strategies described here for several weeks, try following a simpler and less stimulating schedule.

You can do the following:

■ Be aware of how stimulation affects your child. When she becomes overstimulated, step in and help her calm down by taking a break together in a quiet room. View this as a learning experience, not a punishment.

- Reduce stimulation in your home and in the child's room. For example, put half or two-thirds of your child's toys away. Rotate toys weekly for variety.
- Plan less busy days. There should be several days a week when you and your child just "hang out" at home. One class or exciting activity per day is sufficient. This is especially important if your child participates in active play with older siblings, or even just accompanies you on the carpool and shopping circuits.
- Build in periods of regular relaxation, "time-ins," for your child and yourself. Start a star chart and plan to award yourself a star each time you pause for five or ten minutes during the day to relax. When you have twelve stars, reward yourself with something relaxing like a massage.
- Plan simpler vacations in which you stay at a condo, or a motel with a kitchenette, preferably in a single location. You can cook some meals at "home" rather than eating out, which is highly stimulating and makes it harder for your child to use her foot brake to soothe and calm.
- If you are visiting relatives, stay in a hotel for a break or use your room at the relatives' home for "time-ins" several times a day.

Strategy 2: Sucking and Breathing Routines

When a child sucks on a bottle and feeds, the coordination among sucking, swallowing, and breathing is particularly stimulating to the vagus nerve. This is why we say that sucking is the first method a child uses for self-soothing. Sucking coincides with an inhalation of breath, swallowing requires the breath to be held, and the final step is exhaling. "Suck, swallow, breathe" is the phrase I use to refer to this pattern. This strategy works best for a child who is no longer using the bottle; if your child still uses a bottle, you may need to modify what I describe. Your goal is to get your child to follow the suck, swallow, breathe pattern that you demonstrate:

- First, inhale deeply through your mouth, so that your child can hear and see what you are doing.
- Then suck up some liquid loudly through a straw.
- Next, make a gulping sound to show you are swallowing the liquid.

- Finally, let out your breath loudly to alert your child to this action.
- Repeat the entire routine several times, and then have your child mirror you.

Many internationally adopted children suck first without inhaling. They suck rapidly several times, swallow a huge amount of liquid, and then pant for air. This is a sure sign that the child is revving, not calming.

As a child gets older, say four to six years old, and can count, you can help the steps flow smoothly by counting aloud as your child sucks, swallows, and breathes: "Inhale, two, three, four; suck, two, three, four; swallow, two, three, four; breathe out, two, three, four." Getting your child to look in your eyes during this process will help slow down any revving up that occurs.

Suck, Swallow, Breathe Games for Older Children

Yi Sheng, at nearly five years of age, had difficulty soothing and calming himself and he refused to lie in anyone's arms or suck on a bottle. So his father invented several games to help him with the suck, swallow, breathe routine. Kenji purchased a dozen reusable plastic straws, curvy and colorful, and he and Yi Sheng went outside to play, using the straws to suck up water from a water bottle and then to blow it out. Of course, between turns Yi Sheng drank through the straw. When he did so, Kenji drank through his straw, too, and he and Yi Sheng looked at each other as they went through the suck, swallow, breathe routine, mirroring each other's actions. Kenji always made an exaggerated gulping sound when he swallowed, and this made Yi Sheng laugh.

When she was four years old, Sonia and her family discovered that it was fun (and challenging) to use a straw to blow Ping-Pong balls across a table or balloons from one end of the living room floor to the other. Doing this takes a lot of breath control, which itself is necessary as a child learns to focus attention; the foot brake is the source of breath control and therefore attention as well.

Ideally games like these should be cooperative ones, in which parent and child take turns. Asking any child, even a ten-year-old, to play such a game alone is not the point. Learning self-control through interaction with a parent is the key to developing family skills, no matter what the child's chronological age is.

The Bottle Controversy

"My dentist and my pediatrician told me to take Demetri off the bottle immediately," Denise confided.

"My pediatrician was horrified that Sonia still takes a bottle at night," Carolyn added.

Most pediatricians and dentists see primarily non-adopted children, who have had lots of opportunities to develop their co-regulation; it is easy for them to overlook the special meaning of a bottle for an internationally adopted child. In the eyes of these professionals, the bottle and the thumb are the "enemies" that cause cavities and misaligned teeth.

Parents, pediatricians, and dentists need to understand the importance of sucking in a child's overall development and to make thoughtful decisions about the bottle and other sucking opportunities. To put it bluntly, if your child cannot calm down and sit quietly, your dentist will not be able to work on his teeth. Holding a child who is sucking on a bottle while looking at your face is the easiest and most convenient way to help that child develop co-regulation. In this position all the factors that stimulate the vagus nerve and its work are in place. If your child is older than five or six, or is not comfortable on your lap, you can sit side by side (with your child on your left!) and look at each other.

Bottles are important for developing both the feeding connection between child and parent and the basics of self-control. However, pediatricians and dentists are usually adamant about weaning children from bottles by one year of age, for health reasons. I encourage parents of internationally adopted children to use a bottle, if a child will accept it, because it helps the child develop his vagus nerve and self-control. However, there are some important guidelines to prevent health problems such as cavities and ear infections:

- Fill the bottle with water or diluted juice, not with milk or undiluted juice.
- Offer your child a pacifier or other sucking or chewing object at bedtime. Do not let your child fall asleep sucking the bottle.
- Limit your child's use of the bottle to your lap. Do not let your child walk around sucking on a bottle.
- Always associate the bottle with a parent's touch, with face-to-face gazing with a parent, and with a comfort object, such as a stuffed toy or a blanket.

If you decide not to use a bottle to encourage sucking, or if your child simply does not want to use one, you can use a sippy cup, a juice box with a straw, or even an adult water bottle with a top designed for sucking.

From Eating to Other Self-Soothing Behaviors

"Associating the bottle with a comfort object sounds important. Can you explain how this works?" Denise once asked me.

For a young child, a blanket or stuffed toy is often the item of greatest interest beyond food. A special song or rhyme can serve a similar purpose for a child who is more auditory than tactile. For older children, songs and rhymes can evoke, or take the place of, the closeness of being fed. A school-age child or even a teenager can repeat a nighttime rhyme, such as "Nighty-night, don't let the bedbugs bite!" after a parent leaves the room in order to soothe herself.

"I've tried giving Demetri a cuddly toy, but he throws it away," Denise told me. It takes time for cuddle toys and blankets to develop into loved objects. Once in a while a child quickly attaches to some object, but most children move through stages of learning to self-soothe. The first stage is using a parent for comfort. Until a child truly feels safe and soothed by a parent, she cannot transfer that feeling to an object or toy. So a special panda bear or blanket may not be useful until the second year your adopted child is home.

"How long does it take for our children to develop this connection to us? And how do we know when it's occurred?" Nina asked. Carolyn wondered, "What if our child has had a good connection with a foster parent, like our Sonia did. Does that make this process go faster?"

For a birth child, attachment to a cuddly object begins sometime between one and two years of age. Prior to this, however, a child develops a set of behaviors that reflect her connection to a parent. These behaviors include watching Mom or Dad prepare food when she is hungry, handing toys to parents, facing a parent while playing, playing close to a parent, and seeking parental attention regularly. When she is across the room or exploring something new, a child checks in, looking at the parent for guidance, as if to say, "Do you like what I'm doing?" As a culmination of all these connections, a child begins to show signs of missing a parent when the parent is out of sight. Signs of missing include looking for or following a parent from room to room and fussing when a parent leaves. Nine months is the average age when a *non-adopted* child begins to show signs of missing a parent. An adopted child generally needs nine months of family age.

An Eating Game That Connects Parent and Child

"Now that you know how the pieces of soothing work," I say to the First Year Home Group parents, "let's try some things with our children. I think all of you have a bottle or some food with you. We're going to play a game called It Tastes Better When You Look in My Eyes. Since some children are anxious about being fed, we will initially play this game among the parents. Once children see adults play the game, they will realize it's different from the orphanage and will feel safe enough to try it." (This game was introduced in chapter 4.)

I instruct each of the parents to find a partner and decide who will feed and who will be fed. "Then look into each other's eyes and slowly start the feeding," I say. "The feeder says, 'It tastes better when we look at each other.' The person who is being fed says, 'Yummy!' We'll go around the circle, starting with Carolyn and David."

The children have been busy playing, but when all the parents focus on Carolyn feeding David, the children look around to see what is happening. Carolyn smiles while looking into David's eyes and feeding him a piece of apple. "Yummy. Mmmmmm," David says.

The children move a step closer. Sonia, sitting in her mother's lap, looks on and then cranes her neck to watch.

Next, Laura feeds Meg a piece of cookie. "Yummy," Meg says with a smile, looking into Laura's eyes. As the game continues, one by one each child approaches his or her parent and indicates that he or she wants to play this game, too. Demetri is the most hesitant, but he is willing to feed Denise, although he repeatedly tips her head back before he does so.

"What should I do now?" Denise wails as she gazes upon the ceiling and her son peers into her open mouth.

"Tell Demetri that this game is not like the orphanage, not like eating in Russia. This is family eating and you need to look in each other's eyes," I encourage Denise.

Denise faces her son and begins teaching him what family feeding is like.

Meanwhile, Mu Ling sticks out her hand to try to feed her mother Meg, but she accidentally hits Meg's nose. Mu Ling was not paying attention to Meg's face. "You have to look at my face, Mu Ling," Meg says, as she gently turns her daughter's head toward hers.

"Soon An, look at me when you suck your bottle," Joe tells his daughter. "Look at my eyes. I know they are different from your foster mother's eyes."

The room dissolves into the focused chaos of five families teaching their children to eat family style, face to face, eye to eye. After five minutes the children are full of apples and crackers and they gradually return to their individual play. Most are sitting closer to their parents than they were before the eating game.

Strategy 3: Listening to Music

In recent years researchers have provided ample scientific evidence to support the first proposition in the oft-quoted line by William Congreve, "Music has charms to soothe a savage breast, to soften rocks, or bend a knotted oak." They have proved that music is indeed emotionally and physiologically regulating and can soothe, calm, and organize. Both listening and singing activate the vagus nerve and have a calming effect. Music literally teaches the brain to calm itself.

Listening to melodic music such as Mozart is uniquely calming. Lullabies are not merely pretty good-night songs but genuinely effective ways to soothe a child. Eventually a child who hears singing begins to sing to soothe himself.

The simplest strategy is to sing to your child. But not everyone likes to sing, and even those who do are not always in a tuneful mood. An equally good strategy is to pick up a CD, preferably with the music of Mozart, Bach, or similar classical composers. Look for music with an easy-to-follow high (treble) melody in the range of the human voice. Turn down the bass and turn up the treble on your player so that this melody is most audible. This makes the music easier to follow for young ears. Experts on the subject recommend music without lyrics, so that a child can follow the melody without the additional complexity of language. (This rules out most children's songs.)

An hour or two a day of listening to music uninterrupted by conversation is a good goal, according to listening therapists. However, even half an hour is great. A child can play with toys, color, or do other things that do not require words while listening. If you do not want to hear the music yourself, set your child up with a personal music device.

Strategy 4: Singing

Another way of stimulating the foot brake system is for the child herself to sing. Children often sing in imitation of Mom or Dad, so tune up your pipes and break out the songs. Because the emphasis is on the melody, not the words, choose very simple, repetitive songs. Although it is tempting to introduce new songs, as you become bored singing "Twinkle, Twinkle, Little Star" for what seems like the millionth time, remember that a new song is new stimulation and is harder to follow. Repeating songs or a series of songs is more helpful for activating the co-regulated foot brake.

Strategy 5: Movement and Music

Another way to help a child soothe and calm is to combine music and movement.

For example, you and your child can rock forward and back as you sing "Row, Row, Row Your Boat," and you can make a game of stopping your rocking and singing for two or three counts at the end of each line.

Make singing and dancing together a regular part of your day, fitting it into the end of some routine. Denise and Demetri decided to make "Ring around the Rosy" their "coming-home song." Singing the song and dancing to the tune gave them a way to relax after returning from shopping or play and to have a calm way to transition to whatever activity came next.

TIME-INS FOR RELAXATION

Most parents are familiar with time-outs as consequences for poor behavior. We address time-outs and other consequences in chapter 16, but here I would like to introduce the concept of *time-in*. A time-in is a special opportunity to help a child slow down and relax with a parent. It is a period for actively teaching, and not just telling, your child how to relax and take a breather.

One day Mu Ling, nearly three years old, was getting very active in the Group, beginning to throw toys and to grab bottles from other children. Her mother Meg told her several times, "Calm down!" and "Stop throwing toys; we don't do that here." Meg was ready to take Mu Ling home. I commented that Mu Ling might not realize, or care, that this was a consequence of her behavior. Instead I suggested taking Mu Ling to the waiting room for a quiet time-in together.

"Your behavior is telling Mom and me that you need a special quiet time with Mom on the couch in the other room," I told Mu Ling, while removing another potential missile from her hand. Meg got up and led Mu Ling from the playroom to my waiting room.

"You can flip off the lights to help Mu Ling recognize that this is a quieter place. Then help her to calm by rocking in the rocking chair, or blowing bubbles for her to watch," I suggested. I told Meg not to worry about educating Mu Ling immediately about "good behavior"; Mu Ling would listen better to that information after becoming calmer. The time-in worked, and Meg made plans to make time-ins a regular part of Group sessions for Mu Ling.

Some children need a spatial change, such as moving from one room to another, to help them stop revving. Other children do best with oral stimulation such as sucking. Still others prefer movement or singing. As a parent, you are the chief executive of soothing and calming, of the foot brake system, for your child and yourself. You are the CEO of emotional and behavioral control, and as such you must actively guide your child toward the self-calming activities that work best for him.

"I've tried some but not all of these things," Denise once commented to me, "but the one thing that really slows Demetri down is watching the video of his adoption. Why does he watch that over and over again, sitting so calmly, and why is it the one thing that is guaranteed to calm him down?"

In this chapter we have covered a variety of methods for launching the development of self-control in your child. But Denise's comments provide a reminder that telling the child's story coherently from the child's point of view (the subject of chapter 7) in itself is a soothing and calming technique that is tremendously powerful, and central to, the lives of internationally adopted children. Along with telling your child's story, developing the family skills for soothing and calming will help your child with the big and little bumps that inevitably arise on the road of life.

Sensory-Motor Integration and Stimulation Management

IN THE PREVIOUS CHAPTER we explored the roots of self-regulation in the calming and soothing that a child gets from suck, swallow, breathe routines, as well as from music, movement, eating games, and time-ins. In this chapter we look at the way that the five senses become organized by the brain and by the child's experiences, and at how the senses get in sync with the child's growing motor skills. This *sensory organization* also confers a sense of calmness and is an important additional element of self-regulation. As we listen to the parents in the First Year Home Group, we will hear about some of the *sensory disorganization* they observe in their children.

GETTING READY: BEANBAG BATHS AND MASSAGES

Many, although not all, children feel soothed by broad, deep pressure on their bodies. While in utero the fetus experiences pressure from the surrounding fluid and uterine muscles. Parents in many cultures swaddle newborn babies to reproduce this sense of containment. For an older child, parents can duplicate this pressure-induced sense of calm and security in two ways: One is what I call a "beanbag bath" and the other is a spandex "wrap." Both techniques help raise your child's level of Parent Juice (see chapter 9), to encourage your child to stay close to you and feel calm and relaxed.

To start a beanbag bath, lie on the floor and place several large beanbags on your body. (You can order large beanbags, about seven inches square, from http://www.abilitations.com, or you can make your own at home.) If the beanbags are not relaxing for you, try wrapping yourself in a wide piece of spandex material. The pressure of the beanbags or the spandex is soothing and calming.

When the parents in the Group try these methods, the children are fascinated. Demetri walks over, lifts one of the large beanbags off his mother's leg, and then drops it back onto her. "Ooof!" Denise says, and then she laughs. "Would you like a beanbag on your legs, Demetri?" she asks. Her son sits down and drags one of the heavy bags over to his legs and his mom helps him put it on. He gives her a warm smile of connection. Denise covers her own and then Demetri's legs with beanbags and lies back, turning her head to watch her son.

After the children have tried the beanbag bath, we offer to rock each one in a spandex wrap. We place a large rectangle of spandex on the floor and invite a child to sit in the middle. Two parents grasp the four corners of the spandex, and while watching the child's response, they gently lift him or her from the ground; the spandex embraces the child, who is rocked gently. As the child is rocked, he or she feels the pressure of the spandex. Some children like the rocking; others, like Sonia, just want to sit tightly wrapped up and peeking out at Mom and Dad.

These tactile experiences prime the children for the more intimate touch experience of massage.

Next I turn off the lights in the room and ask the parents to whisper or use low voices to create a dim, quiet atmosphere. I invite Meg and Laura to massage each other's feet to demonstrate to the children what massage is. Meg playfully adds "This little piggy went to market..." to her massage routine. Soon Mu Ling and Demetri stick their feet out to their parents. Yi Sheng chooses another approach; he places his feet against his dad's and pushes alternately on each foot. Kenji responds in sync, and the two enjoy a foot-to-foot massage.

CHALLENGES OF SENSORY-MOTOR INTEGRATION

As the parents in the Group begin to think about sensory integration, they share observations about their children's behavior.

"Soon An is so sensitive to sounds, she cries and covers her ears when she hears a truck go by," reported Charlotte. "But oddly enough she loves bright lights and seems to be more alert when it's brighter."

"Demetri," Denise said, "is a picky eater. He doesn't like crunchy foods, only soft ones. In fact, he would like to have soup for all his meals if he could."

"Mu Ling doesn't just run up to me; she rams into me. She seems unaware of pain," said Meg.

"Sonia," commented Carolyn, "can't seem to hold herself up. She slumps over in a chair until she's nearly lying down. The other day we put her on the slide at the playground, but she wouldn't sit up. She began to slide down head first, and she got scared."

According to Kenji, "Yi Sheng has difficulty modulating his voice. When he talks it's always at top volume."

When parents use words like *sensitive*, *picky*, or *unaware*, they are describing sensory-motor issues. When these issues are mild, many parents assume they are merely personality variations. After all, everyone knows someone who is a picky eater or who hates loud noise or who does not like to be hugged tightly. We might think of such a person as a bit eccentric, but in fact he or she may have a sensory-integration or sensory-modulation problem. Many picky, sensitive, or unaware children have some genuine developmental gaps that cause their eccentric or frustrating behaviors, and those gaps may lead to behaviors that are hurtful. Now that we know more about this critical area of development, parents can help their children.

The field of Sensory-Motor Integration (or SI) is the area of research and theory in which professionals address these types of developmental gaps. SI began in the mid-twentieth century with the observations and writings of A. Jean Ayres, an occupational therapist in Los Angeles. Despite the neurological origins of sensory-motor dysfunctions, SI has remained the domain of occupational therapists; medical doctors, such as neurologists and pediatricians, do not use it. I have found that parenting strategies based on SI are quite effective, and I believe that pediatricians who advise parents that a child will "grow out of" these disorganized behaviors are misguided. And I am not alone: Although initially SI was considered a fringe therapy, over the past half-century it has become highly respected, at least outside the medical community, among child-development specialists.

The remainder of this chapter introduces parenting techniques that encourage and support this vital area of development. Even children who do not show signs of difficulty will benefit from these techniques, which literally help organize the brain.

OUR SENSES MUST LEARN TO WORK TOGETHER

The five senses—taste, touch, smell, hearing, and sight—provide information about the world to the brain. Each piece of information is called a stimulus; together, sensory stimuli make up much of the input to the brain. Sensory-motor integration also incorporates two other forms of input that are less well known. The first is our sense of movement and balance in relation to gravity; our abilities in this area come from what is called the vestibular system. The second is our sense of where our body is in space, our body's spatial relation to other people and objects around us. These abilities come from what is known as the *proprioceptive system.*

As the inputs come in, the brain processes all the information. This is referred to as *central processing*. Finally, the person acts or responds. SI practitioners call this response, or output, *praxis*. Praxis consists of the many ways we organize our behavior. It includes our activity level, our self-help skills (feeding and dressing, for example), our sequencing of behaviors (putting one foot in front of another), our motor planning (preparing to go up a stair by lifting a foot), and our overall organization of behavior (including everything from putting objects away neatly to putting on clothing correctly to writing one's own name in the upper right-hand corner of the paper at school). The box below lists the core praxis behaviors that a child must master as she develops; I have adapted the list from the book *SenseAbilities: Understanding Sensory Integration*, by Maryann Colby Trott.

Praxis Behaviors

Imitation:	mimicking others' behavior
Ideation:	basing action on one's own ideas, including new movement possibilities
Initiation:	determining how and where to begin an activity
Construction:	putting things together in new and different ways
Feedback:	using information from proprioception to refine motor skills
Feedforward:	anticipating the next step, and the strength or speed needed to perform it
Gradation of intensity:	deciding how much energy to put into a motor activity
Timing and sequencing:	determining the speed and order in which motor activity occurs
Organization:	putting all these pieces together

TWO TYPES OF SI DYSFUNCTIONS

A. Jean Ayres called an SI dysfunction a "neurological inefficiency" and compared it to a traffic jam in the brain. Maryann Trott identifies two types of SI problems: a *discrimination* dysfunction and a *defensiveness* dysfunction. An example of a discrimination dysfunction is reaching into a pocket and being unable to tell the difference between a piece of tissue and a toothpick. A defensiveness dysfunction would be when your sensitivity is so great that you cannot bear to touch one or more of the items in your pocket. Children who are hypersensitive, for example, avoid certain sounds, textures, or odors. In her book *The Out-of-Sync Child*, Carol Kranowitz describes a child with SI dysfunction as having "a disorganized brain." "His overall development," Kranowitz writes, "is disorderly and his participation in childhood experiences is spotty, reluctant, or inept ... Responding to everyday events can be enormously challenging."

Sensory Integration at Work

Input (Stimulus) →

Central Processing (Brain)

→ **Output (Praxis)**

SI DYSFUNCTION AND THE INTERNATIONALLY ADOPTED CHILD

Unfortunately there is little scientific research on SI dysfunction among internationally adopted children; we have only some anecdotal, observational reports and a few parent surveys, limited to Romanian children and their adoptive parents. Consistent with what other researchers who follow postinstitutionalized Romanian children have found, those examining SI have concluded that the more time a child spent in an orphanage, the greater the severity of the child's problems.

The most severely deprived children, represented by the wave of Romanian adoptees who came to the United States during the 1990s, are likely to have a wide variety of sensory integration and behavioral issues. These children often have tactile problems, such as heightened sensitivity to texture (so that the child will wear only soft cotton clothing with the labels or tags removed), or a dislike of certain food textures. I believe these symptoms indicate general SI dysfunction rather than an isolated problem.

I have observed in my own work with adoptees that internationally adopted children have a mixture of hypersensitivities and hyposensitivities—they sense, or respond to, too much or too little, and the same child may do both at different moments. These hyper- and hyposensitivities appear most when the child is under stress or anxious. I have also seen that some adopted children have problems with balance and movement in relation to gravity, as well as with motor planning, coordination, and muscle tone. These areas, too, deteriorate when a child feels greater stress.

It is important to distinguish between difficulties that are genuinely SI-based and those that are emotionally based. Often a parent observes, for example, that in some settings a child is perfectly capable of motor planning but in other settings (usually the stressful ones) he seems to lose all or part of this skill. The parent might reasonably suspect that stress or emotional issues make the difference, but it is often validating to have an expert in SI evaluation confirm this. SI therapy is unlikely to make a difference in a child whose SI problems are primarily emotional if the stress continues to be present. Instead, a parent needs to manage stressful situations so that the child can more easily integrate his sensory inputs and the resulting behaviors, or praxes.

I have also observed that most internationally adopted children have difficulty with awareness of their energy level—Am I devoting too much or too little energy to this behavior?—and also with learning to move smoothly from one energy level to another.

Finally, it is my belief that, because many adopted children have had a restricted level of stimulation in the past, they are more vulnerable to new or high levels of stimulation in the present; they have trouble processing such intense input and responding with appropriate and calm behaviors.

In the remainder of this chapter I share methods that address the areas of SI difficulty I have just outlined. Be aware that these activities cannot substitute for a full SI assessment and treatment by a professional. However, they do cover the basic areas that children from complex backgrounds generally find challenging.

FIVE SI AREAS FOR PARENTS TO ADDRESS

1. Sensory modulation
2. Working with gravity
3. Regulating activity level
4. Self-awareness of activity level and alert, focused attention
5. The "sensory diet"

STRATEGY 1: DEVELOPING SENSORY MODULATION THROUGH BRUSHING

Soon An is hypersensitive to noise and covers her ears when Charlotte vacuums or a truck goes by. Demetri spits out crunchy foods because of his intense oral-tactile sensitivity. Mu Ling, on the other hand, is hyposensitive. She stuffs her mouth too full because of her lack of oral sensitivity, and she craves swinging and hanging upside down to satisfy her vestibular needs. Because her body does not fully feel, and her mind does not fully process, the stimulation of her actions, she wants to swing extra high and to do so for quite long periods of time.

Sensory modulation is the capacity to turn the intensity of feeling sensations either higher, as in Mu Ling's eating, or lower, as in Soon An's hearing. Telling Soon An or Demetri to "lighten up" or "be less sensitive," or telling Mu Ling to "pay more attention" or to "be more sensitive," would do little to help their sensory-modulation issues. Such phrases instead would make them feel inadequate, unable to change something over which they have no control. In fact, most children with SI problems already experience low self-esteem.

If your child has difficulty with sensory modulation, acknowledge to yourself and to your child that these issues are real and not something your child is making up just to be difficult. "I know your ears hurt," you might say. "It must be hard for you when I run the vacuum cleaner." Continue by acknowledging that sensory issues are difficult, for both you and your child: "Having sensitive ears is hard for you and me." These kinds of statements put you on your child's side and you cease to be the adversary. Finally, assure your child that you have a strategy, a program that can help: "I have a way to help us with this problem."

A method that I recommend highly for parents of both hyper- and hyposensitive children is the Wilbarger Protocol, developed by Patricia and Julia Wilbarger. This program helps a child modulate each of the sensory areas. Using a soft brush, a parent brushes a child's back, arms, and legs on a regular basis throughout the day. How does something so simple work to change a child's brain?

The skin is the largest organ in the body and a primary sense organ. One of the first parts of an infant's body to adjust to the world and to sensory input is the skin. When, as in the Wilbarger Protocol, you condition your child's skin to modulate the experience of tactile input, your child's brain gains a model of how to do this with input from other sense organs. But as simple as the procedure is, parents have to work hard at performing it consistently for several weeks.

I will describe the protocol briefly, but I urge all parents to obtain and read Patricia and Julia Wilbarger's short booklet "Sensory Defensiveness in Children Aged 2–12: An Intervention Guide for Parents and Other Caretakers," available from Avanti Educational Programs (see the Bibliography for details). One caveat: The brushing technique has been widely adopted in sensory-modulation work with children because of observations of pronounced changes, but there is no scientific research that proves a correlation between these changes and the method. Unlike coercive holding therapies (see chapter 13), however, the Wilbarger Protocol carries no risks of shutdown or other negative side effects.

I recommend that you receive instruction initially from an occupational therapist familiar with the treatment, although it is possible to use it successfully on your own.

The Brushing Technique

The Wilbargers recommend a soft surgical brush that is not scratchy. (A good brush for the purpose is available from the Abilitations catalog or at http://www.abilitations.com, where there are other great SI-based materials as well.) You might also try soft brushes sold in drugstores for cosmetic or cleaning purposes, or even a small washcloth. With this soft brush or similar item, it is possible to exert some degree of pressure without scratching or hurting a child. Because each child responds differently to sensation, however, I recommend finding a brush or a cloth about four inches square, approximately the size of your palm, that when rubbed firmly on the skin feels comfortable to your child. Encourage your child to be part of the process of finding and evaluating a brush or cloth; giving a child a sense of control over the experience is particularly important for a child from a complex background.

Each session of brushing is short, just about five minutes. Introduce the brush to your child and let her touch it and try it on her own skin. Then have her lie down in a comfortable position on her tummy. Brush firmly over her back, arms, hands, and legs with a single strong stroke over each section of skin. Brush the front, back, and sides of each limb *just once* each session.

Brushing is never done on the head and face or on the front of the body, especially the stomach area. Avoid brushing the sides of the body, which tend to be ticklish. Avoid feet and hands if they are too ticklish as well, until the child's body begins to adjust to the brushing experience. Avoid a light touch, which is overly stimulating. Do not brush a child under two months of age.

According to the Wilbarger Protocol, brushing should be done every two hours when a child is awake for approximately five to seven days. After that you can decrease the frequency, but you should continue to brush at regular intervals. Professional guidance is helpful as you decide how often to brush.

It may take a while for your internationally adopted child to become comfortable with the brushing. Start slowly, doing just one arm, perhaps, or one part of the back. Let your child choose the area. It is important that your child feel in control and not forced to endure the experience. Let your child brush you, too, either occasionally or during each session.

Brushing is a good time to talk to your child about how it feels to have her body gently cared for by an adult who listens to and cares about her. Brushing is not just a sensory-integration technique, but also an opportunity to connect with your child on an emotional level.

Tell your child that the purpose is to help her body feel the brush or cloth and then to relax. Explain that you realize this might be hard at first. It may be scary because in the past your child may have experienced rough, inconsiderate, or even hurtful touches. Encourage your child to breathe evenly as you brush. Explain that you are going to do this every two or three hours, to help her body feel more comfortable with all kinds of sensations, including sounds, odors, tastes, and things she touches or sees.

Because this practice demands a great deal of commitment from parents, you might want to start during a vacation when you and your child are together all day for several days.

Effects of Brushing

Your child will begin to look forward to these special times with you. Being the center of your attention feels wonderful. In fact, your child is likely to begin looking forward to being brushed and will remind you or even beg you for the treatment.

Within a week your child should begin to relax more during the brushing and may ask for a longer session. More is fine, but it is important that more at one time does not translate into skipping the next planned time. It is the regularity, not the length, of each session that trains the brain to modulate its response to sensation.

Within two to three weeks you may notice that your child's reactions to sensations are beginning to change in the area of touch, but possibly in other sensory modes as well. You need to be the judge of how long you continue the brushing sessions. If you see changes, keep going. If after a while there is no further change, take a break. You can always return to brushing again in two or three months.

Keeping a journal of your child's behavior, starting before you begin the brushing protocol, is an excellent way to determine if changes are real or imaginary. A journal may be as simple as a date and a brief description of a troubling behavior. But do not forget to include times when your child indeed modulates his behavior when you may have been expecting the opposite.

Demetri's mother, Denise, used the brushing protocol when Demetri was two and a half years old. A portion of her journal appears below.

DEMETRI'S REACTIONS TO FOOD

Date	Behavior
11/20	Spit out cooked carrots, choked on pretzel.
11/21	Refused to eat chunky applesauce.
11/22	Began brushing. Lots of squirming.
11/23	Spit out cooked squash, threw cooked carrots on floor.
11/28	Tried to feed himself applesauce with his hands (big mess).
11/30	Went and got the brush and gave it to me early this morning.
12/4	Took cooked carrot off my plate, sucked on it, and then chewed it up proudly.

You must always be the judge of how your child reacts to new parenting strategies. If you see that any part of the brushing experience makes your child's behavior worse, or causes him to revert to coping behaviors, stop and evaluate the situation. Changing the type of brush or cloth may help. For a hypersensitive child the brush may be too rough initially; for a hyposensitive child a rough brush may work just fine, but you may find that you need to use even more pressure. Experiment, with your child's cooperation; listen to his words and sounds, and watch for other reactions.

Ayres and other SI practitioners believe that the sensory system is linked to the part of the brain that senses danger and responds with protective behavior, including aggression. *If your child responds by hitting, biting, or other aggressive behavior, you have overstimulated her.* Therefore parents are advised to go very slowly and to back off when a child seems threatened. If you have any questions or concerns, stop the brushing and consult with an experienced practitioner to help you.

STRATEGY 2: WORKING WITH GRAVITY

In their early lives adopted children with complex backgrounds often missed out on stimulation of the vestibular system, which constantly measures and adjusts the body's movements in relation to gravity. When a caregiver carries a child around, the child must constantly make bodily adjustments to follow the movement of the adult. Babies learn to balance their heavy heads, adjust their muscles, and coordinate their arms and legs during this daily experience. Part of the sensory deprivation of an orphanage consists of fewer opportunities for these important kinds of vestibular experience and practice.

To help your adopted child develop a well-modulated vestibular system it is important, first, to carry her frequently, even if she is no longer an infant. Do not rely on the baby stroller or baby swing. Find a front pack or backpack for those times when you need to have your hands free. Begin slowly, as you would with a newborn. As with all other kinds of physical activity, keep family age in mind. Part of physical play is the child trusting you, the playmate, as well as her own body.

ACTIVITIES TO INCREASE VESTIBULAR SKILLS

Carry your child frequently
Have "tummy time" each day
Crawl together
Play swinging and rocking "womb games"

Carrying is not the only way to activate and tune your child's vestibular skills. "Tummy time"—simply playing on the floor or ground—is a vital experience for a child and one that many internationally adopted children have missed. This is especially true of children who were old enough to walk when they were adopted. Many birth-country cultures do not encourage a child to crawl or to play on the ground, for reasons of sanitation or safety. The lack of tummy time means that internationally adopted children frequently have had little time to explore the world on their bellies and to make all the vestibular adjustments that this experience triggers.

So put your baby or toddler on her tummy, join her on the floor in a similar position, and play with toys and look at each other. Play rolling-over games, reach for things, and push toys back and forth to each other. Practice crawling together, or make an obstacle course through which to crawl. Crawling develops important visual skills, coordination of both sides of the body, and physical strength.

Rocking and swinging are also important vestibular experiences that nurture modulation. As your child moves through space, even if held by a swing, she must adjust and readjust her balance. Learning to do this smoothly is a form of physical modulation. Like tactile modulation, physical work can influence and regulate other sensory and emotional areas. For example, when a parent rocks a crying baby, the parent is activating the child's vestibular system to modulate her emotional system.

Hold your child on your lap and sing a song while rocking forward and backward. Try side-to-side rocking, and determine whether your child prefers that. If your child prefers not to be held, put her in a rocking chair, kneel beside the chair, and gently rock her. Experiment with the speed and the length of rocks to see what pleases your child, and stick with that pattern for a while. Once your child enjoys being held, get out to the park and swing with your child in your lap. I call all these swinging or rocking experiences "womb games," because they re-create the feeling a child had in the womb. While inside her birth mother, your child learned to move with her. Now is an opportunity for your child to learn to move with you.

STRATEGY 3: REGULATING ACTIVITY LEVEL WITH HEAVY WORK

"Mu Ling is always moving things around, even large pieces of furniture!" Meg once commented when Mu Ling was three years old. "She needs an outlet for her energy. I've considered signing her up for swimming or gymnastics lessons."

"Yi Sheng likes to push things around. He won't get on the tricycle we have, but he pushes it up and down the driveway endlessly," Nina said of her five-year-old son.

Both Mu Ling and Yi Sheng were demonstrating the need most young children have to engage in "heavy work," actions that involve their muscles and joints in an effort to defy gravity. Heavy work is taking place when your child throws all the cushions off the couch, or empties the laundry basket or toy chest. Heavy work is moving all the rocks from one side of the yard to the other or dragging a hose over the lawn. Children find heavy work to do all over the home and yard.

Heavy work helps a child modulate the vestibular, tactile, visual, and proprioceptive systems. It releases endorphins, the same "feel-good" chemicals that adults release when exercising. After exercising, a child feels relaxed and can focus quietly—at least for a while. In short, heavy work helps to regulate a child's activity level. Recognizing the importance of heavy work for development motivates parents to choose appropriate activities for their child.

Finding Appropriate Heavy Work

Many parents think of signing up a young child for a physical activity such as gymnastics or swimming because he is so active, but an internationally adopted child with a young family age may not be ready for such a challenge. These classes usually require a child to separate from a parent and to work with a teacher who is a stranger. They also presume that a child has the emotional and physical self-control necessary to follow directions and be in a group. In addition, classes do not address SI issues, and those very issues may interfere with the child's participation and learning. Think carefully about the developmental and emotional needs of your adopted child before filling the week with activities and classes. Instead, consider ways to incorporate heavy work into your child's life at home, so that he can learn to regulate his energy level in a familiar environment.

Here is one example that would be easy to re-create at home. In the playroom connected to my office I have a wagon stacked with about fifteen heavy beanbags, each about eight inches square. These beanbags provide lots of opportunities for heavy work. Children load and unload them from the wagon. They take beanbag baths, as described earlier in this chapter. They put the beanbags on their heads and then bend forward to make them fall to the floor with a resounding *plop!*

One day when he was two years old, Demetri crawled over to the wagon and tugged at the beanbags. Some bags were filled with rice and others with beans, to provide different textures. Demetri pulled a blue bag into his lap, then pushed hard in order to get it off his lap. Three-and-a-half-year-old Mu Ling and five-and-a-half-year-old Yi Sheng joined him. Together the three children unloaded the bags and then reloaded the wagon. Next, Yi Sheng dragged the loaded wagon around the room. It was heavy work, and the flow of endorphins soothed and calmed the children.

It was fascinating to watch how heavy work changed each child's play. Beforehand Demetri had been roaming around the room without pausing long enough to engage with any one toy. After the wagon and beanbag work, he sat down with a truck and began rolling it over one of the big beanbags, playing in an extended and more focused way. In SI terms, his praxis matured and improved. He showed that he knew where to begin with the truck, and he invented new ways to move it around; he even brought over some blocks and constructed a small road. His play became far more elaborate than it had been before he did his heavy work.

Mu Ling made similar changes in her play. She had previously been empty-ing one box of toys after another and leaving them strewn around in a disorga-nized fashion. Meg trailed behind her daughter, trying to straighten up her mess. After the beanbag workout, Mu Ling opened a box of baby toys and took every-thing out of it. But then she arranged the items in a neat pile and began taking them, one at a time, to Meg. She began to show delight at Meg's smile each time she brought over another toy. The heavy work had organized Mu Ling's behavior so that she was able to engage in genuine social and emotional connections.

Within five minutes, however, Mu Ling's newfound organization began to dissolve. "Now what do I do?" Meg asked me as her daughter began to throw the toys over her shoulder instead of handing them to Meg.

The organizational impact of heavy work lasts only so long. Parents should be prepared to move in and help their child resume heavy work when its effects wear off. Over time you will find that you do not need to return so rapidly and often to heavy work as your child develops more skills in this area.

I encouraged Meg to help Mu Ling return to the wagon and unload the bean-bags again. Heavy work makes throwing difficult—those bags are just too weighty to fling about. This time I suggested that Meg stay with Mu Ling, since no other child was doing heavy work. Before long Mu Ling began building a path with the beanbags. It took her less time than in the previous round to get the organiz-ing benefits of the work. Her mother's presence helped her focus as well.

Like the brushing protocol, heavy work requires consistent attention from a parent. Heavy work also requires parents to be proactive in helping their child return to the activity when his behavior begins to fragment into unfocused play.

STRATEGY 4: BUILDING A CHILD'S SELF-AWARENESS OF ACTIVITY LEVEL

"When will Mu Ling know that she needs to do a bit of heavy work?" Meg asked. "Do I have to be watching her all the time?"

Helping a child learn to manage her own activity level is an important aspect of parenting. Children with SI issues are often largely or entirely unaware of what they are doing. In such cases the children must be taught to be aware of their own behavior and to determine when that behavior needs moderation.

In the First Year Home Group I have introduced a simple system that has worked well for teaching self-awareness to children as young as one year of age, as well as older children through school age. You will find the system easy to make and use yourselves at home. This is how it works: I cut a sturdy paper plate in half. I divide the half plate into four sections and color in each of the sections. From left to right the colors are purple, blue, green, and red. This is how I introduce the colors to the children:

- "Purple is when you are hiding inside yourself."
- "Blue is when you are feeling tired or sleepy, like when you first wake up."
- "Green is when you are alert and ready to learn something new."
- "Red is when you are moving a lot or are very busy."

I explain to the children and parents that this is an *activity level plate*. It is not, I tell them, meant to show whether an activity is good or bad, appropriate or inappropriate. I demonstrate examples of the behaviors that go with each color. This play-acting catches the children's attention and makes the plate meaningful to them.

If a child is familiar with the *Winnie the Pooh* characters, it is helpful to associate the colors and behaviors with Pooh characters. Bouncy Tigger is decidedly in the Red Zone. Eeyore is in the Blue Zone, with his sad, sleepy quality. Roo or Piglet, who are withdrawn or shy, can be used for the Purple Zone. Winnie the Pooh himself represents the Green Zone, because he is always thinking about things, asking questions, or listening intently to Christopher Robin, Owl, or Kanga.

I give the parents in the Group supplies to make their own plates. Often the children decide to help. This is great, because it helps them feel part of the process and in control later, when the plate is used. At home you can make one plate yourself to introduce the ideas, and then make a second plate with your child. There can never be too many activity level plates! Keep one in each room, if you like.

When Yi Sheng, at nearly five, comes over to work with Nina, his mother, I ask him what color he is. He looks at me blankly. I realize there are different ways to interpret my question, so I again explain the way the plate colors show how we are acting and feeling. Yi Sheng thinks about my question again and points to the blue. I tell him that he acts more green to me, because he does not look sleepy. But Yi Sheng points to blue again. He may not yet be able to identify how he feels; learning to be self-aware of feelings and behaviors takes time. Or perhaps he is sleepy or withdrawn and I am unaware of that. The conversation, the words, and the concepts, are more important than precision at this point. You are likely to find that you have to work with your child each day for at least a week just to develop an understanding of the categories. Look on these discussions as fun, not work.

When the children return to the Group the following week, Yi Sheng finds the plate from the week before. He sees Demetri begin to crawl rapidly around the room, points to the red section, and smiles at his mom. Then he points to himself and then to the blue section. "Get up," he says.

"That's right, you were sleepy this morning when you got up," Nina confirms. For a preschool-age child such as Yi Sheng, the activity plate is easy and fun. It quickly becomes part of the parent-child communication system, giving the child an additional way to talk about what is going on. Children younger than four years old need more time, perhaps several weeks or even a month, to learn to associate the colors on the plate with their own behavior and with the relevant descriptive words.

Once a child begins to be aware of his own activity level, parents can find activities that help him become more organized and modulated. Of course that requires a parent to know what sorts of things will result in their particular child becoming more alert or less energized. It is like understanding what food provides good nutrition. The Wilbargers have proposed a concept they call a *sensory diet*, which helps parents get a handle on what works for their child.

STRATEGY 5: A SENSORY DIET

You probably have your own set of sensory "supports" that keep you alert or help you to manage excess energy. Some people love to suck a cold drink through a straw, whereas others prefer to jingle the coins in their pocket or swing one leg. We all use sensory-motor tricks to help ourselves. Conscious awareness of what those tricks are can help us stay alert for longer periods of time, or calm us when we are overstimulated or overactive. Internationally adopted children benefit enormously from having a sensory diet that helps them manage their tendency either to rev up or to shut down. Expanding the metaphor, we can say that this group of children tends to be "allergic" (to react with stress) to certain things, such as overstimulation, new experiences, and unfamiliar limits. A sensory diet provides your child with experiences that moderate the "allergic" reactions to common situations such as the first day of school, two birthday parties on the same day, or the introduction of a new family rule. A sensory diet can also help children who have difficulty paying attention and staying focused.

For example, Soon An does well with soft sounds, quiet music, dim lights, and gentle movements. Mu Ling needs higher levels of stimulation and lots of heavy work to help her focus in a quiet, alert way. Her family keeps a set of large, heavy beanbags in the house and has a pile of rocks in the yard for her heavy work. Mu Ling also likes drinking something cold or chewing on frozen bananas to calm herself down.

You may enjoy, and find it useful, to have everyone in the family discover his or her own sensory diet. The questions below will help you get started, either just for your child or for everyone in the family.

A SENSORY DIET: WHAT DO YOU PREFER?

Temperature:	A warm bath or a cold drink of water?
Brightness:	A bright room or a dimly lit one? Natural or fluorescent light?
Texture:	A rough rug or a smooth floor? A cozy blanket; soft, loose clothing; or jeans?
Taste:	Sweet, salty, or sour?
Texture of food:	Smooth, crunchy, chewy, Jello-y?
Beverage:	Warm and sweet (like cocoa), cold and sour (like lemonade), or cold and sweet (like soy milk)?
Physical activity:	Slow swinging or fast swinging? Jumping, sliding, or spinning?

Add things to your routine that help your child calm. Remove activities or sensory experiences that make her shut down or rev up. Incorporate calming activities regularly throughout the day, especially before anything stressful is to occur. For trips out of the house take a package of sensory-stimulating or sensory-soothing items with you. As you and your child talk about the way each activity or item provides sensory support, you will find your child wanting to have those items handy. You might even keep a set of such items in the car.

SHOULD I SEEK ASSESSMENT FOR MY CHILD?

If you have adopted recently and you believe your child is struggling with sensory-motor integration or stimulus management, give him four to six months to settle down before seeking help. Meanwhile, try the strategies in this chapter. If you see little or no improvement, seek help. Seek help sooner if your child's behavior interferes with your relationship with him, or with his ability to play and explore the world or progress developmentally.

To help you understand your child and to help you communicate with a therapist or other professional, the Wilbargers' categorization of three levels of SI dysfunction, described in their booklet "Sensory Defensiveness in Children Aged 2–12," can be a useful tool.

Level 1 is a mild condition. The child appears picky, oversensitive, slightly overreactive, resistant to change, or slightly controlling. He is able to engage in age-appropriate activities, but it requires a lot of effort for him to do so, and he may fall apart emotionally after the activity is done.

At level 2, moderate dysfunction, a child struggles in two or more aspects of his life. Self-care skills are affected along with attention and behavior at day-care, preschool, or school. The child limits exploration or play because those are difficult.

Level 3 is severe dysfunction and at this level the difficulties impact every aspect of a child's life. The child strongly avoids new sensations or, conversely, runs toward new experiences headlong. A child's development and socialization are severely compromised.

If your child is at level 2 or 3, seek help as soon as you can to prevent your relationship from suffering. In addition, get help right away if your child has difficulty with eating or being fed. What health professionals call "failure to thrive" is a dangerous condition. Finally, if you have been home from an adoption for six months or more and the SI-related problem behaviors are getting progressively worse, seek help as soon as you can.

THE SI THERAPY PROCESS

If you decide to consult a sensory-integration specialist, the therapist will want to meet with you and your child for an assessment. You have a right to ask questions about what the therapist is doing and how the evaluation and treatment processes work. Find out in advance if you will receive a videotape of the session and a written or oral report from the therapist. Assessment is often a tiring experience for children, so plan a quiet afternoon at home afterward.

Based on the assessment the therapist may suggest activities to do at home or a series of sessions one-on-one with your child. I recommend that you go along. This is especially important if one therapist does the evaluation and another therapist does the treatment; you want to be sure the therapy provides what the assessment prescribed. Although the activities, whether done at your home or in the therapist's office, are designed to be playful and fun, they are also therapeutic. They will feel challenging to your child. A therapist should be skilled in involving your child on a level that is comfortable for her before presenting more challenging tasks. Sessions should not make the child's behavior worse. Tell your therapist if this is the case, even after a single session.

During both the assessment and the one-on-one sessions, note the way the therapist helps your child reorganize and calm down after a challenge. A successful session with a competent SI therapist should end with the child being calm and alert, more controlled and more organized than before the session began. If this happens to your child, she is making progress in sensory-motor integration and modulation. If you are not satisfied, do not continue to expose your child to an overly challenging, disintegrating experience. Find another therapist.

Baseline Evaluations Are Valuable

If you think your child has SI issues but the level of dysfunction seems minimal, it is worthwhile to have him evaluated by an SI specialist anyway. This is the same idea as a medical checkup. Sometimes a mild SI dysfunction leads to more complicated problems later, during the school years, and a missed diagnosis may eventually lead to a *mis*diagnosis. Suppose your four-year-old child has mild sensory-modulation difficulties; these might well develop into difficulty with writing, drawing, and reading. Two years later the first-grade teacher notes on the report card that your child has an "attention problem" and is overly social; in second grade the reading specialist might do an assessment and send a note home stating that your child is "hyperactive"; the principal speaks to you by phone after observing and concludes that your child needs medication or perhaps needs to repeat first grade. It can take a parent years to untangle the original SI issue from the cascade of behaviors and problems it may cause later.

An SI evaluation at four years of age or younger would pinpoint the mild modulation difficulty and give your child time to work on it before heading for school. Even if the difficulty disappears after intervention, it could reappear when new levels of skill are required and your child experiences more stress.

Having an early diagnosis gives you and your child a better chance of getting effective help.

Consulting a qualified therapist is not an admission that you are failing as a parent or that your child is severely damaged or dysfunctional. Many adopted children with complex backgrounds simply need a little help with managing stimulation and acquiring sensory-motor integration skills. SI work is a valuable way to improve your relationship with your child while supporting his developing abilities to self-regulate.

"Ping-Pong" Interactions for Connection and Reconnection

EVERY CHILD, ADOPTED OR NOT, must find a happy medium between revving up and shutting down. I call this middle ground a *calm-alert state*. It is more than just relaxation or an easygoing state of mind. It is a state in which a child is relaxed but also alert, able to focus attention and to learn from others or the environment.

Finding this calm middle ground is a major challenge for a child who has a stress-shaped brain (see chapter 2). Such a child is highly reactive, emotionally and physically. This means she must calm herself far more frequently than the child next door. The child next door gets up in the morning, gets dressed calmly, and becomes only mildly stressed when saying goodbye as she goes off to daycare or school. The same sequence of events for the child with a stress-shaped brain triggers fight-or-flight responses. The child experiences each new moment in the sequence as a major stressor, not a small and manageable hurdle. This is why the parents of internationally adopted children are often exhausted by nine in the morning, having already lived through several major stress points with their child.

Calmness is a learned skill, which a child acquires through interactions with a soothing, calm parent.

A child learns to find the happy medium of calmness through interactions with a soothing, calm parent. *Calmness is a learned skill.* It begins with the soothing interactions around feeding in infancy. During this feeding process a variety of physical interactions between parent and child causes the child to calm.

We have seen how sucking stimulates the vagus nerve to calm heart rate and breathing, and how, when a parent holds a child on the parent's left side, the connection between the baby's and the parent's left eyes stimulates the soothing capacity of the right side of the baby's brain. We know that the pressure of the parent's arm against the back of the baby's neck and head is especially soothing.

Other movements can induce calm in young children. These include rocking, swinging, being carried, and being swaddled (wrapped firmly in a blanket). These physical interactions between parent and child increase connection and calmness simultaneously.

THE PING-PONG PATTERN OF INTERACTION

When a parent and child interact and connect, energy flows back and forth between them. This pattern is evident in a wide range of behaviors: soothing activities such as rocking; passing a toy or throwing a ball back and forth; and in different modes of communication, such as eye contact and face-to-face interaction, the imitation of sounds, and conversation. I call this pattern *Ping-Pong interaction*, because it resembles the swift exchanges of a Ping-Pong game. The Ping-Pong interaction pattern enables a child to become, and remain, calm and alert. In this chapter we explore a variety of Ping-Pong interactions in which you can engage with your child.

THE YES/NO GAME

One of the first ways an adopted child who has recently become connected with his parents begins to differentiate himself from them is by saying no. This *no* is not merely oppositional, but the earliest way a child asserts his own identity and signals his desire to make independent choices. For example, Yi Sheng was five years old, with six months of family age, when he began to define himself in this way. When offered cereal for breakfast, he would say, "No. I want noodles." When something like this happens, it is all too easy for parents to embark on a series of power struggles with their child, which lead to disconnection between parent and child and elicit fight-or-flight behaviors in the child. When I work with parents who are looking for a way to break out of this vicious cycle, I suggest that they teach their child to play what I call the Yes/No Game. It teaches children to be both connected and independent at the same time.

At a First Year Home Group session during the period in which Yi Sheng was practicing his use of the word *no*, I invited Yi Sheng's father to play a game of Yes/No with me.

"Yes!" I said.

"No," Kenji rejoined.

"Yes." "No." "Yes." "No." Back and forth we went, faster than Ping-Pong balls at a tournament. Yi Sheng came over and watched us. I stepped back to let Yi Sheng and his father play the game.

"Yes!" Kenji said.

"No!" his son replied.

"Y-e-e-e-s-s-s," Kenji returned, coaxing Yi Sheng with his tone of voice and the drawn-out pronunciation of the word.

"N-o-o-o-o-o!" Yi Sheng replied.

Kenji continued the game, mirroring Yi Sheng's tone. After several exchanges, Yi Sheng played a trick on his father and repeated Kenji's "Yes." In response Kenji switched to saying "No." From then on, as father and son continued to play the game, they occasionally tricked each other into switching roles.

This is a very satisfying and engaging game for children who are typically oppositional, as many adopted children are at some point in their development. It gives them an opportunity to play at being oppositional, but without the negative consequences. The game keeps them connected, rather than disconnected, and nurtures in-sync play and playfulness itself. The mirroring of tones that often takes place encourages each person to be in tune with the other.

Playing the game in the manner that Kenji and Yi Sheng eventually did, switching from "Yes" to "No" and "No" to "Yes," requires more sophistication in the parent-child relationship, and usually children do not want to make this switch until six months to a year after adoption.

MORE PING-PONG GAMES

Ping-Pong games demand that the child focus attention on an activity; they also require the child and the parent to have an object or activity of shared attention.

There are other Ping-Pong games you can play with your child. One day Soon An, at nine months old, was waving her bottle around in the air. Then she handed it to her mother. For several moments Charlotte just held the bottle, surprised at her daughter's gift. It occurred to me that this was a Ping-Pong opportunity, so I encouraged Charlotte to hand the bottle back. Within a few minutes Soon An and her mother were playing a Ping-Pong game with the bottle. This simple back-and-forth passing game with a baby is the foundation for future conversations and more complex interactions.

There are all kinds of Ping-Pong games, each modeling a "conversation" between parent and child yet not always involving talk. They include rolling a ball or batting a balloon back and forth, handing each other toys, taking turns taking toys off a shelf, and stacking blocks alternately in a tower. As children grow older, these Ping-Pong games continue to be a way of being close, without, again, having to talk. Handball; catch with a rubber ball, tennis ball, baseball, or softball; and playing Frisbee, not to mention the game of Ping-Pong itself, are great for older school-age children, as are tennis, paddleball, racquetball, and other two-person games that teenagers can enjoy with a parent. No matter how sophisticated these games may be in their rules or in the skills they require, the elemental, back-and-forth, Ping-Pong quality they have provides a deep sense of connection between parent and child. Simple card games like Go Fish or Uno provide the same feeling of alternating interaction, although with more talk built into them.

Older children love returning even to simple Ping-Pong games, in large part, I believe, because they reinforce the parent-child connection. As we have seen, of all the fears that haunt a child with a complex background, the biggest is: Will you leave me, too? Ping-Pong games tell a child, "I'm here, I'm here, I'm here," repeatedly and predictably. That is intensely reassuring.

CHECKING IN

The family skill of checking in may be seen as another sort of Ping-Pong interaction, one that extends a little more slowly over time and ranges a little more widely through space. We have seen that checking in strengthens connection with a parent within the Magic Circle, helps to release Parent Juice, and develops a child's resiliency in the face of stress.

Like most children from an orphanage background, Demetri, at two, needed specific lessons in how to "check in." Although many children check in on their own, internationally adopted children are less likely to do so because they have trouble recognizing their own needs. When a child begins feeling low on Parent Juice, she may switch to coping behaviors instead of checking in. This is why it is important to teach your child explicitly to monitor her own activity level. "When you begin to slow down and run out of gas," you might say to your child, "and when you wonder where I am, then it's time to find me and check in."

Denise modeled check-in behavior for her son. At first she sat quietly near Demetri, and then she leaned over and patted him, saying, "I'm just checking in with you. Do you need some Mommy Juice?" Later she sat across the room from him, quietly reading the paper, and then stood up and walked over to Demetri. Gradually, Demetri began to look up every five to ten minutes, expecting his mother's attention. Denise encouraged him: "Why don't you check in with me and give me a 'high five' or 'thumbs up' when you are done with that toy?" In this way Denise let her son know that checking in is a two-way street, a Ping-Pong interaction. Alternating check-ins is a way of taking turns at reconnecting.

CHECKING IN FOR OLDER CHILDREN

Checking in is a way to reassert the Magic Circle after a period during which a child of any age has lost the sense of the circle's presence. Even older children need to check in. When Mu Ling was seven she would rush home from school, eager to play outside. Within minutes of dropping her backpack in the front hall and heading for the backyard, Meg or Laura would hear her crying. She had fallen off her bike, lost a ball over the fence, or somehow or other gotten in a jam that triggered an emotional meltdown. Clearly the Magic Circle had failed to hold Mu Ling; it had been stretched too far during an entire day at school. Mu Ling needed to fill up on Parent Juice before she went out to play on her own or with friends.

As children play, they run out of emotional energy long before they run out of physical energy. Checking in with a parent provides emotional refueling during gaps in play. A child can play longer, learn more, and develop the ability to tolerate frustration by checking in with a parent and redrawing the Magic Circle on a regular basis.

To help Mu Ling avoid the daily meltdowns, Meg decided to make a ritual of playing ball with her daughter for at least ten minutes when she came home from school. Tossing a ball combined an energetic activity with a connection to Mom, a connection that was repeated over and over again, Ping-Pong style, each time Mu Ling caught or threw the ball. At first Meg had to teach Mu Ling to follow the path of the ball with her eyes and to make eye contact with Meg; over time Meg observed that Mu Ling got better and better at doing these things.

Checking in should involve eye and voice contact, which are especially critical as a child grows older. Ping-Pong games are particularly valuable in this regard, because they create a context in which face-to-face interaction has to occur, even with children who up to that point tended to avoid such contact. At ten years of age Sonia once arrived home from school, dragging her backpack, and said, "I failed the math test, Mom." Carolyn looked across the kitchen at her daughter, then got up, gave her a hug, and looked deep into her daughter's brown eyes. "How about a game of catch to get your mind off that test?" she asked. For internationally adopted children the reconnection in the Magic Circle often takes more than a hug or a friendly look from across the room. Ping-Pong interactions, which are more long-lasting and intense exchanges, are vital to stepping up the flow of Parent Juice, to re-creating for your child the strength of your encompassing embrace and care. The best follow-up to a separation is to play a little Ping-Pong.

Making Rules and Limits Work

"How do we get Yi Sheng to follow the family rules?"
"How old does a child need to be to understand rules?"
"Should we be giving Mu Ling time-outs for bad behavior?"

LIFE IS FILLED WITH RULES, and every child must learn to live with them. Approximately half of all parents who adopt internationally bring home children who are excessively mobile; for safety reasons, these children need to be taught rules immediately. Most parents, adoptive or not, set rules to provide for a child's safety or health needs—"Don't touch the electric outlet" or "Hold my hand when we cross the street," for example. As a child matures, rules reinforce social skills as well: "We sit at the table when we eat." The first part of this chapter discusses strategies for teaching rules and setting limits that parents will find useful from Adoption Day forward. The remainder of the chapter looks at how to handle children who respond to limits and rules with anger and aggression.

INTRODUCING THE RULES ON DAY ONE

Setting rules may not seem like your highest priority on the day you adopt a new child. But a child from another country is like a child from another planet: She has no clue what the rules are on Earth, as it were—in your family and household. The majority of internationally adopted children need to be taught limits on behavior immediately upon joining their new families. Adopting parents often assume their child knows basic rules of behavior based on the child's chronological age, but that may very well not be the case. So Rule One for parents on Day One is: Explain and demonstrate the rules of behavior in your family. Far from being harsh, this approach in fact builds trust and connection between you and your child.

When you assume your child knows the rules, and you then mete out consequences when she fails to follow them, she feels betrayed and caught in an impossible situation. If this has happened in your family, simply sit down with your child and announce that everyone is starting over with rules and limits. Educate your child about rules, assuming she has never encountered them before. You have no idea what your child really understands until you begin this kind of education.

In addition, I have learned over the years that foster parents or orphanage caregivers in a child's birth country may well have told a child about a future full of toys, trips to Disneyland or Disney World, and other delicious fantasies. The child is often shocked and angry to find that family life has more rules than an orphanage.

Children have no particular reason to follow rules or respect limits if they have no real relationship, other than a bare-bones legal one, with their new parents. Therefore, parents need to recognize the importance of incentives and rewards. These are ways to encourage a child's interest in following the rules, even if the parents' opinion is initially of no interest to the child. By using incentives that clearly come from you, the parent, you will teach your child to associate both the incentive and her relationship to you with following the rules. Start with several simple rules, such as "Ask me for food or help" or "We don't hit each other."

"TIME-IN," NOT TIME-OUT

Putting an internationally adopted child on *time-out* may appear to work, but in fact it undermines connection and trust through forced separation. To a child who is sensitive to abandonment or who shuts down or revs up when alone, time-outs fail to provide thought about rules, or about anything else that is particularly constructive. In contrast, *time-ins* provide a child with supervised time as a consequence for being "too young," either chronologically or behaviorally or both, to follow the rules.

A time-in is a chance for a child to think about the rule without losing a parent's attention. Develop a comfortable time-in spot for you and your child. You need to be, or to make yourself be, at ease. Do not make a time-in overly long. Instead, use it to give your child a moment to recuperate emotionally and be ready to make a good choice the next time. Some children may accept a lap and a cuddle as part of this recuperation period, whereas others do better if you sit quietly nearby. Because Yi Sheng at four and a half years old was "lap shy," his mother, Nina, found a red scarf that she and her son could each hold to feel connected during a time-in. Meg found that offering Mu Ling a juice box helped her three-year-old daughter settle and calm enough to consider her own behavior.

Your goal is to help your child calm and then make a good choice about his future behavior in regard to the broken rule. This may happen immediately after a time-in. For example, Mu Ling "earned" a time-in when she repeatedly hit the cat. After she sucked on a box of juice during her time-in, her mother said, "Next time you can make a good choice and not hit the cat." Mu Ling got up, walked to the cat, and then put her hands behind her own back, indicating that she was making the good choice not to hit. This good behavior immediately earned Mu Ling praise from her mother.

GOOD-CHOICE WORK

Here is an example, from a family in our First Year Home Group, of what to say and do when guiding your child to make a good choice. Yi Sheng at five years of age began eating off his parents' plates at meals. Nina responded by teaching her son, not punishing him. "Yi Sheng," she said, "in our family we eat off only our own plates. Maybe in the orphanage it was all right to take other people's food. It's not all right in our family." It took several mealtimes filled with *repeated and consistent explanation* and with *assisted compliance*, which means physically helping a child follow a rule, for Yi Sheng to get the idea. Nina made a game out of feeding Yi Sheng from her plate, but she would not allow him to grab food directly from her plate.

Internationally adopted children often have a strong need to be in control. They often see rules as control by others.

Because internationally adopted children have a strong need to be in control, they often see limits or rules as an undesirable form of control by others. This view can trigger aggressive coping behavior or survival skills. Parents can reduce this "fight response" by emphasizing the *child's choice* in each situation. When Yi Sheng insisted on eating off his mother's plate, she gave him the choice of eating next to her or across the table. When he said nothing, Nina continued, "When you are silent and refuse to make a choice, you are telling me to make the choice for you." Yi Sheng quickly decided to sit across the table, in order to remain in control. Such a focus on the child's power to choose is an excellent way to help her make good choices. When a child feels that she is involved in making the choice, she is less likely to perceive imposed consequences as a personal assault by the parent, and therefore less likely to engage the parent aggressively in a battle over control.

POOR CHOICES, ASSISTED COMPLIANCE, AND CONSEQUENCES

"What happens if Yi Sheng makes a poor choice, such as continuing to sit beside me and grab my food?" Nina asked me. In this case, I told her, she could say, "You made a choice to sit beside me, but you followed that with a poor choice to grab my food. The consequence for making a poor choice is that you must eat at the end of the table, away from Mom. I will help you move there." Nina made the decision to use separation as a consequence because she knew that Yi Sheng wanted to be near her. She believed the prospect of separation would motivate her son to make a better choice and regain his place beside her. Moving the child firmly but gently is another example of assisted compliance: "Next time we have a meal [or in two minutes' time], you will have a chance to make a new choice." Setting a brief time limit, and using a kitchen timer to signal its end, further depersonalizes the consequence. A brief limit also helps a child learn quickly from experience and offers him the opportunity to demonstrate a good choice of behavior, for which a parent can reward him by being close again.

Using an incentive or reward is better than using a consequence. One type of incentive is food. Food is the initial connection between infant and parent; using it as a reward is a way to establish a relationship immediately with your adopted child. When Yi Sheng did not want to come to the table for a meal, his parents offered him his favorite food, noodles, for complying with this family expectation. The noodles were available for the first five minutes after Yi Sheng was called; then they were removed. Yi Sheng quickly learned to join the family for meals. Nina made a friendly game of feeding Yi Sheng the beloved noodles as a way to form a relationship around this good choice her son made.

A more vigorous approach is to set up a system whereby a child "earns" the privilege of participating in pleasant family activities by following the rules of the house. This works only with a child of five years old or more; younger children cannot grasp the "earning" concept. A child might, for example, earn the right to use crayons or toys, or to watch television, if he controls his aggressive language or persistent yelling. A specified time of controlled behavior can earn a child an equal amount of time for the privileged activity. Practicing appropriate behavior also helps a child learn to control inappropriate behaviors. For example, a child who jumps on the furniture may need to practice sitting on the couch several times a day under parental supervision and may be rewarded with a privilege for having done so.

This parenting strategy is described more fully in the chapter "Day-to-Day Parenting" in *Facilitating Developmental Attachment*, a book by Daniel Hughes. He describes privileges as including "unsupervised time [or] unsupervised contact with animals or younger children, use of toys, TV, tools, [or] crayons, and participation in social or sports activities."

A third approach to helping children work with limits is *allowing natural consequences to take effect*. Mu Ling refused to put on her coat on a cold, blustery day. Her parents used the natural consequence of becoming cold to encourage her to ask for her coat. But sometimes natural consequences backfire, especially with internationally adopted children who are accustomed to antagonistic conditions, both physically and interpersonally. In Mu Ling's case, she simply did not feel the cold, because of her survival and coping skills. This third approach is less reliable than the first two.

Incentives and rewards work only when a child recognizes the connection between the choice and the reward. This means that you must narrate the connection and observe carefully to see if your child understands. If your child fails to change his behavior, do not assume that your child is stubborn; instead, teach him anew to make the connection clearer, or pick a more direct incentive.

HELPING YOUR CHILD WITH RULES AND LIMITS

1. Make consistent, repeated explanations of rules.
2. Use assisted compliance.
3. Give your child a choice.
4. Use incentives to encourage good choices, and give rewards for making them.

THE ANGRY AND CONTROLLING CHILD

You may find, as you begin setting limits and educating your child about them, that your child consistently reacts with anger and sees the limits as a threat to her need to be in control. I have found in working with adoptive families that difficulty with accepting rules is often the first clear indication that a child has moderate to severe behavioral difficulties.

A child with severe difficulties after adoption has problems in all of the following areas: interpersonal relationships, cognitive functioning, impulse control, and regulation of aggression. In *Facilitating Developmental Attachment*, Daniel Hughes, who has worked for years with the most challenging adopted and foster care children, offers fifteen specific examples of when and where these problems emerge, which I have paraphrased below:

1. Compulsive need to control others
2. Intense lying, even when "caught in the act"
3. Poor (aggressive or oppositional-defiant) response to discipline
4. Lack of comfort with eye contact, except when lying
5. Desire for either too much or too little physical contact
6. Lack of mutual enjoyment and spontaneity in interactions
7. Disturbances in bodily functions: eating, sleeping, urinating, and defecating
8. Discomfort with and resistance to increased attachment
9. Indiscriminately friendly, charming behavior; relationships easily replaced
10. Poor communication; many nonsense questions and much chatter
11. Difficulty learning cause and effect; poor planning or problem solving
12. Lack of empathy; little evidence of guilt and remorse
13. Ability to see only the extremes: all good or all bad
14. Habitual dissociation (extreme inattentiveness to what is happening in the present) or habitual hypervigilance (extreme attentiveness)
15. Pervasive shame, with extreme difficulty reestablishing a bond following conflict

Note the use of descriptive words such as *compulsive, pervasive, habitual,* and *intense.* The behaviors are taken to an extreme and they happen consistently. Severe problems are extreme and unremitting on a minute-to-minute basis.

A child with only mild to moderate difficulties, which many internationally adopted children have, may show signs of these same behaviors *occasionally*, from several times a day to a few times a week. Such a child exhibits a mixture of appropriate and problematic behaviors during a single day. A child with severe problems exhibits problem behaviors consistently, going long periods without appropriate interactions with parents or others.

How you feel when you are with your child is another way to evaluate her level of difficulty. If you feel, even occasionally each day, a genuine sense of connection with your child, and you sense that she has the same feelings, the child most likely has only mild to moderate difficulties. If your child's behavior makes you feel helpless or angry *consistently*, however, she probably has severe issues that need to be addressed.

Chapter 2 described research on foster children that reveals three ways in which such children can make parents feel helpless or angry: behaving in ways that "fail to elicit nurturance"; engaging in oppositional, defiant, and even destructive behavior; and behaving with extreme and consistent anger. When a child is most needy, these negative behaviors are most in evidence, because the child has an overreactive and aggressive fight-or-flight response to stress. A parent faced with such a child normally feels angry and helpless. The child has "induced" these feelings, which reflect how the child herself feels about life and the family, in the parent. The parents' induced anger becomes, in turn, a further positive reinforcer of the child's behavior, and therefore the child feels "good"—in control, that is— when the parent is angry or even out of control. The twisted nature of this type of relationship can make parents feel they are losing their minds.

First take control of your own feelings. Once you know and can predict that your child will try to incite you to anger with her behavior, you can choose to react differently. Your failure to become angry is the most powerful change agent you have with such a child. Your sense of humor and your awareness that you are parenting therapeutically are your next most powerful tools. Therapeutic parenting requires you to take a step back and stop trying to nurture and love your child in the ways you may have learned in your own family. Therapeutic parenting is done from a slightly impersonal distance. Not surprisingly, a child who has severe behavior problems prefers this distance, for closeness to an adult feels threatening or even dangerous.

THREE WAYS TO BEGIN DEALING WITH SEVERE BEHAVIORS

There are three techniques for dealing with severe behaviors that the adoptive parents with whom I work have found highly effective. First, they *substitute neutral phrases for words of praise.* Second, they provide structured opportunities for their children to *practice being angry, and then practice stopping their anger.* Third, they create sessions in which their children *practice how to have fun with a parent.*

Using Neutral Phrases

Mu Ling went through an extremely angry period at six years of age. She literally cursed at her parents when called to sit down for meals. When Mu Ling did seat herself and her parents praised her, she reacted by spitting on her plate. Quite reasonably, this made her parents feel that it was impossible to reward her good behavior and extinguish the bad.

I encouraged Mu Ling's parents to pick a neutral phrase, such as "Happy birthday," "Have a nice day," "The sky is blue," or "Early bird," to use in place of any praise they might offer Mu Ling. This technique interrupts the child's automatic negative response. The next time Mu Ling sat down at the table at mealtime, Meg responded with "Happy birthday" rather than "Good job." Mu Ling's surprise and puzzlement at Meg's neutral tone and the random nature of the comment disrupted her typical spitting response. She was confused that she could not get her mother to be angry and by the nonsensical nature of the words, although she understood that they must be in response to her good behavior. The neutrality and irrelevance of such a comment create distance between child and parent, allowing the child to become accustomed to praise in small steps.

Practicing Anger, Then Practicing Fun

Mu Ling's parents wanted her to stop cursing as an expression of anger. Being angry has three parts, I suggested to Mu Ling and her parents when they came to my office for a private session. First is becoming angry, second is being angry, and third is stopping angry behavior. Mu Ling, I continued, was good at the first two but needed practice with the third.

This sent Mu Ling into a cursing fit, as if to demonstrate precisely what I had said. I told Meg and Laura that what we were doing together in the office they could do at home as well. While Mu Ling continued her verbal abuse, I demonstrated neutrality and a bit of humor by commenting that Mu Ling had a loud voice for her age and quite an extensive vocabulary. I went on to say again, however, that I doubted Mu Ling was good at stopping her anger. In fact, I said, I was going to test that by setting a kitchen timer for three minutes. When it "dinged" I would see if Mu Ling could become quiet and composed.

Having your child practice being angry and stopping his angry behavior may seem counterintuitive when you consider that your child already seems to be quite proficient at being angry. But the method in fact works, because it teaches a child that his anger is something he can control. Another element of the technique's success may simply be reverse psychology: A few children immediately stop their angry behavior just to contradict a parent's demand. Telling a child to practice stopping angry behavior is another way of saying, "I don't think you can do this." Most children older than eighteen months immediately want to take the challenge and prove a parent wrong: "I can so stop being angry if I want to!"

I provided Mu Ling with several heavy but throwable beanbags and a cardboard box for a target, as a physical but nonabusive way for her to release her rage. I told her that she could throw the beanbags until the timer rang.

When Mu Ling stopped cursing but threw a beanbag at Meg, I told her that if she did not throw the beanbag at or into the cardboard box I would have to help her throw. Rather than accept help, Mu Ling chose to aim at the box. My choice of assisted compliance—helping her throw—as a consequence was based on the knowledge that severely troubled children consistently reject help from others. Then I told her, "Happy birthday," and when she looked at me quizzically I said, "You stopped cursing. Happy birthday," and then turned back to her parents to give her distance from my "praise."

When the timer sounded, Mu Ling continued throwing the beanbags. "Hmm, I guess Mu Ling needs to practice stopping her anger more. She can't stop herself yet," I commented in a neutral voice, as if I were evaluating her ability to stop reading, say, when asked. I reset the timer, and Mu Ling threw more beanbags. But now she did so with less enthusiasm, because I had dictated that she continue. When the timer rang, she laughed unpleasantly and began throwing the beanbags hard against the box.

I set the timer a third time and simply commented that "Mu Ling needs more practice." When the timer rang this time, Mu Ling abruptly put down her toy. She looked confused and uncomfortable. Meg uttered the non sequitur that she and I had planned: "Happy birthday." Mu Ling looked at her mom and gave her the first genuine smile in two weeks.

Having fun or even being relaxed with a parent is uncomfortable for a child like Mu Ling, because fun is a shared, spontaneous interaction in which neither, person, child or adult, is completely in control. Thus children who, like Mu Ling, feel they must be in control need to practice having fun with Mom or Dad.

Once a minimal starting level of having fun has been achieved—which as we have just seen can be quite difficult—parents can demonstrate higher levels of having fun, involving more time together, more intense cooperation, and more laughter. You can suggest that each new level is "too hard" for your child to do; this usually motivates a child to take the challenge. The first level might be "a little fun," which you could demonstrate with smiling. The second level would be "some fun," which you would show with a big grin that shows teeth. "A lot of fun" would be laughing, wiggling one's body with pleasure, and saying, "Oh, boy!"

Meg chose a Slinky to practice playing with her daughter. Mu Ling remembered the toy from her time in the First Year Home Group four years before. Meg demonstrated what different levels of fun look like: smiles, then grins, then wiggling or bouncing with joy. Next she said that Mu Ling could play with one end of the Slinky while Mom held the other. When Mu Ling got angry, Mom suggested that they would need to practice starting and stopping anger again. Mu Ling immediately dropped her angry demeanor and began to play, if soberly, with the Slinky.

"No fun yet," Meg told her daughter. "This may be too hard for you," she added, in an empathetic voice.

Mu Ling's smile looked more like a grimace.

Mom responded with the non sequitur "Happy birthday."

Mu Ling began to relax and explore the Slinky, and finally she smiled a genuine big smile and laughed.

"Kick the can," her mother responded, using a new nonsense phrase. "That's some fun."

At the beginning of this chapter we discussed how earning privileges helps a child learn to respect limits and follow family rules. It would have been inappropriate to teach Mu Ling to earn playful interactions, or any interactions, with her parents, because clearly she did not yet know how to play. However, once she learned to play, and showed that she had mastered this skill along with control of her anger, it would be suitable to have her earn play time by following rules. As it turned out, by the time Mu Ling was ten she knew that demonstrating good manners at the table during an entire meal was a way to earn fifteen minutes of playing catch with her mother.

WHERE TO GO FROM HERE: THERAPY TO SUPPORT EVERYONE

If your child has the type of moderate to severe problems described in this chapter, your family needs a therapist. Do not delay searching for a child and family therapist who can help you and your child. I offer several important guidelines as you begin your search. First, pick someone with whom you feel comfortable, whose voice is soothing, and whom you feel you can trust. Second, choose a therapist who is willing to have you be present in the session with your child at least some of the time and who will meet with you separately when needed. Some therapists want to see the child only. This is not acceptable or effective for helping a severely affected child.

Third, if you feel there is no progress after two or three sessions, talk to the therapist, preferably in an adults-only session. If you feel that you are stuck after six sessions, research on therapeutic efficacy indicates you most likely are. Find a new therapist.

Fourth, if you alone, or you and your partner together, need support and help, find a therapist who will work with you. A child with severe behavior problems can turn even the most well-adjusted, stable, happy adults into basket cases. Get the support you need. You deserve it and you will be in better shape to help your child change.

Finally, know that you are not alone. Many parents suffer in silence and hide their child's angry and controlling behaviors, fearing that they as parents are somehow responsible. Your child arrived with serious problems for reasons you may not even know. Ask your therapist to help you find a group of parents like yourself, and get support from them.

Repairing Disconnection between Child and Parent

"SONIA IGNORED ME FOR A FEW DAYS after I first went out for the evening," Carolyn told the First Year Home Group one day. It was one of several examples that we heard of an intense and extended *disconnection* between parent and child.

"The last few times I've set limits for Demetri he had a tantrum. After the tantrum he treated me so coolly, refusing to make eye contact for several hours," Denise shared.

"Yi Sheng refuses to eat after we've had a verbal disagreement," said Nina. "We were playing Candy Land once and he thought it was his turn, but really it wasn't. We argued and he got so angry he walked away. He stayed upset until dinner, and when he came to the table, he folded his arms and insisted he wasn't hungry."

WHEN THE MAGIC CIRCLE BREAKS

Every adoptive family faces a day or an evening when a child and parent who have been well connected suddenly disconnect. When Carolyn went to her book group that evening, she "broke" the Magic Circle in her daughter's eyes. Sonia reacted by shutting down in response to any approach by either of her parents; she withdrew from the Magic Circle of connection. Whereas a non-adopted two- or three-year-old would whine and cling to Mom, Sonia ignored her mother and became sober and withdrawn.

Yi Sheng and Demetri both held on to the disconnection, shunning eye contact with and refusing to take food from their parents. Internationally adopted children often react to ruptures by resuming reactive coping behaviors (see chapter 5). The adopted child experiences ordinary disruptions, including common kinds of separations, as well as instances of limit setting or defining consequences, and even minor disruptions, such as disagreements or changes in plans, as a potential loss of the parent.

Disconnection with a parent short-circuits the child's ability to remain behaviorally and emotionally balanced. She becomes anxious. When disconnection follows a period of connection, the internationally adopted child asks internally, or out loud, what to her is the most important question: "Are you going to leave me, too?"

Internationally adopted children can experience ordinary and even minor disruptions as the potential loss of a parent.

This was the case for Sonia. The rupture with her foster mother in Guatemala was never repaired, and she transferred her feelings from the past to the present with her adoptive mother. For his part, Yi Sheng did not get the chance to say goodbye to, much less bring closure to his relationships with, his birth parents or his foster family. These past disconnections colored Yi Sheng's feelings about the small rift with his mother over the Candy Land game. Like Yi Sheng, Demetri also had unfinished emotional business with disconnections and separations.

REPAIRING THE DISCONNECTION

It was the parents in the First Year Home Group who found some way to reconnect after emotional arguments or disagreements. Mom came over and rubbed Sonia's back. Dad offered to play ball or give Yi Sheng a piggyback ride. Denise volunteered to play trucks with Demetri. Each of these gestures was a repair of the disconnection.

"Why do we parents always have to make the first move toward repair?" David asked the Group.

The unfinished emotional business of loss makes it exceptionally difficult for internationally adopted children to initiate repair. They just do not expect or believe that the other person will be there waiting for them. They are skeptical that their efforts at repair will be rewarded, and more than that, they feel that they once again have done something bad to make the adult leave or get mad. As a result, the child expects to be abandoned. Parents have to model repair words and behaviors to help their child learn that these are incorrect assumptions.

Parents have to help a child carry and reduce the heavy weight of fear, sadness, and anger that lingers from past abandonment experiences and colors new experiences of disruption and disconnection.

REPAIR IS MORE THAN AN APOLOGY

You must initiate the compassionate repair of a break in your relationship with your child. This is not always easy. When David asked, "Won't Sonia just forget about it?" the answer, I told him, simply is no. When Carolyn protested, "But I didn't do anything wrong. Why should I fix it?" I told her that indeed she did nothing wrong by going out. Nevertheless, Sonia experienced Carolyn's leaving as breaking the Magic Circle. Sonia needed her mother's help to understand that the circle was not in fact broken, only stretched farther than she could bear.

Repair needs to be a delicate, nonjudgmental experience for both parent and child. A child needs the parent to explain what happened, to be in tune with how the child felt, and to reassure the child that the rupture is not permanent.

How do you make a repair? Tell your child with compassion that you can guess how he felt when you left. Carolyn, for example, might say, "Sonia, I bet you thought I would never come back when I left last night. I wonder if you were scared."

Second, you must listen to what your child says and watch his body language, facial expressions, and play. *Whatever* your child does after your opening statement is a response. Knowing that Sonia tended to shut down in difficult situations, Carolyn could comment on this: "Sonia, you are sitting there like a little silent rock. All shut down. I think these feelings are so hard for you that you don't want to feel them."

Just this small amount of conversation is enough to repair a situation with a young child. You do not have to have an hour's worth of discussion. Finally, close the repair conversation by suggesting a hug or a shared activity.

When a child withdraws in an angry, uncooperative, or dismissive manner, many parents feel he should "have a consequence" for misbehaving. But in fact, in instances such as these the child has already had a consequence: the deflated, empty, scared feeling of losing a parent. Your repair conversation with your child should help him react differently, if not immediately then certainly down the road. The repair conversation should be part of a larger conversation stretching between this event and the next time Mom is going out for the evening. Your child will learn to change his behavior if you pick up the threads of the conversation multiple times and anticipate and address your child's behavior beforehand. In this way repair is an important component of proactive parenting and the strengthening and maintenance of the Magic Circle.

Researchers and clinicians agree that repair is a critical part of helping a child to manage emotional control in the present as well as long-term. The key to repair is the parent maintaining a balanced emotional state when the child is upset, thereby conveying to the child that the parent can tolerate his negative feelings. The child, too, learns to tolerate his own negative emotions and the negative emotions of others. When Carolyn acknowledged Sonia's upset and calmly listened to Sonia's expression of feelings, she was teaching Sonia to manage her negative feelings.

Moreover, Carolyn's being emotionally in tune with her daughter reestablished the connection that we call the Magic Circle. "In tune" does not mean feeling the same upset feelings in the same way. It means instead that a parent acknowledges in a sensitive manner how the child feels without losing emotional balance in the process.

The culmination of repair is to re-create the Magic Circle using the strategies described earlier in this book. These include reinitiating the in-tune and in-sync face-to-face behaviors that created the circle in the first place (see chapter 9 on the Magic Circle and chapter 10 on face and eye contact). Thus it is important to find an activity for parent and child that will help this happen. Simply holding a child and rocking might work for some families. With others a game of ball may do the trick. The "Ping-Pong" or back-and-forth interaction is vital (see chapter 15). The face-to-face interaction is critical. The increasing sense of joy is crucial. Each of these pieces contributes to strengthening the Magic Circle.

PRACTICING REPAIR

"I still love you even when you are mad at me. When you finish being mad, I'll hold you," Laura told her three-year-old daughter, Mu Ling, who was having a tantrum because she wanted another cookie.

Staying close by, rather than insisting on a time-out away from Mom, shows the child that the parent is not leaving. Laura told her daughter about the immediate future plan: "I'll hold you." This is a reaffirmation of the Magic Circle. When Mu Ling finally began hiccupping and whimpering instead of shouting and kicking, Laura offered to hold her again. This time Mu Ling crawled into her mother's lap and gripped Laura's shirt tightly in her fist.

Laura took hold of a finger from that hand and started This Little Piggy, watching carefully to see how her daughter reacted. Mu Ling turned her head away. She was not ready to play. So Laura waited and held the finger. She asked, "Can I feed you some cereal?"

Feeding her daughter offered Laura the opportunity for in-tune and in-sync behavior. It was nurturing and promoted face-to-face interaction and eye contact. Mu Ling nodded, and Laura carried her to the kitchen to get the cereal. On the way, Mu Ling held out her hand and wiggled her fingers, indicating that now she was ready to play the Piggy Game.

FAMILY SKILLS FOR CO-REGULATION OF FEELINGS AND BEHAVIOR

1. Learning to replace reactive coping behaviors with a quiet, alert state
2. Learning to co-regulate feelings and behaviors with a parent
3. Learning to participate in repair of child-parent relationship after ruptures

Mu Ling was learning to tolerate and regulate her own strong negative feelings. Rupture and repair are necessary experiences to support this next, and culminating, step in co-regulation and development. The first step toward learning to regulate emotions and behavior for an internationally adopted child is to set aside reactive coping behaviors, including revving up or shutting down. The second step is learning to work with a parent to co-regulate feelings and actions. The third step is to participate in the repair of a rupture in the parent-child relationship, in order to return to co-regulation. I cannot emphasize too much how crucial repair is for strengthening the Magic Circle, and how rewarding the results. If you want your child to be able to be compassionate, to apologize for mistakes, to take responsibility for managing her own negative behavior, begin practicing repair today.

Encouraging Adjustment and Interdependence

AS A CHILD BEGINS to adjust to life with a new family, reactive coping behaviors and survival skills are replaced by interdependent relationships with parents and other caregiving adults. I use the word *adjustment* to refer both to the period of time in which this happens and to the behavioral milestones that occur within that period.

FROM SURVIVAL AND COPING TO ADJUSTMENT

When a child first joins his adoptive family there is a period, sometimes as short as a few hours, sometimes as long as a year or more, during which he sizes up the new situation. Sometimes adoptive parents refer to this period as a "honeymoon" because the child's behavior seems so mature and independent. As this pseudomature behavior begins to reveal the rougher survival skills and more aggressive reactive coping behaviors, parents realize that there is a need for adjustment in the child's behavior.

THE ADJUSTMENT PERIOD

Adoption → "Sizing Up"/"Honeymoon" → Adjustment → Family Skills and Family Life

In addition to the movement toward age-appropriate behaviors, there are changes in the frequency of a child's reliance on survival and reactive coping

207

behaviors. Adjustment begins with survival and coping behaviors in full force and ends when those behaviors occur only rarely, perhaps once a week rather than daily.

STAGES OF ADJUSTMENT DURING THE FIRST YEAR HOME

1. Survival and reactive coping skills predominate in a child's behavior, and the child behaves as though he is "on his own" in the world.
2. A shared, interactive relationship begins to grow between parent and child. Family skills are being learned, in small pockets of time, but survival and coping skills continue to dominate.
3. Family skills within a shared, interactive, co-regulating relationship alternate frequently with survival and coping behaviors. Family skills continue to be learned and are practiced for longer periods of time.
4. Family skills and co-regulation have developed to the point that the Magic Circle feels present for significant periods of time each day. Survival and coping behaviors play a minor role daily.
5. Family skills and co-regulation predominate, with only occasional episodes of survival and coping behaviors, perhaps no more than three each week.

Adjustment behaviors, then, is a general term to describe the progressive development of family skills that replace survival skills and reactive coping behaviors. Family skills develop gradually; rarely does a child move quickly and seamlessly from survival skills to age-appropriate family skills. Instead, the child begins with early forms of family skills. For example, Yi Sheng began "asking" for attention when he was five years old, by tugging at his mother's clothing and whining—the family skills of a two- or three-year-old. Although Yi Sheng could speak some English after being home for six months, he did not use age-appropriate verbal behavior to get his mother's attention. Thus family skills move from a "baby" level through toddler, preschool, and school-age levels until a child can use age-appropriate family skills—until family age catches up with chronological age, in other words. Adjustment behavior always precedes age-appropriate behavior; the need for an adjustment period is one of the reasons that internationally adopted children's development cannot be judged on an ages-and-stages basis.

ADJUSTMENT AS TRANSITIONAL BEHAVIOR

Survival Skills and Reactive Coping Behaviors ➔ Adjustment: Learning Family Skills ➔ Age-Appropriate Behaviors

Parent Juice drives the process of adjustment (see chapter 9). Parent Juice enhances the child's thrill of mobility and exploration throughout childhood, from crawling, walking, and running to going to school and discovering the world beyond parents and home. Naturally a parent's sparkling eyes and smile show pride in the child's blossoming physical and other skills. Simply seeing this parental facial expression releases yet more Parent Juice in the child. A child simultaneously experiences the exhilaration of *in*dependence and, by returning repeatedly for more jolts of Parent Juice, a deeper *inter*dependence. This independence combined with interdependence is quite different from the child's

Interdependence is the core of adjustment.

previous state of feeling on his own or virtually alone in the world. Soon An felt isolated when she lost her foster mother; Charlotte had to help her daughter regain a sense of interdependence. Demetri had been alone essentially since birth, and he knew no other state until Denise, his mother, taught him otherwise. Yi Sheng, with his many losses, had a sense that he could rely only on himself, but his parents found ways to break through this barrier. Achieving a sense of interdependence is at the core of adjustment for an internationally adopted child.

ADJUSTMENT: THE BEGINNINGS OF FAMILY SKILLS

Many adopted children struggle with what psychologists call *global disorganization*, which is a fancy term for being immersed in a sea of uncontrolled behavior and emotion. A parent's job in this situation is to be a life preserver, relieving a child of her reliance on coping and survival skills. When a period of adjustment begins, a child literally just "hangs on" to you by whining, clinging, leading

A relationship always begins at the beginning.

you around by the hand, or repeatedly handing you toys. Although on the surface these simple interactions might seem to indicate distress, they actually indicate that your child's trust in you is growing. These clinging behaviors show that your child recognizes that you are different from other adults.

Your child's adjustment behaviors may seem immature, especially if her prior coping style has been one of premature or pseudomature self-reliance. This immaturity is a reflection of the newness of the child-parent relationship, regardless of the child's chronological age. A relationship always begins at the beginning. Clinging is an early form of staying close to a parent; whining is an early form of communication; leading a parent by the hand and handing a parent toys are both early forms of sharing attention with a parent. Family age is more helpful for understanding adjustment behaviors than chronological age.

In this chapter we take a closer look at seven adjustment behaviors. They are frequently the first adjustment behaviors parents notice. These seven behaviors replace the seven survival skills introduced in chapter 4. The box below shows which adjustment behaviors replace which survival skills. Although family skills are the ultimate goals for our children, adjustment behaviors are transitional behaviors on the way to those goals. For example, we want a child to acquire the family skill of asking for help or attention, but on the way we recognize that a child will whine, tug, or beg as interim skills of adjustment.

From Survival to Adjustment

	Survival Skill	Adjustment Behavior
1.	Eats everything	Becomes a picky eater
2.	Performs or charms adults to get attention	Whines
3.	Treats adults as interchangeable	Clings to parents
4.	Soothes or comforts self	Interacts with parent for comfort
5.	Restricts range of feelings	Expresses a greater range of feelings, in a greater variety of ways
6.	Tolerates being alone for long periods of time	Checks in with parents for emotional refueling
7.	Organizes self by routines	Shows flexibility; creates routines with others

PICKY EATING, WHINING, AND CLINGING

Picky eating, whining, and clinging occur in a predictable order and at predictable times during an adopted child's first year home.

Picky eating reflects a child's recognition that food is abundant and available at almost any time. This availability gives the child a reason to trust his new family, and his picky eating in response to that availability is often the first indication that a child is developing such trust. Picky eating generally occurs by three months of family age, as a child begins to settle in and recognize family routines.

Whining reflects a child's recognition that the new caregivers, his parents, are responsive to his needs and to his efforts at communicating those needs. Whining develops between two and six months of family age.

Clinging expresses a preference for parents over other adults. It may be excessive and it may be accompanied by anxiety around strangers. This preference reflects, of course, a child's increasing connection with a parent. This adjustment behavior emerges as early as three months of family age or as late as a year or more after adoption.

TIMETABLE OF ADJUSTMENT BEHAVIORS

Adjustment Behavior	Timing of Adjustment
Picky eating	Three to four months of family age
Whining	Two to six months of family age
Preferential clinging	Three to twelve or more months of family age

Picky Eating and Abundance

Picky eating seems like a response to food, not to a parent. But food is the substance that psychologically represents a parent's nurturance. Picky eating reflects a child's realization that there is an abundance of food, which often precedes her realization that the parent is abundantly available in many other ways.

It can be difficult for an internationally adopted child to realize that there is an abundance of food in her new home. I once received a phone call from the mother of a four-year-old boy, Boris, adopted from Russia, whose family age was one month. His mother asked me to make a home visit, to see for myself her son's "annoying habit," as she put it, of repeatedly opening the refrigerator. "I need help," she told me, "because Boris is driving me crazy. I can't understand why he does this when I've repeatedly scolded him for disobeying."

During my hour-long visit the boy did just what his mother had described. He opened the refrigerator and gazed at all the food, then he closed the door. A few minutes later he was back, inspecting the food supply again. This went on until I commented to him, "There is a lot of food in there."

The boy nodded with a serious expression.

"I bet there wasn't that much food in Russia."

The boy nodded again in agreement.

"Do you think the food will disappear?" I asked him.

With a worried expression he nodded again and opened the door to check the refrigerator's contents.

"Let's ask your mom if the food will disappear," I suggested, pointing to Mom. The boy looked at his mother.

Mom reassured her son that the refrigerator would always have enough food, and the boy sighed and smiled.

Here is another opportunity to tell the child's story from the child's perspective, incorporating the current behavior and making sense of it, in order to teach a new behavior, which in this case is keeping the refrigerator door closed. "You lived in Russia before now," his mother told him. Quickly recognizing what her son needed to know, she added, "There wasn't enough food in Russia, and you were always hungry. Now you live in America. The refrigerator's full, but you are worried it will disappear. You keep checking on the food. But it won't disappear. You'll see: After a week it will still be full."

Then Mom wanted to explain that opening the door would make the food spoil. I suggested that this would not be meaningful to her son, because it did not relate to his experience. Instead she said, "I bet you never saw a refrigerator in Russia." Again her son nodded. Then he patted the outside of the refrigerator door.

Pickiness about food may be related to a child's desire to be in control of feeding herself. In orphanages children are fed quickly, often in ways that adoptive parents would find abusive. Feeding is rapid, efficient, and rarely a positive social experience. Pickiness is a way for a child to exercise control and to avoid being in a helpless position.

Food is not the area in which to start a control battle with your child. Instead, always have some of her "comfort food" on hand. If you can prepare it yourself, your home will be filled with the scent of familiar food that reassures your child. But if you don't enjoy searching for and trying new recipes, find a local ethnic restaurant serving the cuisine of your child's birth country from which you can get takeout food.

A Parenting Strategy for Managing Picky Eaters

Food choice is an appropriate arena in which to allow a child to explore self-control, as long as you do not end up serving French fries and ice cream for every meal. To permit choice while maintaining good nutrition, I advise parents to select and keep on hand two or three food items that are healthful and nutritious and that their child has expressed the desire to eat. Let your child choose freely from among these preselected favorite items that he has enjoyed in the past. Always have at least one item that does not require cooking. The no-need-to-cook list might include yogurt, tofu, or whole-grain cereal with milk. This strategy provides your child with the experience of control without your having to become a short-order cook.

Parenting a Child Who Hoards

Not all young adoptees are physically capable of checking the food supply or asking in words if the food will always be available. Instead, some children hoard food, in their pockets, in secret places in the house, or even in their mouths. Talk with your child about how she may have lacked sufficient food in the past, and relate that to the hoarding. The mother's conversation with the boy who repeatedly opened the refrigerator is a good model. When parents express a combination of understanding their child's prior experience and reassuring her that things are different now, the child develops trust in a parent's ability to make sense of both the past and the present.

Hoarding is a combination of a survival skill (for a child who had limited food available in the past) and an expression of feeling uncared for, alone, and empty. The key to changing hoarding behavior is helping a child connect the food itself with a parent's loving presence.

It is important that you *treat hoarding behavior seriously*. A child needs to be told that her parents are not angry with her for hoarding and that they understand the feeling of emptiness that caused her behavior. Set up a safe, clean place to keep extra food. Make food always available in some way. Sharing the feelings that lead to hoarding does not encourage the behavior, but instead reduces the child's feelings of emptiness.

In addition to verbal reassurances, engage in the following sensory modalities with the hoarding child:

Touch: Hold your child or sit close by her while she eats. If you notice your child eating hoarded food, offer your lap, or sit close by. This helps her build associations among you, the food, and the experience of filling herself.

Sucking: Sucking is the first source of comfort for a child. If your child who hoards still uses a bottle, let her continue to do so and even increase the frequency of bottles. Use straws or a sippy cup for an older child.

Eye contact: Make eye contact with your child last as long as possible. It may only be a couple of seconds at first. Count the seconds at the beginning of the first week and then again at the end, and try to double your time each week. Over several weeks of practice you will see a dramatic change. (Remember: A five-second "connect" is a 500 percent improvement over one second!) You need to be *extremely* proactive, getting directly in your child's face to encourage a mutual gaze.

During the period in which you are working with your child on eye contact and gazing, tell her repeatedly that *food tastes better when you look at someone you love.* This is a fact. Gazing into the eyes of someone you love and who loves you releases specific hormones and biochemicals that make both people feel good.

Keep up your child's work in all three of these areas—touch, sucking, and eye contact—at least three or four times a day for several weeks. One or two times for a few days will not change feeding behavior. The more practice, the sooner your interdependent relationship with your child will develop and the sooner your child will replace her hoarding behavior with trust in your ability to provide enough food and, by association, enough nurturance generally.

Whining

Whining is a low-level, infantile form of communication designed to get a parent's attention. If like most parents you hate hearing your child whine, remember this: A child who expects neglect does not whine but instead is silent. Whining is a pointless waste of energy in a busy orphanage. When your adopted child whines, it reflects his recognition that his new parent is responsive and available. Whining is a major step away from the coping behaviors of, say, the Royal Boss or the Warm Rock (see chapter 5). It is a major step away from reliance on the survival skills of performing for and charming adults to gain their attention.

I encourage parents to teach their child to whine, if the child has not already started, because it is the easiest way for him to signal for attention.

Whining is only a temporary stage, a steppingstone to more effective communication such as signs, gestures, and words. Many parents try to suppress whining without teaching more appropriate forms of attention getting. Teaching your child to call you, to tug on your clothing, or to use nonverbal signs is a much better way to reduce whining.

Once you have taught your child how to call for you or otherwise get your attention, respond to whining with positive redirection. "If you give me the 'I need you' sign or tug on my pants," you might say, "I'll pay attention. You can do it!" Inject a sense of fun and an appreciation of your child's learning ability into this process.

So, rejoice when your child begins to whine! You have done a great job helping him discard coping and survival skills in favor of an important family skill: two-way communication.

Preferential Clinging

Some children cling from the moment they meet their adoptive parents. It is understandable that a parent would describe such a child as "attached," because the child acts like Velcro. But a Velcro baby in the first three months of family age is clinging out of fear generated by the upheavals of the Big Change—the adoption experience. Clingy behavior in the first few months of family age is probably neither adjustment nor attachment. Rather, it is a survival behavior to avoid further loss.

Preferential clinginess, which means clinging to parents but not to strangers or temporary caregivers, appears only after a child becomes familiar with her new parent. Family skills related to connection and attachment take months and years to grow. Preferential clinging is a signal that your child is ready to work on deeper and more enduring forms of connection.

Clinginess as Connection

Sudden or excessive clingy behavior typically develops during the first year home, frequently accompanied by separation anxiety or stranger anxiety. Suddenly your child does not want you to leave the room, whereas the week before she hardly noticed when you disappeared to unload the dryer. A few days ago anyone could give your child a bottle; now only you can do so without her raising a fuss and calling for you.

Clinginess and separation anxiety usually develop in non-adopted children at nine to ten months of age. Among adopted children, these behaviors develop at a similar time, except on a family-age clock rather than a chronological clock. Clinginess, especially preferential clinging, is an important sign of a child's increasing connection to her new parent. Like whining, it indicates an increasingly interactive relationship between child and parent.

SLOW-TO-DEVELOP ADJUSTMENT BEHAVIORS

Picky eating, whining, and clinging appear on the scene quickly, often without much intervention from parents, and they are hard for a parent to miss. We turn next to four adjustment behaviors that develop more slowly and are more difficult to spot. They are *co-regulated soothing*, which refers to a child using a parent to calm down; an *expanded range of feelings*, including appropriately expressed sadness, anger, fear, excitement, and happiness; *checking in for emotional refueling*; and *flexibility when faced with change*. These four adjustment behaviors may take years to develop into full-fledged family skills, and they definitely need parental encouragement to flourish.

Co-regulated Soothing and Comforting

Children who use survival or coping behaviors, as many internationally adopted children do, find ways to soothe themselves in isolation. But as a child adjusts to family life, he begins to rely on parents for emotional support and balance. You may notice that your child calms when you pick him up or touch him, or when he hears your voice. This is interactive soothing behavior.

At first a child who relies on survival skills rejects or pushes away a parent offering comfort. A parent might comment sympathetically on a bumped head only to have the child ignore the comment or protest that everything is fine. As time goes on and a parent continues to offer soothing, a child reaches a wrenching decision point, torn between sticking with survival behaviors and becoming dependent on parents for comfort. I often see an adopted child approach a parent for comfort and then turn away; this is a child who has come to this point of decision. You need persistence and understanding to break through this conflict to help your child feel at ease with interdependency. Chapters 13 and 15 have more detailed suggestions about developing soothing interactions. Keep in mind that a child using survival skills rejects you when he needs you most. So be persistent in reaching out to meet the real, if unexpressed, need behind his behaviors.

An Expanded Range of Expressed Emotions

Internationally adopted children typically start their lives in their new families with a narrow range of expressed emotions. As we have seen (see chapter 5), where that narrow range lies is different for different children. Over time, each type of child begins to expand her range of emotions in a different way. The Warm

Rock, for example, emerges from her passive and inattentive state and becomes fussy or angry. The Royal Boss may go from a hastily shouted "bye!" to biting her lip and murmuring a nearly inaudible "bye." When these changes happen, we are witnessing the growth of emotion and of its expression. Parents who tenderly nurture the tiny smiles of a coping child will eventually be rewarded with belly laughs. Facial expressions of fear, surprise, distaste (a wrinkled nose), and disgust (the entire face wrinkled), among other emotions, all emerge bit by bit.

Sometimes adopted children who are beyond infancy explore this new emotional territory by "pretending" to express emotions in a self-conscious way. For example, instead of genuine tears after a fall, a child produces a fake sort of cry. Or during play a child pretends to laugh very loud. What differentiates real crying or laughing from pretend is the self-consciousness of the child when she pretends.

When I work with adoptive parents, I suggest that they always support and encourage the expression of feelings, even if the initial expressions are self-conscious and a bit fake, in the following ways:

First, *praise your child for expressing the correct feeling* for the situation. For example, you can say, "Yes, crying is what a person does when she gets hurt," or "When we're having fun, we can laugh so loud!"

Second, *do not point out the "pretending"* or staged quality. Doing so only increases the child's self-consciousness and causes her to retreat.

Third, *offer more ways to express the same feelings,* including facial expressions, gestures, body language, sign language, and different words.

Note that in a child adopted at eighteen months of age or older an expanded range of emotions may take more than a year to appear.

Before a child can express feelings, especially painful, sad, or angry feelings, she must feel that her new family is a sufficiently safe environment in which to do so. The process goes faster if parents make room for those feelings by telling the child's story from the child's perspective (see chapter 7). Nothing seems sad to a child in comparison to having lost a familiar caregiver or foster parent. Endings and leave-takings, especially, evoke the intense past feelings; without a context the sad feelings may go into hiding, leaving a "stone-faced" child who turns away or walks away during moments of separation, or who hurries quickly and inattentively through the leave-taking moment. Sometimes such a child expresses difficult emotions inappropriately, in laughter at sad events or separations, for example. Although it may appear that a child does not understand the concept of "goodbye," I think it is more likely she understands it all too well and wants to avoid the subject.

The Gradual Expression of a Painful Emotion: Sadness

Let us explore further the gradual emergence of expressed sadness. We make an effort to teach the expression of uncomfortable feelings in the First Year Home Group. At the end of each session we sing the "Goodbye Song," which gives each child an opportunity to feel the uncomfortable emotions of sadness, frustration ("I want to stay and play!"), or even anger ("I want to be in control of leaving or not!"). Non-adopted children are generally able to express these feelings in a controlled way as they say or sing goodbye, but internationally adopted children are never at ease, especially in the beginning. Most of the children have in recent months gone through the global psychological disorganization of the adoption. "Goodbye" is not a favorite topic.

In chapter 1 we observed how difficult goodbye is for children with just one month of family age. Without help and guidance, a child remains unable to respond to goodbyes appropriately. I observed a girl named Katie, whose family joined a First Year Home group when she was three years old and had a family age of nine months. When we sang the "Goodbye Song" to her she "sang" goodbye with an overly wide, theatrical smile on her face, alternately kicking her legs and waving one of her feet. This was her performance, to cope with her difficult feelings.

During goodbyes in the second month of the Group, Katie covered her face with her hands, a blanket, or the Eeyore doll (the saddest character in *Winnie the Pooh*, having lost his tail) when the song was sung to her. In the third month Katie responded when the song was sung to anyone in the Group by sucking her fingers, with a crooked smile.

Finally, after four months (sixteen weekly sessions) in the Group, and having recently celebrated her fourth birthday, this little girl showed a genuinely sad face at goodbye time and said clearly and firmly, "I don't want to leave."

It took a lot of patience for Katie's parents to support their daughter through the gradual emergence of an appropriate feeling and its expression. It was hard not to chastise her for hiding her face, for trying to be the center of attention, or for "faking" her expressions. Once she reached the milestone of expressing her sadness clearly, her parents were confused. "Why is she sad now?" her mother asked. "She knows we'll come back."

It was hard for Mom to realize that her child had been sad all along but unable to manage, and appropriately express, that emotion. It took Katie four times as long as it would take a non-adopted child to be able to say goodbye with appropriate feelings and behavioral control. This is exactly what the long-term research on adopted children tells us.

Checking In for Emotional Refueling

Internationally adopted children enter their new families prepared to be "on their own." Many arrive with well-practiced survival skills for managing without consistent caregiving from adults. When an adopted child eventually does begin to reach out, to check in, to get help, to have fun, or merely to connect, it is vital that parents take note of this major change in orientation.

SIGNS OF CONNECTION

Holding hands with parent

Insisting on staying together

Shadowing parent around the house

Checking in with parent by offering a toy, pat, or kiss

Checking in visually by looking across a room to catch parent's eye

Wanting parent nearby in order to fall asleep

Reacting in advance to separations or signs of separation from home, parent, or objects

Reacting after separation, either positively or negatively

Connection in your child begins with small and tentative behaviors, such as taking your hand or handing you a toy, gestures that are seemingly so ordinary that you may take them for granted. They represent, however, a major internal shift in how your child views the world. Instead of feeling alone and untrusting of adults, he is beginning to trust, to look to his parent as an available, nurturing, special person in his life. I cannot emphasize enough how important this shift is. Once it has occurred, connection, identity, and resiliency will blossom; without it, your child is left to rely on survival skills and reactive coping behaviors that will distort and undermine his future development.

Parents must do everything in their power to nurture these small connection steps and recognize them for what they are. Certainly you can teach your child to do each of the connection actions listed in the box above. As your child begins to take these specific steps, acknowledge verbally what he is doing, give praise of a level or type that he can accept, and show appreciation with a smile that you make sure he sees.

Make these tiny connection steps a reason for celebrating your effective parenting. You have been working hard. The fact that your child is engaging you by reaching out for your hand, for example, is evidence that you have enabled him to trust you. This is a monumental step in adjustment and you should be proud that your work made this possible.

Flexibility in the Face of Change

Internationally adopted children frequently lose their emotional and behavioral balance when a routine changes or during transitions from one activity to another. Maintaining balance in these situations is an important adjustment skill for adopted children to learn.

Why are these children so rigid? All children are highly dependent on routines to structure their experience; repetition and predictability give infants and young children a sense of security, safety, and control. To a child, things seem safest and most secure when both the caregiver and the routine are consistent. But when caregivers change, as has happened at least once and usually more than once in the life of an international adoptee, routines alone become the most consistent and predictable, and therefore safest, refuges in life.

Routines give a child a sense of control because she can predict what will happen. Mental control leads to emotional and behavioral control, just as much as being physically in control of a situation would do.

Think for a moment of a day when something in your routine was altered and how you felt. When I find my routine changed because the car suddenly stalls and needs to be repaired, I have trouble organizing and remembering what should happen for the rest of the day. Take one routine away and everything else falls to pieces. This is how internationally adopted children feel about their routines. No wonder they treasure and defend them so fiercely.

The flip side of an adopted child's intense attachment to her routines is the fear or sense of danger she feels when a routine changes.

Imagine the morning of your child's adoption. The caregiver is more rushed than usual, and your child is being dressed more rapidly and in unfamiliar clothing. Instead of moving on to the next child immediately, the caregiver cries and holds your child for a few extra moments. She talks to your child about "the new family" and the importance of being a "good girl." After breakfast everyone stands around and says goodbye, and then your child is given several pieces of candy and a little jar of yogurt or rice milk. In short, changes in the routine are the first indication that this day will be radically different.

Over the next days and weeks, and even months and years, your child's mind will associate these and other small changes with the Big Change, with the trauma of leaving everyone and everything that was familiar. In short, adoptees take little changes quite seriously. By controlling or avoiding transitions or changes in routine, they feel they can avoid the next big surprise, whatever it may be. They feel they can avoid the anxiety and the loss of emotional and behavioral control that they know can accompany the trauma of change.

To a parent a small change in routine seems ordinary, even inconsequential. "What's your problem?" a parent throws out at the hysterical child, who is completely out of control because the parent read the bedtime story before she brushed her teeth, an unforgivable change in routine.

Because routines help your child feel safe and secure, leave them in place for several months at least. Then make a plan to help your child practice tiny changes, as a step toward learning flexibility. For example, at four years of age Mu Ling's routine before naptime was to have her mother Meg cuddle with her on the bed and sing a special lullaby to Mu Ling before she was left to fall asleep. Meg decided to change the routine by cuddling her daughter in a rocking chair and singing the lullaby before placing her in bed. Meg explained to her daughter that in two days they were going to make a small change in naptime; Meg picked Saturday to make the change because it was a low-pressure day. Because Mu Ling knew in advance of the change, she had time to anticipate and predict it.

Developing flexibility takes time and practice. I advise parents to begin working on flexibility with a routine that takes place during the day, not in the morning or at night.

Another aspect of flexibility for a child is being able to trust more than one adult. Meg had always done the wake-up routine with Mu Ling. When Mu Ling was four and a half, her parents decided to practice having Laura, Mu Ling's other mother, wake Mu Ling in the morning. I suggested that this might be difficult because mornings were especially stressful for Mu Ling. Morning difficulty is common among some traumatized children because their biochemical cycles are disrupted; levels of cortisol, a soothing chemical, which in non-adopted children are high in the morning, are significantly lower in internationally adopted children with stress-shaped brains. This makes for cranky, irritable mornings. Sucking on a juice box or sipping a glass of juice in bed can help a child calm for the morning. So Meg added the juice change first and then moved on to preparing Mu Ling in other ways for Laura to be the "wake-up parent."

Adjustment behaviors are challenging for parents. The fact that they are often babylike or less than age-appropriate can be frustrating to parents who want their child to behave in an age-appropriate way. Teaching adjustment behaviors takes a lot of work, mostly involving breaking skills into small and manageable steps. Be patient with your child and yourself. You will not always do it perfectly, and when you do not, you have a chance to practice repair (see chapter 17) with your child. Celebrate your child's and your successes, even if they are very, very small steps toward your ultimate goals.

In the next chapter we will explore the subject of flexibility in the face of change, with a focus specifically on ways that you can structure your and your child's daily lives to make your child's adjustment as smooth and successful as possible.

Structuring Transitions, Separations, and Work/Life Decisions

"I CAN'T GET SONIA TO STOP one activity and move on to another," Carolyn said when she left a phone message for me, asking for an appointment. "She doesn't want to stop playing and take a bath, but once she's in the bath, she doesn't want to get out and have dinner. Every transition is a struggle." Sonia was now three and a half years old, an age when children without complex backgrounds have a degree of ease with everyday transitions like these.

Difficulties with transitions are typical of most children as they become more independent. When a child learns to walk, or develops greater dexterity with his hands, he naturally begins to feel he is able to control a great deal of his life. As a child works on understanding his newfound autonomy and power, he is constantly swinging between feelings of "I'm the boss of the world" and "I am the boss of nothing and therefore completely helpless." As we have learned, young children think in absolute terms.

TRANSITIONS AND AUTONOMY

Transitions challenge a child's sense of autonomy and control. To the child, a transition is a change orchestrated by someone else, usually a parent. Transitions emphasize that a parent, not the child, is the boss.

Naturally, parents view transitions differently. Carolyn had no intention of diminishing her daughter's sense of independence, no thought of making Sonia feel helpless. Transitions are ordinary and simple, and they happen all the time.

They are the rhythm of the day, the necessary starting and stopping of activities and the movement from one activity to another.

PAST TRANSITIONS INFLUENCE NEW ONES

There are three reasons Sonia might have found transitions challenging, even threatening. First, they represent change, and a child like Sonia with a complex background associates even small changes with major life changes, including the adoption itself. It is hard for you to be in tune with your child's previous experiences of such life changes unless you spend time thinking about the loss and disorientation that those changes entailed. Once you focus on that, it should not be surprising that new experiences or transitions can trigger a continual state of hyper-alertness, or other reactive coping behaviors, in your child. These triggered responses can ultimately lead a child to avoid transitions and novelty on a regular basis.

Second, as a child becomes more independent, which of course is developmentally appropriate, transitions orchestrated by others threaten her sense of independence. "I want to decide!" Sonia announced. "I am the boss of my body. That's what my teacher said at school." A young child's literal application of these ideas to family life often leads to power struggles with a parent at transition points.

Third, transitions are stressful, and stress is unpleasant, so a child tries to avoid transitions as a way to minimize stress. This is a natural reaction, especially when a child is already engaged in a pleasant activity. However, it is harder to understand why a child would resist transitioning from breakfast to getting ready to go to the park, where the endpoint of the transition is something the child clearly desires. A child with a stress-shaped brain generalizes her avoidance of change and transitions to all situations, as a way to minimize stress reactions and reactive coping behaviors. Why try on new clothing when that causes stress and a loss of control? Better to stick with the same old corduroy pants or cotton dress and stay calm.

HOW TO MAKE TRANSITIONS EASIER

To help your child learn to handle transitions more easily, reduce the number of transitions and changes of activities to a minimum. This may mean giving up some scheduled activities and spending more extended and unscheduled time at home or at the park. I believe these two locations, along with the grocery store, are really all your child regularly needs during the first five years. There are enough daily transitions at home without creating more by adding multiple classes or playgroups. During the first year home, one special activity per week is enough until your child is comfortable managing transitions. You may have to cut back on your social schedule for a while, but it is worth it. Your child will be much more cooperative and pleasant when he is not overly stressed by frequent changes from one activity to the next.

Carolyn counted the number of daily transitions during which Sonia threw a tantrum. On a typical day, Sonia had swim class in the morning and preschool in the afternoon; then she and her mom went to the market to buy dinner. Swim class and preschool in one day is a lot for a young child, and both activities themselves contain many internal transitions. By the time Sonia got home she was ready to be done with transitions.

Talk to your child each morning about all the events that will happen that day. Conversations like these will increase your sensitivity to your child's experience in general and help your child anticipate the changes of a particular day. You may want to tell your child that you know he probably has to manage many more changes each day than he did in his foster home or orphanage.

"I know a day with swim class, preschool, and shopping must feel pretty busy to you," Carolyn told Sonia. "I remember in Guatemala at *la casa de su primera madre* [the house of your first mother], you spent every day just playing at home. Here with me, your *segunda mamá* [second mama], you have a lot of changes in just one day."

Use routines to make transitions go smoothly. Routines help a child predict what will come next and therefore offer him a sense of mental control. Sometimes a routine is the way a single activity is structured. For example, putting clothing on in a particular order—pants first, then shirt, then socks and shoes last—structures the activity of dressing. Once a given activity is done, you may find a "bridge routine" helpful, such as holding hands while walking to the car. This helps a child feel in control of the passage from one activity to the next one.

Routines help a child remain regulated emotionally and physically. The responsibility for regulation begins with the parent who establishes the routine. As the child follows the routine repeatedly, he learns to remain calm during a transition. In this way the responsibility for regulation shifts over time from the parent to the child.

Preschool teachers have found that combining a song with a transition is an extremely powerful way to help children through the rough spot. Why singing? It activates the "foot brake" (see chapter 13), to help a child slow down and remain in balance emotionally and behaviorally. Use a song you and your child like to sing, or make one up for common transitions such as leaving the house, taking a bath before bedtime, getting dressed, and so on. Carolyn and Sonia liked the singing idea and made up songs for each transition during their day.

MANAGING TRANSITIONS

1. Reduce the number of changes of activity and of location during each day.
2. Talk about how life before adoption was different, with fewer changes, than the child's present life. Listen to how your child feels about the differences.
3. Develop and use routines that act as a predictable, familiar bridge between two different activities.

CREATING AN EFFECTIVE BRIDGE ROUTINE

A routine replaces a direct order ("Clean up," "Take a bath," "Come to dinner") from the parent to the child. It creates a cooperative approach to transitions rather than a hierarchical one. Cooperation is a vital part of an interdependent relationship and an important social skill to model before a child goes to school. A cooperative routine is a unique strategy in that it supports *inter*dependence and *in*dependence simultaneously.

Here is a scheme for a bridge routine that makes use of a kitchen timer and a transitional song. I have seen this basic plan work many times, but feel free to modify the details in a way that works well for your child. A bridge routine begins with a preparation statement, a clear explanation of how the routine will proceed. Use the terms *first*, *next*, and *last* to sequence the routine so that your child knows what will happen at each step. Tell your child what the overall purpose of the bridge routine is. Carolyn, for example, told her daughter, "I have a new plan to help us when it's time to change from one activity to another."

Next, let your child know you are in tune with what is difficult for her. "I know you don't like to stop playing or being in the bathtub," you might say. "I can see that you would like that to go on and on."

Continue being in tune by predicting your child's positive response to the new plan: "I think you will like this plan and be good at it. It will help make changes easier."

Finally, explain the specifics of the plan: "*First*, I'll tell you that soon it will be time to stop playing [or bathing, or being at the park]. If you choose to stop right away, that's fine. But if you choose to keep going, we'll set the timer for three minutes more of fun."

Give your child a choice about when to stop. Stopping anytime before the timer goes off is acceptable. The choice gives some children a greater sense of autonomy. "I can stop myself," the child reasons. Other children prefer to wring every last second of play time from the experience.

Then say, "*Next*, when the timer rings, you and I will sing the cleanup song [or other song you and your child have agreed on for a given transition] as you put away the toys [or get out of the bath]."

At first a child may have difficulty following this step. Help a reluctant child comply. Needing help does not mean your child has failed; she just needs a lot of help because the task is difficult. In the early days or weeks of your bridge routine, count it as a success if your child does not collapse into a tantrum.

If you do need to help your child comply, accompany your actions with positive words, such as "You did a pretty good job. Next time you'll do even better." Or you might say, "It was hard for you, but you held yourself together." Perhaps most important, you, the parent, should remain neutral to positive about your child's behavior. This process takes time to learn.

The final step moves your child into the next activity. As you finish explaining the routine, simply say, "*Last*, you will sit down at the table [get dried off and put on fresh clothes, get in the car to go home, or the like]."

WHEN TRANSITION TROUBLES RETURN

There will be times, even after your child has mastered the key transition routines that divide his day, when he reverts to old transition difficulties. Be prepared for this to happen when there is extra stress or change in your child's life, and respond by modifying the relevant transition routines in a way that makes the change easier for your child. For example, through Sonia's school years, Carolyn noticed that her daughter's transitions from school to homework or from homework to dinnertime were difficult, with one exception. If Carolyn drove the afternoon carpool, Sonia was calmer and more flexible during these transitions. On the days when this was not possible, Carolyn eventually learned that it worked well to take a fifteen- or even thirty-minute break to do some "Ping-Pong" activity (see chapter 15) as a bridge before expecting Sonia to begin her homework. Combining play and a snack with an intensive mom-daughter connection experience released additional Parent Juice, which in turn helped Sonia ease through the transitions of the late afternoon.

TRANSITION AND SEPARATION

The transitions described in this chapter do not involve major physical separations between a parent and child, unlike going to daycare or school. It is important to keep in mind that even transitions that seemingly do not involve separation are in fact experienced as separations by internationally adopted children. Sonia, for example, did not want to separate from her toys and the comfort of her play. She did not want to separate from her cozy spot on the floor and move to a new location. Simply riding in the car, even with her mother, was a separation from home. She experienced getting out of the bath as a separation from the warm water. Although adults see these as ordinary changes of activity and location, a child with a complex background has less Parent Juice stored up and less control of her own behavior and emotions. As a result, internationally adopted children need more parental help and support with transitions.

STRENGTHENING THE MAGIC CIRCLE WITH CONSISTENCY

Just as routines help a child securely predict what will happen next, overall consistency in family life helps a child feel securely held within the Magic Circle (see chapter 9). Consistency means a child can count on a parent doing things the same way, or pretty much the same way, every time. Consistency helps build a child's sense of the safety of the Magic Circle, which extends beyond the immediate interaction between parent and child (which is what is most salient to an infant) to encompass the entirety of family life (which grows in importance as the child matures). A simple but valuable kind of consistency would be eating breakfast every day at the table, although the food may change from day to day. Other details might be consistently linked to this one; perhaps Mom always wears a bathrobe before breakfast and takes a shower in the morning. Later in the day, Dad might always come home before dinner. Along with more complex routines, these simple points of consistency help a child feel there is order and predictability, which is especially comforting to a child with a complex background. Pointing out these consistent parts of family life to your child each day, especially when your family life is particularly busy or in the midst of changes, helps him feel connected to you.

When a child has been overwhelmed with changes, he begins to develop a strong belief that change is the norm. Philosophically this may be an accurate description of the world, but a child from a complex background is too young to engage in philosophical thinking. Such a child needs to have a sense of stability, a sense that the world is consistent, in order to develop family skills. Without consistency, an adopted child relies on survival skills and coping behaviors.

No parent, no matter how organized, can be perfectly consistent. Nor should one try to be. However, more consistency in a family makes adjustment and development easier for a child from a complex background. Even small, ordinary inconsistencies can shake the world of a child who has lived through one or more major life changes. A child with a low-key temperament may be able to adjust to an inconsistent family life, but most children from complex backgrounds are high strung. A highly inconsistent family life can trigger even more controlling, oppositional behaviors, and lessen cooperation and calmness, especially if a child is temperamentally intense to begin with.

The consistent pattern at Sonia's house at bedtime helped her manage separation. At five months of family age, however, by which time Sonia knew the consistent routine well and was calmly in sync with it, she was disturbed when Carolyn began attending a book-group meeting once a month and left Sonia's father in charge. This small change, Carolyn and David could easily see, was an ominous signal to Sonia that bigger changes might be on the way.

Sonia began to shut down on Carolyn's book-club night, in anticipation of the trouble she expected to have at bedtime. When David told her to get ready for bed, she walked out of the bedroom, curled up on the living room couch, and refused to move. Increasingly angry, David pulled out every consequence he could think of, but Sonia ignored him in silence. Sonia frustrated her father for hours until Carolyn arrived home. With consistency restored, Sonia went to bed without fuss. That fixed the problem in the short term, but it was not a long-term solution. Over time David began to acknowledge verbally to Sonia that she must be worried that her mother's leaving was the sign of more changes. He explained that he would carry out the same bedtime routine as Carolyn and reassured Sonia that her mother would return. David began putting Sonia to bed several other nights during the week, even when Carolyn was present. After several weeks Sonia was able to engage in her bedtime routine smoothly with either parent.

Ronald Federici, a developmental psychologist who has worked with internationally adopted children, advocates and has used a method of ultra-consistency that deserves attention at this point. In his article in *International Adoption: Chal-*

lenges and Opportunities, Federici describes his method as "recreating the institutional setting and gradually detoxifying off of the institution." This means, in short, that some adopted children are so accustomed to rigid institutional routines that they simply must have very consistent routines right after their adoptions, until they learn that family life is less "toxic"—has more love, connection, and choice, and less loss, pain, and authoritarianism—than the orphanage. Federici recommends this method for adopted children who have come out of the most deprived, neglectful, and rigid orphanage conditions in Eastern Europe, who typically join their new families with behavioral and adjustment problems that need immediate attention. I strongly agree with Federici that for such children parents should *minimize stimulation*—make everything totally consistent and predictable, with virtually no surprises—in the first weeks home. Sometimes there are situations, as an adopted child grows older, when a return to minimal stimulation and very high consistency is necessary.

Federici's recommendations are for children who are severely affected by their pre-adoption backgrounds. The recommendations I provide here are for children who have been mildly to moderately affected by their complex background. If you feel that your child is severely affected, you may want to read Federici's article "Raising the Post-Institutionalized Child," which is posted on his website at http://www.drfederici.com/raising_child.htm. You may also wish to consult a psychologist or family therapist who specializes in adopted children.

WORK/LIFE ROUTINES

Almost all parents have special challenges connected with integrating child care and work. These challenges must be resolved, but sometimes the best-intentioned solutions turn out to be mistakes. In my work with families I often encounter three solutions that have significant pitfalls, especially in families with internationally adopted children. Decisions you make in these areas—how work hours and workdays are allocated, how many nonparental caregivers a child has, and working at home—have a tremendous impact on how easy or hard it is for a child to adjust to a daily routine and to the transitions within that routine.

A Few Long Workdays versus Working in Smaller Chunks Daily

Many parents decide that the best solution is to work two or three long days in order to have more full days at home with their child or children. For a parent this means switching roles less often. Nina, a mother in our First Year Home Group, once decided to do this, working two very long days per week. She had to get up at six in the morning on workdays, leaving the house before her son, Yi Sheng, awakened. She returned home after his bedtime, after a ten-hour workday. Nina tried this plan for three weeks.

Ultimately Nina realized that Yi Sheng needed to spend time with her every single day, and for at least several hours each day, in order to feel connected with her. He had begun staying up late to see her when she came home, demanding to sleep in her bed, and waking up early to catch her before she left for work. Being only five, he did not know which days were workdays, so he followed his special new schedule every day. He rapidly became sleep-deprived and cranky. He reverted to reactive coping behaviors, and he rarely interacted with Nina without throwing a tantrum. Nina concluded that her new work schedule was undermining Yi Sheng's connection with her.

The majority of internationally adopted infants and young children can manage a maximum of four hours away from Mom or Dad before reverting to coping behaviors. Some cannot tolerate even two or three hours, especially soon after a tentative connection starts to grow. Some infants and toddlers cannot tolerate even shorter amounts of time away—say, one to two hours daily—without failing to thrive. When Denise went to work for four hours a day, her son, Demetri, had six months of family age and had just begun to connect with her. In her absence he refused to eat, play, or sleep. He remained in a hyper-alert state, staring out the front window until she returned.

If you begin leaving your internationally adopted child within a month of becoming a family, she will not protest but will continue with survival skills and coping behaviors. This will be easy on you, but it is a disastrous start to a relationship. If instead you establish a connection by staying home for four to six months before returning to work, your child will become angry with you (because now she cares for you) and will revert to survival and coping behaviors. In short, going back to work, even part-time, when your child is in the process of learning to trust you is a risky decision. I advise the adoptive parents with whom I work to do whatever they can, including taking out a second mortgage or other loan, to cover themselves financially in order for one parent to stay at home during their child's first year.

Both Nina and Denise decided to arrange four-hour days at work. This schedule affected their children much less severely.

Many Caregivers or Just One?

When Denise went back to work, many of her friends wanted to be "aunts" or "uncles" to Demetri, and Denise decided to make use of all these helpers. She arranged a schedule according to which Demetri would be cared for at home by a different "aunt" or "uncle" each day.

Unfortunately, Demetri experienced this arrangement as an extension of the orphanage where he had lived in Russia, albeit a much more luxurious extension. He reverted to his indiscriminately friendly and performing behavior. His new caregivers found this cute and encouraged it, not realizing that it meant Demetri was becoming less, not more, connected with his mother. Fortunately, one of the friends eventually did become concerned and persuaded Denise to reconsider her child-care options. By limiting the number of caregivers to just three, including herself, Denise was able to help her son regain his connection to her. In addition, she worked with the other two caregivers to make sure they did not encourage survival or coping behaviors.

COMMON WORK/LIFE PITFALLS

1. Working fewer, longer days
2. Having too many different caregivers
3. Working at home

Working at Home

After taking her daughter, Mu Ling, out of a family daycare arrangement that was not working out, Meg decided to work at home, thereby combining child care and work. As a CPA she was able to move her small practice into an unoccupied extra bedroom and to do the majority of her client contact by phone. It seemed like a dream; she would save money on office rent and daycare at the same time. But even before the busy tax season rolled around, Meg found that dividing her attention between Mu Ling and her clients was difficult at best.

Mu Ling reverted to coping and survival skills. She engaged in risk taking to secure her mother's attention. Mu Ling's negative methods of controlling her mother's behavior led the two of them down the road from moderate difficulties into the severe realm. Mu Ling began to derive more "pleasure" from annoying than from pleasing her mother, and the family skills she had acquired fell by the wayside as she concentrated on "being bad" as a way to hold on to Mom.

Meg was angry, as she told me, that her best intentions to "be there for Mu Ling" resulted in her daughter "taking advantage of the situation" and "manipulating" her. When Meg and I untangled this upsetting situation together, I explained to her that it is better for a child from a complex background to have the full attention of whoever is caregiving. Thus, although working at home seemed like a good plan, it really was not going to help Mu Ling develop a positive connection with her mother. Meg needed to hire a caregiver for the hours she worked. If she wished to save rent by working at home, she would have to find an out-of-home care situation.

Working at home creates a confusing situation for any child, especially those under the age of five. The working parent is present physically yet not present emotionally or cognitively. This is too hard for even non-adopted children to manage. It is even more difficult for an adopted child, in particular one with fewer than two years of family age who is still working on forming a connection to a new parent. Having daycare and work in two different locations provides clarity for a child, even though separation is involved.

REAPPEARANCE OF COPING AND SURVIVAL SKILLS

Internationally adopted children often mistake daycare centers or preschools for orphanages or foster homes. Because this is so prevalent, it is important to watch for the reappearance of coping or survival skills when your child heads off to a group setting. Certain coping behaviors such as shutting down make a child easier to work with for teachers, who applaud the "quiet, well-behaved" child without recognizing that he has emotionally withdrawn from the present. Revving up or accelerating behaviors may cause a child to be labeled "hyperactive." Still other survival skills, such as clinging or inconsistent or difficult social relationships, can lead to other sorts of misdiagnoses by the staff or teachers.

I strongly encourage parents to limit the length of time a child attends daily preschool or daycare to four hours or less, if at all possible, until the child has been home for two or more years. Your child needs your one-to-one parenting to develop the family skills that will enable him to get the most from a preschool or daycare environment. If your child does not yet have these family skills, he is merely practicing survival and coping behaviors in a fancier but orphanage-like setting.

"I adopted a child because I wanted to be a mom," Denise once said in a gathering of parents from the First Year Home Group, "and I see that this is my time to do that. I'll have to find some financial way to scrape by."

"If I miss this time now with Mu Ling, we can never reclaim it. And we've already missed so much together," Meg said.

"It's hard to hear that I have to stay home and really work at teaching Yi Sheng family skills," Nina admitted. "But I understand that he'll just repeat his survival and coping skills if I send him to preschool. He's a master at cutting in line and getting his snack before anyone, but he isn't making friends."

These parents were coming to terms with the realities of parenting an internationally adopted child who needed extra time with and support from them. The good news, I can report, is that after a year or two of concerted effort, Demetri, Mu Ling, and Yi Sheng were able to attend daycare and preschool, where they used their newly acquired family skills. Their parents were so proud when they saw their children succeeding at what once had seemed an insurmountable task: growing up.

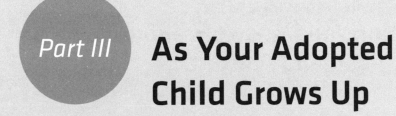

Part III **As Your Adopted Child Grows Up**

Questions and Answers about Birth, Past, and Present

WHEN WE TELL YOUNG ADOPTED CHILDREN their story—for example, when we use the Three-Photo Story or answer the Four Questions (see chapter 7)—we do so in terms of *a sequence of changes of caregivers* rather than in terms of *types of specific relationships*. In large part this is because these children do not have a grasp of basic human reproduction.

However, after a child reaches the age of three, parents can begin to introduce the concept of birth in order to help a child understand more about her own life. If you have adopted a child who is three or older, especially one who lived with a birth parent, you should introduce this information as soon as possible.

WHAT A THREE- TO FIVE-YEAR-OLD CHILD NEEDS TO KNOW

Sometime during a child's third or fourth year, he may ask, "Where did I come from?" If your child does not ask, you should offer the information anyway.

Children of this age need to know first that all people begin as babies. Second, they should be told that all babies grow in a special part of a mommy (not the "tummy" or "stomach") called a *womb* or *uterus*. Third, they should learn that when a baby comes out of the mommy this is called *birth*. Finally, they need to understand that some babies stay with their birth mommy and some babies do not. Once the child understands these two possibilities, you can explain that adoption provides a second mommy with whom a child grows up.

These four points will generate some basic questions from your adopted child for which you need to be prepared. The biggest and most important question of all is: "Mommy, did I grow in your body?" It may be of interest to you that non-adopted children do not ask this question. They know or assume they grew in Mom's body. Internationally adopted children have some deep sense that this is not true for them, so they ask the question.

Sometimes parents find it easier to explain this information using a simple children's book about birth. Nina had several such books for her older daughters which she shared with Yi Sheng, her son. The books were kept in his room. One morning Nina discovered that her son had "illustrated" them more to his liking. Yi Sheng had scribbled across the face of one pregnant mother and decorated several pages showing mothers and babies with Chinese stickers. Nina refrained from chastising her son and instead asked him to describe his feelings about the pictures. "I wonder how you were feeling when you drew over the mommy's face," she began.

"Are you mad, Mommy? I know it is wrong to write in books, but she didn't look Chinese," Yi Sheng explained. Nina found it instructive that although her older daughters were of mixed race, they had not been particularly bothered by the white racial images in the books. Perhaps this was because they still lived with their birth parents, whereas Yi Sheng did not. Thus it was more important for him to connect this book on birth to his own personal experience. "I want her to look like me, like my mommy looked," Yi Sheng told Nina.

Nina said, "I bet your mommy had beautiful black eyes and black hair like you, Yi Sheng. Would you tell me about her?"

"No, just one thing. She had long hair," her son replied, "and yours is short."

"I like the Chinese stickers you put on the book, to show this is about a Chinese boy like you," Nina said.

Yi Sheng smiled and cuddled close to his mother. "Will you read the book?" he asked.

"I WISH YOU HAD GROWN IN MY BODY, TOO"

Of course every adoptive parent must answer, "No you didn't grow inside me." But there is more that you can say. Most adopted children at some point say, "I wish I'd grown in your body." You can acknowledge to your child, "I wish you had grown in my body, too." Your mutual wishes are an important point of connection. The fact that you, the parent, also have a wish that did not come true creates a special connection between you and your child.

Make a connection based on shared loss.

Making connections with your child through loss is vital. Adoption and complex backgrounds are all about loss, about being rejected or feeling alone, about feeling different. If you and your child can share feelings about a loss that you have both experienced, albeit in different ways, you can create an unbreakable relationship. Loss is the yin of your connection's yang.

If you allow your child to be the only one coping with loss, whether the loss of a birth mother or her other losses, you enhance her feelings of being isolated and disconnected from you. I have seen in my work with adoptive families that this small omission can grow to tragic proportions. You think you are doing all the right things. You tell the story, you talk about the loss of the birth mom, and you wait for the child to express sorrow. But instead of moving closer, your child pulls away and stops asking questions. The old adage "A trouble shared is a trouble half endured" is true. Indeed, when the sharing is mutual, the trouble can become not just halfway but completely endurable. Your child needs you to share, just as your child herself needs to share, to make this relationship work.

The implications of this information about birth and reproduction cause children to rethink the Three-Photo Story. Soon An, for example, returned to the first photograph, which was of her foster mother, and reflected on how she was not her birth mother, and how her stay with this woman was just a way station. Although such a fact is obvious to an adult, it brings a new perspective to a young child that can shake her foundations like an earthquake. This emotional and cognitive upheaval is likely to cause fussiness, anger, and the child's rejection of her parent or of the topic.

Because Yi Sheng was older when he was adopted, his parents did not have to wait for him to grow up before explaining about birth parents and foster parents. This information helped him make sense of the jumble of events in his memory. In addition, telling the story helped Yi Sheng know that his adoptive parents were aware of his history, his complicated life. Having someone with whom to share it was a great relief to him; it is likely that no one had ever discussed these facts with him. Having this knowledge in common with his adoptive parents built Yi Sheng's trust and strong connection to them.

"WHY DIDN'T MY BIRTH MOMMY KEEP ME?"

Once a three- to five-year-old child understands that he did not grow inside his adoptive mother, his next move will be to look you in the eye and to ask the hardest question of all: "Why didn't my birth mommy keep me?" The first answer that occurs to many adoptive parents is some form of "It was because she loved you and wanted you to have a better life." I strongly advise against replying in this manner. To put it bluntly, your child will know right away that you are lying and that you have no idea what you are talking about. You, your child's adoptive parent, have modeled being a loving parent. If giving a child away is a sign of love, your child cannot believe all of *your* promises of a "forever family."

In fact, all of the standard answers to this difficult question present problems as a child matures and acquires a higher capacity for rational thought and analysis. Many families in China, for example, indeed keep their daughters, even paying fines in order to be allowed to keep a second, third, or even fourth child. A girl adopted from China will eventually learn this fact and may even discover specifically that her siblings were kept but she was relinquished. More generally, all children eventually notice that many poor mothers keep their children. Therefore, they wonder, how could poverty be the reason for their relinquishment?

Lois Melina, who has written extensively about adoption, has pointed out that no matter how carefully a parent constructs an explanation for a child's relinquishment, the pain is still present. Too facile an explanation to a young child can lead to more problems when he becomes a teenager and is trying to understand and identify with a birth parent.

How, then, does one answer this hardest of all questions? A child less than five cannot understand the precise political, legal, or personal details that were relevant to the birth parent's decision. But children do know about choices. It is a good choice to do what Mom says, for example, and a bad choice to ignore Dad's instructions. It is a good choice to hold hands when you cross the street, and a bad or dangerous choice to run across alone. I encourage parents to talk about how a birth parent had to make a "choice" and a "grownup decision."

No matter how carefully you construct and tell the story of your child's relinquishment, he still feels the pain of that event.

Keep in mind that young children think in absolute terms of good versus bad. If you compare the political or cultural systems of your child's birth country unfavorably to those of your country, your child could misconstrue your account; he may conclude that he was born in a "bad country." Hold off on these comparisons until your child is seven to nine years of age.

A child who was adopted in his toddler years or later may have memories of conversations or activities that shed light on his relinquishment. You can always ask a straightforward question, such as "How old were you when you went to the orphanage for the first time?" or "Were there any other children in your foster home?" Over the years you and your child will put the pieces together, acting as detectives to make sense out of them.

It is worth remembering that very few internationally adopted children came from comfortable homes with loving parents and only minor family problems (unless the children were kidnapped). Most children are from families who faced problems that adoptive parents can hardly imagine—war, widespread chronic and fatal illnesses with no care available, political oppression, or natural or man-made disasters—or from families in which parents made many poor choices, resulting in substance abuse or domestic violence. Although every adopted child eventually has to face the harsh reality that his birth parents were not fully in control of their lives or made bad choices, a three- to five-year-old child cannot achieve this depth of understanding.

"HOW DOES A BABY GET OUT OF THE MOMMY?"

I usually suggest that adoptive parents leave this important detail out of the initial discussion about birth and birth mothers, unless a child brings it up. The first four points that you need to get across are so hugely astounding to adopted children that it takes them a while to think through the implications. However, eventually you do need to answer this question, whether your child brings it up or not.

I encourage you to find a good children's book on birth with good drawings or photographs, such as Joanna Cole and Margaret Miller's *How You Were Born*. Be prepared for your normally careful-with-books child to have some strong feelings about this one, perhaps altering, doctoring, or embellishing it as Yi Sheng did. You can simply comment, "You must have had some strong feelings about this book. Maybe we can select a special drawing pad where you can express those feelings. I bet you know writing in books is not what we do in our family."

If you do not use a book, you can draw a simple picture of a woman's body. Show two spread legs and explain that there are three holes between the legs; expect lots of giggling and squirming as you do this. There is, you can say, the poop hole (this will get a big laugh), the pee hole, and the baby hole, which is between the other two. Explain that the baby hole, the vagina, is very stretchy (like the poop hole, in a child's experience), so that a baby can come out. Most children express both fascination and disgust. These are very appropriate reactions, which you can assure your child are acceptable.

CREATING DISTANCE FOR YOUR CHILD

It takes an adopted child several years to process this information and come to emotional terms with its implications. Questions your child hears, such as "Is that your real mother?" will keep the topic on the table. You need to model positive answers in public that say your child is adopted and is loved as much as any child, and in private you can give your child extra time to talk or draw about feelings. For single parents there are the additional questions about the missing dad or mom, and other questions arise about gay or lesbian couples; I do not address them here because the issues are not unique to internationally adopted children.

Sometimes a child resists discussions of the Big Change or the Four Questions (see chapter 7). The child may feel that the reality is too much; she may need you to help her create some distance from the weighty matters on her mind. You can take the pressure off your child by talking to a doll or puppet as your child's alter ego.

One day Yi Sheng complained that he did not have a real mommy. His adoptive mother spoke to Leo, the lion puppet that Yi Sheng favored. "Leo, it looks like it's hard to play today. Maybe something's on your mind that's troubling you," Nina said. She made the puppet nod. "Will you talk for Leo?" she asked Yi Sheng.

Yi Sheng took the puppet. He had the puppet hide its head and then run away. During this play Nina narrated what the puppet was doing. She took a couple of guesses at his feelings. "I don't think Leo wants to talk. Is he scared or sad?" Nina asked.

"He's scared!" Yi Sheng confided. Nina tuned in to Leo's fear. She reassured him and playfully offered Leo a Popsicle. Soon Leo wanted to talk. Yi Sheng told his mother, through the puppet, that he was scared because she had written a letter to the orphanage the day before. He was afraid the orphanage people would come and take him back. At this revelation Nina was able to reassure her son that he would never go back to the orphanage. Five minutes later Yi Sheng began playing happily again. He spent the afternoon building a long, complicated railroad track and running his train on it. Putting the pieces of the track and the cars of the train together was his way of playing about his feelings concerning the connection with his new parents.

Yi Sheng's healthy play behavior is typically the way internationally adopted children respond to hearing their own story. When a child grasps what happened to her, she is able to move forward with age-appropriate development in all areas. Providing your child with additional information about what happened in the past is good insurance for the future.

Separation and Reunion

AFTER THE EXPERIENCE OF THE BIG CHANGE most internationally adopted children are highly sensitive to even the prospect of separation, let alone the reality. *Separation anxiety*, *relinquishment sensitivity*, *excessive clinginess*, and *school refusal* are terms that therapists and counselors have used to describe separation issues. Separation is the obverse of connection; as a child's sense of connection with a parent increases, so do separation issues. If an internationally adopted child were to have no separation concerns, I would question the connection between that child and his parents. Moreover, a child with a complex background who does not have separation issues is equivalent to an adult who walks away feeling "just fine" from having totaled the car in a collision. This degree of denial about reality is ultimately not in the person's best interest.

There was no denial about separation in many phone calls I received from the former members of the First Year Home Group when their children were three to five. Denise, for example, once called to schedule a checkup appointment for her three-year-old son, Demetri.

"Demetri is being so clingy and difficult," she told me over the phone. "He used to love going to daycare, but now it's impossible to get him out of the house in the morning. He cries and begs me to stay home with him."

I received a call from Nina concerning Yi Sheng's "obsession" about saying goodbye. Once they left the house, Yi Sheng, at age five, waved and yelled goodbye continually until they pulled into the parking lot at school. Then he cried bitterly and told Nina, "I know I have to go to school. You want me to."

A third phone call was from Charlotte. Her daughter, Soon An, had suddenly become fearful of having Mom out of her sight. Charlotte wondered if this was related to an episode a few months earlier when she had sneaked out of the house after Soon An had fallen asleep, leaving Soon An alone with a babysitter.

My educated guess was that all three children were struggling with a combination of *ordinary separation issues* related to the growth of an interdependent connection with their parents, and *traumatic separation issues* associated with a complex background full of losses and separations.

PLAYING DETECTIVE: ASSESSING SEPARATION ISSUES

Parents and therapists, I have learned, need to play detective in order to figure out what is going on with separation. I ask four questions when I investigate separation issues:

1. What new things is your child doing or learning? Has she had a recent leap forward developmentally?
2. Has your child recently developed a deeper connection with a parent?
3. Have there been any changes in the family routine, especially in the comings and goings of the primary caregiving parent?
4. In what way might the current separation context resemble the child's experience of the Big Change or of pre-adoption changes?

If the answer to the first question is yes—the child has just learned to walk, climb, recite the alphabet, read, ride a tricycle or bicycle, ice skate, or swim, for example—I am usually able to reassure the parents that the separation anxiety is related to this new developmental leap forward. It is scary for an internationally adopted child to become more competent and independent. Doing so brings up fears of losing her parents; after all, the last time or times the child lost her caregivers coincided with a further step in growing up. Frequently such fear surfaces when a child awakens in the middle of the night and calls for a parent— another behavior associated with developmental leaps forward.

If this is the case with your child, reassure her that growing up, including the specific skill she has recently mastered, will not change or sever her relationship to you. With patience and reassurance, this kind of separation issue resolves relatively quickly.

If your child has been home for approximately nine months to a year, I expect the answer to question two to be yes. At about a year of family age a child typically has achieved a deep enough connection with a parent to express anxiety about being separated. But this intensification can happen at any time, and it typically does several times between ages three and five. Often when the parent-child relationship deepens, internationally adopted children become more anxious, at least for a while—the stronger the connection, the greater the worry that it will be lost. In contrast to a birth child, an internationally adopted child believes a parent might vanish at any time. When this belief surfaces, I advise parents to revisit with their child, patiently and thoroughly, the Four Questions: What happened to me? Who will take care of me now? Did I make the Big Change happen? Will everything change again, and will I lose you, too? (See chapter 7 for a full discussion of these questions and ways to answer them with a child.)

Denise told me that recently Demetri had been hugging and kissing her with genuine affection, saying, "Me love Mommy!" He also loved getting hugs in return. This intensified relationship was very likely the source of Demetri's clinginess and his reluctance to separate from his mom and go to daycare.

Sometimes the answer to question number three is yes. Mom has recently gone back to work, Dad has begun traveling more frequently, school has started, or some other event has occurred that stirs a child's fears of loss through separation. Charlotte admitted that her sneaking out, and Soon An awakening to the presence of the babysitter, was probably the trigger for Soon An's clingy behavior. In addition, Joe, Soon An's father, had been working more at night and the family schedule was disrupted.

If none of the first three questions elicits information that sheds light on a child's separation anxiety, I assume that question four holds the key. I ask parents to recall everything they can about the day they met their child. Sometimes we must examine every little detail before we discover that something in the present, such as getting new clothes or getting up earlier than usual, is similar to something that happened around the time of Adoption Day and therefore has triggered their child's separation anxiety.

Before we look in greater depth at how to address an internationally adopted child's separation anxiety, let us look briefly at how a child who does not have a complex background learns to deal with separation.

UNCOMPLICATED SEPARATION DEVELOPMENT

The ability to separate physically from a parent is a normal developmental task. An infant separated from a parent begins to cry and fuss; a toddler or preschooler cries when parents leave him with a babysitter in order to go out to eat by themselves. These behaviors are actually signs of physiological and emotional disorganization, or, as it is clinically termed, *dysregulation*, and a reversion to reactive coping behaviors (see chapter 5). Initially, separation causes the child to rev up, and if a parent does not reappear quickly, the child gradually changes gear and shuts down. What were long believed to be normal emotional reactions to a parent's absence are now known to be physiological signs of dysregulation.

As a child matures, he learns to manage emotions and behavior in an interdependent relationship with a parent, and he transitions from physiological reactions to emotional ones. The revving up at separation turns into anger and the shutting down turns into sadness. The developmental challenge of dealing with separation is for a child to manage these feelings and their associated behaviors.

It is appropriate for a young child to be sad or mad at separation and happy at reunion. It is inappropriate for a child to ignore a parent's departure, or to reject a parent or be sad when a parent returns. Successful separation development includes expressing the appropriate emotions in the proper order.

To evaluate separation development we look at how the child acts at the time of separation, how the child behaves when the parent is away, and how the child responds when the parent returns.

Understanding Separation

- How does the child behave at separation?
- How does the child behave when the parent is away?
- How does the child behave when the parent returns?

FIVE STAGES OF SEPARATION FOR INTERNATIONALLY ADOPTED CHILDREN

When Demetri first became Denise's son, he ignored her departures, engaging in his revving behaviors. He gave no sign of noticing when she returned.

Such behavior can mislead parents. Denise was delighted that separations were so easy, and she wondered why there were so many concerns about adopted children and separation. Eighteen months later, however, she discovered that things had changed, and that Demetri now indeed was challenged by separation. He had become connected to Denise, and he objected firmly when she had to go.

Looking back, Denise realized that her son had not been connected with her for the many months during which separations went smoothly. Now he was. From Denise's description I was able to tell her that Demetri had moved from stage one to stage two of the five stages of separation through which most international adoptees pass.

FIVE STAGES OF SEPARATION

1. Child ignores parent's departures and returns. When parent is absent, child's play is the same as when parent is present.
2. Child reverts to coping behaviors of revving up or shutting down when parent leaves; child has difficulty engaging in play during separation; child either rejects parent upon return or becomes very clingy.
3. Child cries sadly, but does not shut down, when parent leaves. Child engages in low-key play during separation and is angry or rejecting at reunion.
4. Child is visibly sad at parent's departure but cries minimally; child recovers quickly and is able to play normally. Child is happy to see parent return.
5. Child is able to separate smoothly without overt sorrow, plays well during parent's absence, and is relaxed and able to reunite smoothly at parent's return.

The second stage of separation is the most volatile. The child engages in uncontrolled coping behaviors (of acceleration or of shutting down) that are difficult to change. The child screams, kicks, clings, throws a tantrum, or begs a parent to stay. While the parent is away the child may shut down and be unable to play, or may rev up and be excessively active. The "foot brake" of emotional control is not engaged (see chapter 13). At reunion the child may cling to the parent and stay extra close for hours. Demetri, for example, threw a tantrum when Denise left, revved up while she was away, and shadowed her closely when she returned.

In the third developmental stage of separation a child shifts from coping to the modulation of intense emotions of sadness or anger. Nina reported this behavior with her son, Yi Sheng, who cried bitterly and clung to her when it was time to go into the school building. But once he went inside, he pulled himself together and participated fully. Reunion at the end of the school day was still difficult: When Mom came to pick him up, he lashed out at her angrily and was uncooperative.

During the fourth stage of separation the child is able to express sadness and anger appropriately when a parent leaves, usually in a fully worded sentence. "You are making me very, very sad, Daddy! I don't like you when you leave," the child might say. However, once the parent departs the child plays comfortably and happily greets the parent when it is time to reunite. This fourth stage features appropriate and well-expressed emotions.

By the fifth stage a child has a level of trust and confidence that enables her to separate without dwelling on sadness or anger. At this stage a child plays comfortably during the parent's absence and experiences a happy reunion. The smooth quality of the transitions, the result of a combination of the child's own emotional self-regulation and her trust in the relationship's continuity, is the key to the fifth stage.

Developmentally, separation continues to be a major issue at many junctures throughout childhood and into adolescence and beyond. It is center stage when a child of any age makes a developmental leap forward. You can expect separation issues when your child starts high school, leaves for college, gets her first job, becomes engaged, gets married, and starts a family.

"INSTITUTIONAL" REMINDERS

As we have seen, because every internationally adopted child experienced permanent separation from former caregivers at least once, every new separation, no matter how small or ordinary, may evoke fear and anxiety. When adoptive parents forget about this aspect of separation, they treat separation development as something easy and ordinary. Denise said to me, "I tried to reassure Demetri it was just a couple of hours at daycare, that it was no big deal, but he became even more anxious." Statements like this can make a child feel dismissed and can lead to a negative self-image. "What's wrong with me? Why can't I just separate comfortably like Mom wants me to?" the child wonders. In turn, the child becomes angry and reverts to coping behaviors, including tantrums and emotional withdrawal, just when we want to encourage him to connect more deeply.

An "institutional" place—one with many children, several adults, and multiple rooms—can be reminiscent of an orphanage or even a foster home. Time and again, adult and older adoptees describe how a school has reminded them of such an institution. This memory triggers post-traumatic stress feelings and behavior, which include outbursts of anger, a sense of déjà vu, and the fear that permanent separation is about to happen again.

If you are fortunate enough to have gone to or learned about your child's orphanage or foster home, examine that setting in your or your child's memory, or in photographs or videos that you might have, for clues to what triggers your child's upset. In the box below are some suggestions to guide you. Use these to open a conversation with your child about what might seem "familiar," or like something one might encounter in Russia, China, Guatemala, and so on.

SOME DAYCARE OR SCHOOL REMINDERS OF PRE-ADOPTION LIFE

- Appearance of teachers, other caregivers: check hair, glasses, age, other characteristics
- Structure of building: wood, concrete, one- or two-story, multiple rooms in a row, and the like
- Several adults, each assigned to a group of children
- Lines of children; silence, or lots of noise, in the line
- Lunchroom, playground, and other common spaces

Nina asked Yi Sheng what bothered him most about school. He told her that the kids running around on the playground, which was what he saw each morning when he arrived at school, reminded him of the orphanage where he had been. Nina sympathized with him concerning how it must feel to go to a place that looked like the orphanage. Together mother and son brainstormed and decided that Yi Sheng would enter the school from the other side of the building, not the playground side, and go directly to the classroom. Doing this helped Yi Sheng feel less anxious about school. But it did not stop him from saying "goodbye" all the way from home until they reached school.

Denise discovered that Demetri thought that his teacher, an older woman with glasses, looked like one of the caregivers at his orphanage. Denise got out her video of the adoption trip and together they looked for that particular caregiver. Although they did not find her, Denise encouraged Demetri to help her draw a picture of the woman at the orphanage and of his teacher. Together they focused on the similarities and differences, in terms of hair, glasses, nose, clothing, the countries in which the women lived, and other features.

Neither of these parental interventions completely solved the children's problems, but they helped put parent and child on the same page and gave them a starting point from which they could work together further. In general, the strongest intervention is to make the present different from the past, even if the present still carries reminders of the past. Making the present different from the past helps reduce the trigger effect and enables the child to be more comfortable.

When an important part of the child's current environment reminds him of the past, his ability to manage separation is diminished. Institutional reminders of this kind can make a child who is at stage four or five of separation regress to stage two or three. To help a child regain the lost skills, parents can use some of these techniques: playing with a Slinky; encouraging the use of cuddlies as a method of scaffolding; and telling social stories.

Using a Slinky to Get a Grip on Separation

As we have seen in our discussions of younger children, the Slinky is an ideal toy for working on separation. There is no reason you cannot bring back the Slinky with three- to five-year-olds who have been home more than a year. When you talk about the Big Change, the Slinky can show "away and *not* back." To establish contrast, when you talk about going to daycare, having a babysitter, or going to school, you can show your child "away and *back*." In both cases your child can use the Slinky to "talk" about a separation beforehand, to play about it during the period of separation, and to talk about it again afterward. Overall, the Slinky helps show your child that she is in control, unlike the past, when she had no control of her fate at all.

Cuddlies, Mental Pictures, and Object Constancy

Child development books often speak about *object constancy*, the ability of a child to remember that an object or person exists even when it is absent or not visible. A simple example is hiding a child's toy under a box. A child without object constancy believes the toy has vanished. A child who has developed object constancy flips over the box and reveals the toy. When a parent goes away, a child with object constancy theoretically should remember the parent and wait for the parent to reappear. But real life is different.

Object constancy depends on a child's ability to form and keep a mental picture of the parent. If he can do so, he can draw comfort from the picture even when the parent is away. But forming a mental picture is an abstract skill. The development of object constancy is usually preceded by a period in which a child is attached to concrete and tactile, not abstract and mental, reminders of a parent. These concrete reminders are often called *cuddlies*. For example, a well-worn blanket or stuffed animal may be a young child's constant companion. Such items substitute for a parent in the parent's absence and offer the child reassurance. A parent can encourage a child to use a cuddly to help the child maintain a "picture" of the parent in his mind.

Object constancy with regard to parents can be delayed in internationally adopted children. The reason is that it is often difficult to get a child with a complex background into and through the cuddly stage. Once an internationally adopted child has connected with a parent, he does not easily accept a cuddly as a parent substitute. Normally a cuddly is acceptable to a child during a parental absence because the child trusts that the parent will return. However, a child who had many "substitute" parents is unlikely to want another substitute now that he has the "real thing." Accepting a substitute may even suggest that the parent can or will vanish. In this case the cuddly evokes loss, not reassurance.

Scaffolding the Acceptance of Cuddlies

To develop the use of a cuddly with your child, you need to put in place a series of preliminary steps in a process called *scaffolding*. The idea of scaffolding is to build a bridge from where the child already is competent to the next level of accomplishment.

The first step is for you and your child to have an interdependent relationship, one that has existed for long enough that the child truly relies on you. You must directly and sensitively address your child's fear of losing you before you will be able to get her to accept a cuddly. This means returning to the Four Questions (see chapter 7) and making sure your child is comfortable with the answers you have worked out. Stage two of separation (see the box on page 246) is an excellent time to *introduce* a cuddly, but do not expect your child actually to *use* it until she is at stage three or even stage four of separation development.

The Sweaty Shirt Strategy

This is a strategy that you can try beginning at stage two of separation development. The parents with whom I work use this when their children reject the introduction of impersonal cuddlies such as stuffed animals or blankets. It is a second step in the scaffolding for your child's eventual acceptance of a blanket or stuffed animal.

The earliest and most powerful way we identify others, especially those with whom we are intimate, is by smell. Each person has a unique scent, and your child will recognize yours if he is connected to you. Make sure your child knows how you smell; play a smelling game and see if you and your child smell the same or different. Do you smell different at different times of day? Do you smell different after eating? Be persistent until your child finds your odor familiar.

Next, take an old T-shirt that you are willing to give up and rub it on your body, especially under your arms. Show your child that this shirt smells like you. Each of you must take a big sniff. Tell your child that this shirt is *for him*, to keep and smell when you are not there. For example, if he wakes in the middle of the night, he can smell the shirt, feel close to you, and go back to sleep.

When you hold your child, hold the shirt as well. Keep it with you when you travel in the car, go to Grandma's house, or simply go from room to room in your house with your child. Put it to bed with your child, and hang it on the high chair while he eats dinner. This imbues the shirt with your relationship as well as your odor. Teach your child to keep the shirt with him when you are apart. It will become his first safe cuddly and his reassurance that you will be back.

This strategy takes time to develop. Begin it as soon as possible, but it is never too late if you have not done so already. If your three- to five-year-old does not yet have a favorite blanket or stuffed animal, try the sweaty shirt strategy.

Choosing or Making a Cuddly

The next scaffolding step involves helping your child to pick out a cuddly animal or blanket for herself. Mu Ling, for example, "fell in love with a black Labrador dog puppet," according to her mother Meg. "She said it has black fur just like she has black hair. She named the dog Lili and carries it everywhere. Somehow this puppet makes her feel safe, even when I have to leave her with the babysitter."

Nina explained that Yi Sheng had no interest in stuffed animals or her sweaty T-shirt. But one day when she happened to be at a fabric store, Yi Sheng figured out his own version of a cuddly. "Yi Sheng pulled me over to the silk department. He pointed to some smooth white silk and said, 'Like China.' It occurred to me that he might like a small silk blanket. So I bought half a yard of the silk and put a soft flannel backing on it to make a small blanket. Yi Sheng loved it and carried it everywhere."

Sonia's mother had brought back lengths of woven Guatemalan material when she adopted Sonia. Sonia chose her favorite pattern and Carolyn made her daughter a small *rebozo*, a Guatemalan shawl, to wear or carry with her. Sonia loved the familiar design from her birth country and the fact that it began to smell like her second mama.

In all of these instances the children became attached to a treasured object. The parents then had to encourage their child to link the object with the image of a parent's soothing presence while the child was separated from the parent. The combination of something old or remembered from a child's homeland and something new made by a parent becomes a tangible bridge connecting the past to the present and the parent to the child. If you did not bring back a length of cloth from your child's home country, look for similar material at your local fabric store or go to an ethnic store to find what you need.

Photo "Cuddlies"

A photograph of your family is a tangible object that a child can carry in his pocket or backpack. A photo cuddly is another scaffolding step toward the child's full internalization of the parent's soothing image during a separation. The photo should be recent and feature all the family members together with your child. Choosing a photograph together is a good way to open a conversation with your child about separation; children from three to five love to talk with parents about photos. Share the feelings that you have when you are separated from your child: sadness, missing him, perhaps anger that you have to part when you would rather be together. Tell your child how you want him to use this cuddly. "You can keep this in your pocket or backpack," you can say. "If you miss me, take it out and say hello. Look at how we are all together. This photo can remind you that every day, at the end of the day, our family will come back together again."

Denise took Demetri to a photo booth and they took a strip of photos for him to keep in his backpack at daycare. They took a second strip of photos for Denise to keep in her purse when she went to work. Demetri loved the fact that he and his mother each had a photo strip—a parallel experience that demonstrated their special connection. When they first looked at the strips together, Denise let her son know she missed him and thought about him when she was at work, just as he missed and thought about her at daycare. This was news to Demetri. He could not imagine that his mother actually thought about him when he was away from her. Many internationally adopted children struggle with the belief that other people remember or care about them. This conversation made the strips even more special; they became a reminder that Demetri's mother did remember him.

Older children extrapolate from this kind of dialogue about remembering and wonder if their birth parents remember them. This poignant worry often exposes the child's belief that no one will remember him, and the child wonders, "If my birth mother doesn't remember me, how can a 'stranger,' an adoptive parent, do so?" The best way to resolve this worry is simply to reassure your child that you do think about him when you are away. A call from work to preschool or home to say hello is a way to confirm this fact.

Getting your child to the point at which he accepts and uses a cuddly involves several scaffolding steps. Beyond that, the use of the cuddly itself is one of many scaffolding steps that will enable your child to progress through the five steps of separation. Putting feelings into words and sharing those feelings help a child move from his present comfort zone to a more advanced developmental level. There are times when a three- to five-year-old child refuses to talk, refuses to elaborate or discuss feelings. Then the very best thing to do is acknowledge to your child that "these feelings are very hard to talk about." Sit together and think about that.

Such conversations may be daily fare for a while, as your child begins to progress through the stages of separation. A particularly good time for conversations like these is at bath time or bedtime, when you and your child can look back over the day and trace the separations, the times apart, and the reunions, along with each person's feelings during each phase.

Social Stories

Social stories help young children develop self-regulation, memory, and empathy. As we have seen, when a child can anticipate and predict what will occur, she feels more in control and is better able to maintain emotional balance. The social story is an excellent tool for helping a child who has difficulties with separations and transitions.

Social stories are told from the child's perspective. A social story talks about a child's feelings, including negative ones, but it also communicates a positive expectation that the child is able to manage those feelings. This perspective helps a child recognize and regulate her own emotions. A social story might begin, for example, with "I feel mad when I have to clean up my toys and I want to keep playing."

Social stories incorporate a parent's point of view as well. The parent and the child decide together what the story will say. It might include cultural values that adults want to convey. "Mommy wants our home to be safe," the story might say. "When I clean up my toys, no one will trip on them. I can help keep my home safe."

Social stories help children recognize social cues, especially those that reinforce a child's positive connection with a parent or teacher. As a child goes through the three-to-five years, she encounters more and more categories of nonparental adults, all of whom have their own sets of cues about limits and expectations. When a child becomes upset about a limit, she often misses positive or encouraging social cues, such as a warm smile. In such a case the social story might emphasize that "my teacher smiles at me when I clean up my desk."

Social stories provide predictability on many levels. A story informs the child what is going to happen, how she may feel, what is expected of her, important social cues to note, and how a good behavior choice will be rewarded.

Here is an example of how Carolyn developed a social story with Sonia when her daughter was four years old.

"Once upon a time there was a little girl named—" Carolyn paused and waited for Sonia to offer a name.

"Sonia!" said Sonia with delight. "Is this story about me?"

"Yes," Carolyn replied. "One evening Sonia was playing with her toys. When it's time for dinner we have to put our toys away." At this point Carolyn began weaving in information about what had just taken place, which was that Sonia had refused to pick up her toys.

"But Sonia didn't want to clean up her toys," Carolyn said. "Sonia was sad. She didn't want to say goodbye to her toys. But Mommy said, 'Putting toys away keeps us safe. We won't trip on toys if they are put away.'"

Sonia jumped in to continue the story, "So Sonia put the toys carefully away."

Then Sonia said she wanted to hear the story again. Over time Carolyn worked with Sonia to tell social stories not just retrospectively, after something had gone wrong, but prospectively, to teach Sonia how to anticipate and predict, and thereby feel a sense of control and balance in the face of a separation from her toys.

As you tell these kinds of social stories to your internationally adopted child, you will find two things. First, you need to repeat the stories often. Second, your child may not be very good at generalizing from a specific story like this one to other kinds of separations and transitions in her life—even ones that seem very similar to you. Instead, you will have to construct new social stories for each unique subject and context.

PUTTING ANGER FIRST

Let us return now to Nina and her son, Yi Sheng. As I worked with them, we explored the possibility that some of Yi Sheng's troubles with separations could be traced to his never having had the chance to say goodbye to the people he had left behind. Internationally adopted children often have a lot of missed goodbyes in their pasts. We found that Yi Sheng wished he had had a chance to say goodbye to his Chinese father. Nina suggested that he write or draw a note to this man, and Yi Sheng agreed.

Nina called to fill me in on the picture-drawing session. Yi Sheng was able to express in the picture, and then in words, how angry he was that a Chinese family did not adopt him in China. Nina pursued the subject with humor. "I guess you were pretty disappointed to get a person like me for your mom," she told him empathetically. "If I were Chinese, I'd want a Chinese mom, too."

Yi Sheng nodded in agreement and, surprisingly for Nina, without apparent hostility.

"Is that why you are so angry whenever I come home? Are you hoping I'll come home and be Chinese?" Nina asked, imagining how a child might use magical thinking to wish for what was lost.

Yi Sheng looked up at Nina with a deeply sad expression, which slowly changed into a big, happy grin. He put his arms around his new mom and said, "I love you."

"What did that mean?" Nina asked me.

Yi Sheng had stored up anger and disappointment, just as Nina had suspected. He was old enough to understand what he had lost and to wish for it to return. But what brought the grin to his face and his heartfelt statement of love was that he now knew that his new mother understood those feelings. Yi Sheng was no longer alone with his sad and angry thoughts; he had an understanding parent with whom he could share his deepest feelings.

When a parent "tunes in" accurately—"hits the nail on the head"—a child often shifts from sad or angry feelings to loving ones. Moments like this require parents to set their own personal feelings aside for a time while they tune in to a child's greater need. Later, you may want to revisit your own feelings about your child's anguish, both your relief that your child has expressed his deepest concerns to you as well as your grief over the losses in his past.

HELPING SOON AN RECUPERATE

Now let us return to Soon An's difficulties with separation. Her excessive clinginess was indeed the result of a rash decision on Charlotte's part to sneak out, leaving a sleeping Soon An with a babysitter. When Soon An woke up, she called for Mom, then searched the house. She became hysterical. The sitter was unable to comfort her, and when Charlotte finally returned, Soon An frantically attached herself to her. Soon An had always been a good sleeper, but now she began to wake up every two hours at night.

As Charlotte and I talked, Charlotte admitted that it was a mistake to sneak out. What puzzled her was how persistent and long-lasting Soon An's response turned out to be. "It was just *one* time," Charlotte wailed. Soon An's nightly awakenings were a symptom of separation anxiety stirred up by her having "lost" Mom for a few hours.

Psychological researchers have been able to determine that it takes just a single deeply fearful triggering event to teach the brain to be on the lookout for similar events in the future. One traumatic event can powerfully affect a person's life far into the future. Soon An was now hyper-alert, actually expecting that Mom would vanish, even though there had been hundreds of days when Mom was consistently present.

Every parent makes mistakes. The important thing is to acknowledge the error and then begin repairing it. Charlotte needed two methods of repair. The first was for her to get in tune with Soon An, to acknowledge Soon An's deep separation anxiety and its origin. The second strategy was to help Soon An reduce her hyper-alert state and desensitize her to separation from Mom in tiny, incremental steps. This strategy would work only if Soon An could be made to believe her mother's promise to never sneak out again.

Sitting together with me and her daughter, Charlotte explained to Soon An how sorry she was that she frightened Soon An by sneaking out. "I won't ever leave without telling you," Charlotte reassured her daughter. Soon An looked at her mother solemnly. Her eyes began to tear up.

Later I suggested to Charlotte that she wait at least several days to give Soon An the opportunity to see and experience that Charlotte was trustworthy again, by making a point of telling Soon An every time she left the room or the house. In addition, Soon An needed to be reminded of Charlotte's promise. I encouraged Charlotte to increase the number of soothing and calming activities to help alleviate Soon An's hyper-alert state.

The *desensitization* process is borrowed from cognitive-behavioral therapy and adapted for use between a parent and a young child. In cognitive-behavioral therapy with adults, visualization is used to help the person become comfortable with anxiety-provoking material. For a child we substitute doll play for visualization.

The first week of the desensitization work began with Charlotte and Soon An each holding a doll. The two dolls were connected by a Slinky. Each day Soon An moved the dolls a little farther apart. During this time Soon An was in control: She could make the dolls stay close together or move farther apart. This play required Soon An and her mother to move apart as well.

The following week Soon An and Charlotte held the dolls, still connected by the Slinky, around the corner of a wall from each other. They peeked at each other whenever they got "nervous" or "anxious." The third week, they were positioned so that one doll was in a hall and the other was in an adjacent room. Again, Soon An and her mother had the dolls check in with each other when they "felt" separated and afraid.

This technique is more effective than, say, using a reward for not being clingy, because it actually creates a new pathway in the brain. The new pathway provides an alternative to hyper-alertness, in the form of a calm response to separation, and repeated practice increases the likelihood that a child will use this alternative pathway. For Charlotte and Soon An, the desensitization method continued to build the interdependent relationship that took a blow when Charlotte snuck out. This method may sound slow and laborious, but it will work if you stick to it.

DOUBLE SEPARATION ANXIETY: CHILD-AND-PARENT SYMMETRY

Sometimes parents, too, struggle with separation anxiety. It is extra difficult for an anxious parent to reassure a child that everything will be all right, because the child is likely to sense the parent's anxiety. Charlotte confided to me sometime later that she herself was anxious about leaving Soon An because of her own frightening experience as a child. Her mother had left her with a neighbor while Charlotte was asleep, and Charlotte woke up and was frightened. "And then," she said, "I went and did a similar thing to my daughter!"

The fact that Charlotte had *not* thought of this incident in years is probably why she repeated it with her own child. When we remember painful past events we are less likely to repeat them. On the other hand, remembering has its own limitations.

For example, Kenji found it hard to take Yi Sheng to school because Kenji's own father had died when he was a boy. It helped Kenji to have Nina, his wife, work on the separation issues with Yi Sheng. Still, Kenji was able to reassure Yi Sheng that even though a father dies, a person can still grow up and have a good, happy life. Kenji was proof of this.

Guiding your internationally adopted child through the stages of separation is likely to open up your own life story, with all of its moments of separation and loss, large or small. This makes separation work with your child doubly difficult but when it is mastered, doubly rewarding.

ADOPTION ISSUES FROM THREE TO FIVE

Dictators and Bosses

"MU LING HAS ALWAYS BEEN DEMANDING," Meg commented to me one day about her daughter, "but her current behavior seems more extreme than it was a year ago. What's going on?"

When you begin to notice that your child is particularly demanding and expects you to do everything for her, you can be assured that you have taught her that you are a consistent and reliable caregiver. In turn, she has learned to depend on you. All joking aside, your child's dictatorial behavior illustrates your success in forming an interdependent relationship with your child. Your child believes she is the center of your world. "Dictatorship" in a baby or young child is a normal stage. So celebrate! You have reached a milestone of interdependence.

DETHRONING THE DICTATOR

A key to parenting your three- to five-year-old internationally adopted child is helping the child learn that the two of you are interdependent people, separate yet interconnected. How far you have—or have not—come in this area emerges in the ways your child pays attention to you and how that attention feels. If you and your child are having fun together, and your child shows interest in you and your activities and follows you, you have an interdependent relationship. If your child generally ignores you, except when struggling with you for control, you have not developed a give-and-take relationship; you are still just living together.

When Meg and her daughter came to my office for a checkup visit eighteen months after adoption, I could see that Meg had done an excellent job of parenting. She had created both an interdependent relationship with her daughter— and a minor dictator.

A recent incident exemplified Mu Ling's behavior at four years of age. Meg began as soon as she came into the playroom at my office. "It just happened on the way over here," she said. "I was driving and Mu Ling wanted some gum. The gum was in my purse on the floor of the front seat. Mu Ling was in her car seat in the back. I told Mu Ling clearly that I couldn't reach the gum and that it was too dangerous to get it while I was driving. I promised she'd have gum when we parked the car. Mu Ling began yelling and kicking the seat in front of her. I am ashamed to say that I ultimately resorted to threatening escalating consequences and shouting at her. I felt angry and helpless," Meg concluded. Then she whispered, "I think she's become a monster."

I assured Meg that Mu Ling was no monster and that her behavior showed me that in fact Mu Ling felt very connected to her mommy. I complimented Meg. The two were so connected that Mu Ling treated her mother like an extension of herself, like an arm that could be commanded and would obey.

But when a part of your body does not respond to your commands, you feel angry and helpless. Because Mu Ling viewed her mom as an extension of herself, she felt angry and helpless and induced the same feelings in Meg.

I suggested to Meg that we first check out my theory with a brief test. This is a test you can use at home to assess your own child, but be careful how you word your questions so that you do not inadvertently suggest the correct answer to your child.

Mu Ling was playing on the floor with a car and some blocks a few feet away from her mother. She made the car roll over the blocks and then crash into them. Then she rearranged the blocks.

"Who is moving the blocks and the car?" I asked Mu Ling. Mu Ling was silent, and then she looked confused and looked at her mother. I gently repeated the question.

"Mommy," Mu Ling answered. She continued moving the car and driving over the blocks.

"You mean Mommy's hand is moving the car and the blocks?"

"Uh-huh," Mu Ling agreed.

Meg looked at me with surprise. I was surprised, too, although I had heard this same kind of response before from other children who behave as if their mom or dad is a "third arm."

"Mu Ling, will you look at your mom's hands?" I asked. Mu Ling looked. "Now look at your own hands," I told her, and she did. "Whose hands are moving the toys?" I asked.

This time Mu Ling looked exceedingly confused. She turned and crawled into Meg's lap. Her behavior revealed the conflict between her internal feelings that Mom was in control of the toys and her observation of her own hands.

I asked Meg what kinds of things Mu Ling asked to do for herself. Meg admitted that more often than not Mu Ling demanded that a parent do things for her. For example, if a toy was across the room, Mu Ling ordered, "Get my doll!" If she felt thirsty she announced, "I want water," with the implied demand for service.

"Don't worry," I told Meg, "We are going to use the Third-Arm Cure. Within a week everything will begin to improve."

THE THIRD-ARM CURE FOR SMALL DICTATORS

When an adopted child becomes a dictator, I encourage the use of what I call the Third-Arm Cure. The cure has two parts. The first is to define the differences between parent and child as they arise during daily routines.

"This is Mommy's nose; this is Mu Ling's nose" points to physical differences.

"Mommy's hands are pouring the soy milk; Mu Ling's hands are holding the cracker" points to differences in activities and roles.

"Mommy wants Mu Ling to drink soy milk; Mu Ling wants to drink juice" points to differences in wants and desires.

The second part of the cure is reassuring the child that difference does not mean a loss of connection or loss of care for the child:

"Mommy's eyes are blue; Mu Ling's are brown. We are different but we still love each other."

"Mommy pours the milk and Mu Ling eats a cracker. We do different things, but we still love each other. We still are connected."

"Mommy likes to drink soy milk and Mu Ling likes juice best. We like different things to drink, but we still love each other."

Although these statements sound simplistic and repetitive, you will be surprised and delighted to find that young children love to hear words like this over and over again. Reassurance of love despite differences is vital. It helps an internationally adopted child distinguish between being different and becoming disconnected. If a child cannot make this distinction, he feels compelled to remain "one" with a parent at all times, either by continually dictating to or perpetually clinging to the parent. In either case, when the drive for autonomy erupts, as it eventually will, there will be negative consequences if it is based on either of these falsely constructed relationships.

Recognizing differences without losing connection provides the foundation for a child's successful adjustment to limits and consequences. If a child experiences a difference with a parent as a loss of love, he will certainly experience a limit as rejection. This can become a particularly difficult situation in the teen years (see chapter 29).

The refusal or hesitation to separate either physically or psychologically from a parent is one of the primary developmental obstacles for an internationally adopted child.

PUTTING THE THIRD-ARM CURE INTO EVERYDAY PRACTICE

I decided to begin the Third-Arm Cure immediately with Meg and Mu Ling. As they sat together on the floor, I encouraged Meg to narrate the differences she observed between herself and her daughter.

Meg said, "I am sitting on the floor. Mu Ling is sitting on the floor. We are both sitting on the floor. But we are doing different things. My hands are holding a notepad, and Mu Ling's hands are holding a block."

My prescription for Meg was to continue narrating as much as possible throughout the day for one week. Narration of whatever happens to be going on is more natural than launching into a speech, as it were, about parent-child differences. I suggested that whenever Mu Ling became demanding, Meg should narrate Mu Ling's desire as compared to her own. She must teach Laura, Mu Ling's other mother, to do the same, so that they could make sure that Mu Ling learned to differentiate from both parents. After Laura, Meg, and Mu Ling had these conversations for a full week, Mu Ling realized that her independence and autonomy would not destroy her relationship with either of her parents. She began to drop her dictatorial stance and revel in differences between herself and her parents.

WHO IS THE BOSS?

As Mu Ling got more comfortable with differences, her exploratory behavior exploded into action. She wanted to do everything herself.

When something like this happens, parents need to switch from setting limits on demanding behavior to scaffolding—breaking tasks into smaller steps that a child can manage, so that she gains confidence in her autonomy. For example, a child wants to dress herself but first needs to learn how to put a shirt on right side out, or to navigate the complexity of buttons. Of course some activities, such as using a ladder to get things off a high shelf, may still need limits for safety reasons, even when a child is able to "do it myself."

New challenging behaviors emerge as demanding behavior subsides and differentiation begins. Expect your child to engage in more autonomous and independent activity and to insist, "I want to do it myself!"

As a child develops autonomy, she needs guidance about what activities she can control and which ones are still the purview of her parents. She needs to know, in short, who the boss is for her various activities. Health and safety determine where to draw some of the lines. For example, Mu Ling is the boss of her play, as long as she does not throw things (safety issue); she can be the boss of what clothing she puts on, as long as it is temperature-appropriate (health issue); she is the boss of what she puts in her mouth and when she closes her eyes, although parents still are the boss of what food is cooked and when bedtime will be.

As your three- to five-year-old begins to accomplish tasks autonomously, you must relinquish control in some areas and tell your child explicitly that you are doing so. Making this change requires flexibility and lots of humor. Because Mu Ling had begun to argue with her parents about who was the boss, I suggested to Meg and Laura that they make up a chart that defined who was the boss of what. The result is shown below. Note that a chart like this could run on forever, covering every aspect of your family's life; it is best, as Mu Ling's parents did, to limit the chart to areas that are especially under discussion (or contention) in your family at a given time.

WHO IS THE BOSS?

Item or Activity	Boss
Mu Ling's mouth and eating	Mu Ling
Mom's mouth and eating	Mom
The television set	Parents
What toys Mu Ling chooses	Mu Ling
Friends Mu Ling plays with	Mu Ling
Books Mu Ling chooses	Mu Ling
Bedtime	Parents
Mu Ling's eyes	Mu Ling

Mu Ling helped create the chart by drawing pictures to represent the items or activities, and she drew a picture of the person who was the boss of each one. This activity focused Mu Ling on her own capabilities. In addition, the chart emphasized the large number of things Mu Ling did control and the few non-negotiable items that her parents controlled.

Sometimes an overly mature or highly intelligent child wants to take on more mature tasks while simultaneously engaging in very young behaviors. Yi Sheng would not put on his own shoes, but he wanted to learn to ride a bike. This type of mixed maturity can be addressed by requiring a child to master the earlier skill (tying shoes, for example) before advancing to a more mature skill (riding a bike, for example, or learning to read), regardless of her capacity to handle the advanced skill.

THE FRAGILE CHILD AND OVERPROTECTIVE PARENTS

Some parents of an adopted child are nurturing to the point of being overprotective. This behavior often has its roots in pre-adoption experiences, including miscarriages, difficult births or stillbirths, delayed adoptions, or adoption miscarriages. As a result of such experiences, the parents perceive the child who is ultimately adopted as a fragile miracle who might disappear at any time. Sometimes a parent's knowledge of, or educated guesses about, the deprivation and losses the child experienced prior to adoption feeds the image of the fragile child. This mantle of fragility that parents project onto a child leads parents to protect both more and for longer than necessary.

When parents realize that they have been overprotecting and babying their child, they often react abruptly. Suddenly they become the biggest limit setters in the neighborhood; Mom is the queen and Dad the king of consequences, the withholding parents. In the blink of an eye, for no reason the child can discern, the wonderful good parent turns into the evil villain. Not surprisingly, the child becomes frightened and worries that this is the prelude to another Big Change.

Should you be concerned that you have been overprotective, take a deep breath and go more slowly. Let your child know that you have been thinking about how you act with him. Explain that he is older now and better able to handle tasks that you have been doing for him.

Prepare your child for your intended changes. Explain that the changes are not because you love him less, but because you do love him and want to help him grow up. You might give an example to make this point clear. "You know," you might say, "how sometimes you say, 'I'm thirsty,' and I run and get you some water?" The child will nod or otherwise acknowledge the service. "Well, you are four years old now," you continue, "and you know how to get a paper cup and use the water cooler, and you can get your own water. But it's not that I've stopped loving you; I just think it's time to learn this."

"Separations" even of this limited sort—separations from familiar little routines—often entail some degree of anger. If you feel forced to maintain your "servant" status, *you* will be angry. If you change your behavior abruptly, *your child* will be angry. This change in parenting will feel to your child like a rupture of his relationship with you. Repair is needed, and reassurance is part of repair. Your child needs plenty of reassurance as he develops more autonomy, because the vast majority of internationally adopted children are scared to grow up. Being on one's own, even in limited spheres, appears to be the road to losing, not maintaining, connection with a parent. This struggle between connection and autonomy is one of the things that make adoptive development a complex challenge for parent and child.

"YOU HATE ME!": WHEN LIMITS FEEL LIKE REJECTION

A child with a complex background fears connection, because she believes the parent sooner or later will disconnect and reject or abandon her. When a parent sets a limit, says no, or in any other way breaks the close connection of an interdependent relationship, the child's fear of loss is triggered. When this happens, three- to five-year-old adopted children often lose control of their "foot brake" (see chapter 13), become enraged, and revert to coping behaviors. Although some children do this from Adoption Day forward, others begin to respond to limits in negative ways after one, two, or more years of family age.

When Meg told five-year-old Mu Ling that she could have only two helpings of noodles, Mu Ling screamed at her mom, "You hate me! But I hate you back first." When Kenji told five-year-old Yi Sheng that he needed to come to the table for dinner, Yi Sheng did as he was told, but he sat at the table refusing to eat. Mu Ling responded with a tantrum, externalizing her uncontrolled intense feelings in inappropriate behaviors. Yi Sheng internalized his feelings by shutting down and denying his own hunger.

What is often shocking to a parent of an internationally adopted child, I have found, is how limits elicit extreme emotional reactions. Mu Ling's sophisticated language skills made it easy to forget that her behavior was little different from the basic revving up of a frustrated infant. This is an example of mixed maturities. Based on Mu Ling's chronological age, Meg might see her daughter as "sassy," "out of line," and in need of firm correction. Yi Sheng's behavior, in contrast, appeared controlled, but his strong feelings were hidden beneath his passive, shut-down exterior.

HOW LIMITS WORK—OR DO NOT WORK

To understand why limits elicit such strong reactions in internationally adopted children, let us look first at how limits operate in a successful interdependent relationship between parent and child. Researchers have discovered that a child's tolerance of limits is related to his experiences of learning to explore the world around him.

Young toddlers are driven to explore their world. They stand up in their cribs and *cannot* sit down. They constantly walk about and do not want to be carried or rolled in a stroller, because their bodily maturation drives them to be mobile. A group of researchers led by Margaret Mahler in the 1960s dubbed this period of exhilarated exploration "the practicing period." For non-adopted children without a complex background, the practicing period begins at around ten months of age and lasts until approximately eighteen months of age. It is a time for exploring autonomy and physical separation from parents through crawling and walking.

A child who has been with his parents since birth has developed the interdependent connections that convey Parent Juice to him, stimulating his exploratory behavior. Equally important is the child's experience with a parent who withdraws or denies the child Parent Juice, such as when a parent averts his or her gaze from a child who is seeking a "jolt" of it. If Mom averts her gaze or Dad has a neutral or serious expression, the child fails to get the expected Parent Juice. This is the beginning of a parent controlling the child's behavior. Imagine a child about to touch a fragile vase who turns to look at Mom and sees her disapproving look. Instantly the toddler drops his hand, comes back to Mom, and works hard to get her to smile and "deliver the juice." Mom, without a word, has set a limit.

Exploration can feel risky for internationally adopted children with complex backgrounds, and such a child may experience as rejection the limits encountered during exploration. An international adoptee may well reach the toddler and preschool years without having passed through the practicing period with his new parents. In general, an internationally adopted child has difficulty receiving Parent Juice even when there is an interdependent relationship. As a result, many appear extremely sensitive to even small corrections. Because they have so little Parent Juice to begin with, any drop in the level is monumental in its impact. This makes limit setting far more complicated, because the child experiences limits as rejection on both a biochemical and an emotional level. The adoptive parents with whom I work often feel, as a consequence, that they are always "walking on eggshells."

RESPONSE BIAS TO ANGRY FACES

Research on how children from complex backgrounds respond to a parent's facial expressions reveals an additional hurdle for limit setting with internationally adopted children. Such children may have difficulty reading a range of emotions in the facial expressions of others. In particular, there is a bias toward seeing an angry face when the child is feeling stressed or threatened; a child is likely to look at a parent and "see" anger if the child feels stressed to even a small degree, regardless of the actual expression on the parent's face.

A child's bias toward seeing anger and criticism in others is an ongoing challenge to parents of internationally adopted children. It is the reason parents need to emphasize and continually work on helping a child read emotional expressions accurately, including looking at the face of a speaker carefully before deciding how the speaker feels.

CHANGING THE BRAIN: FROM ACCELERATOR AND EMERGENCY BRAKE TO FOOT BRAKE

An internationally adopted child frequently reacts to limits with rage rather than modulated anger. Rage is expressed in tantrums, spitting, biting, throwing objects, hitting objects or parents, and the like. Even a stern look or the imposition of a modest limit can cause such physical upset, which to parents seems quite out of proportion. But these reactions are typical for children with complex backgrounds who have a history of reactive coping behaviors.

Now that we have looked at some of the reasons behind these reactions, let us turn to what you can do to make establishing limits with three- to five-year-olds go more smoothly and successfully. The key is to guide your child through limit-setting work that allows her brain to develop new capabilities. These capabilities reduce reactive coping responses, the ones we have called "accelerating," or revving up, and "emergency braking," or shutting down. (See chapter 13 for strategies to use with younger children.) The goal is to substitute a "foot-braking" system that facilitates interdependent and cooperative emotional and behavioral responses.

THREE STRATEGIES

How can you reshape your child's brain in this manner? First, you should remain available and responsive when your child is angry. Second, you should help your child use words and images to respond emotionally to limits. Third, you need to reconnect with your child in order to help him recuperate from a tantrum or other outburst. When used consistently, these three strategies gradually help a child give up the lonely, enraged fight-or-flight reaction; instead, limit setting becomes a shared, albeit challenging, experience. After repeated practice, the child begins to *expect* relief from distress caused by the imposition of a limit. In short, he creates a "story" of what is happening, and that story includes the resumption of Parent Juice and of the relationship with the parent.

Mu Ling told this story about a showdown over noodles. "I wanted more noodles," she said, "but Mommy said, 'No, just three helpings.' I was mad! I shouted at Mommy and kicked her chair. Mommy said, 'I think you are mad, but you can be mad and then stop.' I stopped shouting. Mommy held me and helped me calm down." As a child learns over time to tell such stories, he begins to incorporate the *expectation of relief,* which in turn begins to function as an internal means of self-control when the child meets the next limit. It is not unlike what we as adults do when something goes wrong and we tell ourselves a story that includes a sentence such as "All right, I can handle this, and I will be able to do it better next time."

THREE STRATEGIES FOR LIMIT-SETTING OUTBURSTS

1. Parent remains available and responsive when child is angry.
2. Parent helps child use words and stories to express what happened.
3. Parent uses interactive repair to reconnect with child.

Available and Responsive

What is "available and responsive"? Admittedly it can be a difficult stance to assume in the face of a child's extreme displays of anger. But I strongly advise parents to make the effort. In particular, I encourage them not to react by creating distance between themselves and the child, either by leaving her alone or by putting her in a separate room for a time-out. Being available means being both physically and emotionally present. Sometimes I tell parents to "act like bamboo":

Bend but do not break, and be peacefully centered, despite what your child is going through. Be patient; your child is working and you are standing by.

There is one circumstance, however, when a parent *does* need to separate from an angry child. If you feel that you may lose control physically or emotionally, you need a parental time-out. Tell your child you need time to cool off, that you will be in the next room, and that you will return shortly. Then go and calm yourself down.

Narration: Using Words and Stories

Once you have made it clear to your child that you are available and responsive, it is time to start talking about what happened. While a child is actively raging, of course, it is nearly impossible to have a conversation. You might start by confirming that you are aware of how upset and angry your child is by saying, for example, "I can hear and see that you are very angry." Repeating the limit as part of what you say, however, generally just makes the child more furious. I therefore advise against saying, "I know you are *very* angry because I said no more cookies" and the like. Just stick with reflecting the child's feelings. You can also tell your child that you will stay with him, and keep both of you safe, and that you know he will be able to calm down. "I'm here to help you, to keep you safe," you might say. "I know you'll calm down in a while."

Note that some children do not like to be looked at. You may want to pick another direction in which to look as you begin talking to your child. Although direct face-to-face eye contact is a goal toward which you should be working, this is not the time to insist on it.

I have found that the best way to encourage a child to use appropriate words that express his feelings forthrightly, yet without rage, is to piece together with him a narrative about what has happened. For example:

"Let's tell the story of what happened today. Mommy [Daddy] said no more cookies. How did you feel?" Leave some time for your child to use words to describe his feelings.

"You wanted more cookies. What did Mommy [Daddy] say?" Again, give your child time to verbalize what he saw you do or heard you say.

"Then you calmed down. You and I agreed we don't always want the same things. Sometimes you want more cookies and I say no. Sometimes I want you to wear a jacket and you say no. Even when we are different, I still love you." Give your child an additional chance to make sense of what happened.

These small narratives offer an opportunity to revisit your connections with your child as well as your differences. Over time your child's internalization of these narratives will change the way he reacts to limits that you set in the future.

Reconnection and Repair

After a big blowup over a limit, it is time to reconnect with your child and repair the effects of the outburst. What do "reconnection and repair" mean? Some parents want to transition quickly to hugs and kisses, but this is not always comfortable for a child who has just been raging. A simple, and not intense, interactive activity is best. Some three- to five-year-old children seek to reconnect through infantile behaviors, such as being fed, or playing a game such as Peekaboo or rolling a ball back and forth. Others prefer taking a walk around the block, playing cards, or building something together.

As a child between three and five struggles with limits, she may be drawn to fairy tales with wicked witches or evil fairies. The contrast between good and bad in these stories reflects the work your child is doing to integrate the "good" parent (who supplies Parent Juice) and the "bad" parent (who sets limits and withholds the Parent Juice). Other children who are struggling with limits may be frightened by fairy tales. Such a child may feel overwhelmed by the good-versus-bad parent split and unable to bear hearing about good versus evil in story form.

WHEN THE STRATEGIES DO NOT WORK

Sometimes a child responds negatively to limits because of other things that are going on in his life. I use the following questions to determine whether factors other than a child's adoptive status or his complex background may be interfering with his ability to handle limits:

1. When did the behavior begin?
2. What was happening in the days just before the behavior started?
3. Is the child starting to learn a new skill, such as riding a tricycle or bike, or reading?
4. Has anything changed at home?
5. Is a parent working more or traveling more?
6. Is there any change coming up in the family, such as moving, remodeling, a new babysitter, or a big brother or sister leaving for college?
7. What does the parent think is going on with the child?
8. What positive connecting behaviors is the child engaging in with the parent?

Often the answer to one or more of these questions reveals additional stress on the child, which may well be the reason the child is continuing to struggle angrily with limits. Sometimes a child needs more help than parents realize initially. This is what happened with Yi Sheng. Although he was the oldest child in the First Year Home Group, he acted as though he were the youngest. He dropped his coat on the floor, demanded that his parents carry him in and out of the playroom, and refused to share toys or participate in the Group's games and activities. Eventually his parents reached their wits' end, and despite their experience as parents, they were feeling continually frustrated.

The eight questions seek primarily one of two things: a new developmental stage or a change in the family or the child's life. Answering the questions helps parents focus on what they may have dismissed or overlooked as the source of the child's discomfort. Typically a child is either entering a new developmental stage, such as reading, or facing a new challenge, such as starting kindergarten; or there has been a change in the family—in Mom or Dad's work life, or in a sibling's school or college life.

The questions also seek what a parent thinks is happening. I look for a parent's intuition about what "feels right." Nina, for example, commented that it felt as if Yi Sheng was feeling closer to her and her husband because he was not afraid to test them. This was more than simply an intuition; Nina was able to point to specific details about how Yi Sheng had been cuddling with Kenji when he returned home from work, or how he liked to hold on to Nina's pant leg as she cooked dinner. Sometimes these examples of good connection are forgotten in the heat and residue of big emotional blowups.

As she worked her way through the questions, Nina also realized that the beginning of kindergarten coincided with Yi Sheng's negative and demanding behavior. Many children, especially adopted children, fear that as they grow older and more competent their parents will cease to care for them. Many internationally adopted children remember the pre-adoption experience of being pushed to be more competent at self-care because their caregivers had heavy workloads. Later, even long after their adoptions, they associate self-care or increased skills with disconnection. Yi Sheng's strongly oppositional behavior was clearly a plea for a deeper and more secure connection, albeit in a backward sort of way.

Once again, acknowledge explicitly to your child his stress and its origins, and construct a narrative together about those things. Tell this story repeatedly for several days and weeks. This will bring you and your child together. Be patient, too; you may need some time, as a new family routine gets established or as a child settles into a new developmental stage, to figure out how to establish limits in this now altered situation. During this time make as few additional changes as possible, and focus on limits you have already introduced rather than new ones.

FOCUS ON FAMILY AGE

Many parents of internationally adopted children are indeed mindful of family age as they build a relationship with their child. But I have found that when it comes to limit setting, parents tend to focus on chronological age. So I emphasize again: Use family age as a guide for setting and enforcing limits, and for your expectations about how well your child should, and will, respond to them. Your child's ability to handle limits will increase as you implement the strategies of responsiveness, narration building, and repair described in this chapter.

Making Choices about Race, Culture, Ethnicity, and Identity

"Mom, am I black?" seven-year-old Soon An asked her mother.

"When I grow up will I look more like you?" Mu Ling, nine years old, asked her mother.

"Jeremy said I'm not Russian. If I was born in Russia, and both my birth parents were Russian, then why am I not Russian?" Demetri asked his mom.

INTERNATIONALLY ADOPTED CHILDREN between six and nine struggle with a host of new questions about their identities. Although three-year-olds notice that people have different eyes, hair texture, or skin color, it is not until a child is about six that parents begin to hear questions such as the ones quoted above. These new questions concern race, culture, ethnicity, and nationality. As you read this chapter and as you engage in discussions with your child about these categories, keep in mind that these are *social and cultural constructions* that vary from place to place and from one historical era to another, and that they are not fixed biological categories. Remember, too, that different families and different individuals are free to choose which of these categories—if any—they wish to emphasize as they identify themselves. A person of Japanese ancestry who was born in Brazil might consider herself Japanese in terms of ethnicity or race; Brazilian, Japanese, or both in terms of nationality; and Brazilian, Portuguese, or Japanese in terms of culture; and she might choose to focus on one of these categorizations and not the others. If such a person emigrated to the United States, she might keep none, some, or all of these designations, and she might well become Hispanic or Latina as well, since Americans tend to label all persons from Central or South America that way—even though Brazil was once a Portuguese but never a Spanish colony.

You may be somewhat skeptical about the idea that families and individuals are "free to choose" which designations to use. That kind of freedom is ideal, but it is often difficult to exercise. Social scientists use the expression *white privilege* to describe the usually implicit and unstated but nonetheless real experience of never having to worry that your physical traits will affect how others treat you. Many internationally adopted children do not benefit from white privilege. In your child's early years, up to about age six, during which time she is usually with you, she will be treated as you are and may therefore assume white privilege if you are Caucasian. After six years of age, or when she begins to attend elementary school, she will lose the umbrella of white privilege.

WHO AM I?

When Soon An, who was born in Korea, asked her mother, "Mom, am I black?" her question revealed how the concept of race is often confusing to children less than ten or eleven years of age. As we have seen, the good/bad, either/or thinking of six- to nine-year-olds is very concrete. The logic of a seven-year-old dictates that if you are not "white" then you must be "black." This makes life more challenging for an Asian or Hispanic child, who now must face some of the same difficulties that an African or African-American child faces. Many adoptive parents discover that their internationally adopted children think of themselves as "black," because their classmates tell them they are definitely not "white."

Six- to nine-year-olds are still concrete thinkers and cannot fully understand the history or sociology of prejudice and racial discrimination.

Early and careful education of your child is your best approach. Expose your child to lots of other people, especially children, who look like him. In connection with these situations, use the descriptive terms that you prefer—Asian, Hispanic, Guatemalan, Korean, Chinese, and the like—and teach your child to which group he belongs. Help your child become familiar with the vocabulary you want him to use to build a positive identity. Define yourself, too, and other members of your family, neighborhood, and community. Remember when your child was two and he labeled everyone he met as a mommy, a daddy, or a dog? This is the same sort of categorization on a more sophisticated level.

Between six and nine years of age, children need to find their place. They do not need a wide-ranging lecture on racism, the roots of prejudice, or the history of discrimination. These terms are too abstract for the concrete thinking of this age.

Mu Ling's question "When I grow up will I look more like you?" illustrates how children of even nine years of age still have a fluid sense of who they are. Gender concepts stabilize around four or five years old, and often earlier, but race and ethnicity take longer to become permanent in a child's mind. This is especially true for multiracial children or a child in a multiracial family. Thus, Mu Ling, who had Caucasian parents, was not certain that her Asian appearance was permanent. Perhaps, she reasoned, her identity would change as she grew older. After all, just about everything else in her life had changed at one time or another.

Demetri's question about if, and why, he was "not Russian" leads us into the area of competing or overlapping realms of identity. Demetri was trying to understand who he was. He knew that he was born in Russia. Did that not make him Russian? He knew his birth parents were Russian but his adoptive mother was American. Was he Russian, American, or a Russian-American combination?

MAKING SENSE OF CATEGORIES

Combined or hyphenated descriptors often dilute the sense of identity for a child in this age range. A six-year-old who hears that she is "Chinese-American" may feel neither Chinese nor American. At this age each heritage needs its own individual space. We know from research studies that rather than experiencing their identities as dual, biracial children or children in multiracial homes instead identify alternately with one race and then with the other. Internationally adopted children between six and nine oscillate or alternate in a similar manner. Your adopted child needs to have distinct opportunities to develop each part of her heritage, without having to combine them or to choose one over the other. Do not expect or require loyalty to one identity or another; instead, let your child, and the rest of your family as well, enjoy the exploration of each of her available identities in turn.

Once you have acknowledged openly with your child the two main sources that contribute to her identity—birth parents and adoptive family—help her with words that describe the ethnic, cultural, and national characteristics that stem from these sources. In addition, identify words that will encourage your child to describe, and feel positively about, her physical traits and appearance, as well as the physical traits of others. Remember that children probably do not use racial terms to describe themselves until they are seven years of age or older. Typically they use color or texture terms instead. Denise helped Demetri take pride in the way his stocky build and blond hair revealed his Russian heritage. She pointed out the contrast with her own dark hair and eyes, which came from her family's Mediterranean heritage. After looking in the mirror together, Denise and her son consulted a map of Europe and found that their original families were not so very far apart after all!

Discuss these matters frequently with the whole family, so that your adopted child feels welcome to talk about them. Sitting down together and looking at advertisements, books (illustrations and words), and classroom materials, or watching movies, in order to find examples of different people and groups is a good way to get the conversation started. It is all too easy for parents to let this topic slip by; often this happens because of the parents' own white privilege, or because children wish to protect their parents' innocence. I have found that even six-year-olds already know that their parents would be upset to hear, for example, that a classmate told Mu Ling her eyes were too small to see out of, or that an older child commented that her daddy said "beaners like Sonia" were taking over the world.

MINORITY AND MAINSTREAM

Internationally adopted children and their parents must learn to navigate through two different realms of experience: minority and mainstream. This is true even for internationally adopted children who share their adoptive family's racial, ethnic, and cultural identities. How can this be? Because every internationally adopted child is part of a unique minority group: international adoptees. International adoptees experience discrimination from those who expect them to identify with a particular nationality or race in specific ways. For example, when Demetri was in class with a child of Russian immigrants, the Russian child told Demetri, "You can't be Russian; you don't speak the language." When Demetri protested, the child persisted: "What do you eat for dinner? Hot dogs or pirozhki?" Finally the child delivered his final condemnation: "You don't look Russian." Such tests of language, custom, or appearance are frequently used to discriminate against international adoptees in the same way that they are used to discriminate against or harass biracial or multiracial children. In this situation Demetri had to learn how to handle himself as a member of a minority, coping with prejudice, discrimination, and racism.

The educational psychologist H. C. Stevenson has written that parents need to "communicate messages and behaviors to children and adolescents to bolster their sense of identity, given the possibility and reality that their life experiences may include racially hostile encounters." Talking with your child positively about his traits and connecting them to his heritage are part of this training. If your child is five or six years of age or older, you also need to protect him from surprises by warning him that some children will disrespect his heritage through "tests" or outright insults. This is the beginning of supporting your child in his travels through the experience of belonging to a minority, and perhaps more than one minority.

Only a non-adopted white person can fully partake of white privilege. Even a "white" internationally adopted child has to learn to engage with mainstream society with a bicultural orientation. This was Demetri's challenge. An internationally adopted child, whether white or nonwhite, must be able to switch from the mainstream culture to his birth culture according to circumstances. When Yi Sheng ate with his friends from school at the cafeteria, he had pizza; when he visited his Chinese friend, he ate pot stickers; and when he was at home, he joined his Japanese-Chinese-Jewish-American family eating sukiyaki and challah for Friday night dinner. At least in relation to food, Yi Sheng moved easily between the mainstream and several different cultures.

In order for Yi Sheng to have this ability to move between cultures, his parents had to make sure he was exposed to and had a positive feeling about each of the cultures with which he was connected. Arranging for a breadth of experiences took time, energy, and ingenuity on their part. Instead of having Yi Sheng take tae kwon do near their home, for example, Nina arranged to drive him to a largely Chinese neighborhood where he would meet and befriend other Chinese children. Once a month the family went out to dinner at a Chinese restaurant. Yi Sheng's father, Kenji, whose heritage is Japanese, learned to make several Chinese noodle dishes that became family favorites. These intentionally planned activities exposed Yi Sheng to his birth culture and created a strong positive sense of identification.

Yi Sheng's relationship with his family was the nurturing foundation for his developing multicultural identity. The family created a buffer against negative comments, experiences, or images that Yi Sheng encountered. Your family should be a place to talk about your child's negative experiences and process them, turning them into empowering rather than secretive or undermining experiences.

WHERE ARE YOU FROM?

All parents of internationally adopted children of color need to prepare their child for the not-so-infrequent experience of having an adult assume that the child does not speak English and is an immigrant. This begins to happen when such a child is not standing with white middle-class parents beside her.

"Where are you from?" the stranger asked, enunciating loudly and slowly, directly into Sonia's face.

"Seattle," replied Sonia, who was seven and had been in the United States for six years.

"No! I mean where are you from? Do you speak English?"

A child who has to process such an experience alone begins to feel disconnected from parents. A child tries to protect parents from knowing about uncomfortable situations that may happen at school or in other public places like parks and stores.

As an adoptive parent, you need to anticipate events like these, talking with your child before and after they happen to help her make sense of them and to give her the opportunity to express her feelings about them. This is the time to explore the concept of being and feeling "different" and to come to grips with all the ramifications of being different in your child's daily life. Together, you and your child can decide on a shorthand name to label the range of situations in which she is tested, challenged, or insulted about her identity. This name will help both of you to refer to new and similar situations as they arise and will evoke all your previous discussions and understandings. Sonia and her mother, for example, chose the word *testing* to cover these situations.

"PASSING" AND HYPER-IDENTIFICATION

Some six- to nine-year-old children avoid addressing issues of race, culture, and discrimination. In particular, they ignore or reject their heritage and even their physical traits. Some people may view this negatively as "passing as white"; others may perceive this neutrally, or positively, as evidence that the child is simply comfortable with the styles and appearances of the white middle class. In recent years adoption experts have begun to look more favorably on a nonwhite child's assimilation of the values and styles of his white parents, if indeed he has white parents, and have rejected the word *passing* with its pejorative implications. Instead, they use the more neutral term *symbolic white*.

Other children in this age range choose instead to focus on their racial or ethnic appearance and may begin to prefer ethnic music, food, clothing, and hairstyles, among other things. Sometimes these children unwittingly play into stereotypes about their birth country and culture. I call this phase, when a child intensely takes on the traits of his birth culture, *hyper-identification*.

Your role is to provide a consistent, positive presentation of *all* the races, cultures, or ethnicities that are present in your child's birth and present families. You might think of your family as putting out a smorgasbord of experiences from which the child can choose, returning throughout childhood as often as he wishes to try out new tastes and experiences. If, for example, Mu Ling decided to drop her Chinese dance class and take gymnastics instead, her parents need not feel they must pressure her to engage in an activity connected with her birth country. There will be periods in her life when she wants to engage in such activities and periods in which she does not.

When your child goes through a period of intense identification with his birth country, you do not need to rein him in. Sonia went through a stage in which she wanted to eat tortillas for breakfast every single day. "This is my Guatemalan time," she told her parents. As long as she ate an otherwise balanced diet, it was fine to allow this phase to run its course.

Parents and family provide a safe haven in which a child can explore and experiment with different identities. Between six and nine, children need to do their exploration close to home, of course, with a parent's guidance and participation.

IDENTIFICATION AND LOSS

There were days when Demetri wanted Denise to answer him using the Russian words for *yes* and *no*, and there were other days when he preferred English. Some days Sonia ate tortillas and other days she asked for bread. Yi Sheng wanted noodles for breakfast five days a week and cold cereal on the other two days. Oscillation is the healthy norm for a child with a multiracial, multiethnic, or multicultural heritage.

For parents this often seems like having to indulge a child. "I can't keep tortillas and bread in the house all the time," Sonia's mother sighed. "I never know what Sonia will want for breakfast. I feel I'm a short-order cook."

But when tortillas were not available or Denise forgot to use Russian words, Sonia and Demetri lost their emotional and behavioral control. Their identification with their birth country was a way to soothe their sense of loss. Eating a tortilla soothed Sonia's feelings of missing her birth country and her foster mother. Hearing his mom use *da* and *nyet* helped Demetri feel he was really a Russian boy and had not lost his roots. When tortillas were missing, Sonia was forced to be more in touch with her feelings of loss. When Denise forgot to use Russian words, Demetri was forced to confront his loss of birth country and language, and he expressed those feelings in a fury beyond what seemed appropriate for the circumstances.

A child who is not exposed to her birth culture is not able to explore what that culture means to her until adulthood.

With a six- to nine-year-old child, conversation is the best way to address such issues. Pulling out the Three-Photo Story (see chapter 7) is one way to start the dialogue. The parent can interweave the importance of tortillas, or language, or whatever else the child cares deeply about into the story. Storytelling helps the child connect her strong emotions to her real losses early on in her life and reveals the smaller current losses—such as there being no tortillas available—as triggers that recall those deep old feelings.

CULTURE CAMPS

Internationally adopted youngsters and preteenagers naturally turn to their families when they want a safe haven to be themselves. But as children grow older they want to turn to their peers as well. This is why internationally adopted children need groups in which they feel known and secure, groups that support their complex backgrounds and kaleidoscopic heritages.

Many parents look to "culture camps," gatherings of other internationally adopted families, often from the same country, as one place that a child can find this type of connection. Most culture camps are run by parents and are affiliated with specific ethnic or cultural groups. Examples include the Korean Identity Development Society (KIDS), the Korean American Adoptee Adoptive Family Network (KAAN), Guatemala Adoptive Families Network, Families for Russian and Ukrainian Adoption (FRUA), and Families with Children from China (FCC). You can find a comprehensive list at http://www.karensadoptionlinks.com. Other culture camps are sponsored by large adoption agencies, such as Holt International Children's Services, or adoption education groups, such as the Center for Adoption Support and Education.

Typically children and parents attend camp together for a weekend each year, usually in the summer. The camps serve two major purposes, both equally important: they provide opportunities to learn about a child's birth culture; and they present abundant opportunities to meet, interact with, and become friends with other children who are adopted from the same country. Sometimes children who were adopted together (that is, their adoptive parents arrived in the birth country in the same travel group) or from the same city or province reunite at these gatherings.

Internationally adopted children in this age range look forward excitedly to culture camp. "It's a place where everyone looks like me and my family!" they say. Culture camp fulfills a child's need to fit in and not to be seen as different.

Unfortunately these camps and the occasional holiday parties or picnics sponsored by adoption groups take place just a few times each year. Many of the parties and picnics, and even the camps, are geared more toward children of five to seven years of age, who are just beginning to need this kind of support from peers. Older children, who crave even more peer support, may find the camp experience or parties less than satisfying. Just when children need the camps more, they tend to offer less.

FORMING YOUR OWN MULTICULTURAL GROUP

Because family is the source of each child's best support, it is in the family that the multicultural haven must be rooted. If you do not live in a multiracial, multiethnic, or multicultural neighborhood, or if your child does not attend a school with a mixed population, you need to help build a social circle that will feel uniquely comfortable for your child.

Put together a group of multiethnic or multicultural families and meet together regularly. Children who meet "similar" children and whose parents socialize regularly in the group find the support they need in this "extended family." When the preteen years of cliques and the tough years of adolescence arrive, this special group of families will provide the solid haven that young people need.

For some families such a group emerges naturally. Carolyn with her Southern friends and David with his Latino friends had a mixed cultural and social group before they adopted Sonia. It was natural to continue those friendships, and eventually one or two other families who had adopted internationally joined the group. Carolyn organized monthly gatherings for a potluck dinner. By the time Sonia was twelve, she had a dependable group of multiracial friends that extended her family. Although she attended a predominantly white private school and struggled with cliques and feeling out of place, she always had her family's social life for support and friendship.

Denise relied heavily on the Families for Russian and Ukrainian Adoption group, which had a chapter in her town, for extending her son's (and her own) circle of friends and peers. Denise decided to make her home the center for regular celebrations of Russian holidays. When Demetri turned nine, Denise decided to start a monthly bowling night for the group. By the time her son was twelve, he had a core group of good friends, separate from his school friends, to play with. Having more than one social group is particularly important for internationally adopted children.

A TRIP TO YOUR CHILD'S BIRTH COUNTRY: IF AND WHEN

There is a strong belief among many families that traveling to a child's birth country is an important way to help the child identify with his cultural background. However, I have found that it is a good idea for parents to think carefully about their motives for the trip and what they hope their child will gain from it. Is the plan driven by a parent's guilt over being unable to supply cultural connections at home? Can parents provide enough preparation on an age-appropriate level to make visiting the home country emotionally safe?

Laura and Meg decided to travel to China with their daughter and joined a special tour that had been set up for returning adoptees. Mu Ling was excited and proud to see her birth country. But in the days following the visit to her orphanage she was distinctly depressed. Her parents wanted to discuss her feelings with her, but she rejected their openings. Also, when they returned from the trip, Laura and Meg commented that the entire tour seemed to be a shopping trip for the parents, as the tour leader took them to all her friends' shops.

Nina and Kenji decided to spend a month living in China with Yi Sheng and their daughters to acquire a deeper appreciation of the country. Kenji took a job teaching English. But after having read many positive reports about how children loved returning to their birth country, Kenji and Nina were dismayed by Yi Sheng's reaction. His response to China was a regression to his original coping skills, combined with periods of silent grief and of clinging to Nina. He refused to go on sightseeing trips and wanted only to watch the English-language videotapes he had brought from home. Yi Sheng refused to talk about his behavior or his feelings, despite the earlier progress he and his parents had made in that

Children with explicit memories of their pre-adoption lives need to have greater maturity and emotional stability before visiting their birth country.

department. Nina returned home early with Yi Sheng and immediately sought therapy to deal with his emotional collapse.

As Nina and Kenji learned, children with explicit memories of pre-adoption life have a much more difficult time when confronted with the land, language, and faces of their birth country. For these children it is more appropriate to wait until they have greater maturity and emotional stability to make such a trip. Yi Sheng, at eight, simply was not ready.

Nearly all internationally adopted children over the age of six have some sense that although they look the same as most of the people in their birth country, they are also different because of their experiences with their adoptive family in another country. A child with a mixed heritage due to adoption is undeniably different from a native resident of his birth country. A child's realization of this, and other feelings about adoption that surface, can make a birth-country trip an emotionally demanding experience for children in this age range.

But if your child seems positively inclined toward such a venture and you can swing it financially, the experience can be enjoyable and rewarding. A trip to a birth country is often the first time an internationally adopted child may feel he "looks like everyone else" and is part of the mainstream. Seven-year-old Sonia found it delightful that her mother was different-looking from everyone in Guatemala, whereas she, Sonia, was "just like all the other Guatemalan girls" and could converse in Spanish. Even Demetri, who is Caucasian in appearance like his mother, experienced a deep sense of fitting in and of belonging when he visited Russia. By nine years of age most children can begin to appreciate the beauty and culture of another country.

Despite the strong feelings among many adoptive parents that such a trip will build a child's self-esteem and cultural pride, adoption experts do not believe these trips are mandatory for every adopted child's well-being and development. What is more important than a two-week trip, or even living in a birth country for a few months, is the day-in and day-out, year-after-year experience you offer your child of sharing in the various cultures and ethnic traditions that are represented in your family. Even relatively small exposures to different cultures can make a deep and lasting impact on a child's self-esteem and identity.

ADOPTION ISSUES FROM SIX TO NINE

Creating a Deeper
and More Detailed Adoption Story

FROM SIX TO NINE YEARS OF AGE, adopted children begin to use their greater intellectual and emotional abilities to grapple with the issue of who was responsible for their relinquishment and adoption. A parent needs to help a child recognize that the birth parent, not the child herself, was responsible for the relinquishment and that other adults (adoption workers and adoptive parents, chiefly) also made the choices that led to the adoption. This new perspective enables a child to set aside feelings of shame (innate badness) or guilt (badness for having done something) so that she can begin to feel that she is deserving of good things, including a good family.

In this chapter we cover what your six- to nine-year-old child wants and needs to know about her pre-adoption and adoption stories, and how her story now needs to have more specific facts and more emotional nuance than the story she worked on at five or younger.

"I DESERVE A GOOD FAMILY"

A major task for a parent of an adopted child between six and nine is to help the child progress from a sense of shame toward feeling good and deserving. This process is not like a developmental milestone that a child passes completely, such as learning to ride a bike. Rather it is a series of explorations over a wide expanse of territory. As the exploration proceeds, you help your child learn to recognize the "sinkholes of shame" and the "pits of guilt," how to climb out of these places, and ultimately how to avoid them. Some days a child may revert to feeling shameful and blameworthy, and on other days—which ideally become more frequent as the child ages from six toward nine—he thinks, "I'm a good person. It's all right to make mistakes and not be perfect. Nothing terrible will happen. I deserve a good, loving family."

THE LOGIC OF MISDIRECTED ANGER

Explaining adoption to a six- to nine-year-old is made more complicated by the ways in which many adopted children base their images of their birth mothers on their adoptive mothers. After all, the child reasons, a mother is a mother, and what one expects from one mother is what one expects from all mothers. Mu Ling applied this youthful logic to what Laura told her: "Your birth mother loved you and wanted you to have a better life." Mu Ling thought about this and concluded that since Laura and Meg, Mu Ling's other mother, loved her, they, too, might relinquish her to some other family for "a better life." She became worried and extra clingy at bedtime, until Meg unraveled the source of her fears. I have found that telling an adopted child that her birth mother relinquished her out of love inevitably leads to problems. Instead, it is better to say that a birth parent relinquished a child because of grownup problems, not because of love. But note that once you have made this point, you can expect your child to observe "grownup problems" in your own home; she may wonder how serious these are and whether they will lead to another relinquishment. Honest answers, even if difficult, are more reassuring than lies. If parents are considering a separation or divorce, for example, they need to deal with their child openly, and in the context of the child's previous losses, not sweep the problem under the rug.

Increasing emotional awareness and increasingly complex cognitive and logical skills lead to changes in a child's view of, and questions about, adoption. Sonia as a six-year-old was "happy to be 'dopted," she said. But by nine years of age her increasingly sophisticated thinking had transformed her into a sullen child whenever adoption was discussed. When told she was "lucky" to be adopted, Sonia looked at the ground and muttered, "Adoption isn't lucky. It's bad luck to lose your first family." Demetri began to deny that he was adopted. Sonia, Soon An, and Mu Ling all spent time mourning their respective birth mothers. Yi Sheng wanted more information about population policies in China and became incensed that such rules could force separations between parents and children.

Be prepared for this shift toward a gloomier or angrier outlook and do not hold it against your child. A child's changing feelings may be primarily directed at birth parents, but she may also displace and misdirect them onto the adoptive parents. You can clear up this confusion simply by wondering aloud to your child that perhaps the feelings she is expressing—"You are a stupid head, Mom"— are really more about her birth mom than *this* mom. Be prepared to be told off during this period. This is when you need to distance yourself a bit, to refrain from taking your child's criticisms personally, and to cultivate a sense of humor about your own "flaws" and "faults," which your child insists on pointing out.

THE FOUR QUESTIONS FOR SIX- TO NINE-YEAR-OLDS

Between six and nine years of age, children learn more about the world and human relationships, and as a result they need to revisit and refine answers to the Four Questions (see chapter 7). Children often hear personal questions from their friends, peers, and teachers and receive school assignments that lead them to be more curious about their life story and their complex background. The fact that this curiosity exists, even if your child does not articulate it, is the reason that you need to be proactive about guiding your child back to the Four Questions.

Question 1: What Happened to Me?

Most children in this age range answer this question with the action-based narrative that leads from the birth mother to the interim caregiver (foster parent or orphanage caregiver) to the adoptive family. But as they progress toward age nine they want more details added to the story. You can fill in the specifics of the timing of changes in your child's life. This is a good opportunity, for example, to point out a young child and say, "See that baby over there? She's about two months old. That was the age you were when you went to the orphanage."

You can also describe in more detail the reasons (or the presumed or alleged reasons) for the birth parents' decision. "We think your mother was too young and too poor," you might say, or you might mention China's "one-child" policy. The prefacing words *we think* tell the child that the reason for relinquishment is not certain, which indeed is often the case. If on the other hand you are reasonably certain, you can say, for example, "We are pretty sure your mother was an alcoholic [drank too much beer or wine] and the Russian government took you away because she couldn't take care of you."

> No matter how carefully we explain a birth parent's reasons for relinquishment, we cannot erase our child's emotional responses to this loss of connection.

Most children in this age range ask, "*Why* was my mom too poor or too young?" "What is the reason for this one-child policy?" and similar follow-up questions. Through these questions your child is exploring who or what was "good" or "bad" in his birth family and country. No matter how carefully we explain, a child of this age is looking to assign responsibility. Poverty, alcoholism, and youth are "bad," because such a mother cannot care for a child. China and its one-child policy are "bad," too, because they separate mothers and children. Mu Ling and Yi Sheng both opined that the people of China should take a vote about the one-child policy, just as students in their respective classes at school sometimes voted in order to reach a decision. Each of them went through a period of "hating" China and everything Chinese.

Parents need to be patient when they provide these new details, and they need to allow their children to struggle with their new, emerging feelings. It is hard to listen to a child rail against birth parents when, as an adult, you realize that the parents (or the government) made a good decision. And it can be difficult to hear your child say that he "hates" his birth country, when you are simultaneously trying to instill in him a sense of pride in his origins.

Keep in mind, too, that some of the relevant information that would help answer the first question most fully may simply be too abstract or complex for your child. Even at the upper end of this age range, at eight or nine years of age, children have trouble grasping the complexities of how a government, let alone a foreign government, works. They are barely aware that there are governmental or private social-service agencies, much less ones that have the authority to remove a child from a birth parent's care. Finally, although they are likely to be familiar with single-mother households among their peers or in their neighborhood, they are unlikely to be able to appreciate the religious or cultural reasons that unwed mothers are shunned in other countries.

Focus on the Birth Parent's Choice

The concept of choice is something a child of this age can understand, so it is a good concept to use when answering the first question. It also helps a child think about her own capability of choosing. A child in this age range is old enough to understand, too, that everyone, including parents, makes poor or bad choices in their lives at times. She is therefore less likely to split her two sets of parents into the absolutely good adoptive parents and the absolutely bad birth parents.

"But I don't think that Mu Ling's birth mother had a choice, given Chinese family-planning laws," Meg once protested to me as we were discussing this matter. Many adoptive parents gravitate toward this view, because it absolves the birth parents of guilt. However, in China as in other countries there are in fact other choices. For example, a Chinese woman has access to free abortions, and Mu Ling's mother chose not to make use of that option. In addition, many Chinese families choose to pay fines rather than relinquish their child.

> **Adopted children need to feel angry or hurt by their birth parent's choice to relinquish them. This is how they absolve themselves of the shame of causing their own abandonment.**

From the child's perspective, the birth parent's worst choice was to relinquish the child. As we have seen, when a child can conceive of a birth parent making a "poor" choice, the child is relieved of the shame of being bad. As such, it is a healthy step for adopted children to become angry at a birth parent. With this responsibility off the child's shoulders, she can begin to feel that she is intrinsically good and deserves a good family and home.

Looking for Comfort to Balance the Pain

Sonia, at age eight, told her parents, "My birth mother made the wrong choice to grow a baby when she was poor. She should have gotten a job and *then* grown me in her body. Now I bet she's real sad she lost me. But I'm mad at her. I deserve a good home and family." By this logic Sonia was able to comfort herself. Allowing a child to work out ways like this to comfort himself or to explain or support his own feelings is important, even if there is no direct evidence for some of the components of the story he tells. Facing the feelings of abandonment head-on is too hard for a child to do alone, which is why you are there listening and talking about it.

> **Being emotionally present for your child as he faces feelings of abandonment means your child is no longer alone with those feelings.**

Yi Sheng swung from hating to loving his birth mother, depending on which choice he considered. "I love her because she didn't get an abortion. Abortions are free in China," he said. On other occasions he pounded his stuffed panda—for him a stand-in for his Chinese birth mother—and yelled, "You dumb jerk, why did you let me go? You should have kept me!"

Telling the adoption story ultimately helps a child regulate emotions and behavior, but be aware that a six- to nine-year-old has strong feelings about birth parents he has never seen. Children tend to take out their feelings of anger at birth parents on the only available parents, the adoptive ones. As Yi Sheng's parents did, it helps to provide surrogates, such as ethnic adult-looking dolls, or animals or toys associated with your child's country of origin, toward which your child can direct his anger. You can also encourage your child to draw a picture of his birth mother, and give him permission to express his feelings on the paper by scribbling on it, blacking it out, or writing words full of feeling.

Do not be surprised if your child expresses a mixture of strong angry and loving feelings toward his birth parents, and do your best to keep your own reactions to these feelings neutral, or if not neutral, private.

Question 2: Who Will Take Care of Me Now?

Most children in this age range are comfortable answering this question by repeating that "Mom or Dad takes care of me now," along with other extended family members such as grandparents, aunts, and uncles. However, some adopted children between six and nine test their adoptive parents' commitment to their care by assuming too much independence and engaging in risky behavior, such as riding a skateboard down the middle of the street. Or they revert to coping behaviors to check if, and how, their parents will continue to deliver care under trying circumstances.

When Demetri began riding in a carpool to soccer practice at age six, he began to be hyperactive in the car, and then at practice, in ways that were reminiscent of his coping behaviors when he was first adopted. On particularly difficult days he asked his mother to drive him to practice, knowing that he would have problems in the carpool. Denise had to work with Demetri to help him still feel connected to her and emotionally in control—to convince him, in short, that she was always going to take care of him, even if she was temporarily absent and he was under the supervision of another adult. To this end she suggested that Demetri carry a photo of the two of them together to remind him of their connection. She also encouraged Demetri to hum their special "I Love You" song to himself to relax when he was missing her in the carpool.

Question 3: Did I Make the Big Change Happen?

This question is the kernel of the struggle for a child between six and nine years of age. Sonia, for example, understood intellectually that she was not responsible for her own abandonment. However, emotionally and irrationally she still felt as if she was somehow "bad" and that was why both her birth and foster mothers had let her go. This combination of feeling both bad and rejected came up a lot when a clique of girls in her class shut her out. It came up when her team lost at soccer, or when she lost at the card games she and her parents often played.

Rejection and uncertainty seemed to haunt her. During this period Sonia described her birth mother as just the outline of a woman. "I can see her clothing but never her face," she told her adoptive mother. It was then that Carolyn led

Sonia to a mirror to look at her own face and features. Without going into specific details about inheritance, Carolyn explained that Sonia's appearance was a gift from her mother. Together they explored what her birth mother had contributed to Sonia's life. Sonia began to imagine her mother as looking like Sonia herself, only older.

Ordinary experiences of rejection at school or in playgroups can trigger an adopted child's feelings of adoption-related shame.

Sonia struggled to feel good about herself and to accept her adoptive mother's assurances that she was not to blame for her birth mother's "grownup" problems and decisions. As she began to feel more independent, Sonia became more hesitant about accepting her mother's words. And with only a featureless outline of her birth mother with which to work, she became withdrawn and unwilling to try new things. These were signals to her adoptive parents that Sonia was continuing to feel responsible for her own adoption. Each activity that Carolyn tried seemed to bring Sonia some comfort, but not permanent good cheer. "I'm beginning to understand what is meant by adoption being a lifelong process," Carolyn confided to me. "This is hard work for all of us." Like other parents of internationally adopted children of this age, Carolyn had to accept her daughter's unease and sadness as she struggled with newfound understanding of her complex life story.

Question 4: Will Everything Change Again, and Will I Lose You, Too?

By age six children can apply some fairly sophisticated logic to the information they have about themselves and their adoption stories. When Charlotte, for example, explained to her daughter, Soon An, that Soon An's birth mother was not married and therefore could not raise her, Soon An replied that her cousin Sophie was nineteen and unmarried but kept *her* baby. A few weeks later Soon An asked whether, if Daddy and Mommy ever divorced, an unmarried Charlotte would place Soon An for adoption. Sometimes it is hard not to laugh at a child's confusion, but it is important to treat these questions seriously. Later you can share the craziness with another adult, or jot down memorable questions in a little notebook.

Demetri began to wonder, because his mother was a nurse, that Denise might leave him at the hospital one day, just as his birth mother had once done. Although a child between six and nine is capable of logical thinking, there is often a large amount of irrational feeling and thought, not to mention missing information, associated with how the child applies this logic to her life's story. Sorting out such confusion is important, because the child's fantasies, even irrational ones, about what *could* happen make her fears seem more real. These fears in turn can lead to emotional and behavioral acting out.

When she was nine years old, Sonia worried that she might be kidnapped and given to another family. She had difficulty falling asleep every night unless she knew that her windows were locked. Young children often have phobias that can linger, or intensify, as they get older. If your adopted child has strong irrational fears about being given away again, talk about how this once really did happen and about how scary it was. "You know, there was a time when it must have felt like you were kidnapped, when we took you and left Guatemala," you might say, to acknowledge to your child that her fears are not entirely baseless. You can also promise your child that you will prepare her for any changes or surprises of a similar nature should they ever occur. This degree of frankness will reassure your child that you are honest and can be trusted.

BUILDING A COHERENT STORY OF HONEST FEELINGS

Between six and nine years of age, internationally adopted children need to have their story reexplained to them with more sophisticated language and concepts. Children of this age should learn the meaning of *abandonment, relinquishment, foster parent, single mother, orphanage, adoption agency,* and any other terms they may hear used in reference to their complex background.

Children at this age are no longer willing to parrot the party line and smile about adoption. If they have not already begun to have negative feelings about adoption, they are certain to begin to experience and express such feelings.

Although children of this age have an expanded range of concepts and feelings, this does not always mean that they will be able to understand adult ideas or points of view. Understanding and supporting a child's changing notions and feelings about his complex background is challenging. Talking through each piece of your child's complex background with him helps him to continue feeling connected to you. Talking about the Four Questions continues to build a coherent story. Together, building connection and building coherence help your child develop greater emotional and behavioral control.

A six- to nine-year-old internationally adopted child faces two new challenges. First, he will hear many new questions from other children and from teachers, parents of friends, and other adults; and he will have to construct answers without the help of a parent. Typical questions include the following: "Are you adopted?" "Where do you come from?" "Why don't you speak your own language?" "Who is your *real* mother?" "What happened to your *real* parents?"

The second challenge comes in the form of school assignments that require a child to present information about his background to an audience. Such assignments often include bringing in baby pictures, making a family tree, or reporting on one's family's ethnic connections and heritage.

PREPARING YOUR CHILD TO HANDLE CHALLENGING QUESTIONS

You need to provide your adopted child with guidelines for handling the questions she will be asked. Make a list of the challenging questions you know she is likely to hear, and ask your child if anyone has asked her a hard question. Then read your list together and say something like "Let's make a plan for how to handle these hard questions." This offer assures your child that you are not leaving her alone to struggle with how the world at large seeks to uncover her complex background.

Offer your child a set of choices for how to respond to difficult questions. The three general choices are keeping information private; answering, explaining, and educating; or deflecting the question by using humor or another kind of distracting response. It is a good idea to use a set of dolls or stuffed animals as characters (questioners and answerers) to create some emotional distance as you help your child work on these responses.

THREE WAYS TO ANSWER DIFFICULT QUESTIONS

1. Say, "It's private," and then walk away or change the subject.
2. Offer an explanation that informs the other person.
3. Respond with humor or a distracting response.

Have your child practice each of these responses, or similar ones that you create with her, until she can reel them off automatically without thinking. For the first option she might say, "That's my private business; I don't want to share that now." She might have ready a way to change the subject, such as the question "What's your favorite game at recess?"

For the second option, when a child feels comfortable and wants to share information, she can offer a brief explanation such as "I don't speak Korean, because I have lived with my English-speaking parents since I was a baby." Work with your child on brief answers to the other most common questions, about her "real" parents and so on.

For the third option, when a child feels confident but is unwilling at the time he is asked to answer a question, a humorous or distracting response such as "I have an *imaginary* mother and a *real* mother; what about you?" can be empowering.

Sometimes parents of adopted children in the early grades are asked to do a class presentation about different kinds of families, or about a holiday or a special food from a child's birth country. These presentations can provide information about international adoption and provide an opportunity for a child's classmates to ask questions. At Easter time Denise came to Demetri's second-grade class and showed everyone how *pysanky* eggs are made. During the presentation Denise told the class that Demetri came from Russia, and she explained how he came to be her son. She let the children ask questions, and in her answers she modeled how to use positive adoption language. When one child asked, "Why was Demetri abandoned?" Denise explained that the word *abandoned* sounded like the birth mom did not make any plan for her child. In fact, she pointed out, Demetri's birth mother did have a plan: She left Demetri at the hospital so that the staff there would take care of him.

PREPARING YOUR CHILD TO HANDLE CHALLENGING SCHOOL ASSIGNMENTS

Children in kindergarten and the early elementary grades are often asked to write or talk about, or assemble visual materials that illustrate, their family and its ethnic and cultural background. Such assignments can be difficult for an internationally adopted child. Indeed, sometimes assignments that simply resonate with a child's complex background, without addressing it directly, can be challenging. Soon An, for example, once came home unwilling to do her reading homework. Charlotte discovered that her daughter's assignment was the story of Hansel and Gretel, the terrifying fairy tale about children who are sent away by their parents and must confront a cannibalistic witch. Any reading that is about a baby or child who is separated from a parent can trigger a child's adoption-related feelings.

It is a huge challenge for internationally adopted children between six and nine years of age to present something from their birth culture or their personal history. The prospect of doing so without a parent present provokes overwhelming feelings. In response to such assignments, many adopted children have an emotional or behavioral meltdown. If this happens to your child, take it as an indication that the assignment is too hard, because your child has so much more information to process than other children. Do what you can to reduce your child's stress. This may include talking to the teacher. If you do so, bring your child along for the discussion. If your child is not melting down but nevertheless seems to be struggling with the assignment, spend some time reviewing his adoption story with him. Then explore together why the assignment is challenging—perhaps your child has no baby pictures, for example. Finally, try to come up with ways that your child can complete the assignment successfully, such as by telling only those parts of the story that he feels comfortable sharing, or drawing a picture of himself in lieu of missing photographs. (I have found that if a child wants to do the assignment in a slightly modified manner, it is a good idea for the parent to alert the teacher in advance, so that the child does not have to explain or ask permission himself.) If you cannot come up with a good solution, it may be time to talk to the teacher about skipping the assignment altogether or replacing it with something different.

If your child is melting down over a school assignment, find out if the work involves themes of family, babyhood, parent-and-child separation, abandonment, loss, or death.

Assignments that require children to share the ethnic or cultural background of their family often make internationally adopted children feel that they must choose between their birth family and their adoptive family. This can raise issues of loyalty. Many internationally adopted children choose to present information about their adoptive family. Soon An, who was born in Korea, told her first-grade class all about her family's Swedish culture, and how at Christmastime she participated in the candlelight Santa Lucia festival. Yi Sheng, who was born in China, talked about how his paternal grandmother (Kenji's mother) made the best sukiyaki, a Japanese dish that Yi Sheng loved.

Even when your child successfully completes an assignment of this kind, the issues of identity and loyalty that it brings up should remain open for discussion in your family. Talking openly and frequently about these matters now will pave the way for similar, yet more complex, conversations you will have when your child enters the preteen and teen years.

FINDING TIME TO MAKE SENSE OF THE PAST

School assignments and challenging questions are opportunities for you to help your child make sense of her complex background and process the feelings associated with the new information and understanding she acquires as she matures. Because a child of this age is often busy with school, friends, and activities, you need to make space in your family life for talking and thinking about the past.

It is all too common for children to have back-to-back activities during this period of development. Swimming, soccer, piano lessons, dance classes, tae kwon do, and the like can fill every waking minute. A heavy schedule is highly stimulating and does not allow for much "down time." Children who have complex backgrounds and difficulty with regulation need more down time (see chapters 2 and 13) than other children do. As a child works on developing a deeper and more nuanced story about her complex background, she requires more down time as well.

Every parent knows that making a place and time to do homework is necessary for the work to be accomplished well. The same is true for the work that a child must do to construct an adoption story and life story appropriate to this age range. The seemingly simple task of integrating newly mastered terms such as *orphanage* or *foster mother* into a life story can take a great deal of repetition and practice. You cannot expect your child to make sense of a complex background unless she has the time and the emotional energy to do so, and it is your responsibility to make sure she has these resources. This is likely to mean that you must go against the prevailing trend of overscheduling children's lives.

Charlotte brought Soon An to see me at the beginning of first grade because Soon An cried herself to sleep each night thinking about her birth mother. She was also becoming a perfectionist. When I heard what Soon An's weekly schedule was, I discovered that the only time she had to process her feelings about her current or past life was at bedtime. Every other minute was filled with classes and activities. "But Soon An loves all her classes and excels at them," Charlotte protested. This might be true, I responded, but I suggested that Soon An was missing out on other important work, and this was leading to problems. Working regularly with a six- to nine-year-old on a coherent story of the past helps prevent perfectionism, obsessive grieving, and other issues from growing into more serious problems.

I explained to Charlotte that just as infants, toddlers, and preschoolers need to hear their story during the daytime, or else they will dream about it at night, Soon An, too, needed time during the day to process her thoughts and feelings about adoption in order to keep her from obsessing about them at night. Charlotte and Joe agreed to reduce Soon An's planned activities, to talk about the Four Questions again and in greater detail, and to make sure Soon An had more time to process her feelings. Eventually, however, they gave in to Soon An's protestations and resumed the activities they had stopped. Soon An's nighttime problems returned, along with some other behavioral and emotional problems. In the next chapter we will see how Charlotte and Joe dealt with these, and how other parents help children who act out and are otherwise troubled as a result of not having worked out a coherent and emotionally satisfying adoption story.

ADOPTION ISSUES FROM SIX TO NINE

Acting Out, Being "Perfect," and Other Challenging Behaviors

"Soon An has turned into a terrible tattletale."
"Demetri is starting to lie when I catch him breaking a rule."
"Mu Ling has turned into a perfectionist!"
"Yi Sheng constantly tells us and his friends, 'I know that already.'"

THE ELEMENTARY-SCHOOL YEARS present many challenges for parents of children adopted internationally. Challenging behaviors in children between six and nine years of age include telling tales on others, telling lies about one's own behavior, and stealing. These negative behaviors seem all the worse because in most cases a six-year-old child understands clearly that such behavior is wrong, yet he persists in doing it. When Denise, for example, asked six-year-old Demetri to put some sticks of kindling by the fireplace, he scattered them all over the living room rug, fully aware that it was the wrong thing to do.

Whereas some children work very hard to be worse than bad, another group works very hard to be better than good. These children strive for perfection, assuming the role of behavior "police" and often becoming unbearable "know-it-alls." Soon An, for example, at age seven, was constantly running to the teacher or her mother to report on her friends' alleged misbehavior. Despite losing those friendships, she persisted in telling tales.

Because much of this behavior is typical of children younger than six to nine, it is wise to consider the child's family age as well as chronological age. Adopted children who may be older chronologically but have a family age of

297

between two and six years, just like birth children with a chronological age of two to six years, are busy trying out good and bad behavior choices. They need lots of clear and consistent guidelines and corrections of their behavior over several years in order to develop full self-control and to make good choices.

Young children rely on parental reactions to their behaviors to form a sense of self. By the time a child is six or so, he has usually processed enough of these reactions to have a generally positive self-image with room for both his good and his bad behaviors. By the time Mu Ling was six years of age chronologically, she knew she was a "good girl" if she put on her coat and shoes to leave for school and that she was a "bad girl" if she dropped food on the floor **Family age is important to consider before judging the meaning of a child's challenging behaviors.** for the dog. But because her family age was only three and a half years, she did not have a typical six-year-old's well-integrated self-image, full of pride in following the rules. Instead, she had the self-image of a three-and-a-half-year old, and a child of this age still breaks rules frequently, because of forgetfulness, experimentation, or playfulness.

HOW THE SIX- TO NINE-YEAR-OLD CHILD THINKS

Children between six and nine years old think in an either/or framework, just as younger children do. Something is either right or wrong; someone is good or bad. There is very little nuanced understanding of things between the two poles. In the early years of this age range, children are often bossy and act like little police officers, informing others of the rules and tattling on those who do not comply. A child in early elementary school is not fully comfortable with the concept that basically good people sometimes make poor choices or occasionally engage in bad behavior. Because of their younger family age and because of their notion that someone (either the child herself or some adult) must have been a "bad person" to cause their relinquishment, internationally adopted children persist longer in having an either/or concept of good and bad. So, when some nine-year-olds already grasp the idea that good and bad may coexist—that it may be acceptable, for example, to tell a social lie—an internationally adopted child may still think in very concrete, either/or terms. This polarization makes forming a positive self-image difficult, because each of us has both good and bad tendencies and moments.

ADOPTION ISSUES AND SELF-IMAGE

The process of integrating good and bad behaviors into a generally positive self-concept is made even more difficult when a child's feelings of shame for his relinquishment intrude. Internationally adopted children feel more strongly and dramatically than other children the pressure to be good and do what is right, because deep down they still fear that they "did something wrong" that resulted in their relinquishment. An adopted child between six and nine faces a cognitive and moral choice, either to blame the birth parent or to blame himself for the abandonment. A child at this age cannot imagine an adult making a mistake, so the child concludes that he was indeed responsible for his own relinquishment. At this cognitive stage the child first "blames the victim"—himself. The weight of such blame, and the shame that follows from it, is hard to bear, and so some children try to hide it by becoming perfectionists or know-it-alls. Or they resort to acting out their shameful image of themselves, engaging knowingly in lying, stealing, and disruptive or disrespectful behavior to prove they are really as bad as they feel. Parents who lecture, punish, or set consequences for such a child only confirm his negative self-image, which leads to even more outrageous behavior.

By understanding this intellectual and emotional tangle, parents can help a child make it through this difficult period. Without this insight into the child's internal turmoil, parents tend to rely on an ages-and-stages approach to discipline and parenting, which drives a wedge between them and their child. This is often the root of more volatile problems of disconnection, and of emotional and behavioral lack of control, when the child reaches the preteen or teen years.

CONSEQUENCES OF FEELING GUILTY ABOUT THE ABANDONMENT

The adopted child's feelings of guilt for her own abandonment foster a strongly held belief of being bad. Many children begin lying to avoid responsibility for bad behavior or mistakes. Mu Ling blamed the dog for eating the cookies she secretly took from the kitchen. She stole the cookies because she felt like a "bad person." Eating the cookies both made her feel better and simultaneously proved her belief that she was bad. Sonia assured her parents that she never tattled on her classmates at school, but her teacher reported that it was a daily problem. Sonia was so worried about her own behavior that she could not stop correcting others.

Some internationally adopted children become perfectionists. They fear that any error or bad behavior will reveal how bad they really are and how responsible they are for their own complex past. Soon An became the model kindergarten student. Demetri worked incessantly on printing his name, sure that it was never quite right, although his writing was remarkably developed for his age. Mu Ling obsessed about getting each and every spelling word correct on the Friday tests.

Although it is tempting to admire a child for having such high standards, perfectionism has its costs. One is that the child often refuses to learn new things, because of deep fears of making a mistake. Yi Sheng began avoiding difficult tasks or challenges, and he announced repeatedly, "I *knew* that," in a self-satisfied tone, every time his parents tried to tell him something new or share some interesting piece of information.

This need to be correct, perfect, and all-knowing can affect social relationships, too. No child wants to be friends with a "know-it-all" or a bossy tattletale. For this reason each of the five First Year Home Group children we have been following struggled at one time or another, between six and nine years of age, with friendships. The important thing for parents to keep in mind is that the root of the matter is each child's anxiety about her inner goodness, not a true lack of social skills.

INTEGRATING GOOD AND BAD CHOICES
INTO A POSITIVE SELF-CONCEPT

A non-adopted child in this age group works on integrating his good and bad behaviors into an acceptable self-concept. He eventually understands that a good behavior happens not because he is perfect, but because he made one good choice; that a bad behavior happens not because he is terrible, but because he made one bad choice; and that the same integrated self can sometimes make good choices and sometimes make poor ones. The internationally adopted child struggles with this task longer and harder, resulting in mixed maturities. When Soon An, for example, had just turned six, she was advanced in her language skills and was beginning to read, but she had not yet integrated her good and bad behavior choices into a positive self-concept. She blamed the dog, a friend, or even her parents for errors to which she could not admit. Charlotte and Joe were horrified that their daughter was beginning to lie.

Understanding why an internationally adopted child suddenly begins lying, stealing, and avoiding responsibility for his actions is a critical part of parenting during the elementary-school years. Tell your child's story again, reconciling his misperceptions about responsibility with the reality. And even though you think you have covered this ground well before your child was six, you must come back to the story again, not as a once- or twice-told tale but as a tale told daily. "I know you may not believe this, but your relinquishing wasn't your fault. It was a grownup decision and choice by your birth parent," you can say, adding emphatically, "I'm going to tell you this until you believe it!" This is an important way for you to maintain a connection with your child. You cannot let your child live with the shame of the secret belief that he is innately bad and therefore responsible for his own complex background. Shame is one of the most toxic emotions.

DO ADULTS MAKE MISTAKES?

From birth to nine years of age children find it almost inconceivable that adults might make bad choices or mistakes. You have to teach your child explicitly that the opposite is true, using yourself as an example. Tell your child, too, that not only do you make mistakes, but you also admit them and, if possible, rectify them. In addition, your ability to maintain your emotional and behavioral balance is a critical model for how your child can maintain a similar balance when she makes an error. For example, if you get on the wrong freeway entrance, or burn dinner, admit, "I made a mistake. I may not be able to rectify it completely, but I'll try." Other aspects of your response are equally important. How do you respond emotionally? Does the mistake lead to verbal self-abuse or name calling, such as "I am such a stupid idiot! How could I get on the freeway going north instead of south?" Do you act out and lose control of feelings and behavior? If you shout and pound the steering wheel, or fling the pot across the kitchen, you are not offering a model that will help your child when she makes a mistake.

Parents may, of course, do all these things, but the really important modeling then is how they pull themselves back together and recover emotional equilibrium. "Well, sometimes I make mistakes," you can say. "I don't like it, but I'll survive and live with myself. I'm still a good person." Acknowledging a lack of perfection is important. All too often an internationally adopted child responds to a parent's loss of control with the question "Was it my fault?" in a tone that conveys she thinks it was.

If taking a wrong turn in the car or making a mistake in the kitchen can cause a parent to lose control, it is no wonder that a child loses emotional and behavioral control at something as monumental as the thought that she was responsible for her own abandonment. This is why a tiny mistake leads to a full-blown tantrum, or refusal to go to school, or obsessive perfectionism.

THE BIRTH PARENT'S RESPONSIBILITY ABSOLVES THE CHILD

You hold the adult knowledge that the birth parents' choice ultimately was a good one, in the child's best interest. But your child has no way to understand that. Rather, at this age, and for most of childhood, he is going to feel that his birth parent or parents "made a big mistake." This means your child will be understandably furious at this adult choice. Although from your perspective this anger may seem extreme, and although as your child gets older he will need to acquire a more nuanced and at least partly positive view about his birth parents' decision, for the time being anger has the healthy effect of relieving your child of the impossibly heavy responsibility for having caused his own abandonment.

> **You hold the knowledge that the birth parents' choice ultimately was a good one, in your child's best interest. But your six- to nine-year-old child does not understand this.**

To help your child get to this important place, tell him something like this: "I know it's hard for you to imagine that a grownup would make mistakes or bad choices. But grownups aren't perfect. Sometimes grownups make choices that children feel are wrong or bad. I know that's how you feel right now about your birth mother's decision to have you be adopted."

Mu Ling's mother Meg told me that when her daughter was in first grade she said she "hated China," because it made such "stupid, mean laws that made mommies give up their baby girls." This is a healthy attitude for an elementary-school-age child. In a similar vein Demetri once proclaimed, "I hate that drinking is so common in Russia; I hate all beer companies. It's their fault my parents couldn't take care of me!" These solutions to questions of "blame" are never completely accurate, but that is not the point. It is most important at this age that the child blames someone or something other than himself for what happened.

MANAGING YOUR OWN EMOTIONS AND BEHAVIORS

A parent who focuses on punishment for lying and stealing at this age exacerbates emotional and behavioral control problems and ends up with a defiant, furious child. Meting out consequences for your child's reactions to her mixed-up thinking (that she was responsible for the adoption) needs to take a back seat to helping her recognize the thinking in the first place and then manage her emotional and behavioral reactions to mistakes or errors. Setting a consequence for lying before your child can honestly admit to having lied just about guarantees she will avoid this responsibility ever after. So hold on to your own emotions about lying and stealing and take a time-out for yourself if you need one. Your child will be waiting for you when you are calm enough to deal with this complex issue.

Proactive parenting is necessary to break the cycle of lying or stealing. Instead of just retelling the child's adoption story and emphasizing the birth parent's responsibility, the parent must explicitly link the child's acting-out behaviors to her negative or shameful feelings.

Your goals are, first, to maintain and strengthen your connection with your child; second, to help your child get her own story straight; and third, to help her manage her own feelings in response to the straightened-out story. Only after you have made it through these three steps can you move on to helping your child learn to tell the truth, admit to having made a bad choice, and make amends. In fact, making amends is the most effective consequence in such situations. The amends that you teach your child to make should not involve shame or be presented as a punishment that might elicit shame.

Making amends simply means taking responsibility. Many six- to nine-year-old internationally adopted children have difficulty in this area, as we have seen; and although they may be quite mature in some areas of their lives, they may need help in admitting that they made a poor choice and committing to make a different choice next time. Often drawing a picture or two, or using dolls or action figures, helps a child to play out various scenarios of engaging in challenging behaviors, making amends for them, and choosing better alternatives.

If your child continues to misbehave purposely in the hours or days following your discussion, it is likely to be because she feels disconnected and still feels overly responsible for her own relinquishment. "I think you need to stay close to me so I can keep you safe and not let you get into trouble," a parent says to such a child. The parent needs to take responsibility explicitly for a child's behavior when the child shows that she is *too young emotionally* to do so; the way to do this is to keep the child, as much as possible, constantly in sight. This reassures the child that he is cared for and is not "bad," but merely needs more guidance and help from a parent. The caring and guiding parent is not the scary parent who would relinquish a child for being bad. Increasing connection in this way stems and then reverses the child's irresponsible behavior.

WHEN ARE EXPECTATIONS FOR ACHIEVEMENT TOO HIGH?

Although many internationally adopted children are successful in school and in extracurricular activities such as music, dance, art, and sports, all this success can come at a price. When a child is so busy, there is little time for him to explore and understand the feelings of confusion, responsibility, and shame that begin to arise from his own story. To know if this is the case for your child, ask yourself these questions:

1. Does your child have less than an hour of free time to relax each day?
2. Is your child struggling with negative self-esteem or perfectionism?
3. Is your child lying, stealing, or engaging in other negative behaviors?
4. Does your child seem overly sensitive to, and reactive to, stress?
5. Does your child have a difficult time recuperating from stress?

If you answer yes to one or more of these questions, you need to consider carefully the level of expectations you have for your child, or that your child feels you have. You need to rearrange your child's schedule and your time together. A child who grapples with feelings of shame related to adoption acts out in the ways described in this chapter, and therefore needs more consistent attention and guidance, and more free time, than a parent might expect given the child's chronological age.

A child who acts out negative feelings, or feelings of excessive responsibility for his own relinquishment, or feelings simply of excessive responsibility for too many activities, needs his parent to make time for him to process his own story. In addition, any child who overreacts to ordinary stress or has difficulty calming down from stressful situations needs a parent to readjust his schedule of activities.

In chapter 2 I referred to a study from the Netherlands that showed that adopted children with parents from a high socioeconomic class had the greatest number of problems, presumably from the stress of too-high expectations. The six-to-nine age range is the time to take that research seriously and evaluate your child's daily and weekly schedule. Is there time for him to think about, talk about, and play about his life story with you? Is there time available in which you can help your child integrate his feelings about being good and bad, and develop clarity about who was responsible for the choices that led to his relinquishment and adoption?

Often the parents who set high expectations for their children, enrolling them in multiple classes and encouraging them to participate in multiple sports, are also trying desperately to meet their own high expectations. Once again, a parent must be a positive role model for a child, in this case by setting reasonable expectations for the time and energy available. Reversing a pattern of high expectations—of the child, of the parent or parents, or both—requires commitment and resolve.

PUZZLES FOR SOOTHING AND CLOSURE

School-age children struggle to put the pieces of their life story together. Fitting together the pieces of a real jigsaw puzzle can give a child a sense of accomplishment that eludes her when she tries to piece together her own life story. Puzzles are soothing for this reason and help bring closure when a child feels stuck. Puzzles should not be additional challenges for your child; instead, they should offer an easy to moderate level of challenge and should help her develop a sense of comfort and competence.

Puzzles can be turned into a "Ping-Pong game" (see chapter 15) with a parent and child taking turns to place a piece. This type of play is especially soothing and connecting, and it provides a more grownup way for you and your child to strengthen your relationship.

PING-PONG MOMENTS

Children who are perfectionists or know-it-alls have trouble accepting new ideas or tackling new skills. Ping-Pong interactions, through a game of catch, a puzzle, or another game of your choice, can be a good preface to introducing a new idea or challenge to your child. Just as for a younger child sucking on a straw in a juice box served as preparation for a transition, a Ping-Pong interaction can help you and your child get ready for something more challenging.

Soon An at six years old was just beginning to learn the rules of the game Candy Land. But she became hysterical when she had to go back to an earlier section of the board. This loss of control happens to all children at some times, but it is worse and more frequent in internationally adopted children who cannot bear to lose. They associate losing with earlier losses in their lives, and they feel that they have had enough of those.

Charlotte used a Ping-Pong game, involving patting a balloon back and forth across the floor, to help Soon An. They played this side game during a game of Candy Land; each time Soon An's turn came, Charlotte and her daughter patted the balloon back and forth between them three times. Then Soon An spun the Candy Land spinner to see what her move was. After her move, they played another round of balloon Ping-Pong. The distraction of the Ping-Pong game was soothing and connecting, and it helped Soon An avoid meltdowns when she had to go backward on the Candy Land board. It did not take long for Soon An to be able to tolerate her level of frustration and move on to playing the game without the extra support.

SELF-TALK

By the time children are in elementary school they are old enough to use *self-talk* strategies for soothing and calming. These are occasions when a child uses the same encouraging and supportive words that a parent has used in the past. Because the child is imitating the parent, there is a strong sense of connection. Yi Sheng, for example, balked at learning new things. His parents always used the words "Take baby steps, go slowly, you can do it." This was a special mantra that Yi Sheng had heard for years. Now, at nine, Nina taught him to say the same words to himself as he did his math homework. When Yi Sheng called for Mom because he was stuck on a problem, Nina first asked him to repeat the self-talk mantra: *Take baby steps, go slowly, you can do it.* Then she listened to him explain the problem. Repeating the mantra first helped Yi Sheng connect with his mother and soothed his emotions. He relaxed visibly and he was able to focus his attention on the problem. Sometimes Nina offered him a Popsicle to help him focus. Often internationally adopted children in this age range can do challenging work when they are calm, but getting to calmness is the hard part.

"I find Yi Sheng really knows everything he needs to know to do the work, but when he gets anxious he can't think straight, or even think at all," Nina told me. "He loses his concentration and then he decides he's stupid. That ties into his fears that he was a bad child who deserved abandonment. Suddenly, the math homework has become proof that his whole life is his fault. At that point he explodes and rips up the paper."

Helping your child stay calm with puzzles, Ping-Pong games, and self-talk strategies is an important part of parenting during this period, and indeed throughout your child's school years.

BABY STEPS AND SCAFFOLDING

I have used the term *scaffolding* (see chapter 21) to describe how parents can break down a skill into manageable parts, evaluate what the child has already mastered, and add new components of the skill slowly and comfortably. A folksier term for this process is *taking baby steps*. For adopted children from six to nine who are easily overwhelmed and prone to losing emotional and behavioral control, baby steps and scaffolding are important parenting tools, especially when it comes to helping them with schoolwork challenges. Some parents, for example, put a paper over half of a spelling word list, simply to make it more manageable.

Others have a child do half of a set of math problems, and then take a break to calm down and refocus.

Sometimes a parent has to become involved in explaining new material. This was especially important for the parents of Yi Sheng, a boy who vividly recalled how it felt to "not know anything" when he was adopted and his whole world became new, and therefore now lacked confidence in his ability to learn new things. But even internationally adopted children without such explicit memories can have trouble learning new things. New things can be hard for any child, and they are especially difficult for a child who struggles with emotional control.

More so than with a birth child in this age range, you will find yourself grappling with the choice between helping your adopted child with new school skills and making him do the new task himself. When Sonia had a challenging new assignment, she withdrew and refused to look at the paper. Her father knew she was able to read the brief instructions, but Sonia withdrew and refused to try. So David decided on one occasion to play a scaffolding game with her. He began to read the paper, but left out a word here and there, just to get Sonia's attention. Within a few moments Sonia exclaimed, "Daddy, you're reading it wrong!" She took the paper and read it correctly.

David continued to play dumb. "What does that mean?" he asked. His daughter patiently explained the assignment to him, discovering how much she knew in the process.

If David had insisted that Sonia "do it herself," the outcome would have been less positive. Often an internationally adopted child needs to maintain a connection with a parent in order to get started on a task, especially a new task, or to continue or finish some work. A parent who is supportive in this way builds connection and encourages a calm focus. A parent who demands too much independence too soon undermines both of these areas.

When your child is six to nine years of age, you need to find—and adjust as needed—the right rhythm of oscillating closer to and farther away from him as he explores independence. This is part of learning to be in sync with your child. As much as he may appear not to want your help, either withdrawing into inactivity or boldly claiming to be able to do everything himself, he will eventually recognize and respond to your support. I have found that most internationally adopted children seem to know that they have extra challenges when learning new skills, and their deep love and appreciation comes out in tender ways.

Sonia, for example, began to insist that Daddy put her to bed at night because he helped her so much on her homework. Demetri drew flowers for his mom as a thank-you for helping him in an encouraging, nonjudgmental way. Yi Sheng asked if he could help his mom cook dinner. Each of the children was aware of how much special and extra effort the parent was making.

"I don't think everyone works as hard as you do to help their child," Yi Sheng told Nina, half happily yet half afraid that he was "too much trouble." His mom hugged him closely and said, "I love doing things for you," which served to reassure him and thank him simultaneously.

Most adoptive parents are pleasantly surprised at how quickly challenging behaviors disappear when the parents make the effort to understand their child's feelings about such matters as being good, being bad, being responsible, and learning new things.

ADOPTION ISSUES FROM TEN TO TWELVE

New Bodies, New Pressures

BETWEEN TEN AND TWELVE YEARS of age, your child's body begins to change dramatically. The changes of puberty lead to many questions and concerns from all children, but especially from internationally adopted children. If your child is not talking about bodily changes, you need to begin strengthening the Magic Circle (see chapter 9) to enhance your parent-child connection. Your child needs to feel comfortable asking you just about anything. Once you have created this comfort zone, get ready for a flood of questions, such as "Do you still have sex?"

Your child may already be asking questions like "Will I look more like you as I grow up?" (meaning more like your racial type) or "Will my breasts [or body hair, or facial hair] look like yours?" Whether your child is relatively silent, or has already taken the lead, it is time to begin talking about physical differences in your family and the genetic contributions of your child's birth parents.

THE FACTS FIRST

When your child was three or four years old, she needed to learn some basic facts of reproduction in order to understand the concept of adoption—to understand how she grew inside one woman's body but was being raised by different parents. As a preteen your child needs much more information about how and why her body is changing, and about the details of human sexual reproduction in general. She needs this information for the same reason that any other preteen does, but in addition it will lead her to understand that she began with a sexual connection between her birth parents. When a preteen revisits the question "What happened to me?" she goes back not only to her birth and early childhood but all the way to her conception. She speculates about her birth parents' relationship, both sexual and emotional, and she tries to understand her place in this newly expanded context.

Preteens need lots of information. They need to understand the biology of sexual development and the mechanics of human reproduction. It is usually hard for a child to frame questions about this subject, so parents need to take the lead. Finding a good age-appropriate book at the library or bookstore is an easy way to open the subject. Charlotte got a book for ten-year-old Soon An, and they began reading a chapter together every night at bedtime. Each chapter generated questions and discussion. The book and the regular nightly reading provided a structure to help Charlotte and Soon An cover this complicated topic. Soon An occasionally requested that they reread a chapter. Just as a four-year-old might struggle to understand the basic concept that all babies grow in a woman's body, preteens struggle with what to them are the seemingly bizarre facts of human sexual development and reproduction.

"You mean the sperm gets into the woman's body with the man's penis?" a preteen might say, surprised if not shocked. A preteen needs time to move from the abstract ideas to the more personal realities of what this all means.

"That's icky!"

"Do you and Daddy do that?"

"What about families with two mommies or two daddies? Can they make babies?"

"Did my birth parents really have sex to make me?"

Questions like these do not emerge all at once. They are the result of long periods of thought as your child digests the information you share with her.

WITH PUBERTY, THE BIRTH PARENTS COME TO VISIT—FOR GOOD

In your child's younger years you may have had the feeling that there were two sets of parents living in your home. Now, with a preteen child, that feeling will grow even stronger, because as your child enters puberty his changing appearance will suggest what his birth parents might have looked like.

For your internationally adopted child, the bodily changes of puberty are more than just the acceleration of physical and sexual development. They also force your child to confront more intensively than in his younger years the fact that he is profoundly different—from his beloved parents and from other relatives, friends, and peers. This is true both for racial features and for other traits that have genetic roots.

Mu Ling at twelve was constantly reminded of her difference from her parents. Her breasts seemed to be small in proportion to her frame, whereas her two mothers have large breasts. "Did you nurse me and [her sister] Clara with your breasts?" Mu Ling wanted to know. When her mothers said no, and explained why, Mu Ling asked "Can I try nursing now, since I missed it with you?"

When an internationally adopted child enters puberty, his changing appearance brings up anew questions about what his birth parents looked like.

A boy at this age wants to know if his voice will be as deep as his adoptive dad's, or if his beard will come in with the same thickness as his dad's beard, or if he will develop in a way that is more like his birth father. A boy may wonder if his penis will look like his birth father's.

Adopted children wonder what the various emerging differences or samenesses, relative to adoptive parents and especially to birth parents, mean. The child's changing body is a constant reminder of his birth parents, and in particular a reminder of just how little he or his adoptive parents know about the birth parents.

Adopted children at this age begin to feel, and exercise, more independence—from both sets of parents. In order to feel fully independent from their birth parents, however, they must first know who those parents were. In part this knowledge comes from their understanding of their adoption stories, as we have discussed elsewhere in this book. During this period, when their bodily changes make them think more concretely and thoroughly about their biological parents, they begin drawing a more complete picture of who those parents were, what they looked like, and what genetic traits they passed on to their children. Only when they have drawn this more complete picture can adopted children successfully differentiate themselves from their birth parents. Of course, in the same age range children also begin to feel a disconnection from their adoptive parents, who the children now understand are not a physical model for what they themselves will grow up to be. Adoptive parents and children together must address both kinds of connections and disconnections.

ADDRESSING DIFFERENCE AND DISCONNECTION

Although your child is beginning to feel disconnected from both her birth parents and her adoptive parents, she is not likely to be able to articulate such feelings.

For this reason you need to address them proactively, talking in detail about your child's physical features and those of her birth parents and her adoptive family. By bringing up and talking about disconnections with your child, you provide vital emotional support; your child feels "held" by you in the Magic Circle. This support, in the context of a long-term connection, is invaluable because it can come only from a parent. At this stage of a child's life, repairing and strengthening the Magic Circle, which has been stretched too far because of these disconnections, prevents a child from being left alone with a deep sense of difference and distance from her parents and family.

There are many things that a parent can say to bridge such disconnections. Charlotte, for example, told Soon An, "It must be hard to see your body changing and wonder what it will look like when you stop growing. I wish we had a photograph of your birth mother. The information that we do have only tells us how tall she was, just five feet, and that she was small-boned."

On another occasion Joe, Soon An's father, suggested to her, "Let's look at some Korean teenagers or women and see what they look like," as he and Soon An headed for their favorite Korean grocery store.

"Daaa-deeee!" Soon An protested. But her father would not be put off.

"I saw Korean women," Joe said to Soon An after they had shopped, "with beautiful moon-shaped faces and thick, dark hair, and with small breasts and strong legs, like great soccer players. I bet your birth mother looked like them, and so will you."

Joe purchased a copy of a fashion magazine for Asian women, and he picked up an English-language copy of the local Korean American paper. He left these on the coffee table at home. One night Charlotte went through the magazines and cut out a couple of photos of Asian women, which she stuck on the refrigerator. "I like how these women look," she commented to Soon An and the rest of the family. These experiences and conversations made it much easier for Soon An to think and talk about her Korean appearance. She also began to make comments indicating that she felt positive about her appearance.

"Demetri looks Caucasian, like me, even though we have different skin tones and hair and eye color," Denise said to me one day. "Do I have to worry about his feelings of being different from me?" All preteens and teenagers feel they are different, even when they live with their birth parents. Every adolescent thinks, at one time or another, "I'm different from everyone in the world, and so very alone." Being adopted adds an extra layer of difference. Being a child of color adopted by Caucasian parents, or any adopted child noticeably different in appearance from the adoptive parents, means yet another layer of difference. Demetri, I suggested to Denise, would always be aware that he is "passing" as non-adopted, as his mother's birth child, as a child born in America. Frequently, adults who were internationally adopted as children say such things as "I always felt different in my family, but I didn't want anyone to know."

Parents need to address these various kinds of difference within the family in order to maintain a connection with their adopted preteen. Several of the parents with whom I have worked have said that the picture book *Horace*, by Holly Keller, which their children loved at six or seven years of age, resurfaced as a favorite in the preteen years. *Horace* is about a leopard adopted by tigers who feels he does not fit in with his family. First he tries to change his spots to stripes. Then he pins up photos of important leopards. Finally he runs away from home to look for a family where he will "belong." He realizes in the process that a family that loves him is more important than a family that looks like him. His mother had been telling him, ever since he was little, "We loved your spots and wanted you to be our child," and finally Horace is able to hear her. "If you chose me, can I choose you?" Horace asks his mother.

This kind of reconnection is what adoptive parents hope will happen during the ten-to-twelve years. After all the differences have been explored and acknowledged, after some disconnecting in other words, the child discovers that her adoptive parents truly are her real parents, and she chooses them back.

FINDING THE RIGHT TIME TO TALK

Parents need to look for openings for conversations about difference and create opportunities to talk if openings do not appear. Many parents report that drive time is a great time to bring up difficult subjects; neither person can leave, but, assuming the child is in the back seat, neither one has to look directly at the other. A parent can make a casual comment and then let it drop, giving the child a chance to digest the comment.

This was how the subject of having parents of two different races came up while Yi Sheng and his father, Kenji, were running errands one Saturday afternoon. Yi Sheng wondered aloud what it would be like to have a "white" dad. Kenji and he talked about this and then shared the conversation with Nina when they got home. This discussion brought the three of them closer. Only then did Yi Sheng confess that some boys at school had made fun of him because he had so little facial or body hair. Finally a bigger secret came out: Yi Sheng had never told his middle-school friends that he was adopted. The middle-school kids assumed that Kenji and Nina were his birth parents, because Kenji looked Asian, as Yi Sheng did. This story is an example of how easily things can get buried with a preteen child, but they can be unearthed if parents take the time to dig a bit.

Sometimes preteens approach a subject indirectly. Mu Ling, at age twelve, was nervous about bringing up the subject of body hair with her two mothers. All of Mu Ling's school friends were showing off their shaved armpits and legs, and Mu Ling felt embarrassed by her relatively hairless body. She was not yet aware that Asian people tend to have less body hair than people from other groups. Meg and Laura, her mothers, both had "furry legs," as Mu Ling put it, and they did not shave them. Mu Ling had first used the expression "furry legs" long ago, but now that she was a preteen it took on new meaning. She began teasing her mothers, as an oblique way to approach the topic of shaving legs. Gradually Meg and Laura realized that Mu Ling did not know that it was "normal" for her to have smooth, hairless underarms and very little pubic hair. Talking about this, and also looking at photos of nude Asian men and women, made Mu Ling and her sister Clara nervous and giggly, but it also reassured them that their development was normal. The conversations strengthened the girls' connection with their moms and each other, making the family stronger.

Parents, too, need to bring up subjects that they themselves find difficult or awkward. Once your preteen has a solid grasp of human sexual development and reproduction, you need to address the more complex and troubling aspects of sexuality. All preteens should learn about topics such as abortion, rape, premature birth, birth control, out-of-wedlock birth, extramarital affairs, prostitution and human trafficking, and the sexual abuse of children and women, as well as about religious, cultural, and political strictures concerning sexuality and conception. If you do not address these matters, you can be sure your child will hear about them from others.

Just as you were asked intrusive questions when your child was younger ("Is that your child?" and "How much did he cost?" for example), and your child heard similar questions (such as "Is that your real mother?"), your preteen child will encounter similar comments and questions. Some examples that I have heard include: "I heard they kill baby girls in China." "In Guatemala there are women who sell their own kids." "Why didn't your real mom just have an abortion if she couldn't keep you?"

Preteens who hear such questions from their peers are unlikely to share these experiences at home, so parents must anticipate them. Discussing such matters with your child and providing him with knowledge about them buffer the negative effect of intrusive questions. Because of their drive to make sense of the past and of their parents' choices, internationally adopted children need clear, honest information and opportunities for discussion.

IMAGINATION AND MISSING INFORMATION

A child who is searching for answers imagines all sorts of possibilities in the absence of hard facts. For example, with no firm proof of why his birth mother left him at the hospital, Demetri imagined many different scenarios. When he learned that unmarried couples could conceive babies, he imagined that his mother was unmarried and ashamed to keep him. He sometimes wondered if his birth father even knew he existed. Did his birth mother tell his birth father? Was their relationship a long-term one or a one-night stand? Things he had read, movies, television programs, and comments from peers had informed Demetri about some of these possibilities and he imagined the rest. Although your preteen may be able to keep fantasy and reality separate in some areas of life, internationally adopted children find this difficult when the subject is birth parents. Your job is to help your child realize and remember that poor choices or bad luck on the part of birth parents is not inherited.

Because they often know so little about their birth parents, internationally adopted children tell stories about them that combine fantasy and reality.

When Mu Ling learned about rape on a news broadcast she began imagining that her birth mother was a rape victim. Mu Ling casually commented to Meg, "I think my birth mom was raped." Meg realized that it was time to talk with her daughter about rape, and other difficult sexual topics, to make sure that Mu Ling understood what she was talking about. Mu Ling asked questions about how rape happens, whose fault it is, how it is punished, and whether rape was more common in China than in the United States. In the end Mu Ling admitted that she really did not know what had happened to her birth mother, but she remained afraid that "something bad happened to her" and that was why she was adopted. This is an example of how the question "Did I make the Big Change happen?" continues to haunt internationally adopted children as they learn more about the world.

I have found that when preteens and teens keep these kinds of thoughts private and continue to be mixed up about the circumstances of their conception and birth, their identification with their birth parents focuses on negative choices or unfortunate circumstances. As a result a child may identify with her birth parents by making poor sexual choices (too-early exploration of sexuality, promiscuity, getting pregnant, engaging in sexually risky behavior or relationships). By talking frequently and openly about birth parents' sexual choices and the consequences thereof, and addressing your child's fantasies about those choices, you give your child the opportunity to use words rather than actions to explore her own sexual identity, and you help her develop an identity that is based on good, safe choices, regardless of what birth parents may have done.

Admittedly, these topics are not easy. Here are some basic guidelines for finding your way. First, make sure you cover the basics of sexual development and reproduction by the time your child is eleven years old. Figure on a full year of discussion. Next, find a book that clearly explains some of these harder and more complex topics. Take it slowly, one topic at a time. If you feel truly unable to do this alone, involve your partner or a close friend. Or consider finding a family therapist who will broach these subjects with you and your child.

FACTS AND CULTURES

Non-adopted children apply information about parental sexuality to a single pair of parents. Internationally adopted children must apply this information to two sets of parents and grasp two different cultures' views of sexuality.

"Why is it all right for a mom without a husband to keep her baby in the United States but not in Korea?" Soon An asked her parents.

Sonia queried her parents, "Why doesn't the Catholic Church let Guatemalan women use birth control?"

"If it was illegal to have more than one child in China, why didn't my birth mother use birth control or get an abortion?" Mu Ling asked.

In order to grasp his own story fully your child needs to understand that his birth parents lived in a country and culture with unique attitudes, prohibitions, and laws that shaped their choices. Internationally adopted preteens not only must learn about sexuality, as all preteens do, but they also must understand sexuality within a particular culture that is different from the one in which they have been raised for most of their lives. You may need to do research on specific cultural beliefs and specific countries' laws to help you piece together with your child the pressures and influences on his birth parents at the origin of his life.

GENETICS

Along with sexuality, preteens need to learn about the inheritance of genetic traits. These matters are especially important for internationally adopted children to grasp. Carolyn and David found that the topic of genetics provided a positive way to talk to Sonia about her birth parents. David found a list of genetically inherited traits on the Internet. Together he, Sonia, and Carolyn went through the list and talked about what each of them had inherited from their birth parents. They talked about how looking in the mirror was one way to "see" what their birth parents contributed. Among the traits they discussed were height; hair color and texture; eye color and shape; nose size and shape; tooth size, arrangement, and bite; earlobes; dimples; and breast size and shape. They also discussed things like athletic and artistic abilities, and math skills, which might have a genetic component along with environmental and cultural roots.

As she considered these traits, Sonia decided that she could draw pictures of her birth parents based on her own features. Although David and Carolyn realized there was little real chance of Sonia drawing an accurate picture, they did not interfere with her efforts. They knew how painful the lack of knowledge had been for Sonia. They remembered the nights she cried herself to sleep, sobbing and saying, "I'll never know what she looked like, and she'll never know how I turned out!" Now Sonia could create an image of family members that would comfort her. Accuracy, in this case, was not the point.

IDENTIFICATION, FACTS, AND FANTASY

As children approach their teens they experience a strong drive to form their own identities. For any child this process involves identifying similarities to and differences from their parents. When there are two sets of parents, the process is more complex. Sometimes, because so little is known about birth parents, children focus on the "bad choices" they made, particularly in the sex-and-reproduction department. "Why did they have sex and make me if they didn't want me?" the child may ask. Sex, according to this logic, becomes the birth parents' "bad choice," which led to the child's adoption.

Watch for your child's negative identification with her birth parents. If she twists fantasy and reality for the purpose of negative identification, you need to untangle the confusion and redirect your child toward positive ways to identify with her birth parents.

Fantasy that creates positive identification with birth parents is always welcome. Preteens become interested in their birth parents as physical bodies, people with breasts, beards, body hair, and other features of adulthood. Drawing pictures of birth parents, looking in the mirror and creating a self-portrait, or looking at magazines with photos of ethnically or racially similar adults are good ways for your preteen to expand her thoughts about herself, her birth parents, and her relationship with them.

THE FOUR QUESTIONS FOR PRETEENS

As a child embarks on puberty and sexual maturity he needs to construct new and more elaborate answers to the Four Questions (see chapter 7): What happened to me? Who will take care of me now? Did I make the Big Change happen? Will everything change again, and will I lose you, too? Many ten- to twelve-year-olds show a particular concern with the second and fourth questions. One day when she was eleven years old, Sonia asked her mother, "If you die, Mom, who do I ask for birth-control information?" It took Carolyn several minutes to recover and construct an adequate answer. She was surprised that Sonia was asking about birth control, but she was positively shocked to think that Sonia worried about her death, that Sonia still felt that her world could be turned upside down again. Carolyn had forgotten over the years that a child with a complex background *always* believes that "anything can happen."

Carolyn's first instinct was to reassure her daughter that she would not die. But, of course, anything can happen, so Carolyn acknowledged Sonia's fear. "I know you are worried something might happen to me, that I could die soon," she said. Then she reassured her daughter—and herself—by adding, "But I don't think that's very likely." Finally Carolyn answered the question: "You can always ask Dad or your Aunt Ellen, my sister."

Perhaps, for adopted children, puberty feels a little too much like the world turning upside down again.

"Does Aunt Ellen know about birth control?" Sonia asked in response.

"Yes, she's forty-eight years old, and married, and has a kid," Carolyn said. "She knows."

"OK," said Sonia. She was silent for a while. Then she pulled her mother close and whispered in her ear, "Mom, don't disappear on me like my first mother did. I love you so much, I'd die if you left me."

Sonia's question clearly reflects the gut-level fears of many, if not all, internationally adopted children. Sonia had fears of abandonment, fears of having no caregiver, and fears of having to face big adult questions, like birth control, alone. She still feared the uncertainty of the world, no matter how well things seemed to be going. Perhaps, for an adopted child, puberty feels a little too much like the world turning upside down once again.

As parents we need to keep in mind that growing up and becoming independent are a double-edged sword for internationally adopted children. Much as a child desires to grow up, from the earliest days or months of life he has associated becoming more independent with losses, and specifically with the loss of a parent. For this reason he may alternately act quite mature and then regress to childish behaviors. We need to make it clear to our internationally adopted children that there is nothing about their growing older and becoming more independent that makes it more likely that they will lose us. As their bodies and personalities mature, we will still be there to teach, support, and love them, and the interdependent connection between us will grow.

FAMILY-LIFE AND SEXUALITY CLASSES

Internationally adopted children in the preteen and early teen years experience several school-related challenges that are important for parents to know about. Many schools offer a family-life and sexuality class in fifth or sixth grade, and then a human biology and reproduction class in seventh or eighth grade. Both classes bring up challenging material for internationally adopted children, as you can imagine. It helps to prepare your child for this material ahead of time by discussing it at home. Whether you do or not, though, your child will come home with new questions for you, about such things as HIV, abortion, sexual abuse, and premarital sex.

Soon An, for example, asked her parents if she might have HIV. "Was that why my first family didn't want me?" she inquired. During this period Soon An had revealed concerns about feeling unwanted in other ways, too. In cases like this, parents need to attend not only to the specific question the child asks but also to the basic fear of not being lovable, which all adoptees have. As Soon An learned more about sex and family matters, she continued to relate what she learned to the first of the Four Questions: What happened to me? Being sick with HIV, for example, was in her mind a plausible reason for being unwanted by her first family.

Sometimes in class another child raises a question about adoption, or links adoption to a topic that the class is discussing. An internationally adopted child, whose adoption history is likely to be known to her classmates, can feel as if the whole class is watching her, waiting for her to provide an answer. When Mu Ling's class learned about premarital sex, for example, and learned that unmarried women could have babies that they might decide to place for adoption, "every head in the room turned my way," Mu Ling reported to her parents.

There is no way to avoid this type of school experience, but there are ways to help your child through it. First, good preparation about your child's own adoption story, including whatever facts you may know about the circumstances of her conception and birth, is essential—because one day an entire roomful of seventh or eighth graders is going to look at your child and demand to know, "Was premarital sex why you were placed for adoption?" Your child should have a short, clear answer at the ready.

Second, make sure as each new school year begins that your child's short, clear explanation is one with which she is still comfortable. A ten-year-old child wants to answer differently from a twelve-year-old.

Third, ask the teacher if there are any components of the family-life or sexuality curriculum that are likely to be blatantly disturbing for your child, and find out when the class will be taught. For example, if you know the class will be discussing sexual abuse, and you know that your child was sexually abused, you will want to prepare her in advance. Some children may not want to go to school or to that class on that particular day. Abused children, and children with complex backgrounds in general, need to feel in control of their lives. Giving a formerly abused child control over being present or not in a class discussing abuse is a positive step toward recovery.

Fourth, tell your child that she can leave a class at any time if disturbing material comes up. She can, for example, just raise her hand and ask to be excused to go to the bathroom. Or, if she needs a longer absence from the class, she can ask to speak with the teacher privately, or she can call you and ask you to contact the school. Most children do not realize that they can leave a class discussion if it is upsetting. Again, knowing that this is possible, even if it is difficult and embarrassing, empowers the child.

Most children do not in fact choose to stay home from school. But having the option to do so says to a child, "My parent is taking care of me. My parent knows this is a hard topic for me." Simply knowing that she can stay out of school, or exit a class for a while, gives a child a choice, and having a choice means the child feels less helpless, less trapped by the past.

Some parents balk at this advice and say that their child needs to "learn to face reality." In such instances I always tell parents that their child *has* faced reality, and has done so multiple times—first when she was separated from her birth parents, next when she was adopted, and then again when the parents and child have discussed adoption together. Facing reality is not the issue. Rape, abortion, abuse, abandoning or otherwise handing over babies, foster care, and so on are disturbing realities of which your child is well aware. The issue is rather that your child does not want to feel alone, without a beloved adult, when these issues are discussed and does not want to be singled out as an example of someone whose life history includes such events.

Demetri, for example, came home one day, kicked the couch, and said to his mother, "I hate having everyone tell me that kids who are adopted probably had parents who used drugs and got AIDS. It's so stupid. I know my birth mom drank, but she didn't do drugs." Denise discovered that Demetri's teacher that day had invited several homeless children to speak with the class. These children explained the reasons they left home, including incest, parental drug use, alcoholism, and extreme poverty. Demetri felt stigmatized by his own birth mother's alcoholism, even though his classmates did not know she was an alcoholic. Nevertheless, the class conversation following the homeless children's visit included comments that there would not be homeless kids, or kids needing to be adopted, if parents did not use drugs. Demetri spent the rest of the day fearful that someone would ask him if his birth mother died of AIDS.

The fifth way to help your child is to listen compassionately and provide support to help her express what was difficult about the conversations at school. Compassionate listening means listening with your heart as well as your head, and it means making an effort to see the world from your child's point of view.

THE "FLOUR BABY" ASSIGNMENT

Some schools try to help preteens face what it is like to have a tiny baby to care for, in order to help them think about the reality of sexual reproduction. The curriculum calls for each child to care for a "baby" (a five-pound sack of flour, for instance) for one week, being responsible for it at all times. In a typical assignment the young "parents" can hire a babysitter when they take a shower, but they must feed the baby three times a day and keep the baby with them at all times, whether at school, at home, or out in public. It is a powerful experience, and most preteens come out of it convinced that they want to wait a *long* time before having children.

Assignments like this can bring out buried or unconscious feelings in internationally adopted children. Mu Ling, for example, was excited to get her flour baby. She was hoping for twins—two three-pound bags—but instead she got a little boy. "I wish it wasn't flour," she told Meg when she got into the car after school. "I want a rice baby, like me, from China." Mu Ling decided to give the baby a Chinese name. She went to the library to look for a book on Chinese names, and she picked Li Po, the name of a famous Chinese poet.

After the first day back at school, Mu Ling reported a startling discovery. "I was the only person whose baby didn't have a toy! Why didn't I buy a toy for my baby?" she asked her parents.

Mu Ling had played out, if unconsciously, her own beginnings as a baby who had had a minimum number of toys and little stimulation in the orphanage. Fortunately her parents were able to help her recognize that her "parenting" of Li Po imitated her own early experience. They were able to help her learn and practice how to parent a baby "family style," with more stimulation and interaction.

Mu Ling also played out her abandonment issues with Li Po. One afternoon she left Li Po downstairs while she did her homework upstairs. When she came down she saw the "baby" and suddenly became angry. "You died on me, Li Po," she shouted, "and I hate you!" This dramatic talk with its inverted logic expressed Mu Ling's deep, intense feelings about abandonment, which are typical of internationally adopted children. For several hours Mu Ling refused to care for Li Po.

Meanwhile Meg and Laura, Mu Ling's mothers, debated whether to intervene. Meg thought they should encourage Mu Ling to resume her care for Li Po. Laura thought they needed to talk about Mu Ling's story and took it upon herself to open the subject with Mu Ling. When Laura said, "You know you were left by your first mother, just like you left Li Po," Mu Ling covered her ears, squeezed her eyes shut, and yelled, "I can't hear you!" This was a sure sign that Laura had touched on a tender but important topic.

"I bet you felt rejected and like you were dead when you were a tiny infant with no mommy to care for you," Laura continued, weaving Mu Ling's earlier comments into her own story of loss. Mu Ling gave Laura the "thumbs up" sign and then hid her head under a pillow on the couch. "Having a baby can bring out your feelings of what you experienced when you were a baby," Laura added. "Feeling this way is normal, given your life. I'm here to help you now and in the future . . . if you ever have your own real baby."

"I'm never, ever going to have a baby!" Mu Ling shouted.

"That's fine, you don't have to," Laura reassured her. "Meanwhile, let me hold your hand for a moment." She took Mu Ling's hand and said, "I love you just the way you are."

It was several hours before Mu Ling could resume caring for Li Po. But with her parents' understanding and support she completed the project, eventually giving Li Po careful and attentive care.

Soon An gave her flour baby two names—one Korean, Jin, that she used at home, and the other an English name, Horace, that she used at school. Soon An insisted to her teacher and classmates that her baby had had a foster mommy and a birth mommy earlier in his life and that she, Soon An, had adopted Horace.

Every night at home she told Jin his story, of being with his first mom, "who couldn't take care of any baby," and then moving in with his foster parents, "two old people who loved you," and finally flying across the ocean to live with "Mommy Charlotte and Daddy Joe," the names of Soon An's own adoptive parents. Her parents found that Soon An's notions about Jin included some misperceptions, including that foster and birth parents were one and the same. After a week of sitting at Soon An's bedside, listening to the story unfold, Charlotte and Joe were both more than ready to be done with the flour baby assignment.

The flour baby assignment demanded more time, energy, and work from the adopted children than from non-adopted children. Additionally, the parents of the adopted children needed to be present and observant in order to pick up on how their child was working through and making sense of her own story in the context of the assignment.

Demetri and Sonia also received the flour baby assignment. They had heavier after-school schedules than the other children, and for this and other reasons they were less engaged and attentive in caring for their babies. As the assignment proceeded, both began to show other signs of difficulties, seemingly unrelated to the curriculum. Demetri developed stomachaches and headaches and sometimes asked to come home from school just before the class in which the flour baby assignment had been given. Sonia developed sleep problems, and she wanted to sleep in her parents' room each night. The mothers of both Sonia and Demetri called me for consultation. After hearing about their situations, I suggested to each that the flour baby project had awakened implicit memories in both children. Stomachaches and headaches and sleep difficulties are typical physical signs, or what psychologists and counselors call *somatic symptoms*, of unresolved feelings.

> **Somatic symptoms replace acting-out behaviors. A child who has tantrums at times of separation may learn to suppress those feelings, but instead has somatic symptoms, such as stomachaches.**

I suggested to the two mothers that the somatic symptoms would ease if Sonia and Demetri had more time to process the feelings and thoughts elicited by their flour babies. Denise and Demetri decided that Demetri would take a few days off from some of his sports activities during the week when this assignment was running. Carolyn decided to make time each evening to talk to Sonia about her own past life, and about the story of her flour baby's young life.

About a month after the project ended, both Denise and Carolyn called to report that both children continued to talk about their flour babies. Although Demetri's headaches and Sonia's sleep difficulties had vanished, their talk about adoption had increased, as had emotional outbursts. After the project ended, both children continued to keep their flour babies in their rooms; the flour babies helped them think through, and feel more deeply, their own early childhood experiences. In contrast, the non-adopted children in their classes were relieved to leave the big sacks of flour in the kitchen, without a backward glance.

CHANGING BODIES, CHANGING REACTIONS TO STRESS

During the ten- to twelve-year-old period, internationally adopted children often grow to look very different from their adoptive parents. Preteens are very aware of these differences, which remind them of their complex backgrounds. Each child from our First Year Home Group struggled with, and occasionally collapsed under, the combined pressure of ordinary puberty issues and specifically adoption-related issues. The Netherlands study (see chapter 2), as we have seen, found that internationally adopted teens who faced high expectations from parents were especially likely to have difficulties with anxiety, depression, and substance abuse. As we look into the lives of the children we have been following, we can see various ways in which this happens.

Soon An, who attended a private middle school with a heavy academic emphasis and a minimum of diversity, kept busy every minute, using perfectionism as a way to avoid facing how her complex background set her apart from her classmates. Demetri kept extra busy as well, using his participation in a selective soccer team that practiced every day and traveled to tournaments most weekends as his way to "fit in." Yi Sheng became involved in an all-ages music club and found friends there among some older, more sophisticated teens. Sonia became an avid reader, burying herself in a literary world and withdrawing socially. Mu Ling became a preteen clothes horse in an effort to win social acceptance by following the latest fashion trends.

From time to time each of these busy, seemingly successful preteens complained of headaches, stomachaches, and nervousness. Some picked at their skin and engaged in extreme nail biting. They had periods of explosive anger and of sullen withdrawal. Their parents were concerned, alternating between the hope that nothing was seriously wrong and the fear that their child was deeply troubled. They delayed addressing their concerns, instead assuming that their child fell within the normal range of preteen behavior.

When I work with parents of internationally adopted preteens, I remind them that their children have more to deal with emotionally and socially than their non-adopted peers. I suggest that these early indications of excessive stress should be taken seriously, and that parental attention and support at this time, and efforts to reduce the amount of stress, would prevent the behaviors and negative emotions from getting worse.

Unfortunately, several of the First Year Home Group children did develop more difficult problems. By eighth grade Demetri began to have trouble falling asleep at night and waking up for school the next morning, and he was exceptionally moody. Sonia began to have panic attacks when a school project was due. Yi Sheng's parents noticed that his clothes often smelled of smoke and alcohol when he came home from seeing his older friends, and they wondered if he was "experimenting." Signs of depression, anxiety, and substance abuse were becoming a part of these children's daily lives.

Demetri, Sonia, and Yi Sheng wanted to act mature and to meet their parents' high expectations, and so they pushed themselves to keep going. Their old fear that they caused their own abandonment and adoption hooked them into trying to prove that they were especially "good" at something or many things—particularly when they saw how high their parents' expectations for them were. But when they took on more than they were ready to handle, stress overwhelmed them.

REDUCING STRESS BY STRENGTHENING THE MAGIC CIRCLE

When I look at youngsters like these, I sense that the Magic Circle, their connection with their parents, is stretched too far. Their emotional and behavioral controls are stretched as well, particularly because of the late hours they keep, their travel schedules, and the disruption of their regular routines. When the circle is stretched thin, preteens begin to worry anew about two of the Four Questions (see chapter 7). They wonder about the second question, whether someone is really there to take care of them. They also revisit the third question, which asks whether they are the cause of their own abandonment; they push themselves to be extra busy and successful in order to prove that they are not failures—people, that is, who would deserve to be abandoned.

Parents are responsible for strengthening the Magic Circle and answering the Four Questions. This proactive parenting reduces a preteen's stress level.

I encourage parents of internationally adopted preteens to address directly with their children such underlying feelings of aloneness and unworthiness. Sonia, for example, had put on twenty extra pounds. Her parents talked with her about how she still needed them to take care of her, and they linked her overeating to her trying too hard to take care of herself before she was really ready. "I do still need you," Sonia sighed. "I just hate to admit it. I feel like being dependent on you means I'm a failure, a bad person, which is probably why my first mother didn't want me." Her parents helped Sonia see that her behavior resulted from her fears. Sonia was still struggling with feeling responsible for her losses and was still unsure about who would take care of her as she matured. Talking with her parents about the Four Questions and about her behavior enabled Sonia and her parents to deepen their connection. Sonia's parents also made a point of cooking meals together with Sonia and exercising with her in order to strengthen the Magic Circle and to demonstrate that they would continue to care for her actively.

Setting limits is another way to strengthen the Magic Circle, express parental care, and let a child know that he is worthwhile. Sometimes this involves not only limits on a child's behavior, but limits on a parent's expectations for the child as well. Demetri's mother was so proud of her son's accomplishments in soccer that she failed to see that he was getting too little sleep and was spending too much time away from home for his age. In order to reduce Demetri's commitments and adjust his schedule to allow him to get enough sleep, Denise had to confront her own feelings as well as her son's. Demetri, for his part, feared that Denise would leave him if he did not excel at something. But what finally motivated Denise to take action was her discovery that Demetri had been using amphetamines and coffee to stay awake at school. Despite his loud protestations, Demetri was relieved, and reassured about his mother's devotion to him, when she finally set limits on his athletic involvement and his bedtime.

MANAGING FEELINGS WITHOUT SUBSTANCE ABUSE

As Denise discovered, it is not premature to talk to preteens about the use of legal and illegal drugs or alcohol as means to prop up energy levels or numb negative, anxious, or depressed feelings. Talking about feelings and fears, along with setting appropriate limits and expectations, can prevent or stop such dangerous behavior.

Ten or eleven years old is not too young for you to begin educating your child about drugs and alcohol. This is true even if your child has gone through D.A.R.E. (Drug Abuse Resistance Education) or a similar antidrug education program at school.

Programs like D.A.R.E. focus on peer pressure, but what you need to teach your child is different. Make it clear that you are aware of youngsters your child's age and older who use alcohol and legal or illegal drugs as a way to "have fun," "relax," or "calm down and feel better." Substance abuse, you need to say, does not happen only because of peer pressure. It can happen to good kids, highly capable kids who are working hard to meet parents' expectations and goals. Under pressure at school, in extracurricular activities, or even at home, these kids feel they are "falling apart" or "can't do it anymore" and need a boost to help them continue on what they perceive is a required path. Talk with your child not just about the peer pressure she might feel but also about moderating the pressure in her life.

Denise asked her son, "Do you ever feel that you desperately need a break from all this pressure—that if you could take a magic pill and make it all go away, you would?" Denise just about fell over when her twelve-year-old son looked relieved and said, "Mom, I didn't think you knew how I felt. I'd give anything just to be ordinary and not have to perform all the time." Denise realized that her son's intense participation in soccer had become a kind of performance, like his charm when he first came from the orphanage. Soccer had become his survival skill. Demetri's fatigue began to lift and his self-medicating ended once he was spending less time playing soccer and was enjoying the exploration of other interests and activities.

Yi Sheng's parents had a similar conversation with their son. Although Yi Sheng was motivated in part by peer pressure to emulate the older boys with whom he was spending time, the conversation also revealed that Yi Sheng was feeling "parentless," unsure of who his real parents were and fearful of losing his adoptive parents, when he was hanging out with his older friends. Nina and Kenji told him frankly that they felt he was unsafe with his older friends and that they suspected him of using tobacco and alcohol. Yi Sheng, who was just turning thirteen at the time, was furious at first. But, surprisingly to his parents, he quickly accepted the new limits they placed on his nighttime excursions and on the company he kept. "When you are sixteen or seventeen you can return to these activities at night," they told him, "but for now it's days only, and only in our company." It turned out that he was thrilled to share his interests with his parents and had never imagined they would want to be involved.

INDEPENDENCE AND LIMITS

When your child was three or four years old, you did not respond to signs of excessive independence or maturity by withdrawing from his presence or relinquishing your parental role. When your child is a preteen, however, those responses become more tempting. You are proud of his newfound independence and maturity, and on top of that he frequently *asks* you to step back and get out of the way. But in many instances you need to resist this temptation. Your preteen needs you to make firm decisions that create a strong Magic Circle of connection and care. Your adopted child is still wondering, "Who is going to take care of me?" Changing bodies and changing emotions leave children with complex backgrounds feeling vulnerable and alone. Setting safe limits and reasonable, unpressured expectations are ways to answer that question in a truly reassuring way.

Identity Challenged and Reinforced

DURING THE FIRST DECADE of your child's life, you were your child's chief advocate and spokesperson in public. As your child enters her second decade, the responsibility for advocating and speaking up for her falls more and more on her own shoulders. She must speak on her own behalf, especially when she faces intrusive, curious questions about her adoption and her complex background. Your child must take control of her own story, deciding when to share it, and how much of it to share, with other people.

Consciously take a step back and give your child the space to take on this responsibility, taking into account all the good conversations you have had with her about her story and her identity. If your child seems to need a refresher course in how to handle situations in which she is asked to say where she "came from" and who her "real parents" are, consider buying a copy of the workbook called the *W.I.S.E. Up! Powerbook*, created by Marilyn Schoettle for the Center for Adoption Support and Education. The premise of the *W.I.S.E. Up! Powerbook* is that an adopted child knows more and is wiser about adoption than others and can therefore share information and inform others—when she so chooses. The workbook, which is written at a level that appeals to preteens, leads children through the steps of deciding how to handle a variety of difficult questions. Parents, too, are encouraged to participate as their child works through the book.

Make sure your child has your permission and support whenever she needs to draw a firm, clear boundary that protects her private thoughts and feelings from others. Find out what your child says when questions become overly intrusive, and ask if she needs stronger words or other kinds of help. But do not be too pushy; she may not need extra help. If the lines of communication with your child are open, she may ask for help a few days after you introduce the subject. This is a new way of using the Magic Circle: A parent waits to be asked.

MUST INDIVIDUALS STAND FOR AN ENTIRE GROUP?

All internationally adopted children at some point have the experience of a teacher pointing them out in class as representatives of national, racial, ethnic, or cultural groups. The teacher expects such a child to represent and speak for an entire demographic category. This category may be one that the child no longer thinks much about, or it may be one with which he still identifies strongly. This kind of calling out in class happens to preteens and teens in even the most forward-looking schools. Here are some examples that children from our First Year Home Group encountered:

> *"We are studying the Cold War, a conflict between Russia and the United States from 1950 through 1970. Demetri, you were born in Russia. What can you tell us about Russia and the Cold War?"*

> *"This semester we will be reading a book about Japan's invasion of Korea,* So Far from the Bamboo Grove *by Yoko Kawashima Watkins. Since you are from Korea, Soon An, could you tell us how Koreans feel about the Japanese?"*

> *"Mu Ling, can you explain why Chinese people forget to use plurals when they learn English?"*

Fellow students, too, ask similar questions. "Sonia," one classmate inquired of her one day, "why does everyone fight in Guatemala? That's all I hear about your country." In another instance Yi Sheng was asked, "How come Chinese celebrate New Year's at a different time every year? Can't Chinese people count?" Comments like these from teachers and peers stamp a child as "different" from his classmates, aiming a spotlight at him as a person with a minority status and as a resident expert of sorts on that minority group. It is akin to asking the one African-American child in a class to talk about what slavery was like.

The expectation that a single person, a child, is able to represent and speak for an entire group is far more common than many parents realize. Your internationally adopted child will run into this type of situation more than once. Prepare him for such situations, first by identifying the phenomenon of "spotlighting" or calling on a "resident expert" and pointing out that this happens to many other people as well, not to adopted children only. Then provide your child with verbal tools for handling such situations and minimizing their emotional impact. Your child could learn to say, for example, "I wasn't even alive during the Cold War, so I have no idea," or "Just because I was born in Guatemala doesn't mean I know what people there think. I've lived here since I was a baby."

Just as when your child was younger you helped him respond to people's assumptions that he must be able speak the native language of his birth country, so, too, must you prepare him now for "spotlighting." No one person is responsible for representing an entire country, race, ethnic group, or culture. This understanding is part of learning how to navigate between the mainstream and the minority.

CLIQUES AND PREJUDICE

Cliques, which arrive on the scene for many children in the ten- to twelve-year-old period, are by nature exclusive, and they can heighten your child's sense of being a member of a minority or of being an "other," as social scientists put it. In fact, cliques during these years can be breeding grounds for outright bullying, ostracism, and prejudice, all of which can be emotionally devastating for the internationally adopted child who already feels that "there is something wrong with me."

Cliques form because children want to associate with other children they consider to be the "same" as themselves, for the simple reason that this helps them avoid uncomfortable feelings of difference. Preteens and teens are prone to feeling "different," of course, and cliques protect against that feeling. Cliques exclude others, sometimes for a particular reason and sometimes for no explicit or discernible reason at all. They operate by demanding that everyone in the clique be the same, by using a common greeting, perhaps, or a similar squeal or laugh, and by encouraging a uniformity of taste—in music, dress, sports, movies or television shows, and other friends, for example. They exclude children who are perceived as different or those who are more outspoken and individual in their lifestyles and preferences. Although cliques may begin in late elementary school, they are most prevalent in the sixth to eighth grades and into the beginning of high school.

Unfortunately, during this period internationally adopted children may easily stand out and be labeled as different. Such children experience extra levels of feeling different: being adopted, being born in another country, having lived in a foster home or orphanage, having a family in which not everyone "matches," and in many instances being racially distinct from their classmates and from their neighborhood peers. When Yi Sheng heard that a group of homeless children had been invited to visit as part of a class project at his school, he was deeply affected. "I've been homeless," he told his parents. "But I don't want anyone at school to know, because then people will make fun of me." His parents discussed the issue with him, but it was not until several weeks later that they figured out that the day on which Yi Sheng stayed home with "a terrible headache" happened to be the same day the homeless children spoke to the class. Stomachaches and headaches are often ways that preteens respond to feeling stressed or different.

For a child who previously felt comfortable being with her family, suddenly a parent who "doesn't match" creates a sense of difference and discomfort. "I'd like to go eat at the Korean restaurant without you, Mom. I'd feel more comfortable if no one was staring at us because you're white," Soon An announced one day when she was twelve. Her mother bit her tongue and did not chastise Soon An for being insensitive. Instead Charlotte simply commented, "I'm glad that you trust me enough to tell me that and that you were thoughtful enough to do so in private."

A preteen's increased level of independence is another cause of her feeling "different." A preteen child turns more often to friends and less often to family for support and emotional inclusion. Preteens look for ways to feel connected and identical to peers. Sometimes two children "twin" themselves, dressing, talking, and looking as much alike as possible. Mu Ling and another Chinese adoptee in her class twinned themselves throughout middle school. Other children, like Demetri, join a sports team to feel part of a group. Others become part of a clique. And still others, like Soon An, become "outsiders" or "loners."

FINDING SUPPORT AS AN "OUTSIDER"

When Soon An's mother complained to the school about the cliques in Soon An's class, she was told that this behavior was normal for this age and that every child felt left out. When Soon An came home one day and complained that some kids had told her that her eyes were "too small to see out of," her mother went back to school for a more serious talk. The otherwise supportive administrators responded that this type of comment was typical of the age. Charlotte refused to accept this. "Racism, put-downs, and bullying are not developmental stages," she insisted.

Around this time Soon An decided that she wanted to keep her mother out of her school life, and she began to insist that she could handle the kids at school on her own. But Charlotte noticed day after day that her daughter left the school building alone, while all her classmates left in groups. Charlotte grew angry and bitter. When she tried to reopen the subject with Soon An, her daughter shut her down. "I don't want to talk about it," Soon An said. She shut herself in her room and devoted herself obsessively to her homework.

Painful as it was for her to do so, Charlotte stepped back and let her daughter manage on her own. However, when she learned that the school nurse, a Native American woman, had been supportive of Soon An, Charlotte initiated a relationship with her. Through this relationship Charlotte kept tabs on what was happening in school, and she felt confident that the nurse was giving Soon An good advice on this issue. Thanks to this trusting relationship with the school nurse, Soon An began to develop a stronger, more independent self-concept.

One day near the end of eighth grade Soon An announced to her parents, "I've gotten used to having people stare at me all the time, to being an outsider." At first Charlotte and Joe took this to be a sign of poor self-image, but gradually they realized that it was an important step in their daughter's coming to terms with her own complex identity. For her middle-school graduation Soon An chose to wear a traditional Korean outfit. This act of individual courage reassured her parents that Soon An would continue to develop her identity as she entered high school. Whereas some children acquire this self-confidence early on, as Soon An did, others need more time.

PREJUDICE, DIVERSITY, AND "AUTHENTICITY TESTS"

According to the sociologist Heather Dalmage, groups of children, beginning in the middle-school years, often use racial or ethnic "authenticity tests" to determine who can be "in" a given peer group or clique. Dalmage lists five areas that are typically "patrolled," as she puts it, by preteens as they decide who is in or out: physical appearance; the kinds of slang a child knows, and what language the child speaks at home; whom the child interacts with outside the group; what neighborhood the child lives in and where the child hangs out, shops, and so on; and "cultural capital" (taste in music, sports, television, Internet sites, magazines, for example). Internationally adopted children, like non-adopted children of mixed race or mixed ethnicity, often "fail" these tests as being "too Chinese" or "not Chinese enough," "too white" or "not white enough," and the like, depending on the circumstances and the makeup of the group or clique.

Many preteen groups use "border patrols" to decide who can be allowed in. Yi Sheng had expected to be included in a group of Jewish children because his mother, Nina, was Jewish and his family celebrated Shabbat each Friday evening. However, the "border patrol" of the Jewish group determined that Yi Sheng did not belong in the group, because he "didn't look Jewish."

Like Soon An, Yi Sheng felt excluded from racial and ethnic groups. He complained to his parents, "I don't fit in *any* group." It was not only the Jewish group that had not accepted him. "I went to eat with the Chinese kids," he reported to his parents. "You know how they all sit around together at lunch? Well, they made fun of me." "You look like you're a white guy," one of the Chinese boys had jeered. "Where'd you get your haircut?"

Parents need to talk about cliques, "border patrol" behavior, and authenticity tests with their internationally adopted children beginning in the preteen years and continuing through adolescence. Sometimes this means helping your child find a group that fully accepts him, and sometimes this means helping your child feel positively about his individual identity, without regard to groups and cliques.

Charlotte helped Soon An find local organizations that promoted diversity in schools, churches, and the wider community. Together they read newsletters from these organizations and articles that dealt with the topic in the local English-language Korean immigrants' newspaper. Over time, Soon An's interest in diversity and community building became an important part of her growing self-identity. Her negative experiences as a preteen eventually became the basis for her strong self-confidence in the years to come.

Soon An discovered that the cruelty of cliques could be reduced with adult encouragement and support. Her teachers introduced community-building games, in which the class had to complete a project without splitting into subgroups, and a

Each child's path to identity is unique. Sometimes it involves fitting in with a group, and sometimes it means standing alone, apart from a group.

technique called "compassionate-listening training," which teaches children to listen empathetically to children with other points of view. Soon An noticed that for a short while the atmosphere in her classes was better, and less exclusive, after the teachers used community-building techniques or taught the class to be aware of racial or other epithets. But once the teachers moved on to other material, the same old cliques were reestablished and prejudiced remarks were heard once again.

IDENTITY FROM THE INSIDE

Preteens and teenagers readily recognize the unfairness of identity assigned from the outside. Most young people of this age like the idea of taking control of their own identity, rather than letting others determine it based solely on stereotypes ("Wow, you must be Asian because you're great in math!") or physical appearance ("What are you? You're so *brown!*").

"What is personal identity good for?" Carolyn asked her family one evening at the dinner table. Everyone chewed silently, and finally Sonia, twelve years old at the time, said, "I guess it helps me know who I am and what I want to do, how I want to act. It's my north star."

Self-assigned identity is a way for a person to structure and give meaning to her life. Seeking a less abstract statement, David asked Sonia for an example. "Well, you know, I like music. Sometimes I love the Beatles. That's pretty white, I guess! But other times I'm into salsa dancing, and that makes sense because I'm Hispanic. I guess having a *mixed* identity helps me navigate in a music store!"

Preteens and teens often come up with very concrete and practical responses to their parents' questions about abstract topics. The important thing is to give them an opportunity to explore and discuss their ideas. Articulating her concept of identity with her parents gave Sonia a boost in self-esteem. Offer your preteen self-concept opportunities much as you would offer healthful food, on a regular basis.

Naturally each child must find her own route to identity. Each child's path is unique. It includes exploration of her own ethnic background and of the ethnic background of her adoptive parents as well as interests unique to her. Mu Ling sought to surround herself with other international adoptees and became involved in activities for older children in her local Families with Children from China organization. Sonia explored her connections to the southern United States, and especially Georgia, where her adoptive mother's roots lay. Yi Sheng found his niche following anime cartoons and finding friends at film festivals and other anime events who shared his interest. Demetri developed his identity through practicing hard and excelling at sports; even when he had to cut back his involvement on a championship soccer team, he went on to become the sportswriter for his school newspaper.

DISCUSSING DIFFICULT OR MISSING INFORMATION

By age ten internationally adopted children are cognitively and emotionally ready for additional information about their adoption histories. There are two things that are hard for parents to share and hard for children to digest: difficult information, and the likelihood that there is a vast quantity of missing information.

Some parents possess difficult information about their child's history. Difficult information includes facts about the less savory circumstances that led to a child's adoption. Each of the First Year Home Group families had some information that they hesitated to share with their child. Denise knew that Demetri's birth mother was an alcoholic and that his birth father had been in prison. When Sonia was five years old, Carolyn and David's adoption lawyer told them Sonia's birth mother had made it known that she had another child available, should they want a sister for Sonia. This suggested to them that the birth mother or the lawyer was in the business of selling babies. Nina and Kenji had reason to believe that the paperwork they received on Yi Sheng was false or partially false, based on Yi Sheng's own memories and on things the orphanage director had told them at the time of adoption.

Other adoptive parents (although none in our Group) have information that their child was rescued from child traffickers, that birth parents lost their parental rights because of neglect or abuse, or that a previous adoption had dissolved before the child was placed. Some parents have learned that their child was a result of incest or rape. Some parents had first been assigned one child, who may have died or been adopted preemptively (and illegally) by another family, before the parents arrived, in which case the adopted child they took home was a "replacement."

In fact, *there is missing information about all internationally adopted children.* The missing information leaves large blanks in the child's early history about such matters as the reason he was available for adoption, the medical or psychological background of the birth family, the birth mother's health and the quality of prenatal care, the child's condition at birth (prematurity or low-birth-weight problems, for example) as well as the precise date and time of the birth, and other things a preteen might want to know. There may be minimal or no information about the birth parents' educational or work backgrounds; about learning difficulties that might be hereditary (dyslexia, for example); or about the parents' appearance, abilities or disabilities, interests, skills, or personalities.

For an internationally adopted child, missing information is often worse than difficult information. As we have seen in the previous chapter, when there is missing information there is instead a blank slate upon which a child can, mixing fantasy and reality, mentally paste any and all problems or scenarios. Specific information, no matter how painful, is something to hang on to, to struggle with. Specific information such as knowing that a birth parent was unwed, or raped, or faced with punishment for having more than the legal number of children (as can happen in China), though this information may be painful to a preteen, limits the free play of fantasy. But when there is no information at all, anything could be possible. As you work through these issues with your child, and as you read the remainder of this chapter, keep in mind that through the preteen and teen years your child will dream up and consider a whole host of possibilities about the past whenever the relevant facts are missing.

NEW INFORMATION YOU CAN SUPPLY

To help the parents with whom I work fill in gaps in their preteen child's adoption story, and to help them address "grownup" matters that their child was not mature enough to handle before the preteen years, I give them the following list of questions. Parents often do not think to address these questions, or they think that they should wait to do so until their child is older. But omitting this kind of information leads to confusion as a preteen processes her adoption story and attempts to understand the events that led up to her adoption. Therefore, I encourage you to take the time to discover if your child knows the answers to these questions.

1. Do you know that you have a birth father as well as a birth mother? Both were involved in your conception and possibly in the decision to place you for adoption.
2. Do you know that a woman or girl can be pregnant and not be married? How young do you think a girl can be when she gets pregnant?
3. Do you know that in [name of birth country] people have different cultural or religious beliefs about what is appropriate or inappropriate sexual behavior? Would you like an example from your birth country of how people think about sexuality, and how that's different from this country?
4. What options do you think your birth parents had for getting care for you if they couldn't care for you themselves?
5. Do you know that international adoption is a legal agreement, not only between two sets of parents but also between two countries as well, about who will raise and be responsible for the child?
6. Did you know that to become adoptive parents we needed to prove we would be good parents—by having a "home study," by having our fingerprints checked to make sure we had never been in trouble with

the law, and by demonstrating that we had enough money to take care of you?

Answering these questions provides preteens with opportunities for deeper, more mature thinking about their birth parents and the reasons for their adoption. The answers help them think more logically and more realistically about adoption, and they help fill in missing information. The facts that the answers to these questions reveal help children separate fantasy ("You kidnapped me!") from reality ("They really checked to see if you were a criminal?").

Preteens want to examine the details of what was revealed during the adoption process, so be ready to pull out your paperwork and your communications from the agency or lawyer. Be willing and prepared to share everything: the referral papers with the child's name and photographs, other documents that relate to the relinquishment, notes you wrote during phone calls, and more. All these bits and pieces are part of the life puzzle your child is piecing together and thinking about.

DIFFICULT INFORMATION: WHY NOW?

If you have withheld specific information from your child about his birth family or the circumstances surrounding the adoption, the preteen period, according to most adoption experts, is the right time to share it. Remind yourself how important honesty is when it comes to keeping a child's trust. Do not lie to your child if you have information, either written or orally communicated, that fills in his adoption story. Before your child reaches the teen years, all the information you have about the adoption, no matter how troubling or even shocking it is, should be shared, unless the child is particularly fragile emotionally or is cognitively impaired.

Why now? The answer is simply because eventually the secret will come out. When your child eventually does learn the truth, as a teenager or young adult, your having withheld it now will undermine his trust in you. This information belongs to him.

I have encountered over the years a variety of information that is withheld from adopted children. Parents are understandably reluctant to share that a child was the result of incest, rape, or an extramarital affair. They often keep secret the fact that the child has siblings or half siblings who remained with the birth parents. Parents hesitate to share their suspicion that the birth mother was selling her babies, or that the child was stolen, sold, or used for sexual purposes.

Parents do not want to put into words the grim reality that the child was "on the street" or sexually abused prior to adoption. Some parents do not want to remember, or reveal, that the birth parents lost parental rights because of neglect, drug or alcohol abuse, mental illness, or incarceration.

These can be painful realities to reveal. But secrets in the family are harmful to everyone. Over time they create serious family problems that may include uncontrolled emotions and behaviors; these may seem to be unrelated to adoption or adoption secrets, but in fact they are related. Healthy families share information. If you feel you need extra support to reveal troubling information to your child, it is wise to enlist the help of a mental health professional specializing in family therapy.

ANSWERING DIFFICULT QUESTIONS

By age twelve most children know that babies can be conceived out of wedlock, by rape, "accident," and other ways that do not fit the standard adoption story. Be prepared for your child to ask startling questions such as "Do you think my birth father raped my birth mother?" It is easy to freeze up and say, "Of course not!" But this reaction shuts down the conversation and your connection to your child. Instead, take a deep breath and ask a question in return, such as "What makes you think about that possibility?" Usually the source turns out to be the plot of a book or movie your child has encountered.

Whatever the source, your child needs you to discuss and clarify this kind of worry. Your answers should open the subject wider, too, so that you can find out if there is something else that your child is really thinking and worrying about. Why is your child considering this? What may have come up in her life to spark this idea? What would it mean to your child if she were the product of a rape? Helping your child to share her thoughts, worries, and guesses is important. Adopted preteens often worry that their birth parents were "bad people," and they are concerned that this badness might rub off magically on themselves. They need to explore these possibilities *with you* in order to discover that "bad luck" or "bad choices" on the part of birth parents cannot be passed on like eye color or a cute dimple.

Among internationally adopted preteens and teens, magical thinking about birth parents happens quite often. It is an example of mixed maturities, for a child who most of the time is very mature cognitively and has good reasoning skills may revert to magical fantasy when the subject at hand is her birth parents.

What is vital for your child to know is that *you* accepted her, loved her, and cared for her—and still do!—regardless of whatever truths she now knows about her past and her birth parents' choices or experiences. Your unconditional acceptance of your child is the key to her accepting herself. Your love is the model for your child's self-acceptance and self-love.

Your unconditional acceptance of your child is the key to your child's ability to accept and love herself.

As your child absorbs difficult information about her birth parents' sexual and reproductive histories, about their legal status, and about their cultural background, your job is to remain steadfastly caring. Your child may express feelings that range from fury at her birth parents to hatred of herself, with a detour through anger at her adoptive parents. Remember that you are the only available parental figure toward whom your child can vent her feelings and emotions. You should not be surprised if your child has a delayed reaction to difficult information. All may seem fine for a few days or even weeks, but eventually the feelings will be expressed. The trigger might be a parent's setting a limit or enforcing a consequence for misbehavior. Suddenly the child explodes with words like "I'm just like my birth mother; you can't trust me. I hate you. I wish you'd never adopted me." Words like these really mean "I'm scared that I'm a bad person and that you will abandon me."

In response to an outburst like this, challenge your child's confused identification with the birth parent. "You and your birth mother [or father] are two different people," you can say. "You may have made a poor choice, but that doesn't make you a bad person. You forgot to call home when you knew you would be late, but that is not at all the same thing as deciding to have a baby outside of marriage. You can learn from your choice and make a different choice next time."

Introduce the birth parents into the conversation occasionally when you set limits or define expectations for your child. "Your birth mother would want you to call home if you were going to be late, and I do, too," you might say.

A deep-seated belief of adopted children, illogical as it may be, is that if the adoption had not occurred the child would not now have sad, mad, or upset feelings. The child imagines a magical division of her life between the good life with her birth family and the bad life with her adoptive family. One of the best ways to respond to a preteen who professes to think this way is to create a hypothetical double parental unit that *combines* the power of both birth and adoptive parents. I suggest to parents that they say something like this: "I think that if your birth mother were here she would want you to be responsible and call home if you were late. Your birth mother and I would agree: If you don't call home, you have to do extra chores to make amends." An answer like this is akin to the common situation in which one parent points out that the other parent agrees about a consequence or expectation; in both cases the child is discouraged from dividing the world into "good" parents and "bad" ones.

In the heat of an argument or a meltdown it is not uncommon for a preteen adopted child to show that she fears she is "just like" her birth mother—irresponsible and prone to making bad choices. Your job is to bring this fear into a safe conversation and reassure your child that what she says is not true. It is especially not true, you must say, because you are planning to make sure your child has all the help and support she needs to make good decisions. In addition, point out that you will continue to work with her to identify good things about her birth parents with which she can identify. When you do this, you are also assuring your child that you will be there for her far into the future.

STAND-INS FOR BIRTH PARENTS

It is hard for a child with little or no information about his birth family to identify positively with his birth parents. Therefore, he needs other role models who in significant ways are like his birth parents. You need to help your child as he seeks out role models that reflect his ethnic, racial, or cultural background. These role models can serve as stand-ins for the birth parents.

Parents need to be on the lookout for opportunities to provide such role models for their child. The Olympic Games offer an opportunity for children and parents to view the most accomplished athletes from a child's birth country. Finding posters or photographs of the competitors and hanging them on the refrigerator or in the child's room is a good way to help your child identify with the physical traits of his own ethnic group. Members of music groups and dance groups, and others such as movie stars or political figures, who represent your child's heritage may be depicted in posters or photos as well. The preteen years are an important time to go to concerts, theatrical performances, street fairs, and holiday celebrations that include adults from your child's birth country, so that your child has a variety of role models from which to choose. Yi Sheng identified with Yao Ming, the first Chinese basketball player to gain prominence in the United States, and Sonia identified with several well-known Hispanic recording artists. Both children fantasized that their birth parents might be like these cultural icons.

MANAGING CHALLENGES TO IDENTITY

During the preteen period parents should begin taking a new role in their child's life in regard to bias, prejudice, name calling, and other identity-related challenges that the child faces at school and among her peers. I have suggested several approaches in this chapter, all of which rely on a parent's working closely with a child. The first approach is to prepare your child for what lies ahead, including educating your internationally adopted child that she will be seen as a member of a minority, as a person who is outside the mainstream. Adoption itself confers minority status; international adoption creates a second, separate minority status; and each group of children from a single birth country is a smaller minority within the larger group of international adoptees. Helping your child recognize ways in which she can get along with the "mainstream" is the beginning of helping her advocate for herself in challenging situations.

The second step is helping your child process the strong feelings and thoughts that arise from challenges at school and in other social contexts. This includes making sufficient time available, talking things over, and inquiring about a child's emotional reactions—as opposed to waiting to be told.

The third step is helping your child find an adult mentor who can help her navigate challenges. Children often find such a mentor at school. This can be a teacher or a counselor, or even a janitor, bus driver, or front-desk staff person.

Soon An made friends with the school nurse, a Native American woman, who helped her deal with being the only Korean adoptee in the school. Demetri discovered that the Philippine-born gym teacher, who had emigrated to the United States as a teenager, really understood what it was like to be "different," and this man became an ally in some social situations that were hard for Demetri to resolve. Mu Ling made a deep connection with the head of the middle school, a Caucasian woman who "clicked" with Mu Ling and helped her to master strong emotional outbursts at school. In each case the child's parent eventually approached the adult to make a connection, to make sure the person was a good mentor, and to show appreciation for the role this person was playing in the child's life.

The final step is to rejoice with your child as she begins to stand up to challenges and manage them on her own. This independence is a vital part of preteen development. And it is important for you to compliment your child for handling a situation on her own. "You did a great job just speaking up and saying, 'I don't know,' when everyone was looking at you and expecting you to know everything about Korea," you might say. "I'm proud of you."

28

ADOPTION ISSUES FROM TEN TO TWELVE
Independence without Disconnection

"Sonia is ten and loves to have overnights with her friends, but the next day she is totally a mess emotionally. The slightest comment from us sets off a tantrum. Then she says, 'You're not my real parents! You can't tell me what to do.'"

"Demetri is twelve and wants to be the best at soccer, kickboxing, and baseball. It seems he's so busy that we are never together for a quiet family evening. I feel like we are becoming two separate people with nothing in common except driving in the car together and sharing a house."

"Mu Ling will redo her homework papers if she doesn't think they are perfect. She stays up late working and then can't get up the next morning. Her perfectionism seems to be getting worse, even though she already gets top grades."

"Soon An would rather clean the basement than play with a friend."

"Yi Sheng prefers school to summer vacation because he likes having a highly scheduled life. But we're worried that he doesn't know how to relax and just play."

INDEPENDENCE, CONNECTION, AND CONTROL

Our culture's emphasis on packing in as many activities as possible causes nearly every child to be extremely busy. Internationally adopted children seem to crave this type of scheduled life. Researchers have shown, in fact, that such children are more socially active and more involved with extracurricular activities than their non-adopted peers. Yi Sheng, who prefers a busy school day to a leisurely summer day, is typical.

As we have seen elsewhere in this book, internationally adopted children have more difficulty than non-adopted children when it comes to modulating their emotions and behavior. When they are young, these children depend on routines and predictability for feeling mentally in control and for being able to manage emotions and behavior. Spending many hours a day within the Magic Circle of connection with parents also helps a child maintain control of emotions and behavior.

As a preteen, however, a child begins to be more independent and begins to develop a separate identity from parents. The Magic Circle stretches too far, the safe routines are discarded, and distance grows between child and parent. Greater independence diminishes the child's sense of connection with parents and with other reliable and predictable features of life. The life of a preteen, especially in a home with pressure to succeed in academics, music, sports, art, and other areas, is anything but predictable.

This feeling of disconnection, along with the stresses that come from growing up and from pressures to succeed, leaves the preteen internationally adopted child vulnerable to emotional and behavioral outbursts. The child may return to coping behaviors that his parents thought he discarded years ago. For example, Sonia, who had not had tantrums for many years, fell apart after being at an overnight and began having tantrums again. Demetri and Mu Ling reverted to their bossy, know-it-all ways, keeping excessively busy as a way of managing their response to independence and stress.

DRAMATIC STATEMENTS AS EXPRESSIONS OF FEAR

"I'm going to run away." Meaning: *I'm afraid you don't want me or will leave me.*

"You're not my real parents." Meaning: *I'm afraid I don't belong here.*

"I wish I were dead." Meaning: *I'm afraid of my intense feelings about all this.*

"I hate myself." Meaning: *I feel unlovable.*

"I hate you." Meaning: *I fear you hate me.*

Loss of behavioral and emotional control can take new forms in preteens. Preteens express their fears through dramatic statements and threats; the box above lists some examples. At their root the fears are of losing connection with a parent or losing control of one's own feelings, and both fears represent a pre-teen's sense that life is out of control. The dramatic threats are misguided attempts to gain control, using the illogical logic, as it were, of youngsters. "If I run away from home, then you can't leave me—I'm in control because I left first. If I tell you that you aren't my real parents, then I am in control of this heartbreaking information, not you. If I kill myself, I can control my upset feelings and have no feelings at all, and then you'll be sorry."

Unfortunately, many parents do not hear the fear that underlies these dra-matic statements. Instead, they often dismiss the child's words as overreactions, as signs of hypersensitivity, or simply as the hysterical ravings of a soon-to-be teenager. At other times parents respond to the dramatic statements by explod-ing with their own strong statements and feelings, and by using time-outs, grounding, or other distancing tactics that stretch the Magic Circle further.

As difficult as it may seem, it is possible to avoid such crises, or at least to avoid making them worse. Because internationally adopted children have less of a grip on their emotions and behavior than their non-adopted peers, and they also have stronger emotions to deal with in the first place, what seem like ex-treme comments fall into what is a "normal" range *for them* and are not overreac-tive, oversensitive, or hysterical. Your task is to discern the important requests for information and help that these dramatic statements contain. As you strug-gle with your preteen's crises, remember that what he is asking for is more con-nection with you, not less, and more help with emotional control. Isolating your child and making him struggle alone with overwhelming feelings is never the right course.

THE PURPOSES OF A TOO-BUSY LIFE

Why might your internationally adopted preteen seek to have an extraordinarily busy life? I have seen this longing in many adopted preteens, and I call it the *busy schedule syndrome*. A highly scheduled life helps a child to predict what will happen next and thereby feel in control mentally. A child between ten and twelve often substitutes more scheduled activities for the stretched Magic Circle. The activities provide the security of a routine, which fills the void created by a preteen's distancing herself from her secure connection with her parents, and they provide, more directly, new people with whom to be connected.

When there are large chunks of time with nothing scheduled, a preteen child begins to feel disconnected and out of control. Yi Sheng spent his summer vacation days complaining of boredom, begging Mom or Dad to do something with him. When Soon An had "nothing to do," she spent hours and hours orga-nizing her room, expressing her perfectionism through obsessive neatness.

Internationally adopted preteens, in short, overextend themselves either by joining numerous groups and activities or by isolating themselves and doing things in obsessively "perfect" ways. When I work with parents of such children, I point them to two strategies. The first involves guiding their child toward a life that offers less stimulation—less overstimulation, to be precise. The second involves increasing connection with their child, without smothering her desire for independence. In both cases the goal is to help the child achieve better emo-tional and behavioral regulation, even as she undergoes the scary process of becoming more independent.

LESS STIMULATION WITH MORE CONNECTION

When Soon An, Demetri, Mu Ling, Sonia, and Yi Sheng first came home from their respective birth countries, they were not able to remain calmly alert for long without revving up or shutting down. Even something as simple as having grandparents over for dinner was just too stimulating for them. They could not stay calm and connect with their parents during the first year home unless their parents deliberately minimized the stimulation they experienced.

When these children were much older, their parents found that reducing stimulation was still the best first step for minimizing tantrums, emotional outbursts, and perfectionistic behaviors. For internationally adopted preteens, a sleepover, a soccer practice, or a night at the movies with friends can be highly stimulating. The stimulation is exacerbated by the fight-or-flight responses that such children experience anytime they are away from their parents. There are two ways you can minimize these difficulties for your child. First, get your child a cell phone and encourage him to check in with you on an agreed-upon sched-ule, perhaps once every three hours, when you are apart. Second, cut down on the number of sleepovers (or the number of children at each sleepover), and reduce the number of sports commitments and other extracurricular activities. Even as your child fights you for setting the limit, you will see relief in his face or in the set of his shoulders.

Although it may seem to you that your child should be more independent and separate from you with each passing year, the fact is that internationally adopted preteens need to have even more connection with their parents than they might have had at eight or nine years of age. Of course, your preteen child does not see things this way, at least at first. "Mom, I don't want to spend time with *you*. I want to be with *my friends*," your soon-to-be-teen will protest. To counter this plea, you need to be deeply convinced that more family time will help your child become more responsible for his own emotional control, especially as he embarks on the more challenging and longer-lasting kinds of separations that preteens begin to experience. Family time releases Parent Juice (see chapter 9), tightens the Magic Circle, incorporates routines, and reassures the child that he will not be abandoned as he grows more independent and mature.

Parents must be deeply convinced that more family time will help a child become more responsible for his own emotional control.

When an infant or toddler or young child rejects parents or has tantrums, parents need to keep that little one more connected and more closely supervised. It is the same with preteens.

The first three years in a new family are the foundation of the first decade of an adopted child's development. Likewise, the three preteen years from ten through twelve are the foundation for an older child's second decade, from thirteen to early adulthood. When parents are not aware of an adventurous preteen's need for extra connection with them, they inadvertently let the child revert to using coping skills as a way to manage emotions and behavior. Expecting too much independence on the part of your preteen in fact weakens the child-parent connection and disengages the "foot brake" (see chapter 13) of emotional and behavioral control that is so important for internationally adopted children of all ages.

FAMILY TIME AND FAMILY CONNECTIONS

What are age-appropriate ways to create family connections for preteens? Parents need to work at getting together with their children and planning a range of age-appropriate activities that suit their children's tastes. Soon An's family decided to have a weekly bowling night when the whole family would eat dinner out and then go bowling. Denise and Demetri decided to have game night every Friday. Each of them got to choose two games to play. Because at first they did not have many games, Denise scheduled a monthly visit, on a Saturday afternoon, to the game store, giving Demetri a chance to pick a new family game and to spend his allowance on other items at the store. By the time Demetri turned eleven, game night was well established, and they began inviting one, and then two, of Demetri's friends to join them.

During the summer vacation from school, several of the families planned weekly outdoor activities. Sonia's family revived an activity they had done when

Sonia was little, going on "U-pick" expeditions. Sonia helped plan a meal based on what the family picked on a given day's outing. Other families went hiking or to the beach.

Most of the families in the First Year Home Group instituted a weekly family meeting when their children reached the preteen years. These meetings strengthened family connections and provided opportunities for the preteens to propose things that they wanted to do independently, from chores around the house to activities with friends away from home. Mu Ling suggested in one meeting that the family buy pizza every Friday night, and that she would be responsible for finding out what everyone wanted and for making the call to the takeout restaurant.

Having fun and laughing together are powerful ways to reestablish the Magic Circle. Some preteen children do not know how to have fun with parents; they may once have known how to do so, when they were very young, but they have not learned how to do so in an age-appropriate way as preteens.

To encourage fun and laughter together, find noncompetitive games, or other cooperative activities, for the family. Sonia's parents decided to make one night a week a family cooking night, with a focus on the foods of Guatemala, where Sonia was born. Everyone tried to learn how to make tortillas by hand. The first several weeks' efforts yielded tortillas that were either soft and doughy or too hard. Sonia was the one to discover the trick to making really good ones. As they practiced and learned, David, Sonia's father, proposed a "museum of bad tortillas." Each week the family voted for the most disastrous tortilla, which then was placed in the "museum." For a long time thereafter, just the mention of the "tortilla museum" set the whole family laughing.

Activities such as visiting museums, state or national parks, or historical sites every month provide the kind of family connection that preteens enjoy. Mu Ling's mother Laura decided that once each month a member of the family would choose a place to visit within a two-hour drive of home. That person got to be the "tour leader," which meant helping with directions and talking, as a tour guide would, about several of the notable features of that week's destination.

> "If you're too busy for family night, then you aren't really a family."

You need to think creatively and with humor about connecting with your preteen child. Doing so will deepen the vital connection between you in a way that both of you will enjoy—and that your child might even find "cool." Your connection with your child can easily break under the intensity of adolescent concerns and too-busy schedules, but fortunately family time can keep the connections strong. As Mu Ling once said to her mother, "If you're too busy for family night, then you aren't really a family."

WHEN OLD COPING BEHAVIORS RETURN

As we have seen, researchers have shown that the process of developing self-control of feelings and behaviors extends for a longer time in internationally adopted children than in non-adopted children—all the way, in fact, into young adulthood. The preteen years are pivotal ones in this process. During these years old coping behaviors may return, and when this happens it is important to help the child so that the development of self-control does not derail.

One evening at the bowling alley, Soon An was frustrated about not finding a bowling ball that fit her small hands. She lost emotional control, kicking at some of the bowling-alley equipment and retreating to the parking lot and into the family car. Joe and Charlotte recognized the return of Soon An's old coping behavior of withdrawal. They sat with her in the car for a few minutes to help her calm down and work through the frustration. Then they encouraged her to come back inside with them and ask at the front desk for a smaller ball. Later, Soon An's parents commented to her that her withdrawal was an old behavior that had its origin in the Big Change experience. "You mean I acted this way when I first met you?" Soon An marveled. "You remember all that about me?" Soon An was able to understand her reactions, and the help she received made her better able to manage strong feelings. The conversations she had with her parents during and after this incident revealed to her how deeply and how long her parents had cared for her. She even said at the end of the evening, "Mom, I know this sounds stupid, but this is the happiest day of my life, just knowing you've loved me all this time."

A non-adopted child might be able to handle a parent's simply forbidding behavior such as Soon An's. Words like "If you don't pull yourself together, bowling night is over" might do the trick. But Charlotte and Joe knew this parenting strategy would only create a deeper rift between themselves and their child. Soon An, at eleven, would experience firm limits as rejection and blame. The experience would distance her from her parents and further encourage her tendency to withdraw, along with other coping behaviors, as a way to manage her emotions.

When Demetri, on his first visit to the game store, was overwhelmed by the many choices of games, he reverted to hyperactivity, one of his old coping behaviors. Fortunately, Denise had anticipated this reaction and knew what to do to help her son. She recognized that the crowded shelves and bright lights of the store were too stimulating for him, and that he could not relax and focus enough to make a choice. She suggested a walk around the block, and while they were walking she bought Demetri a drink that he could use for the suck, swallow, breathe technique (see chapter 13). "Mom, I don't need that anymore!" he protested. But Denise insisted he try it a few times. She jokingly offering to try the suck, swallow, breathe technique herself, saying, "*I* need to calm down *myself!*" Demetri tried it and found that he could calm down. When they reentered the store he was able to pick a game after all.

Recognizing old coping or survival skills as they resurface in your preteen offers you and your child important opportunities. A preteen is old enough to begin recognizing, naming, and talking about her own coping behaviors in a way that a younger child could not do. She is old enough to ask for help to overcome them and to work with Mom or Dad to find alternative methods for soothing and calming herself. In addition, a child of this age can begin to recognize the kinds of challenging and overstimulating activities that trigger the coping behaviors, and to make choices (see the discussion of "family behavior" in chapter 18) that reduce the frequency of these triggers.

How a Preteen Copes with Coping Behaviors

1. Child recognizes own old coping behavior.
2. Child has name for old coping behavior, can talk about it, and knows what triggers it.
3. Child chooses family behaviors to substitute for coping behaviors.

On their walk around the block, Denise later told me, she and her son had a conversation that went like this: "Having too many choices is overstimulating," Denise began. "Do you know how your body feels when you get overstimulated?" she asked Demetri.

Demetri knew immediately what his mother was talking about. "Yes, I get extra active," he said. "Sometimes that happens during school—there are so many things going on, and then the teacher tells me to settle down."

"You're old enough to catch yourself feeling this way, and *you* need to begin telling *yourself* to settle down," Denise told her son.

Talking with your child about how the coping behaviors first emerged when she was a young child, and about the feelings that lay behind the behaviors, is important. It helps a preteen make more sense of her own adoption story. Charlotte, for example, reminded Soon An that when she first arrived from Korea as a six-month-old baby, she was so withdrawn she would fall asleep, as a way to avoid new or difficult things.

"You know, Mom," Soon An replied, "I think I still do that. Hiding in my room and organizing and rearranging things puts my feelings to sleep."

"Maybe together we can find some other ways you can manage your feelings," her mother suggested, "because sometimes you're not able to spend time by yourself cleaning your room. When we are all together at the bowling alley, you can't be alone and you can't organize anything. What might help in that situation?"

"Remember that little ball I used to squeeze, and that blanket I had that smelled like you?" Soon An recalled. "I wish I had some things like that."

"Let's make a trip to the toy store and see if we can find some squishy, squeezy toys you can carry in your pocket," Charlotte proposed. "And I know a catalog that has a lot of those sorts of things in it. You could skim through and pick some out." (The catalog to which Charlotte referred, called Abilitations—http://www.abilitations.com—is one that I frequently recommend to adoptive parents.)

Soon An took her mom's hand and squeezed it gently. "What if I just hold on to the best mom in the world?" she said, smiling.

After these incidents and conversations, both Soon An and Demetri began taking more responsibility for managing their own feelings and behaviors, primarily because their parents first helped them find alternatives to their coping behaviors. An internationally adopted preteen continues to need parental guidance and support in this area. Even after recognizing what they had to do, Soon An and Demetri needed to practice self-awareness and self-control, with some subtle but steady encouragement from their parents.

SLEEP

In the preteen years children begin to challenge the established rules of their families. One of the first limits they seek to overthrow, of course, is bedtime. "I'm twelve now, and I can decide when it's my bedtime. It's my body!" Demetri argued to his mother.

Children everywhere mark their advancement in age by having new bedtime rituals and hours, but it is wise to be vigilant to make sure your child gets enough sleep. Regular and sufficient sleep is especially important for internationally adopted children, who are more vulnerable to overstimulation and stress than their non-adopted peers. Sleep resets levels of the hormone cortisol. Make sure your child gets enough rest each night to help him maintain proper levels and therefore reduce coping behaviors.

You should feel free to agree to move your preteen's bedtime later to signify his maturity. But do not move it very much later, especially if your child must get up early for school. Even fifteen minutes is a lot, given the sophisticated stalling abilities of preteens. If your child argues that he does not have enough time before bedtime to get done what he needs to do, think again about reducing his extracurricular activities rather than pushing the bedtime later. Completing homework, practicing an instrument, eating dinner, and having time to relax alone and with parents do not leave much additional time for after-school activities.

Too little sleep makes a child overreactive to stimulation and less capable of managing behaviors and emotions in response to stress. A sleepless, cranky, irritable, or withdrawn preteen is unable to take full advantage of the new life opportunities that await him as he matures, and he cannot connect happily and smoothly with his peers and parents.

REPAIRING BROKEN CONNECTIONS: PRACTICING ANGER AND MAKING AMENDS

"Yi Sheng gets out of control, yells at me, and then collapses in a storm of tears of regret," Nina, his mother, said to me one day. "I don't know what to do. I feel there should be a consequence for his behavior, yet I don't want to punish him for his difficulties with emotional control."

There are two aspects of Yi Sheng's difficulty. First, he had trouble controlling his upset feelings, which overcame him, for example, after he argued with his friends at school or got frustrated over a computer game. He knew how to express the feelings but not how or when to stop. He needed to practice stopping the feelings and calming himself down. Second, although Yi Sheng felt remorse for his uncontrolled behavior, he did not know how take the next step and make amends to Nina and the rest of his family. Learning these two things—how to stop negative feelings and how to make amends—will strengthen Yi Sheng's connection to his parents and family, not to mention his friends.

Learning to stop being angry, grumpy, critical, and the like is a skill. Like any other skill it must be practiced, and practicing requires a conscious, focused effort. Following some suggestions of mine, Nina got a pad of paper on which Yi Sheng would be able to "draw" angry feelings, and a pillow on which he would be able to act out such feelings, along with a kitchen timer. She introduced these items to Yi Sheng on an occasion when he was not truly angry, and she told him he would use them for "practicing" his anger. Then she explained that he needed to choose an activity, such as doing a puzzle or shooting baskets outside, that he would engage in calmly when he stopped being angry.

The practice would begin with five minutes, timed by the kitchen timer, during which Yi Sheng would use the drawing pad and the pillow to express his anger. He also was free to express his feelings verbally. When the timer rang, Yi Sheng would "practice stopping" his anger. If he switched to the activity he had chosen, or even if he just took a deep breath and began talking about a different subject in a pleasant way, the practice would be over. If he could not control his anger and switch to the chosen activity or the pleasant topic of conversation, Nina would reset the timer and Yi Sheng would practice his anger for another five minutes and then have a second opportunity to practice stopping.

Typically, preteens need only two or three rounds of practice before they succeed. Of course, it is relatively easy to "stop" being angry when you are not truly mad. The point is that if a child practices when she is not in fact angry, she will gain confidence and skills for the times when she is actually upset. Nina found that Yi Sheng's practice was especially effective when he imagined one or another of the frustrating things in his life as he practiced.

Yi Sheng also needed to learn to make amends, which would repair the disconnection he had caused with his upset behavior. The best way, I believe, for a preteen to make amends and reconnect is to perform what a parent with whom I worked called "community service chores." If everyone in the family has been negatively affected or disrupted, the child needs to do something that helps everyone; clearing the table, washing the dishes, and taking out the trash are age-appropriate examples of such chores. If only one person has been affected, the child would do a community service chore to benefit that person. For example, if Mom normally walks the dog in the morning, the child would do that job for an agreed-upon number of times to make amends.

Making amends builds good feeling between people. The key is to get to the point where both or all of the parties feel good, and not to load the child down with a punishing amount of work from which she emerges upset all over again. Moderation is called for as you teach this family skill.

If you find this approach difficult or find yourself wanting to punish rather than help your child, consider short-term counseling to resolve your own feelings.

Learning how to stop being angry and learning to make amends are two important family skills on which many internationally adopted preteens need to work. You need to take proactive steps to encourage these skills in your child, even though this means negotiating with your preteen as she declares her independence. Continue working with your child to strengthen the Magic Circle you worked so hard to create, firming up your connection with your child but allowing the circle to expand as your preteen ventures into new terrain. This flexibility will serve you and your child well through the challenges that lie ahead.

29

ADOPTION ISSUES IN THE TEEN YEARS
In the Shadow of Independence

"I hope Demetri will be ready for college by the time he's eighteen. He's sixteen now and has quit all his sports teams. His favorite activities are sitting around the house reading sports magazine and taking long bike rides alone."

"We thought Soon An was completely ready for high school. But now that she is in her sophomore year she has reverted to her old coping behaviors—she just watches the world, instead of participating in it."

"Mu Ling is a fifteen-year-old social butterfly, but she's letting her academics falter."

"We finally got Yi Sheng to use words to share his feelings, and now, at sixteen, he is letting us have it! He tells us we aren't his real parents, and that we never will be, and that he wants to search for his birth family. He says we are just 'temporary.'"

INDEPENDENCE FOR A TEENAGER is equivalent to standing in a spotlight on the stage of life. To step confidently and comfortably into this spotlight a teen needs to have a clear sense of his identity, solid self-control, and a deep sense of connection to parents. Many non-adopted teens move into this spotlight eager for new adventures, but internationally adopted teens are highly conflicted because, for them, shadows of the past intrude on the glow from the spotlight. They still associate independence and separation with early experiences of abandonment, loss, and grief. Identity remains a complex, changing puzzle.

Self-control and resiliency, already fragile, are put to the test by hormonal changes. The teen years, in short, force internationally adopted children to grapple with vulnerabilities in the areas of identity, connection, and resiliency—all three of the core areas of development on which we have focused in this book. As a result these teens often hesitate on the eve of separation, remaining in the shadows at the side of the stage. At other times they rush toward premature independence and they flounder in a different kind of shadowy world, engaging in inappropriate or even dangerous behaviors and relationships.

In the teen years a child's cognitive abilities grow and enable him to think deeply about big, abstract concepts and their real-life expressions. Some of the big concepts a teenager tackles are loyalty, trust, loss, grief (including what psychologists call *non-finite grief,* which is grief without closure), ethnicity, race, and all aspects of what it means to be adopted. Along with thinking deeply, a teenager is also awash in strong feelings, specifically feelings of sexuality and of aggression or competition, all brought on by flooding hormones. The teen years are a cauldron of disorganization and experimentation in every aspect of life. All this work is directed toward ultimately learning to control strong new feelings, making deeper connections with peers both in friendship and romantically, and preparing to leave home and function in the world as a young adult.

FIVE DEVELOPMENTAL TASKS FOR TEENS

1. Learn to control and express strong feelings appropriately, especially feelings of sexuality and aggression.
2. Make deeper, more lasting connections with peers both in friendship and romantically.
3. Become an individual by identifying with, and also separating physically and psychologically from, parents.
4. Prepare intellectually, emotionally, and physically to enter the adult world, whether through college, a trade school, or a job.
5. Become a flexible and resilient person, able to handle setbacks, disappointments, surprises, and changes in course.

I sometimes think of teens as extra-large toddlers or preschool kids. They are goofy, clumsy, brutally honest, curious, extra active, and emotionally intense.

They are alternately loudly social and quietly withdrawn. And, like toddlers and preschoolers, teens need firm limits.

Although teens can be much like toddlers, I think that you will find raising your teenager easier than raising your toddler. For one thing, teens *do* use their words—though often at high volume or in a low mumble. Teens are interested in talking things over and appreciate a parent who listens. Teens push parents to be better people, to stick to professed values and morals, to "walk the walk," and to be honest and open. Your teen needs you as a positive role model, someone whose identity he can reflect on in order to shape his own identity, either by emulating you or by differentiating himself from you. Teens make us grow as human beings and make family life an adventure.

All teens go through periods of being terribly self-conscious and self-critical. And although they would never admit it, of course, they really treasure a hug every so often. All teens want to know that you still love them.

UNIQUE DEVELOPMENTAL CHALLENGES

What makes parenting an internationally adopted teenager different? All teens, adopted or not, regress. Instead of using their words they whine or act out. Doors slam, voices are raised. Instead of communicating information, teenagers expect you to read their mind about their needs and preferences. "You know I hate pink!" a teen might say. They interrupt, become messy, and fail to follow simple directions—"I never heard you tell me to set the table!"

Internationally adopted teens regress, too. Sometimes their regressive behaviors are more extreme, even overtly infantile. In addition, they may revert to their old coping and survival skills (see chapters 4 and 5). They become performers and charmers again; they are by turns hyperactive and withdrawn; they become moody dictators. They may stop eating, or they may eat too much. They may stray too far away from home too often, or they may spend every day at home in bed. Some stay out too late or run away from home and family. They have difficulty sleeping, and they rant about broken routines and how things "should be." Their behavior seems to be a throwback to when they were one, two, or three years old.

Teens in general exhibit a mixture of maturities, especially as they struggle with the appropriate control and expression of strong feelings. They alternate between stunning immaturity and astonishing maturity, between clingy dependence and defiant independence. Internationally adopted teens have this kind of mixed maturity in the extreme. Often they are most immature and dependent just before they make a significant leap forward toward greater independence.

All teenagers need both to identify with and to separate from their parents, and they often do the latter by arguing with and rejecting their parents. For internationally adopted teens, the strain of this process is doubled: They have to identify with and reject two sets of parents, one set of which is virtually unknown. How does a teenager identify with unknown parents who disappeared in another country before the child was able get acquainted with them or say goodbye to them? How do teens identify with parents who made the "bad" or "wrong" choice not to raise them? Relating to a person who is physically absent but psychologically present involves what psychologists call *boundary ambiguity*. Boundary ambiguity tends to generate extreme and confusing feelings. An internationally adopted teen who identifies with physically absent birth parents may display puzzling or extreme behaviors, from excessive and obsessive identification with the birth parents' ethnicity, race, or culture to complete withdrawal from or denial of the same.

Non-adopted teens develop their identity by creating a sense of self from a coherent story of their past, present, and future. Feeling different is part of this identity-formation process, but for most teens difference is not a permanent state. Internationally adopted teens have to create a coherent story and sense of self based on a complex background from which much important information is missing. This fact marks them as permanently different from other teens who know their family's history (including their family's medical history, about which doctors begin asking children when they are in their teen years). In addition, differences in appearance distinguish the teen from her parents and, in most cases, from many of her peers. A sense of being different must be integrated into an internationally adopted person's sense of self. For a teen who has little or no knowledge of her birth parents and who never had the chance to say goodbye to them, there is an additional sense of open-ended, non-finite loss, a territory of loss and grief that is without closure. It is for this reason that many internationally adopted teenagers often declare that they are planning to go overseas someday and look for their birth parents.

Because identity formation and other developmental challenges are bigger and more complicated for internationally adopted teenagers, some feel overwhelmed with their own emotions or overly pressured by their family's expectations. These stressors lead to more acting out, which may include uncontrolled or dangerous behaviors such as running away from home and abusing or becoming dependent on drugs or alcohol.

With so much to accomplish, it is no wonder that many internationally adopted teens are not ready at eighteen years of age to venture out into the world. Keep in mind that her lack of readiness, her fears, and her unwillingness to become an adult are unlikely to emerge directly in conversations with you. Instead, watch for indirect signals: Your child may fall behind academically, forget to mail or e-mail college applications, or use other ways to delay leaving home.

Many parents respond to the challenging behaviors of internationally adopted teenagers by setting stricter limits and expecting their children to assume more responsibility for themselves and their choices. There will always be situations in which stricter limits are needed, but keep in mind that for adopted teens increased limits and greater responsibilities can backfire. Limits, as we have seen (see chapter 16), can cause adopted children to feel rejected. For adopted teens, limits may bring up questions about an adoptive parent's right to parent the child and the child's loyalty to birth parents instead of adoptive parents. Similarly, increased responsibility triggers feelings of being on one's own, alone in the world. Feelings of separation and abandonment are easily triggered in teens. To counteract and minimize such fears and concerns, you must find ways to increase your teen's connection with you. In the teen years, open and honest communication is more important than ever before.

LISTENING AND TALKING WITH AND WITHOUT WORDS

As in many other relationships—marriage and work, for example—much of the success you have in providing guidance, intervention, and other kinds of parental support for your adopted teen depends on how well the two of you communicate. Parent-teen communication is famously difficult, of course, and it can be especially tough with an internationally adopted teen. This is the case even when parents think they have done everything they can to bring up and delve into a subject. Consider this exchange I once had with a sixteen-year-old international adoptee, an academically and socially successful, and seemingly well-adjusted, high-school student:

"I'd like more information about my birth family," this girl told me.

"Have you asked your mom or dad what they know?" I asked.

"Uh . . . not really, no," was her answer.

"You could do that," I suggested.

"Would you do it for me?" she inquired.

A few days later I talked to this girl's mother, and it turned out that she had been over the story of her daughter's birth family with her daughter repeatedly over the years. In her mind, she had already covered the key facts, and she expressed frustration that her daughter felt the subject had not been discussed.

Parents need to intervene actively in building better lines of communication with their adopted teenagers. Often this means learning new ways both to listen to and to talk to your child.

HOW TEENS COMMUNICATE WITHOUT TALKING

"Yi Sheng listens to this one song, 'What Becomes of the Broken Hearted?' over and over again. He told me that he's played it five hundred times on his computer."

"Sonia listens to a song, 'Heal Me, I'm Heartsick,' from the soundtrack to the movie School of Rock, *which she also loves. It pains me to think Sonia identifies with that song. Why can't she just be happy?"*

"Demetri read the book Holes, *which is about a homesick boy who has mistakenly been sent to a boot camp for delinquent teens, and now he rereads it once a week. And he obsessively watches the movie that's based on the book. Why can't he move on to other books or movies?"*

"Don't laugh, but even though Mu Ling is starting high school next year, she wants me to read her the picture book Corduroy *every night. It was her favorite book when she was five. It's about a department-store teddy bear with a missing button that no one wants to buy. I don't understand why she's so taken with this book now."*

When children are young they communicate their thoughts and feelings through their play. As a child grows older, music, movies, and books begin to replace the blocks, toys, and dolls. The songs, books, and movies with which teens are preoccupied, such as the ones mentioned in the quotations from parents above, communicate the thoughts, feelings, and concerns of this age group. We as adults need to know how to listen and interpret these communications.

Repetitive play in a younger child indicates that the child is working on a particular feeling or concept. In the same way, a teen obsessed with a certain song, book, or movie is engaged in emotional work. The themes are familiar ones in adoptive families: separation, loss, grief, connection and disconnection, identity, trust, and loyalty. Teens use these other media because they sometimes lack sophisticated words, such as *permanence* or *loyalty*, to express their feelings. At other times they have the words but fear to use them, afraid of hurting a parent's feelings by sharing their own.

Sometimes a title alone is a tip-off, such as the songs Yi Sheng and Sonia listened to over and over. Both Sonia and Yi Sheng told their parents on occasion, "You're not my real parents," suggesting that as teens they still had strong feelings about their birth families. The songs to which they listened repeatedly suggested they were grieving for and wounded by the loss of their birth parents.

In the song "What Becomes of the Broken Hearted?" a line from the chorus suggests the search for recovery from grief. Yi Sheng's parents wondered, as they heard this line, what their son's real focus was as he listened to the song—the loss, the recovery from loss, or both.

I often suggest to parents that they listen for the specific lines their teen sings from his favorite song, or which lines he sings the loudest, for a start. Sonia, for example, sang just the first lines of her favorite song in a loop—lines that describe feeling heartsick, broken, and in need of healing. Her parents naturally wanted to know for what or whom she was heartsick, why she felt broken, and what kind of healing she sought.

OPENING UP A CONVERSATION

Sonia's father, David, who is a professional musician, sometimes hummed along or joined in singing the lyrics when Sonia sang. At first Sonia gave her Dad a sour look, but eventually he determined that if he asked permission, she would acquiesce. After that, they sang together frequently, and these times gave David the opportunity to ask Sonia about the song's references in later lines to drugs, suicide, and alcohol. At first Sonia insisted she knew what the references meant, saying, "I know that!" But David was not so sure. Eventually he was able to start a candid talk about how people use drugs, alcohol, and even suicide to deal with overwhelmingly painful feelings. The mutual humming and singing, and the father-daughter conversations, were spread over a period of several weeks.

Carolyn and David did not know much about the movie *School of Rock* from which Sonia's song came. One day they asked her about the movie and expressed interest in watching it with her. "You'll hate it," she told them. But the desire to remain connected with parents who were reaching out to her was irresistible. A couple of days later they did watch the movie together and found a shared pleasure in the way the characters in the film, with the help of an oddball substitute teacher, rebelled against their parents' expectations, yet in the end found their own identities and earned their parents' respect.

"I really like the song when you sing it," Carolyn told Sonia. "I think you sing it with more feeling than it had in the movie, as if you know what it really feels like to be heartsick." Sonia ducked her head; she felt good that her mom recognized why this song was so special for her.

"I guess you're thinking a lot about your first family and foster family," David commented. "I didn't realize that you thought about them so often."

Once David caught on to Sonia's form of "talking" through music and movies, his eagerness became intrusive. Sonia shut him down, saying, "You ask too many questions, Dad." So David asked her if they could decide on a hand signal that would mean that it was all right to open a tough topic—any tough topic. The hand signal gave Sonia a sense of control. She could decide if she wanted to expose her feelings or keep them private. But the fact that she sometimes did open up and share her thoughts and feelings meant that David had found a new and valuable way to launch a conversation with her.

CONTROL ISSUES IN COMMUNICATION

Teenagers are deeply aware of who is in control, whether they are with another teen or with an adult. A parent's starting a conversation about difficult subjects such as loss and abandonment may make a teen feel out of control, both of the conversation and of her own feelings. David and Sonia's nonverbal sign to indicate whether a difficult topic was manageable at a given moment was an important tool for helping Sonia to feel in control of her feelings. To help your teen feel more in control, try to open a discussion about adoption concerns in a way that indicates that you are not demanding an immediate answer. You can simply say that a given topic is on your mind. "Sometime we might talk some more about your birth parents. But I know this isn't an easy subject," you might say.

Yi Sheng in his early teen years often exploded with foul language when his parents tried to talk about his memories and his past. "You know you can calmly tell us that you prefer not to talk about a certain topic, just as you would do with your friends or teachers," Kenji pointed out one day after one of his son's typical outbursts. One evening shortly after this conversation, Kenji joined his son as Yi Sheng watched the movie *Finding Buck McHenry* for what seemed to Kenji to be the hundredth time. Kenji commented on the poignant and heart-wrenching quality of the film to his son. (Kenji did not say anything about the fact that the movie seemed to be directed toward younger children, perhaps eight to twelve.)

Yi Sheng nodded silently as he continued to focus intently on the film, which is about a preteen African-American boy, Aaron, who has been orphaned and lives with his grandparents. With the help of Jason, a Caucasian friend, Aaron discovers that his grandfather, Buck McHenry, was a star baseball player in the Negro Leagues. But Buck has kept his past hidden, even from his wife. Eventually, Buck's past, and the reasons he kept it secret for so long, are revealed.

Starting a conversation about deeply felt subjects such as loss and abandonment can make an adopted teen feel out of control—both of the conversation and of her feelings about those subjects.

When the movie began to explain why Aaron was an orphan, Yi Sheng fast-forwarded the film. "I guess that must be hard to watch," his dad said. They continued watching in silence. As the plot unfolded and Buck's past was revealed, Yi Sheng muttered, "He's so lucky it all comes out right in the end."

"I guess this movie isn't too realistic," Kenji replied. Kenji chose not to say any more at the time about his son's revealing comment, but he kept it in mind. It provided an opening for several conversations in the next week, during one of which Yi Sheng at last shared what was most on his mind. "I want to start searching for my birth parents," he told his father. "I'm thinking of looking on the Internet."

Kenji suggested that they talk about what that might be like, and about what Yi Sheng hoped—or feared—would be revealed, before his son actually started searching. Kenji also asked Yi Sheng how he thought his birth parents might feel if he successfully tracked them down and contacted them. Together father and son began discussing several important topics, all because Kenji had "listened" to what his son was communicating by means of his choice of a movie to watch and rewatch.

When a teenager expresses, directly or indirectly, the desire to search for birth parents, adoptive parents can take the cue, as Kenji did, to open up wider discussions with their teen about loyalty, the permanence or impermanence of family, and the loss of one's parents. These topics, along with the basic question of whether birth parents want to be found, are big and deep, and they take time to discuss and digest. Kenji needed to give Yi Sheng extra time to think through these feelings with his parents, rather giving a quick yes-or-no reaction to his son's desire to search for his birth parents.

As a result of their conversations about birth parents and related topics, Yi Sheng's behavior at school when the subject of adoption arose changed. He was no longer surly and angry but open and confident. One day he called Kenji at work and said, "A kid in my class said he thought adopting unwanted children was the answer to overpopulation problems! I raised my hand and said that adopted children are *not* unwanted, even by their birth parents. And I explained why adoption is *not* a solution to overpopulation. They are not related. I couldn't believe it; after class the teacher thanked me!"

Much of parenting a teen is about laying the groundwork for the moment when your teen is finally ready to talk. And once your teen learns to be comfortably in control of his own story and of how and when he talks with you about it, he will be able to handle situations on his own, away from home, with greater confidence and skill. Sometimes what happens at home is a dress rehearsal for when your teen takes on the wider world at school or work or with peers.

WHEN YOUR TEEN NEEDS TO TALK BUT WILL NOT

Giving a teen control of the topic does not mean that you are allowing her to shut the topic down permanently. You may need, patiently but persistently, to find creative ways to invite your child to open up about difficult topics.

One day, Demetri was walking around the house reading his favorite book, *Holes*, out loud. Denise tried to talk to Demetri about why the book was so meaningful to him. But Demetri ignored her inquiry and instead began reading louder, following his mother and bombarding her with passages from the book. Denise knew she could not stand the auditory assault any longer, so she shut herself in the bathroom and stuck in earplugs to think things through.

Five minutes later, Denise emerged, tossed aside the earplugs, and asked, "Can I read that chapter with you? I want to understand why this book is so important to you."

Demetri was reading a description of how Stanley, the boy in the story, feels when he first arrives at the camp for delinquent teens. Denise linked arms with Demetri as he paced around the house. He continued to read the chapter aloud, but now in a less strident voice. "Wait," Denise said. "I bet you know how Stanley felt because you were in an orphanage, which is sort of like the camp." Demetri said nothing, and Denise continued, "You were sent to that place for no good reason. It was an accidental twist of fate, just like it was for Stanley."

Still, Demetri could not or would not acknowledge with words his feelings or thoughts. So Denise backed up and commented on how hard it must be for him to put his feelings into words. "I think it must be so hard to share these feelings. It's easier just to read about Stanley," she said. "I'd do the same if I were you."

Demetri turned away, but not before Denise got in a quick hug. As she hugged him he whispered, "I love you, Mom."

When a parent grasps the situation from a child's viewpoint, the child or teen responds with appreciation and love.

WHAT TO DO WHEN A TEEN WILL NOT TALK

- Acknowledge how painful and difficult it is for your child to have these thoughts or feelings about adoption and early loss.
- Spend some silent time together if that is what your child wants, but reach out physically for a touch or hug.
- When the time seems right, comment on the parallels between the indirect "language" (such as the plot of a book or movie) that your teen is using and the real-life events of your teen's life.

Three days later, while Demetri and Denise were riding in the car together, Demetri started up the conversation again. "I have it harder than Stanley," he said softly. "He got his family back in the end. I'll *never* see my first parents."

As teenagers begin to think more abstractly, they fully grasp the concept of permanence—both of things lost and of things gained—and of time flowing only forward, never backward. With this concept mastered, adopted teens engage more deeply with their own early losses. But sometimes a teen needs to have parents name the concept. In response to Demetri's comment about never seeing his birth parents, Denise said, "When you were younger you used to think you could roll time backward, like a movie that you can rewind, and that you could go back and meet your birth parents. But now you understand the idea of one-way time, and *permanent* loss."

Not long afterward Denise overheard Demetri, in another room, listening to Joni Mitchell's song "The Circle Game," which deals with themes of loss and time passing. When Denise looked in on him, Demetri greeted her and said, "I think Joni Mitchell must have been adopted."

With patient and careful listening, you will find that your teenager eventually will give you openings for talking about issues that matter deeply to him. The "cue" will not always come from a book, movie, or song that your child likes. It could come in the form of an offhand comment about what is happening in the life of a friend or classmate; it could come in the form of a sudden change in your child's preferences concerning whether, and how much, he wants to spend time with other international adoptees; or it could come in the form of your child suddenly wanting to spend more time with family and less time with peers. Your job is first to notice and read the cues, and then to use those signals as starting points for getting your teen to talk about how it feels to approach adulthood as an adopted person.

MANAGING LIMITS AND RESPONSIBILITIES

Carolyn told me one day that she had a hard time setting limits on the time Sonia, age fifteen, devoted to talking on the phone and socializing with her friends. "She says, 'You're not my real mom so you can't tell me what to do,' and sometimes I wonder if she's right," Carolyn reported.

"I feel like I've lost connection with her. She's always with her friends or on the phone," Carolyn continued. "That's what gets us into one of our fights, and she loses control and has tantrums like a little kid. She never did that before; she was always so good!"

Carolyn was facing a double challenge that I have found to be typical among parents of adopted teens. On one hand, Carolyn questioned the legitimacy of her own claim to Sonia. On the other hand, Sonia questioned her loyalty to her adoptive parents. When a family gets stuck in this position, it is not uncommon for the parents to seek therapy, for the child, for themselves, or for the whole family. Although I can understand this impulse, I have seen many successful examples of families getting through this impasse successfully on their own.

Adopted teenagers use the "real parent" argument to defeat parental limits. But underneath, Sonia was fearful that she had no parent who loved her, and therefore she was testing the parents she happened to have. If Carolyn continued to worry that she was not her daughter's "real" mother, her indecisive parenting would "prove" to Sonia that Sonia was not worthy of having, and did not in fact have, any real mother. Carolyn had to face and conquer her own feelings. She had to claim her right to parent Sonia.

Carolyn and David discussed how to work the phone limits. They realized there was no magic number of hours, that any limit would necessarily be arbitrary. They decided to solve the problem by proposing a tradeoff: For every hour Sonia was on the phone, she needed to spend an equal amount of time helping one of her parents. Together the parents predicted what Sonia would say when she heard the new rule. After a few minutes Carolyn and David were laughing and joking about the comments they expected. "Yeah, we're not her real parents, we're imaginary!" Carolyn said. "It's amazing how an imaginary family can have so much money for clothes and phone bills!" David added. Letting off steam this way, preparing for the inevitable upset, gave both parents a sense of unity and strength.

Sonia was angry. "You hate me! My real mother wouldn't do this to me," she muttered. David and Carolyn let this comment pass. "I need your help cleaning out the basement," Carolyn told her daughter. "You can 'buy' an hour of phone time ahead, if you help me now."

Sonia sulked at first but eventually agreed, and in the following weeks she began to spend time regularly with Carolyn doing enjoyable and useful activities, such as walking the dog, weeding the garden, and, at Sonia's request, painting the bathroom next to Sonia's room. As mother and daughter began to have fun together, Carolyn felt the Magic Circle beginning to reassert itself. She and Sonia began to communicate more, sharing conversations and jokes. Their relationship blossomed into a new level of connection, with a reassuring sense of interdependence on a more mature level.

David, too, began to plan special father-daughter activities with Sonia. She was fascinated by the mixed-race people in David's music group and asked to listen to the group's practices. For the first time Sonia began to ask David about their shared Latino heritage. David had to hold himself back from talking too much. Sonia needed to be in control of these discussions; when they got too emotional for her she put her hands over her ears and chanted, "I can't hear you, I can't hear you." David acknowledged to her that he understood that it was difficult for her to talk about race and ethnicity. He knew there was a breakthrough, that she was happy to discuss being Hispanic, the day she chanted the refrain in Spanish.

INTERDEPENDENCE BEFORE INDEPENDENCE

A teenager's academic performance can decline for a variety of reasons. Some internationally adopted children let their academics slide specifically as a way to avoid, or at least delay, their separation from home and their independence. After all, without the grades, you cannot go to college. This was what Mu Ling, at seventeen and in her junior year, did.

When Meg and Laura saw that Mu Ling's grades were slipping, they decided to pull in the Magic Circle. One night Meg asked Mu Ling if she might fold laundry in Mu Ling's room while her daughter did her schoolwork. At first Mu Ling was suspicious. "Why do you want to do that?" she inquired.

"I miss being with you, and I thought I could just hang around, you know, like old times," Meg said. "Remember how you always wanted me to sit by you when you did your math?"

Using enormous self-control, Meg at first refrained from questioning Mu Ling or making her feel pressured in any way to talk about her schoolwork. Each night for a week Meg found a reason to spend some time in Mu Ling's room. Mu Ling began to ask her mom to help her with math problems. Meg helped but continued to hold herself back from addressing larger issues such as Mu Ling's grades and goals. In the second week Mu Ling invited her mother into her room specifically to talk about her post–high school plans.

Meg and Mu Ling's new routine soothed some of Mu Ling's fears about her growing independence. Eventually she was able to put her fears into words. "Will you still be my mom when I'm at college?" Mu Ling asked.

Meg was surprised at such a childish question. But she realized that this was a sign of her daughter's mixed maturities. She answered the question rather more as if her daughter were seven than seventeen. "Yes, Mu Ling," she said. "I will be your mom when you're at college, and I will be your mom until you are an old lady—like me!"

Mu Ling snuggled up against her mom and said, "Well, if you promise that, then I will promise to keep on growing up."

30

ADOPTION ISSUES IN THE TEEN YEARS

How Self-Control Happens, and What to Do When It Does Not

WE NOW KNOW, BASED ON ACADEMIC RESEARCH and on anecdotal reports by parents, that internationally adopted teens have a harder time controlling and managing their feelings and behaviors than their non-adopted peers. We also know that these difficulties often worsen as an adopted child advances through the teen years, whereas for non-adoptees self-control usually improves with time. The good news is that by young adulthood most international adoptees match non-adopted young people in their ability to control their behavior and emotions. The further good news, as you will see in the examples in this chapter, is that teens are much better able than preteens and younger children to reflect on and talk about the challenges they face, and to work with their parents on practical solutions. However, those adopted teens who do continue to struggle with self-control have a higher rate of depression, anxiety disorders, and substance-abuse problems than do other teens.

In the first part of this chapter I introduce six specific strategies that you can use to help your teen with emotional and behavioral control. In the latter part of the chapter I address what you can do if, despite your best efforts, your child still struggles with self-control and how you can effectively handle wildly out-of-control behavior or threatening situations. For the most part, the six techniques are teenage-appropriate versions of parenting strategies that were introduced earlier in this book for younger children. Here are the six approaches:

1. Teaching and modeling *soothing and calming* techniques.
2. Planning regular *check-in times* for communication.

3. *Limiting physical separation* from home and parents.
4. Planning *routine family activities* for connection with parents.
5. Focusing on *natural consequences*, not *imposed consequences or punishments*, to build responsibility for good choices.
6. Using *family service* for repair and reconnection when poor choices are made.

Throughout the teen years, and possibly into young adulthood, your child will continue to need your active help and support to control her behaviors and emotions. This is true even for teenagers who are quite mature in some domains, such as academics, sports, the arts, or part-time jobs. This need for extra support from parents (and also from teachers) is normal for internationally adopted teens. Imagine that your adopted child is the Tortoise in the fable of the Tortoise and the Hare; you need to be there to keep your teen on track and moving forward in the race to attain behavioral and emotional control by adulthood, when it really counts. My own observations, as well as longitudinal research by academic experts in adoption, strongly suggest that the keys to success as you provide this support—in general, and specifically as you engage in any of the six strategies I have listed—are twofold. First, you need to maintain moderate expectations for your teenager's accomplishments, in all areas of her life and particularly as she works to achieve good self-control. Second, you need to be proactive about introducing the six family skills and about practicing and reinforcing them on a daily basis.

SOOTHING AND CALMING:
SUCK, SWALLOW, BREATHE FOR TEENS

Because of their greater mobility, their wider range of social interactions, and their burgeoning independence, teenagers find themselves meeting a host of new challenges on their own. Internationally adopted teens, who often have less control of their emotions and behaviors than their non-adopted peers, can easily find themselves spiraling downward, even when confronting what may seem like the ordinary frustrations and difficulties of teenage life. Getting a low grade on a paper, being disrespected by a friend, or being involved in a small traffic accident can send an adopted teenager into fight-or-flight mode, shutdown mode, or both. Such reactions prevent these teens, even highly intelligent ones, from handling challenges wisely and learning from their experiences. Although you will not always be able to keep your teenager from spiraling downward in this way, you will be able to prevent it some of the time if you teach him how to get his initial agitation under physiological control. The way you do this is by teaching your teen age-appropriate methods for soothing his emotions and calming his behavior. Once a teen has gotten himself under control, he will be better able to face the challenge and learn from it. If your teen is not able to calm down and focus, trying to educate him about what he should do in a challenging situation is doomed to be ineffective.

Yi Sheng was seventeen years old when he got into his first automobile accident. Another car ran a stop sign, smashed into the passenger door of the car Yi Sheng was driving, and sped off. This frightening situation undermined Yi Sheng's emotional control; he sat on the curb for half an hour, shutting down and trying to get a grip on his feelings. Finally he was able to call his mother, but he was unable to explain what had happened. He simply growled into the phone, "Come get me." Then he hung up abruptly. His mother called him back to find out where he was and what had happened to make Yi Sheng shut down so completely that he could hardly speak. After she heard the facts, she told her son that she needed to do a few rounds of deep breathing, and that she then would be able to drive safely to where he was. She suggested to Yi Sheng that he do some deep breathing, too, while he waited for her to arrive. After calming herself, Nina jumped into her car and went to her son.

Because of their complex backgrounds, internationally adopted teenagers are especially reactive to stress. They can lose control both in response to truly frightening situations, such as a car accident, and in response to relatively minor incidents that they perceive as threatening.

When Nina arrived about ten minutes later, Yi Sheng exploded. "What took you so long?" he shouted. His fear and frustration had distorted his sense of time and he had shifted to his revved-up, fight-or-flight mode. "How come you're always late?" he yelled at her while kicking viciously at his damaged car. Nina refused to respond directly to his emotional outburst and instead invited her son to walk with her to a convenience store a block away and get something to drink.

For Nina, getting her son to walk to the store was not merely a distraction from the smashed car but a deliberate plan to help him calm down. When Yi Sheng was younger, he and his mother discovered that sipping a cold drink helped him to calm down. Now that he was seventeen, Nina did not hand him a juice box, of course, but instead steered him in the direction of the cold-drink cooler at the store and asked him to get a couple of his favorite drinks.

As they walked back to the car, Nina linked Yi Sheng's accusation about her lateness to its early origins in his complex background. "I know you've always felt I was late to get you," Nina said. "The first time it was from the orphanage. I think you were mad I didn't come sooner. Then it was when I picked you up at school. Now it's this time."

"I know, I know," Yi Sheng said, still impatiently but now more calmly. "I know about my past, and I know I hate your being late. But when I feel overwhelmed *now* I'm not really thinking about the orphanage anymore. So how come I still get so upset?"

"Your body is extra reactive to stress because of what happened in the past," his mother suggested. "But you know you have some tricks for calming down that you've developed since you were small," she reminded him.

"Yeah, you'd hand me a juice box and make me do the 'suck, swallow, breathe' routine," Yi Sheng recalled. "And I hated it."

"And if you want to know what I think," his mother replied, "the cold fruit drink you're sipping is doing the trick right now."

Teens can make use of a variety of techniques to soothe, calm, and relax. Drinking sodas or milkshakes with straws, sipping lattes, chewing gum, sucking Popsicles or ice-cream bars, and even whistling or singing are age-appropriate versions of the suck, swallow, breathe process. These oral techniques are often the most effective ones for defusing a teen's agitation during a moment of crisis. But not all calming methods are oral ones for emergency situations; focusing solely on oral self-soothing runs the risk of encouraging your teen to turn to or rely on tobacco, marijuana, alcohol, or junk food. Breathing and stretching exercises, yoga, and regular walking or hiking are effective non-oral strategies for practicing self-soothing and for building relaxation into your teen's everyday life. Some schools or recreation centers have yoga classes for teenagers; these classes are excellent ways to help a teen develop a regular calming practice. Even counting to one hundred, combing or brushing the dog, or doing some "heavy work" like mowing the lawn can help teens restore their equilibrium.

Nina *modeled* calming behavior when she told Yi Sheng she needed to breathe deeply and calm herself before driving anywhere, and also when she got a drink for herself at the convenience store near the accident. Modeling works best when your child is able to observe your practice. If possible, for example, do your own relaxation exercises when your teenager is at home and able to observe your activity.

If your adopted child seems to be unable to relax, even if he has tried various soothing and calming techniques, it may be time to take him to the doctor and have his level of the hormone cortisol checked. Cortisol is part of the normal human stress-response system, responsible for calming the body in the face of stress. If cortisol follows an abnormal 24-hour pattern, your physician will discuss treatment options with you.

CHECKING IN

Mu Ling was sixteen when she came home from playing Frisbee at about eight o'clock one Friday evening and found her parents and her sister, Clara, her only sibling, gone. She searched the house and by nine o'clock was frantic with worry. She called her parents' cell phones but no one answered. At ten o'clock her family came home. Mu Ling lashed out. Between sobs she shouted at her parents, "How come you *abandoned* me here? Where were you? I've called and called!"

Meg and Laura, Mu Ling's two mothers, admitted that they had forgotten to check in with Mu Ling about their plan to go with Clara to the movies. Although both parents noticed that Mu Ling used the word *abandoned*, they decided not to link this comment, for the moment, back to Mu Ling's early experiences with abandonment or to conversations they had had with Mu Ling over the years about this subject.

"I'll never trust you again!" Mu Ling screamed and ran to her room.

Checking in regularly is especially important for internationally adopted children. They need to have constant reminders that they can trust that you will not abandon them—or, in the context of a particular day or evening when you are away from home, that you are not right then in the process of abandoning them. Conversely, when they are away from home they need to check in with you in order to be able to trust that their absence has not weakened their connection with you. Adoptive families with teenagers need to schedule check-in times, and each member of the family needs to be very clear about his or her plans on a given day. Although all families with teenagers build trust by requiring that the teens communicate their plans and check in often, in adoptive families it is important for the parents to check in as well. Otherwise, the child's fear of abandonment will lead to a loss of trust in the parents.

The next day Mu Ling and her family set out to create a plan for checking in and communicating their whereabouts when they were away from the house. Mu Ling was especially insistent on nighttime check-ins. "I mean, what if you go to a movie and then decide to have a coffee? That could get late. How will I know where you are?" she said, sounding rather more like a typical parent than a typical teen.

The family agreed that anyone who was out of the house at night would call home approximately every two hours. "This will help me not feel abandoned the next time you're out," Mu Ling commented. "Don't ever do that again!"

This time Laura decided to respond to Mu Ling's comment, from the evening before, that everyone had abandoned her. "It must have been so scary not to know where we were," Laura said. "And I know that's extra hard for you, after your experience of losing your first family. That must have been the scariest of all."

"No. It wasn't. It was much scarier to think of losing you now, after thinking I was safe," Mu Ling said, correcting her mother.

"I'm glad you told me, honey. I had no idea this was worse," Laura replied. Laura gave her daughter a hug, and Mu Ling hugged her back, saying, "I don't want to lose *two* families. One was enough." In this way Mu Ling let her family know that she was continuing to struggle with the fourth of the Four Questions: Will everything change again, and will I lose you, too?

All teens need to check in with their parents. Adopted teens need to do it more often, and they need their parents to check in with them.

Many adoptive parents I know have told me about occasions when they were just five or ten minutes late picking up their child from an after-school activity, and their child had a tantrum or meltdown as a result. A reciprocal commitment to checking in with each other and fully communicating plans will help you and your teenager continue to feel connected with each other. This commitment helps your teen feel secure in her trust in you, and it goes a long way toward preventing her fears of loss and abandonment from getting out of control.

LIMITING SEPARATIONS FROM PARENTS AND HOME

As teenagers grow older, they spend more time with friends, away from the supervision of parents and of other adults. Teenagers spend longer hours at school, and a host of other activities, such as social gatherings, overnight camps, and sports events, offer additional opportunities for teens to spend time independently, away from home. For internationally adopted teenagers, independent activities bring up the Four Questions in new contexts. "Who will take care of me if I twist my ankle during the weekend tennis tournament?" Yi Sheng asked. Sonia wondered, "Will it be all my fault if my cabin's team loses the scavenger hunt?" These questions, reported to me by Yi Sheng's and Sonia's parents, focus, respectively, on the teen's uncertainty about the continuity of his or her parents' care and the fear of losing them, or on old fears about being responsible for bad outcomes. It would be rare to hear such worries from a non-adopted child.

When internationally adopted teenagers are faced with increasing separation from their home and family, they express their deeper fears and concerns, as in the quotations above, by referring to relatively narrow and specific situations. They also resort to acting out their fears in indirect ways that may seem confusing to parents. Yi Sheng, for example, avidly signed up for every out-of-town weekend tennis tournament he could find. His enthusiasm for these tournaments approached elation, such that his mother wondered if he had become hyperactive and his father worried that he was using drugs. But, in fact, Yi Sheng was deeply fearful of separations, and beyond that of losing his parents completely. Instead of confronting those fears head on and separating slowly, step by step, he denied them and rushed headlong toward more independence than he could handle.

As Sonia looked ahead to a week at an overnight camp, she, too, was afraid of separation, but she expressed her fear in a different way. She told her mother to "tell the camp I won't participate in things like scavenger hunts and races, and I don't want to be in any skits or plays." When her mother responded that she could not pick and choose activities at camp, Sonia became angry and cursed crudely at her mother. As someone who was prone to feel ashamed and responsible for performing badly, as for example in a camp competition or play, Sonia was especially fearful that she would do things wrong when her parents were not there to help her. She was overwhelmed by the thought of being away for a whole week and tried to manage her feelings by taking control and picking which activities she would do and which ones she would avoid.

If your teenager engages in out-of-control behavior while he is away from home, it is probably time to start setting limits on his separations from you. Yi Sheng's parents had let him go to several weekend tournaments before learning from his coach that Yi Sheng had uncharacteristically challenged the coach's authority, and also that he was leading his teammates on midnight excursions outside the hotels or dorms they occupied. When his parents brought up the subject, Yi Sheng acknowledged that his behavior was wrong and out of control. His parents wanted to understand, and address with Yi Sheng, both why he chose to go away from home so often and how these separations were causing him to be out of control. Yi Sheng said that in fact he did not like to be away so often, and he went on to explain, using the illogical logic of a teenager, that he had decided to cope with his fear of losing his parents by spending more, not less, time away from home. "I was mad at the coach because I wanted you there taking care of me, not him," he said. "And I think I went out at night to find out who would really take care of me if I got into trouble."

Yi Sheng's parents made the decision to limit not only the number of weekend tournaments, but also the amount of time Yi Sheng spent away from home on weekdays. They agreed to revisit the decision in two months and determine then if Yi Sheng's self-control had improved and if his separation fears were still an issue. Several days after this decision was made, Yi Sheng told his parents that he was relieved, that too much independence really was scary.

Sonia's parents talked with her about her reluctance to participate in camp activities and about her swearing at her mother when she broached the subject. Because the very subject seemed to make her lose control, and because of her other fears about the week away, they proposed limiting her separation from home. They offered her the option of going to a challenging day camp for teens or working as a counselor at a local day camp for younger children. She, too, was relieved to know that her parents would support her if she decided to back out of the overnight camp. More broadly, she was comforted to realize that her parents would continue to take care of her even as she grew up and became more independent.

> **Adopted teenagers do not need to be kept at home, on a short leash, unable to engage in activities that their non-adopted peers get to enjoy. But sometimes they need to move a little more slowly toward independence.**

Adopted teenagers do not need to be kept at home, on a short leash, unable to engage in activities that their non-adopted peers get to enjoy. But sometimes they need to move a little more slowly. Their fears about separation and loss, and their tendency to lose control either when they are away, as in Yi Sheng's case, or even when they simply think or talk about going away, as in Sonia's case, are legitimate reasons for parents to step in and make their children's path toward independence a notch or two more gradual.

ROUTINES AND RITUALS

When your child was young, routines provided structure and security in her world. In the early childhood years routines are done with a parent, and that fact, combined with their very predictability, is what gives them the power to create security.

Teenagers like routines, too. If you break a routine, your teen will call you on it. Teens like security in a period of life that is so full of change. Internationally adopted teens are even more sensitive to change. Something as simple as a teacher changing the due date for an assignment, or a picnic being rained out, can make such teens lose self-control and act like a child half their age. Adopted teenagers therefore are even more dependent on routines, which reassure them that their world is not turning upside down and that they are not losing control of their lives.

Some routines are just short, ritual exchanges between parent and child. For example, every night at bedtime, which was getting progressively later during her teen years, Sonia and her Dad had a routine of saying to each other, "Nighty-night, don't let the bedbugs bite!" The back-and-forth exchange of the verbal chant, like earlier "Ping-Pong" games (see chapter 15), and its predictable nightly repetition were enough to reassure and soothe sixteen-year-old Sonia at bedtime.

Other family rituals are more complex. Denise and Demetri, for example, decided to go on a bike ride every Sunday morning, which served as a weekly connection point between them. They always stopped for lunch midway through the ride, and every week they shared a Caesar salad and a BLT sandwich. This soothing combination of activity and food helped them feel connected through a week of separate schedules. Some families make doing chores together a ritual, such as cleaning the house together on Saturdays or washing the car together every Sunday during the summer.

Working with your adopted teenager to build rituals and routines into her daily, weekly, and monthly schedules will help her feel more secure and in control of her life. The turmoil of everyday life and the upheaval of the teen years always present new situations that threaten your child's self-control, but her ability to return to and touch base with predictable routines will help her manage her feelings and behaviors.

USING NATURAL CONSEQUENCES

For most teenagers, parentally imposed consequences or punishments for bad behavior or willful disobedience are standard and effective procedures. However, with many internationally adopted children, especially teenagers, these traditional methods of parenting often fail. Not only do punishments fail to improve a teen's behavior, but even modest consequences can lead to a teen losing control, often in extreme ways. The reason behind such exaggerated negative reactions to consequences and punishments is the adopted teen's fear that he is an unworthy, unlovable person. He experiences the consequence or punishment as verification that he is in fact a bad person. In a similar way, poor choices and small and large mistakes that the teen makes, and occasions on which he loses control of emotions or behavior, are further confirmation in his eyes of his shameful nature. As we have noted, such convictions are rooted in the teen's fear that he was responsible for his own relinquishment long ago.

What parenting experts call *natural consequences* provide a more effective way to respond to bad behavior, disobedience, or exaggerated reactions to mistakes on the part of an internationally adopted teenager. When a teen loses control, he is likely to focus on his own or someone else's mistake; a parent should redirect the teen's attention away from the causes and toward the results of his actions. Punishments or imposed consequences tend to make teens feel ashamed, and they make teens get bogged down in arguments about who is "right" and who is "wrong." Natural consequences, in contrast, make the teenager aware that his own choices are the cause of his current pain and give him the best background against which to make better choices in the future.

When teens lose control, they focus other people's mistakes or injustices; the job of parents is to redirect the teens' attention away from the sources and toward the results of their actions.

At seventeen Demetri often acted out his anger by slamming doors and punching walls. One day he received a B, and not his usual A, on a math assignment, and he came home and punched the wall in his room. He hit it so hard that he cut his hand and left a hole in the drywall.

In the past Denise had imposed time-outs and removed privileges when her son erupted in such violent behavior. Sometimes she grounded him, for periods as long as a week. But nothing had worked. After the episode with the math assignment, Denise locked herself in the bathroom and called me for help.

I suggested to Denise that the B on Demetri's paper triggered his hidden feelings of shame, and also that losing control and breaking the wall, far from combating those feelings, served to accentuate them and confirm his sense of worthlessness. (For a more extended discussion of the pervasive role of shame in the lives of adopted children, consider reading Sherrie Eldridge's book *Twenty Things Adopted Kids Wish Their Adoptive Parents Knew*.)

I proposed to Denise that in order to reduce Demetri's angry outbursts, she eventually would have to tackle his feelings of shame. But because a teen's sense of shame disconnects him from others, the parent's first task is to regain connection. This means a parent must set aside blame and anger for a while, as difficult as that may be, and instead empathize with and draw the teen's attention to the immediate feelings that resulted from his rash behavior. In this case, I suggested, Denise needed to point out to Demetri that his hand was in pain—the natural consequence of his having hit a wall.

A statement such as "I bet that hand really hurts. Would you like some help bandaging it?" would be a simple first step toward helping your child reconnect with you after such an incident. Although they express legitimate anger, statements such as "I guess you got what you deserved" or "You can't go around destroying walls when you're angry!" would push your child farther away from you and make her feel more ashamed. Focusing empathetically on the immediate natural consequences of your child's actions, on the other hand, restores connection and calms your teen's raging emotions. By centering the conversation on the painful consequence of the choice your child has made, you are effectively focusing her on the very fact that she does have choices—that she is not intrinsically given to being a bad person or a victim of someone else's badness.

Shame encompasses both a sense of worthlessness and a lack of belief in a good future—in short, shame fosters a sense of hopelessness. As his mother bandaged his hand, Demetri expressed his own helpless, hopeless feelings, saying, "I feel like I'm doomed to be a failure." In my experience, when a minor mishap or mistake leads to such a global expression of hopelessness, the teen in question is operating from a sense of shame.

To change your child's negative feelings about the future, you need to remind her that she will have the opportunity to make a better choice the next time. Express explicitly your confidence in your child's ability to make a better choice, and be precisely focused on the subject of consequences—as Denise was when she told Demetri, "I think the next time you get a lower-than-expected grade on your test you will be able to react in a way that is not so destructive and painful."

When minor mishaps or mistakes lead a teen to utter global expressions of hopelessness, the underlying issue is the teen's sense of shame.

"Maybe that means we ought to get a punching bag then," Demetri said to his mother, leaping ahead with a proposed solution. Together mother and son decided to share the cost of a punching bag—and they also decided to fix the wall together over the upcoming weekend.

Natural consequences do not have to involve pain in order to be effective. Sonia's mother, Carolyn, called me one afternoon to share an incident in which she made use of such consequences, a topic I had discussed with her on an earlier occasion. Fifteen-year-old Sonia had forgotten to separate the whites and the colors when she did her own laundry, and when Sonia saw the result she blamed her mother, saying, "You never told me this would happen!" Sonia also announced that she would not be taking on this responsibility in the future, telling Carolyn, "I'm never doing my wash again." Then Sonia threw the entire wad of wet clothing in the trash and retreated to her room.

When Carolyn saw the clothing in the garbage, she was tempted to blame her daughter. "Didn't you know you were supposed to separate colors and whites?" naturally came to her mind. Instead, she decided to slip a note under Sonia's door. In the note she empathized with how frustrated and upset Sonia felt and said that she herself had once made the same mistake. But Carolyn also wrote that Sonia needed to take responsibility for the natural consequences of her actions and not look for someone to blame. When Sonia came out of her room ten minutes later, she hugged her mother and said, "There's nothing like a big pile of pink clothes to make you lose control. But trust me; I'll remember next time. And I'm sorry I got so upset." Carolyn's decision not to lash out at or punish Sonia, but instead to let her daughter learn from the natural consequences of her actions, allowed Sonia to focus on her own responsibilities and her own power to make good choices.

Imposed consequences keep you on the opposite side of the table from your teen; natural consequences put you on the same side of the table, coaching and guiding your teen as she approaches adulthood and grows into the realization that she has the power to choose and the responsibility to choose well. Your empathetic guidance for the painful emotions your teen feels, combined with your confidence that she can and will do better in the future, are powerful tools. They keep your teen's shame and anger to a minimum, and they help her develop self-control.

REPAIR THROUGH FAMILY SERVICE

Repair is an important means of restoring connection between parent and child. Demetri working to fix the wall that he had hit is one direct and literal example of repair. When a teenager works alongside a parent repairing damage, the experience itself is the teacher, more effective than parents blaming, chastising, or issuing warnings about future behavior.

Another option is having a teenager perform *family service* when he has failed to act responsibly. Unlike the example with Demetri, this form of repair is not literally about fixing physical damage. But as in that example, it is about taking responsibility and restoring connection. In Mu Ling's family, if someone who was away from home failed to check in at ten o'clock at night, that person had to perform two hours of family service to restore trust between the individual and the family. Mu Ling's family kept a list of family service jobs on the refrigerator. The list included cleaning the basement, emptying the trash cans, washing the car, and cleaning the front porch. In Sonia's family, a person who broke the family's rule against name calling had to do another person's chores.

Modeling this system, by applying the rule to yourself and not just to your teen, sends a powerful message. For example, when David, Sonia's father, lashed out and called Sonia "stupid" when she forgot to pass on a phone message, he had to cook dinner for the family two nights in a row, relieving Carolyn of that duty.

A teenager's ability to separate and claim greater independence is anchored by two things: a strong capacity for self-control and a deep connection to parents.

Although our first instinct is usually to think of a verbal apology as a sufficient form of repair, I have found that a concrete service activity accomplishes more. Family service tasks provide internationally adopted teenagers with a period of time to refocus attention, recover emotional equilibrium, and regain a feeling of control over their own behavior.

It can be challenging for you to teach your teenager the six skills of emotional and behavioral self-control that we have just reviewed. However, when you work closely with your teen on these skills, through both coaching and modeling them, the connection between you and your child deepens. This deeper connection provides a secure foundation for your child's increasing independence and his eventual physical separation from home and family. Healthy separation is rooted in this connection, and in the teenager's capacity for self-control. You will be richly rewarded for your efforts, not only by seeing your child mature and achieve independence, but also by receiving your child's affection and respect.

Internationally adopted children can be exceptionally demonstrative when they realize they are receiving the extra support that they need. "It always amazes me," Carolyn said to me one day, "that Sonia insists on buying me little gifts and leaving me love notes." In my experience working with families, I have observed that adoptive teens are less likely to take their parents for granted than their non-adoptive peers. Internationally adopted teens treasure parents who provide close and active care.

STRONG FEELINGS AND BEHAVIORS
MAY REFLECT EARLIER ISSUES

Adolescents are known for having strong feelings, of course, and they often engage in equally forceful actions, or say quite dramatic things, that reflect those feelings. You may have been doing a wonderful job working on self-control, using techniques like the six we have just discussed, but this does not mean that the road ahead is straight and smooth all the way to the horizon. Suddenly the road may take an unexpected turn, because internationally adopted teens tend to be exceptionally reactive.

When a teenager acts out, some parents are dismissive ("That's what teens do") or punitive ("I'll ground you if you do that again"). Neither of these approaches addresses the fact that such behaviors are genuine calls for help from teens, adopted or not.

Clinicians and researchers have concluded that internationally adopted teenagers are particularly vulnerable to the stresses of developing intellectually, emotionally, socially, and physiologically. As a group, internationally adopted teens and young adults are one and a half times more likely than their non-adopted peers to have the symptoms that warrant a psychiatric diagnosis, and they are more than twice as likely to have substance-abuse diagnoses. (See the discussion of Verhulst's research in chapter 2.) As an adoptive parent, you would be wise not to view your teen's acting-out behaviors simply as typical adolescent traits; instead, try to determine how your teen's behavior and her complex background are intertwined. Although acting-out behaviors are not always adoption related, it is a good idea to explore the possibility that they are.

Adopted teens who act or speak in challenging or threatening ways are often expressing earlier difficulties or feelings in new, teenage forms. For example, a teen who threatens to run away is struggling with the same feelings of disconnection from parents as a toddler who wanders too far from his parents or is constantly taking risks. Both the toddler and the teen are worried about the same question: Who will take care of me? Both children question the permanence of the parent-child relationship.

Just as young children express their thoughts and feelings through play, teens also "play" about their concerns. The typical exploratory, identity-changing, friendship-making and friendship-breaking, and risk-taking behaviors of teens as they experiment with greater independence are forms of play that express much about a teen's inner life. However, teen play may have serious, even life-changing or life-threatening, consequences.

Because teens look like adults physically, parents tend to assume that they think like adults and have the understanding of the world that adults have. However, teens' thought processes, and the range of experiences that underlies those processes, are not those of an adult. Teenagers are notorious for having a self-centered focus and a genuine belief in their own immortality. They tend to think that their parents can fix any problem.

A teen may understand something cognitively without grasping the same idea on an emotional level or in a wider perspective. Teens can understand the idea of permanence cognitively, yet they may worry that their family relationship will end when high school ends; or they may imagine that death will "just take away my upset feelings *for a while.*" The magical thinking that we associate with early childhood often lasts longer in internationally adopted teens.

INTERPRETING CALLS FOR HELP

Internationally adopted teens continue to see the world through the lens of the Four Questions (see chapter 7), and they experience a whole variety of strong feelings, from fear and longing to anger and depression, that are connected to their doubts about whether the questions have been fully answered. But they do not always have these doubts on a conscious level, and they do not always express the doubts literally and directly. (It is *very* unlikely that your teen will come up to you and say, "Excuse me, Mom, but I'd like to talk to you about Question Number Two, 'Who will take care of me now?'") Consider these statements from some parents:

> *"We found Yi Sheng crying on his bed one night when he was nearly ready to graduate from high school. 'I just want to die and not face all this,' he told us."*

> *"Sonia just turned fifteen, and she's threatening to run away from home!"*

> *"At fourteen Mu Ling started dressing so provocatively that I feared she was getting propositioned on every street corner."*

> *"Soon An has had the same steady boyfriend since ninth grade, and she insists that they are going to get married the day after they finish high school."*

> *"Demetri got caught shoplifting from the drugstore, and I suspect he's done it other times. What's going on?"*

When Yi Sheng said, "I just want to die," he may have been thinking magically, not grasping the permanence of his own death. Rather he thought of "death" as a way to manage overwhelmingly painful and confusing feelings about his family in China and about what his life might have been with them. Expressing the wish to die is a way to express the wish to shut down, a coping behavior familiar to many adoptees. A toddler may cope by literally shutting down (see chapter 5); a teen talks about suicide, or turns to drugs or alcohol, to shut down feelings she cannot control. Because we know that internationally adopted teens have a harder time managing emotions, we can assume that they mean "I need help managing my overwhelming feelings" when they talk of death.

Sonia's thoughts of running away from home were a way to avoid the painful feelings of separating from her family. As a teen gradually separates from parents and family, a process that may last through young adulthood, she must confront each of the Four Questions. Just as they thought deeply, when they were young, about what happened that led to their adoption, teens now reflect consciously about what is happening to them and what emancipation from home will mean. Their earlier ambivalence about what happened during the separation that occurred when they were adopted reemerges in a new ambivalence about separating from home.

In addition, teens need to explore with their parents their changing, yet continuing, mutual relationship, and to examine the question of how their parents will (or will not) continue to care for them. Some caregiving may be long-term—"We'll continue to pay your health insurance"; some may be new—"We'll lend you money to buy a car"; and some may end—"You know you're going to have to learn how to cook when you get your own apartment." Your adopted teenager's biggest fear is the fourth question: "Will everything change again, and will I lose you, too?" Even if she knows there will still be some kind of connection with you, she fears that you will stop loving her once she is gone from home, or has otherwise become more grownup and independent.

Since these questions and fears can feel overwhelming, some adopted teenagers are tempted to skip working on the answers and embrace independence rapidly and prematurely. Running away, engaging in sex, moving in with friends, or even spending as little time as possible at home are ways a teen imagines she is "in control" of her life and avoids the hard issues. In my experience, a threat to run away or a request to move in with a friend rather than continue living at home is a signal that you and your teen need to address the roots of her ambivalence about growing up.

While some old coping behaviors reappear, new ones may be added as well to a teen's behavioral repertoire. Mu Ling's provocative dressing was the appearance in teenage form of two survival skills: charming or performing to gain attention, and taking control of every situation or relationship. Mu Ling had anxieties and fears about the question "Who will take care of me now?" In a sophisticated teenage way, she was answering the question herself by saying, in effect, "I don't trust our connection, and I am returning to the charming behavior I know will provide me with attention and care." Of course, provocative dressing is not just a charming performance; it is also a form of risk taking. Risky behavior of this sort can be a way to play about abandonment and control issues. A teasing, provocative girl can feel in control of others and also feel confident that she will be able to leave them behind before they decide to leave her. Mu Ling was using her sexualized persona to gain a sense of control over others and to test whether her parents would remain committed and connected to her.

Soon An chose to be in control of her worries about abandonment by keeping a steady boyfriend over several years and by planning to marry at the end of high school. Issues of permanence—"Will someone be a steady, reliable presence in my life?"—and independence—"What will happen to me if I cannot cope when I am out on my own?"—were so overwhelming that Soon An sought immediate, but premature, closure, rather than exploring and coming to grips with her fears of abandonment directly.

In some areas of his life, Demetri revealed a maturity beyond his years. He often did the grocery shopping for his family and he held down a weekend job busing tables at a pizza parlor. But he did not always act responsibly, and in fact he often told his mother that he was not as good as she believed and that beneath his responsible exterior he was an "ugly, stupid creep who just got lucky." Shoplifting was Demetri's way of acting out his feelings of shame, that somehow he was intrinsically bad and unworthy of love and care—a fear that is common among adoptees. If your teenager engages in "bad behavior" she is asking indirectly whether you will continue to love her when she matures, even if she does something bad, and whether there is a chance that she will lose you, too.

Now that you have a feel for how to interpret what your child is expressing when she acts out or uses threatening language, we turn next to ways to respond and cope with these difficult situations. As you respond, keep a cool head. Because it's easy to lose control, I begin with a brief look at *inducement*, a common pitfall in parent-teen relations. Inducement can easily disrupt the parent-child connection and send a parent off in the wrong direction.

INDUCEMENT

Inducement, as we have seen (see chapter 5), occurs when a child creates in a parent the same feelings the child is experiencing. Nina and Kenji, for example, felt at least as helpless as Yi Sheng did the evening he announced that he wished he were dead. When Mu Ling began dressing provocatively, she was using the coping skill of performing as a way to gain control over others, all of which expressed her fear that she was losing control of her life and that she would be abandoned by her family when she reached adulthood. Her parents, in turn, felt their own set of fears about her future when they witnessed her behavior.

Inducement makes parents have feelings that are identical to their children's feelings, but it also makes both parents and children feel miles apart from each other. Denise was furious at her son because she felt that his shoplifting reflected upon her as a parent, and she was ashamed because of that. As a result she found herself withdrawing from Demetri, becoming cold and angry. Demetri's behavior had induced these feelings, which accurately reflected how Demetri had been feeling for months.

You must be wise enough to recognize inducement. In situations in which your own strong feelings are induced by your teenager's feelings (and

Inducement can lead parents quickly to angry, shaming, or out-of-control outbursts.

by the words and behaviors that result from those), you need to keep a tight rein on your own emotional reactions. Inducement can lead you quickly to angry, shaming, or out-of-control responses—"You're grounded for life!" is but one example. Once you recognize the inducement and get a grip on how it is affecting you, you can respond more calmly and directly to your child's hidden feelings and restore the connection with him. As always, remember that when a child is at his worst, he needs his parents the most.

HOW TO RESPOND TO SUICIDE THREATS

"I want to kill myself," "I wish I were dead," and similar statements can either strike terror in a parent's heart or elicit a dismissive reaction. One parent debates whether to call the police or go to the emergency room for help while the other tells the teen to "get over it" and "stop being hysterical." Neither reaction is appropriate and each is likely to make the situation worse.

When Yi Sheng said that he wanted to die, Nina took note of her induced feelings of helplessness and used this insight to guide her response to Yi Sheng. "I wonder, are you are feeling overwhelmed and helpless?" she asked.

Yi Sheng was surprised that his mother recognized how he felt. He had expected that she would be angry with him for saying that he wanted to die.

"I just can't handle all these feelings anymore. I don't know what to do," he confessed, sensing his mother's empathy.

"I know you want me to take what you're telling me very seriously, and I do," Nina reassured her son. Nina did not respond by trying to talk Yi Sheng out of suicide. Instead, she listened with compassion and let Yi Sheng know that she took his need for help seriously. Once she had made that clear, she addressed the suicide issue more directly. She did what mental health professionals call a *suicide check*. This is a set of questions that probes how serious a person's suicide ideas are and evaluates how safe that person is. People who have made suicide threats and who underwent a suicide check of this sort have told mental health researchers that the process made them feel less likely to commit suicide.

Nina told her son, "I want to help you stay safe, so I need you to answer honestly the questions about suicide that I am going to I ask you." An adult talking openly about suicide generally gets a teen's complete attention and honesty. If you mince your words, your teen will respond in kind.

A suicide check consists of two primary questions. The first one is "Do you have a plan for how to kill yourself?" The second question is "Do you have a weapon, or do you have any medicines, drugs, or chemicals that could harm you?" If the answer to either question is yes, follow up immediately to determine what the plan is and what the weapons, drugs, or other instruments are. Remove the instrument from your child's possession and secure it safely. You must take your child to an emergency room (I recommend the emergency room at a children's hospital, if your community has one) or to an emergency appointment with a psychiatrist. When you ask for an appointment be sure to say that the matter is urgent. Specifically use the words *suicide plan*. This will get you immediate attention.

If your teen answers no to both of the suicide-check questions, she is likely to be safe in the short term. But do make sure that all medicines and all weapons are secured; it also helps to ask your child what items in the house she would like you to put away. Then set up an appointment with a psychiatrist and make sure that you talk regularly with your child in the coming days and weeks about the issues that led to the threat.

After a suicide threat, many parents choose to take their teen to the family's primary-care physician. I have found that suicide-related matters are often beyond the scope of practice of family physicians, but your family physician may be able to refer you to a good psychiatrist and get you an appointment sooner than you would on your own. I do recommend a psychiatrist rather than another kind of mental health professional because it may be helpful for your child to be prescribed medication as she gets through this difficult stage in her life. I also recommend a psychiatrist who specializes in adolescence and, if possible, one who has expertise in treating trauma-related issues. Because such specialists are often heavily booked, you may need to work with a non-MD therapist for the most part, with an occasional consultation with an MD psychiatrist for medication.

You also need to talk with your child yourself. Tell her about the permanence of death. This is what Nina did, saying to her son, "Yi Sheng, if you were to kill yourself, you'd never see me or Dad or your dog again. Death is permanent. You can't come back."

Yi Sheng was silent for a while, digesting this. "I never thought of suicide that way," he replied. "I thought it was like going to sleep for a long time, and that I wouldn't feel bad. But I don't want to die forever."

Even though Yi Sheng was a high-school senior, neither his experience nor his considerable intelligence had prepared him to grasp the permanence of *his own* death. Certainly he understood cognitively, in the abstract, that death was permanent,

Cognitively, teenagers understand that death is permanent. Emotionally, they believe they are invulnerable and will live forever.

but that did not mean that he was able emotionally to apply that reality to himself. Teens believe they are invulnerable and will live forever. Educating your child or teen about the real-life consequences of suicide will help ensure her safety.

AFTER A SUICIDE THREAT: REDUCING STRESS AND GETTING HELP

A suicide threat is a desperate cry for help that requires parental intervention. In addition to taking the steps I have just described, relieve as much pressure as possible from your teen's life. Discuss with him how to minimize stress in his life, focusing on extracurricular activities, overstimulating social engagements, and difficult academic commitments that place especially strenuous demands on his energy and time. Temper your own expectations for your child's achievements, and make it clear to your child that for the time being he may need to rein in some of his own ambitions; if he objects, point out that if he does not take a break at this juncture, he may never realize his longer-term plans.

In the weeks after Yi Sheng revealed that he wanted to die Nina and Kenji began talking to him about the possibility of taking a year off after high school.

"Why don't you stay home and live here for another year or two?" they asked him. "You could work at a job. You could start with a couple of classes at the community college when you feel ready."

"Really? I don't have to go to college right away?" Yi Sheng replied. "I can decide when to go?" Yi Sheng was incredulous. He seemed relieved, Nina reported to me, and he appeared to relish the greater sense of control that he now felt over his life.

Work together to replace stressful commitments with activities your child finds soothing and calming and that strengthen his connections with you and the rest of the family. If your child cannot think of activities he wants to do with you, make the decisions for him, for his own health and safety. Although your teen may in the past have resisted your making such decisions, in this situation you are likely to find that he appreciates your efforts and feels safer and more secure as a result. Do not be surprised if your teen wants to spend more time with you.

In the previous section we described how to seek immediate intervention to ensure your teen's safety in the short term. You should lay the groundwork for longer-term therapy for your child, the goal of which is to sort out the issues that led to his suicide threats. In my experience these issues are often adoption specific, and therefore I recommend that you find a therapist who has worked with internationally adopted teens or at least adopted teens. The psychiatrist you saw for the initial intervention may have such a background, or he or she may be able to recommend someone who does. This new therapist need not be a medical psychiatrist but can be a psychologist, social worker, or family therapist. (If your child is receiving medication, you will need to continue consulting with the psychiatrist.) Although it is tempting to send your teen alone to these long-term therapy appointments, the fact is that he needs you to be there. You need to help your teen face and share the critical issues without withdrawing into denial. You need to help explain the therapeutic process to your child, and because most teens do not like the process, you need to provide motivation and help your child recognize when progress is made. Because adopted teens tend to be fearful of autonomy and vulnerable to feeling ashamed of themselves, parents of adoptees especially need to participate in the therapy, so that the teen feels it to be a familial and not just an individual experience.

Many teens who threaten suicide receive a diagnosis of a depressive disorder or an anxiety disorder. The diagnosis itself can help both you and your child make sense of the overwhelming feelings that led to the threat. If your child gets one of these diagnoses, do not dismiss the value of medication. Taking medication is not a sign of failure for you or your child. Taking medication for mental health reasons is just like taking medication for a physical illness, such as diabetes. In both cases the body is out of balance and the medication helps. Although the doctor and pharmacist should inform you about the side effects and withdrawal symptoms of any prescribed drug, it is also wise to check sites on the Internet that also provide such information.

WHAT TO DO WHEN A TEEN THREATENS TO RUN AWAY

Sonia was fifteen when she threatened to run away from home. Her threat sent the entire family into an uproar. David and Carolyn felt deeply rejected. I learned in subsequent conversations with Carolyn that she and David had been unaware of the phenomenon of induced emotions, and that therefore they did not take steps to rein in those feelings. Instead, as Carolyn reported, both parents responded harshly.

"Why would you leave just when everything is getting better? You'll get to leave in three years anyhow, when you go to college!" David shouted.

"We've done everything for you. Why are you abandoning us now?" Carolyn asked tearfully.

"I hate you!" Sonia shouted. "My birth mom got rid of me and now I'm going to leave you first, so that you don't get rid of me, too."

Although it appears illogical to an adult, the idea that one might leave first in order to avoid being left fits with the logic of a teenager. David and Carolyn pulled themselves together and addressed Sonia's statement directly.

Adopted teens continue to struggle with fears of being abandoned. Running away seems to them a way to abandon their parents *before* their parents abandon them.

"But we don't want to abandon you, and we aren't going to," Carolyn said. "We love you."

"But why do you stay at work so late, Mom? You keep working longer and longer hours. I come home and make my own dinner. I might as well be living alone," Sonia retorted.

Sonia's increasing maturity and independence elicited fears of losing connection with her parents. Hurt by Carolyn's increased workload and longer absences and fearful of losing her, Sonia interpreted Carolyn's new work schedule as abandonment. Running away was a "tit for tat" sort of plan; it made her feel in control of the situation. She was going to abandon her parents just as her birth parents had abandoned her and as her adoptive parents seemed to be doing to her right now.

Carolyn was about to justify her new workload and tell Sonia how grownup she was, but she caught herself and pressed her lips together hard. What could she say to connect with Sonia?

"I had no idea my working longer hours made you feel as if I was abandoning you," she said.

"Yeah, well, it did," Sonia answered sourly. "No one is here when I come home from school. No one shops for food or makes dinner anymore."

David recognized the teenage habit of generalizing, or overgeneralizing, and did his best not to correct this obvious exaggeration. Instead he tried to listen compassionately to how Sonia experienced the family changes.

"I can see how our new schedules would trigger some of your old feelings of being left," he acknowledged. "Now I understand why you wanted to run away."

As with other kinds of threats you may hear from your teenage child, you can learn a lot by patiently asking your teen to explain why she wants to run away. Typically teens answer in loud, angry voices, and the explanation is likely to include many observations of the parents' shortcomings. Swallow your pride, and rein in your induced anger, in order to focus on your teen's feelings and ignore the insults.

If you focus on the volume and the foul language, and if you utter the comeback "We're talking about you, not me!" teens, like younger children, will take these comments as evidence that you "hate" them. Not only will this end the productive direction of your conversation, but your punitive tone will trigger feelings of shame in your child, which in turn will lead to more threats and outrageous behavior.

Taking a *family time-out* is a helpful way to avoid this kind of confrontation and give everyone a chance to cool down. If your conversation with your teen about her threat to run away gets off to an angry and unproductive start, take a fifteen-minute break to allow everyone to calm down and collect his or her thoughts. Then have a family meeting over a bowl of popcorn to talk further. Patiently, and without anger on your part, get to the heart of why your teen is threatening to run away. You may have to continue the conversation on and off over several weeks, and there may be additional angry outbursts from your teenager. I think you will find that with internationally adopted children the core issues tend to be, as they were for Sonia, fears of loss and abandonment, anger at what the teen perceives as neglect and indifference when parents expect more independence from the child, and sadness at what feels to the teen like a weakened connection with her parents.

HOW TO RESPOND TO PROVOCATIVE BEHAVIOR

Both Mu Ling and Soon An had fears, rooted in their adoption histories, of being abandoned. As teenagers they expressed these fears in different ways. Mu Ling dressed provocatively and used her appearance and sexuality to give herself a sense of control over her relationships with peers and a sense of power over her parents—an echo of her old coping behaviors, which involved being a performer and asserting control over others. Beyond her abandonment concerns, she was simply trying very hard to be popular. Teenagers, and especially internationally adopted teens who tend to harbor feelings of not fitting in, desperately want to be accepted by their peers. Soon An, on the other hand, coped with her fears of abandonment by keeping a steady boyfriend and planning to marry him at the end of high school. This premature commitment effectively shut down and froze Soon An's explorations of other connections, and also of her own identity.

Teens who engage in provocative behavior are *performing*, as a way both to fit in with their peers and to gain control over others.

Mu Ling's provocative dress, including her very short skirts, exposed underwear, and see-through fabrics, shocked her parents and had them stymied. When Meg brought up the topic, Mu Ling strutted about, taunting her mother and refusing to talk. When Laura, Soon An's other mother, said that she was going to set a limit on Mu Ling's clothing allowance, Mu Ling covered her ears and marched around the house chanting, "I don't care! I don't care! I'll go naked! I don't care!"

Laura and Meg talked over the situation when they were alone. They recognized that some of their daughter's old coping and survival behaviors were back in play; Mu Ling was exerting control, playing the role of "the Royal Boss" (see chapter 5) both by her provocative performance and by her refusal to talk. But they could not figure out how to help their daughter. Finally, they decided to change their tactics. They told Mu Ling how much they admired the colors and fabrics she had chosen and said, in a matter-of-fact way, how effective the short skirts and glimpses of underwear must be at getting the attention of others, especially boys.

Mu Ling was suspicious at first of her parents' interest in her attire. "I thought you hated me and how I dressed," she snapped. Mu Ling's confrontational response gave Meg an opening for showing that she preferred, for her part, listening and responding compassionately, not angrily. "We don't hate you," she said quietly and calmly, "even if your dress choice makes us uncomfortable. Remember how we always used to tell you, 'We love you just the way you are'?"

"Yeah, right," Mu Ling retorted.

Meg ignored her daughter's sarcasm and hesitated before responding. She used her own induced feelings as a clue to how her daughter was feeling. "Now that you're a teenager, and becoming more of your own person, I wonder if you're feeling a bit disconnected from us," she said.

"Yup, that's right," said Mu Ling. "I'm shut out, so I'm making my own way."

Once Meg and Laura heard the words *shut out* they realized that the fear of being shut out or abandoned was the source of their daughter's provocative, attention-getting behavior. Over the next several months they pursued this theme with Mu Ling. They empathized with her fears of being shut out socially at school. They also discovered that Mu Ling was afraid that her lesbian mothers would not welcome her heterosexual preference. (To this latter fear Meg and Laura responded that most teens worry about how their parents will respond to a child's emerging sexuality, regardless of whether the child shares the parents' sexual preferences.) As the three of them continued to untangle and explore Mu Ling's fears, Mu Ling's desperate need for acceptance and her fear of abandonment gradually lessened. Mu Ling's need to perform and control diminished as her sense of safety and connection increased, and over the next year her provocative dressing and behavior diminished.

When internationally adopted teens are working on old adoption-related fears, they often miss the social meaning and impact of their behavior. As most parents would be, Meg and Laura were concerned about the sexual communication of provocative dress. But Mu Ling was simply acting out her own internal, and highly self-centered, feelings and needs by relying on her attention-getting and controlling coping skills. Such behaviors can blur the boundaries of what is socially appropriate or expected. Mu Ling's provocative dressing was the teenage equivalent of her taking the hands of strangers or crawling into their laps when she was a little girl.

Charlotte and Joe recognized that Soon An was shutting down her opportunities for connection with new friends and other young men by keeping a steady boyfriend and planning to marry right after her high-school graduation. Shutting down had been Soon An's modus operandi from the moment they first held their six-month-old daughter in their arms. Now they were looking on as she shut down in a new, teenage way.

PARENTING TECHNIQUES WHEN
THINGS ARE OUT OF CONTROL

---

1. Reduce demands, activities, and stimulation for your teenager.
2. Use empathy. At first, listen more than you talk.
3. Use your own induced feelings as a guide to your child's feelings.
4. Have all-family time-outs.
5. Call family meetings.
6. Help your child understand that survival or coping behaviors are counterproductive.
7. Revisit the Four Questions.
8. Arrange for family therapy.

One evening they asked Soon An to talk about her plans. After listening patiently, Charlotte expressed how she felt about the situation. "I don't know any other way to say it, except this: I feel stuck and overwhelmed, because I don't think you want to hear what I have to say," she told her daughter. At that moment she did not go into any more detail about what she thought Soon An should be doing at her age.

"I guess I feel a little stuck and overwhelmed, too," Soon An confessed. "I want to grow up, but I'm afraid to do it alone. Staying with Conrad and marrying him seems like the answer. But secretly, I'm not so sure." Soon An stared off into space, the way she used to do when she first came from Korea.

"You look as if it's overwhelming, this thought of being independent. It must feel a bit like when you first came to America," Charlotte said.

"I never thought of that," Soon An replied. "It was so long ago. But I guess growing up is kind of like going to a new country; everything is going to be different. I'm afraid it will mean that I'll lose you."

"Those were big fears when you were six months old and they are still big fears when you are sixteen years old. Your mom and I will always be here for you," Joe reassured his daughter. "And you know that means we'll be here for you even if you move out and get a job or go to college. You don't need to get married in order to save yourself from being abandoned. You're not going to be abandoned."

Although Soon An's behavior did not have the overt sexual provocation that characterized Mu Ling's choice of clothing, her steadfast insistence that she would marry the day after her high-school graduation certainly provoked a strong reaction from her parents. Parents respond to their adopted teenagers' provocative, manipulative, and risky behaviors most effectively when they are conscious of how their children's fears arise in connection with the Four Questions. Using empathy, parents can often elicit comments from their teens that reveal which of the questions are troubling their minds and hearts. Once these feelings are out in the open, parents and teens together can connect the feelings more calmly to the provocative behaviors in question.

HOW TO COPE WITH "BAD" OR RISKY BEHAVIOR

The teen years, when a child's identity is rapidly developing and changing, are when an adoptee's sense of shame for having caused his own relinquishment is most sharply experienced and acted out. Adopted teens sometimes put their feelings of shame to the test, engaging in bad behavior as a way to force their parents to validate their alleged badness. When they do so, they are asking one or both of these questions: "If I do bad things, will you still love and care for me?" and "My birth parents made bad choices; am I bad in the same way?" At other times adopted teens engage in risky behavior as they contemplate the changes in their relationship with their parents; their behavior is a way of asking, "Will my parents take care of me now that I am more grown up, even if I am doing scary things all on my own?"

Risky or bad behavior on the part of an internationally adopted teenager implies the question "Will my parents take care of me now that I am more grown up, even if I am doing wrong or scary things?"

When Denise confronted Demetri about his shoplifting, his answer was "So what? What did you expect from the son of a thief?"

"What do you mean by *that*?" Denise demanded.

"I saw it on my adoption records," her son replied. "My birth dad was in prison. I'll bet he was a thief."

"What were you doing in my private files?" Denise raged.

"That's not *your* information; it's *mine*. You stole it, and now I can't ever trust you again. And all you want to talk about is how *I'm* a thief!" Demetri shouted back.

Denise was chagrined. She had decided to share some but not all of the information about Demetri's birth parents. Now that omission was thrown in her face and labeled stealing.

"Look, you're right," Denise said. "It is your information. I shouldn't have kept it from you. I'm sorry." Denise took a deep breath.

Denise tried to hold herself together. She felt guilty for hiding the information, angry that her son was caught stealing, and fearful that she had made a terrible decision when she adopted a child with an alcoholic mother and an incarcerated father. "What was I thinking?" she wondered.

Demetri was having similar feelings. He felt guilty about stealing. He felt guilty about treating his mother cruelly, yet he felt angry at her for hiding the truth about his birth father. He secretly feared he would turn out like his birth parents and that the adoption, like his brief experience in his first family, would end with his abandonment. Demetri was scared. He went upstairs to his room.

A short while later Denise sent a text message to Demetri's cell phone. The message said, "You are not your birth parents. I believe in you and want to help. Love, Mom. P.S. Could we have dinner together in about half an hour?"

Over dinner Demetri was able to ask his mother a question that had been troubling him. "Did you adopt me and then find out my dad was in prison, or did you know that before you decided you would be my mom?" he inquired. On learning that Denise received the background information about Demetri's birth parents several months after the adoption, Demetri asked, "Didn't you want to return me?"

"No way. Absolutely no way would I return you," Denise replied emphatically. "I loved you and you loved me back. Yes, I found out your father had some serious problems, but you are not your father. You are different. You are yourself." During the several months after this conversation, Demetri and Denise continued to talk about Demetri's concerns about his intrinsic self-worth. Each time Denise affirmed her unconditional love for her son, and each time she clarified again that the choices Demetri's birth father had made in no way tainted Demetri.

Identification with birth parents is an important developmental step for adopted teenagers. This identification has positive aspects, but in some cases it can lead to bad or risky behavior—based on the teenager's supposition that the birth parents were "bad people." If your child does something loud or risky, determine if the motivation for the behavior is adoption-related, or if it is just the typical rebelliousness or risk taking of a teenager who is trying to test the limits of independence.

During their conversations Denise discovered that Demetri's concept of the consequences of bad or risky behavior was limited, a shortcoming for nearly all teenagers, adopted or not. Although Demetri knew that shoplifting, as well as lying and talking back to authorities—which he did once he was caught—were wrong, he did not fully grasp the serious consequences of these actions in a public setting, such as a store. He said he thought that a shoplifting incident could "just be erased" if he "apologized and paid the store back" for what he had stolen. When he learned that this act might go on a permanent police record and that he might be banned from the local drugstore, he was horrified and he vowed never to do that kind of thing again. Demetri's naiveté in this regard reminded Denise of an incident the summer before, when Demetri had swum after a rubber raft that was being driven across the lake by a strong wind. He never considered how he would swim back, towing the raft, with the wind pushing him away from the dock. His friends were concerned for his safety, yet they too swam out to help him retrieve the raft without considering the risks of their own actions. All of the teens were rescued by a concerned stranger who happened along in a motorboat and towed them to shore.

Because they have survived so much as infants, toddlers, or youngsters, adopted teenagers feel an especially strong sense of invincibility.

Risk can be an unreal concept to teenagers who, aside from being convinced of their own immortality as teens have always been, are raised nowadays in a virtual-reality world of video games and action movies. Adopted teens are especially vulnerable to underestimating or missing the presence of risk. All of them have had the intensely frightening experience of being taken from familiar caregivers and handed to strangers, of losing their familiar surroundings and traveling to a new and unfamiliar residence. As such, because they have survived so much as infants, toddlers, or youngsters, they feel an especially strong sense of invincibility. "I've handled worse than this," they think to themselves, as they engage in the kinds of risky activities that a teen thinks up. Therefore, keep in mind that the issue that arises when your child engages in bad or risky behavior is not whether he knows it is wrong but whether he fully grasps the consequences. Question your teen carefully, in a neutral but friendly manner, to determine his true level of understanding. Next, walk him through the realities of the consequences of his behavior—in terms of the legal system, the educational system, or the employment system, as well as of his own health, well-being, and self-image.

THIRTY-SECOND SOLUTIONS?

Perhaps it seems to you as if the vignettes in this chapter about the five teenagers from our First Year Home Group all end too quickly, too simply, and too well. In a way you are correct; family life is often messier than these examples, which I have abbreviated and simplified for illustrative purposes. But if there are open lines of communication and a trusting connection between parent and child, often what seems to be a crisis resolves remarkably quickly. The key is for parents to look at the world through their teen's eyes and to communicate their empathy and their ability to see things as their teen does. In most cases teens are waiting and hoping their parents will reach out to them. Above all, teens, and in particular internationally adopted teens, do not want to be abandoned by the parents they have grown to love.

The vignettes in this chapter summarize conversations that took place over a period of months and even years following an initial blowup. The parents had to be both persistent and consistent; if they had gone back to ignoring their teens, or angrily dismissing them, or punishing them, the children would have continued to resort to dramatic means to make their parents listen, to the point of actually carrying out their threats. Do not imagine that a single week of conversation will "cure" the "problem." International adoption is a challenging lifelong adventure for everyone, parents included. Despite your child's newfound independence, the teen years are not a time in which you can step back and take a break. If at all possible, do not take on a more demanding job or begin traveling more frequently during your child's teenage years. Teens, I believe, need their parents around even more than school-age children do.

ADOPTION ISSUES IN THE TEEN YEARS

Mixed Heritages, Fluid Identities

"I'm Korean. I'm American. I'm an immigrant from one country, and a citizen of another."

"I am Russian by birth and American by adoption. How do I make sense of the fact that my birth country and my adoptive country were bitter enemies during the Cold War?"

"I'm a Chinese person adopted by white folks. But I really want to learn Spanish, not Mandarin."

"Some days I feel more Hispanic; other days I feel more white."

"I feel like I'm a white person, regardless of what race or ethnic group other people think I belong to."

WHO AM I? FINDING A MIXED-HERITAGE IDENTITY

In the teen years issues of adoption, race, and ethnicity come together simultaneously as a child begins to go through the process of adult-identity formation. Of course, a child's identity has been developing since birth, and adoptive families almost certainly have discussed ethnicity and race before the teen years (see chapter 23 for a look at these matters in the preteen years). Teenagers, however, have more cognitive tools available for exploring identity, and they also engage in a wider range of social interactions in which issues of identity might arise. When international adoptees are interviewed as young adults, they report that as they progressed through the teen years and broadened their horizons of social interaction, race and ethnicity concerns gradually came to occupy them more than adoption concerns.

We can trace this change over time using Demetri's own words. When he was five, Demetri described himself by saying, "I am adopted. I am a boy. I came from Russia." At ten he wrote an autobiography that began, "I was born far away in Russia and my mom adopted me when I was one year old. I live with my mom in the blue house two blocks from school." By the time Demetri was fifteen, he described himself as "a performer on two ethnic trapezes, one Russian and one American. I flip back and forth. Sometimes I slip, but there's no safety net." Over time his description of himself went from "adopted," to "adopted" and "from Russia," to "Russian and American."

THE EITHER/OR DILEMMA AND THE MIXED-HERITAGE SOLUTION

Living in a society and among a peer group that is acutely aware of appearance, ethnicity, race, and other markers of human difference, internationally adopted teens often feel trapped in an either/or dilemma—either they have one ethnic identity or they have another. And, as Demetri's words suggest, there is no safe haven from this forced choice. The pressure to choose an identity, to choose one or another ethnic affiliation, is a problem all internationally adopted persons face, even those who, like Demetri, appear to "match" their adoptive parents racially.

When Denise first planned to adopt Demetri from Russia, she gave little thought to the possibility that her son would struggle with issues of ethnic and national identity. She thought the fact that he looked like her racially would take care of that. As Denise says now, "I thought there would be fewer adjustment problems if we were both of the same racial background. But he never lets me forget that he is Russian and I am not." Life becomes complex when a child has to integrate two ethnicities, two sets of parents, two countries, and two cultures.

Children such as Soon An and Mu Ling, whose Asian appearance differed in obvious ways from that of their white adoptive parents, faced the either/or dilemma in a more concrete and immediate manner. Yi Sheng and Sonia joined families that were already multiracial and multiethnic, but they too faced the pressure to commit to one identity. Not surprisingly, as an adopted teenager tries to adjust to these pressures, issues of competing loyalties—to birth family versus adoptive family—make the process emotionally stressful.

In the United States the concept that a person must choose either one identity or another has been strongly influenced by the history of race relations over the past four hundred years. Until very recently, anyone who claimed to be both African-American and Caucasian was likely to be treated as an outcast. Not only has this concept held sway in the culture at large, but it has also been influential among adoption professionals. There has been a strong belief in the adoption community that an internationally adopted child, especially a child of color, would have self-esteem and identity problems if forced to live in a mixed family headed by white adoptive parents. As a result, there was strong pressure among adoption professionals to place African-American or Asian children only in African-American or Asian homes. It was assumed that white parents could not help their adopted child of color, or of any different ethnicity, fully identify with her own ethnic and racial background.

In more recent years some adoption professionals have criticized these assumptions, labeling them *monoracial bias*. They point out that there is no research that proves that parents and families are this limited, unable to cope with diversity within their family. In addition, extensive interviews with people who have a mixed heritage, either because they are biologically of mixed race or because they grew up in mixed-race families, reveal that racial and ethnic identities are not fixed and immutable categories; people are capable of juggling multiple identities, and multiple components of a given identity, and of emphasizing one or another identity in different social contexts and at different stages in their lives. This fluidity of identity is especially pronounced during the teen years, when identity formation is a major developmental focus.

Persons with a mixed heritage are capable of juggling multiple identities, and multiple components of a given identity.

All teenagers play with, or "try on," different identities in order to discover which self-image feels most comfortable. One week a teen may dress all in black, in the Goth style, and the next week she may try a hippie look, in a long skirt and a tie-dyed top. A month later the same teen may mix these two styles to create her own unique outfit. Internationally adopted teenagers do this, too, of course, not just with styles and tastes but also with ethnic, racial, and cultural identities. One week, for example, Soon An decided to eat only Swedish food, thereby identifying with the heritage of her adoptive parents; but the next week she wanted to eat *kimchi* and rice every day, as she explored her own Korean roots.

Virtually all internationally adopted children are in families consisting of two or more ethnic groups. Frequently there are two or more racial groups as well. When parents of one country and culture adopt a child of another country and culture, the family can no longer be monocultural, monoracial, or mono-ethnic. Because of this simple reality, adoption professionals now look more favorably on what may be called the *mixed-heritage solution*. Moreover, many, many internationally adopted children have become well-adjusted adults after having been raised in a family in which multiple racial or ethnic identities co-existed peacefully and in which they were free to choose which identity to focus on at a given moment. Therefore, adoption experts say, there are no psycho-logical or social grounds on which to insist that a family—or an individual—be of one race or one culture only.

The term *mixed heritage* can apply to an individual or to a family. It encom-passes mixed-race, mixed-ethnicity, and mixed-culture situations. In my view the virtue of a mixed-heritage approach goes beyond the fact that it accurately describes the multicultural reality of many adoptive families; in addition, it is a key component of an internationally adopted teenager's overall development into a self-reliant adult. The mixed-heritage solution allows room for the inter-national adoptee to explore and choose an identity or identities. It gives her, as a growing child, the freedom (and the responsibility) to construct an identity from the inside out. Her self-image and self-esteem will eventually be based not on how others categorize or label her but on what she herself has chosen over the course of her development.

To say this is not to deny that the world, including the parts of the world—schools, neighborhoods, social venues, and so on—that your teenager inhabits, is made up of specific ethnic and racial groups, and that these groups often define sharply and narrowly who belongs in a group and who must be excluded. The first time Soon An sat down to eat lunch with a group of Korean-American stu-dents at her high school, some of them told Soon An that she did not eat enough *kimchi* to be Korean and therefore was "too white." These comments reflect the limited idea of identity that members of a group often use to define their boundaries. As an adoptive parent, be aware that this is the type of experience your teenager is likely to face. Bring up the topic yourself to start the conversation with your child, because the majority of internationally adopted teenagers do not share this information with their parents. A teen may be silent on this subject for fear of upsetting her parents or because she feels her

Internationally adopted children and their families are mixed-heritage families. Adopted teenagers like hearing that their parents deliberately chose to create such a family.

parents (especially white parents) have never faced a similar situation and would not understand or be able to offer solutions.

Recognizing that your family has a mixed heritage makes an important contribution to your teen's identity formation. In addition to offering support as your teenager explores and chooses among the several identities available to her, you should also point out that when you made the decision to adopt internationally, you consciously chose to create a *mixed-heritage family*. You build a powerful connection with your teen when you acknowledge that you chose to change the family's ethnic identity by adopting a child internationally.

TALKING WITH YOUR TEEN ABOUT MIXED-HERITAGE IDENTITY

Your internationally adopted teenager may be reluctant, as I have said, to open a conversation with you about matters of ethnic identity. But such issues are almost certainly on his mind, and they are important topics for discussion. One strategy for starting the dialogue is to talk not about abstractions but about concrete things he may have heard or experienced. A list of some possibilities, which I have adapted from a similar list in Maria P. P. Root and Matt Kelley's book *The Multiracial Child Resource Book*, follows. These are the kind of experiences that force identity issues into a teen's consciousness, even if he is hesitant to talk about them with you.

> *You have been asked about your ethnic or racial heritage as an object of curiosity.*
>
> *Your ethnicity has been mistakenly identified.*
>
> *You have been told, for example, "You have to choose; you can't be both Russian and American" or "You can't be both from Guatemala and from the U.S."*
>
> *You have been told, for example, "You don't look Korean."*
>
> *You have been told, "You are a mistake."*
>
> *You have been told, "Those can't be your siblings. You don't look alike."*
>
> *You are well liked by peers but you are not asked for dates.*
>
> *Your parents identify your race or ethnicity differently from the way you identify it.*
>
> *Your mother was assumed to be your nanny or babysitter.*

A stranger assumes you are dating an older woman or older man when you are seen with one of your parents.

When people see your mother or father they change how they treat you.

You have tried to hide one or both parents from view when you are among your friends.

Consider showing this list to your teen, or post such a list on the refrigerator so that your teen can keep a tally of when these things happen. Your doing so will provide the starting point for conversations about identity and will signal to your teen that you empathize with his experiences.

As you talk with your teen about ethnicity, race, nationality, and culture, communicate clearly that these are more matters of his own choosing than he might have been led to believe. How or why a person constructs a particular mixed identity does not have to be justified to anyone, and no one can dictate how it will be accomplished. Choosing an identity is based on an individual's aspirations for himself, as well as on his feelings about his birth parents and country, his adoptive parents and country, the social contexts in which he finds himself, and other things as well. Emphasize to your teen, too, that he does not need to make one big "for now and forever more" decision about his identity. Exploration and change are normal and healthy, and the process does not have to end with a singular, frozen identification. Trying out different identities during the teen years is not a sign of low self-esteem or confusion about self.

Many cultures, including that of the United States, overemphasize physical appearance when they categorize (or judge) people. They do this in many different ways, but especially in terms of race. If and when this happens to your teen, he will be forced into making a fixed, either/or decision about his identity. Communicate to him that there is an alternative view, the mixed-heritage approach, which rejects physical appearance as the sole or main criterion for identity. Instead, he can explore and choose from a variety of features—culture, history, nationality, and regional identity ("East Asian," for example), as well as the traits that he discerns in his birth family and adoptive family—as he begins to construct his adult identity.

Convincing your child that he is capable of having a mixed identity founded on a mixed heritage will take proactive efforts on your part. After seventeen-year-old Soon An had talked one day about being a "Korean immigrant" and an "American citizen," as well as an "ethnic Swede," Charlotte decided to e-mail her daughter a list of the various identities that appeared to be available to her. (Over her years as a mother Charlotte had developed numerous ways to get a teen's attention, including sending e-mails and text messages, posting information on the refrigerator, taping a note to the teen's pillow, bringing up topics while driving the teen to the mall, and setting up a family meeting.) Charlotte wrote in her e-mail:

Dear Soon An,
I thought you'd find the list below interesting.
Love, Mom

Who Are You?
1. Korean
2. American
3. Swedish
4. Asian
5. Caucasian or White
6. "Symbolic White." This means you aren't really white but you act like it
because your parents are white.
7. Blended, mixed, fluid, multi-, bi-

After a few days Soon An sent back an e-mail response with a question: "What is 'blended'?" The following afternoon they began talking.

"I never thought about all the ways I can identify myself," Soon An admitted. "I showed this to my friends and the ones who are mixed race got really excited, but the girls who are one hundred percent Korean and live with Korean parents didn't get it. They told me that if I couldn't speak Korean, I was just a banana."

"What's that?" Joe, her father, asked, as he overheard the conversation.

"Daddy, a banana is an Asian person who acts white." Soon An sighed. "It means yellow on the outside and white inside."

"I don't see anything wrong with acting white," Joe responded.

"Yeah, but where do I fit?" Soon An asked. "The Korean girls tell me I'm not Korean enough; the white kids tell me I'm *so* Asian."

"What if you tell them you're a blend?" Charlotte suggested.

"I don't want to blend. It sounds like putting all the ingredients in the food processor and coming out as an ethnic pesto. I'm not a pesto. I'm a mixture, like a multiethnic meal. Some days I like meatballs served with *kimchi* and ketchup! And other days I want *bulgogi* [Korean barbecued beef]—with dilled potatoes and apple pie for dessert." Soon An took off on her metaphor with gusto.

Soon An had begun to grasp the idea of a flexible, fluid identity as a positive way to see herself. It helped her to recognize that mixed-race or mixed-ethnicity

persons have more variety and choice in their identity than monoracial or mo-
noethnic people have, and she found that she fit in more with other teenagers
who themselves came from mixed-heritage families. Although Charlotte helped
by offering vocabulary such as *mixed, flexible,* and *fluid,* Soon An reached these
conclusions on her own.

Sometimes a picture, graph, or map is worth a thousand words. Yi Sheng,
too, was curious about his own mixed identity, and he wondered whether it put
him in a small minority or whether he was part of a larger trend. Nina suggested
to her son that he go online to the MAVIN Foundation website (http://www.
mavinfoundation.org; the foundation supports a variety of mixed-heritage educational endeavors), where, she happened to know, he could order a map of the
United States, based on the 2000 U.S. Census, that showed, county by county,
where mixed-race families lived. Yi Sheng ordered the map, and when it arrived
he posted it on the refrigerator. When Kenji came home he noticed the map and
began studying it. "I guess we're not so weird after all," he concluded. "The western half of the United States is a lot more mixed than anywhere else. I guess we're
living in the right place!"

"Gee, Dad, didn't you know the west was full of mixed-race families like
ours?" Yi Sheng replied. "You are so lame."

"I think your father is worried about standing out," Nina commented. "You
know the old Asian proverb 'The nail that stands up gets hit'? Dad doesn't want
to be a nail."

Yi Sheng smiled. "It's not a white-versus-nonwhite, either/or world anymore.
There are a lot of other 'nail' families out there," he said.

Parenting a teen often means knowing about educational resources and then
letting your teen explore them independently. Just as Charlotte's e-mail gave
Soon An the opportunity to think about ethnic identity and sparked her interest
to the point that she brought up the subject on her own a few days later, so Yi
Sheng was energized and motivated to talk about ethnicity by his own research,
which was based on the lead his mother had suggested. When teens are empow-
ered by the process of doing their own thinking on a subject, they are more willing to discuss it openly. This is especially important for the topic of ethnic identity, which they are often reticent about addressing with their parents.

"W.H.O.S.E. IDENTITY?"

Even when they are strong and resilient, and even when their search for an adult
identity is proceeding relatively smoothly, internationally adopted teenagers

still encounter jarring situations in which their race, culture, or ethnicity is challenged. They may face aggressive, intrusive, or just plain dumb questions; they may hear offhand comments that reveal a speaker's ignorance; or they may be the target of a direct insult. They may face prejudice from people in the majority culture who see them as minorities, and they may endure tests ("authenticity tests"; see chapter 27) from other members of their own minority group who accuse them of not being authentic enough. As a parent, you need to continue teaching your teen the skills to respond to, or calmly walk away from, all of these situations.

One evening Mu Ling's family was discussing how both Mu Ling and her older sister, Clara, could handle the authenticity tests to which Chinese "border patrols" (also see chapter 27) were subjecting them. Clara, who like Mu Ling was adopted from China, was challenged about her family's surname: "You can't be Chinese with a name like Miller," one of her peers had said. Mu Ling had been told by the Chinese kids' border patrol to go hang out with the white kids because, according to them, she acted white, sounded white, and liked white music (whatever that is!). Meg and Laura, their two mothers, asked them how they felt about these encounters.

> **Internationally adopted teenagers may face aggressive, intrusive, or just plain dumb questions; they may hear offhand comments that reveal a speaker's ignorance; or they may be the target of a direct insult.**

"I felt embarrassed and then angry when she told me that I wasn't Chinese enough because I had an English last name," Clara shared.

"I feel hurt and rejected when they challenge who I am," Mu Ling explained. "Then I just find myself bouncing around, trying to get the group's attention, to somehow get in with them."

Meg retrieved the family's copy of *The W.I.S.E. Up! Powerbook*, published by the Center for Adoption Support and Education, which the family had found useful when the girls were younger and first began having to answer difficult questions about their backgrounds. The initials in the title stand for four different tactics an adopted child can choose when faced with challenging comments or questions: **W**alk away; **I**t's private; **S**hare something; **E**ducate them. Meg suggested to Mu Ling that *W*, walking away, might be the appropriate response.

"But you have to have somewhere or somebody to walk toward. You need some other group to join," Mu Ling pointed out.

"How about *I*, it's private?" Laura asked. "You can just say it's private, and then change the subject."

W.H.O.S.E. Identity Is It?

How Mu Ling's Family Responds to Authenticity Tests
Walk away
Humor
Off-topic
Share
Educate

"That won't work with the border patrol," Mu Ling sighed. "They think everything about you is public."

"What if we replace *I* with *O*, for *off-topic*?" Clara suggested. "Your parents are not the issue—that's off-topic. Your hairstyle or choice of slang is irrelevant—that's off-topic, too. What really counts is: Can you join their group?"

"I guess I could just ask that, point blank," Mu Ling conceded. "That would get them to focus on what the issue really is. When I just change the subject and say something like 'Hey, did anyone finish the math homework from last night?' all they do is turn and walk away. But I do like *S*, sharing. I could share with them that I was adopted and didn't get a chance to choose my parents . . . the way all of *them* did! That would get a laugh."

"You're right. Maybe if changing the subject to something else that is serious doesn't work, saying something funny might. Humor is always a good way to go," Laura commented. "So far we have *W*, walk away; *O*, off-topic; *S*, share; and *H*, humor."

"I always liked the *E*, educate, part of the W.I.S.E. plan. Sometimes people treat you badly just because they are ignorant. What about educate? Would that work with the border patrol?" Mu Ling wondered aloud.

"I like that," Clara replied. "What if you told them that there are millions of mixed-heritage families like ours? Tell them that 'mixed' is going to be the next big thing. It's already cool—think about all the mixed-heritage TV and movie stars they all worship."

"I don't know. You're probably right. Even if I don't convince them, at least I would have stood up to their silly test. And then I'll go hang out with the mixed group; I know where they eat lunch. I'll bet they've had the same experiences as I have," Mu Ling said, planning aloud.

"Hey, look, if we rearrange the letters we spell *W-H-O-S-E*. Like *Whose* identity is it anyway?" Clara pointed out.

"I like that," Mu Ling said. "My identity is mine, and I won't let some group or stranger tell me who I am!"

EXOTIC, SEXUAL, OR SHUNNED: DATING AND SOCIAL PRESSURES

Both internationally adopted teens and mixed-race teens experience the negative perceptions of strangers. Internationally adopted teens and young people are sometimes viewed as exotics or as desirable sexual conquests. Some people are attracted to the stereotypic view of other racial or ethnic groups. White boys asked Soon An out for lots of dates when she began high school, but she found that the boys' expectations were for exotic, kinky, and readily available sex. So she made her limits clear, but thereafter she was shunned in the dating world. If Soon An was not a sexual conquest, she became a liability to those same white boys. In addition, no Korean-American boys would ask her out either, fearing she was "too white" and therefore would not pass the authenticity test of their families.

Demetri found in high school that, once he was known to be of Russian origin, girls' parents were hesitant to let him take their daughters out on dates. As far as he could tell, the reason was that he had fallen victim to a stereotype. A ring of Russian immigrant car thieves had been arrested in the area, and the girls' parents imagined that he might be "like them" or somehow "connected to them."

Yi Sheng, for his part, was turned down by the Chinese-American girls he asked out. "I guess they want their Chinese boyfriends to come from a family that's a hundred percent Chinese," he sighed. The white girls saw Yi Sheng as curious, exotic, and funny, but not as a serious partner for the senior prom.

The job of anticipating, and helping teenagers manage their feelings about, such personal rejections falls to parents. Because rejection is a sensitive area for international adoptees, talking about this subject can be like treading across a volatile minefield. Nina tried to prepare Yi Sheng for being left out of the prom, having seen that happen to her two older daughters, both of whom were of mixed race though not adopted. The older girls did not, however, have the same sensitivity to rejection that Yi Sheng had because of his complex background.

Yi Sheng did not want to hear what Nina had to say. "I'm not like my sisters! I'm myself and I'll go to the prom!" he shouted. He held out hope of finding a date until the very last minute, and then, when he was unable to do so, he withdrew into his familiar sullenness. Nina knew that she and Kenji had made the correct choice to be on hand to support their dejected son on prom night.

Another uncomfortable problem arises when strangers assume that an internationally adopted teen daughter is her father's trophy girlfriend. This is what happened to Soon An when Joe took her to visit his relatives in another state. "Why are people on the plane giving me such weird looks?" Soon An asked her father. That is when it dawned on Joe that strangers might think they were lovers. He was revolted, shocked, and angry. He decided to ring for the flight attendant and then loudly asked for a ginger ale for his "adopted daughter!" to satisfy the curiosity of everyone who was eyeing them.

Demetri had a similar experience when some of his friends who had never met Denise saw her driving with Demetri. The friends assumed she was an older woman paramour, and they later complimented Demetri on his taste in "older broads." Demetri was puzzled. But when he realized his friends' error he was embarrassed and angry. He corrected them, saying emphatically, "That's my mom!" The friends launched into a frenzy of teasing, saying, among other things, "Yeah, right! How come she doesn't look like you?" Finally Demetri had to choose between throwing a few punches and explaining that he was an adoptee. "I'm adopted," he said simply. "Of course my mom and I don't look alike." In responding to situations similar to Demetri's, you, as the parent in a mixed-heritage family, need to engage your teen in a conversation about some fairly sophisticated sexual assumptions, prejudices, and tastes in our culture.

LOYALTY CONCERNS

Some teenagers feel they must make a choice between their two sets of parents. The result may be that they cast one set as "bad" parents and the other set as the "good guys." Sometimes, of course, teens cast adoptive parents as the "bad guys" when those parents refuse to let a teen do something she wants. A teen imagines—and asserts defiantly to her adoptive parents—that her birth parents would give her what she wants. The teen idealizes the birth parents and exaggerates what is "wrong" with the adoptive parents. If this has happened to you, you probably have had the reverse experience as well. Hours or days later the same teen denounces her birth parents for leaving her at the orphanage or being unable to care for her, then glorifies you, the adoptive parents.

> **Some adopted teenagers feel they must make a choice between their two sets of parents.**

Teenagers in general explore the concept of loyalty, and especially what it means to be loyal to a friend or to one's family. Some adopted teenagers worry that loyalty to birth parents, as expressed by their interest in or research on their birth cultures or birth countries, is an insult to their adoptive parents. Such a teen may try to conceal her interest in learning more about her past. Internationally adopted teenagers struggle more with their own identity when they perceive loyalty as something that follows an either/or model, in which one choice automatically precludes the other. With increasing maturity and with support from her adoptive parents, a teenager can reconcile her loyalty to her two families without having to choose one over the other. The process of identifying with one set of parents or another, and the loyalty struggle that occurs as part of this process, is, I have found, one of the hardest subjects for teens to talk about.

Two types of comments can help open up the topics of loyalty and identification in conversations with your teenager. First, look for opportunities to remark favorably upon your child's physical resemblance to her birth parents. For example, you might comment, "Your birth mother must have had cute dimples, just like you do." Second, when you speak positively about your child's skills and talents, such as athletic, musical, artistic, or mathematical abilities, note those that she may have inherited from her birth family. Such comments will enable your child to feel loyal to her birth family without feeling that she is pushing you, the adoptive parent, aside. Conversely, you also can comment on what you and your child have accomplished together, what activities you both enjoy, and what traits you share, even though, of course, these were not inherited. Such comments about both birth and adoptive families will open your teenager's heart to sharing her thoughts about identity, loyalty, and family.

A few months after Charlotte and Joe began their campaign of comments like these, fourteen-year-old Soon An cuddled up by her mother one evening and whispered, "I have a secret to tell you, but I'm afraid you'll be mad."

The "Standard Positive Response": "I'm glad you told me. And you know, I think if I were adopted I'd feel the same way."

"I won't be mad," Charlotte reassured her daughter, while she got a firm grip on her feelings and wondered what was coming next.

"I think I'll always love my first mother best," Soon An confessed.

Charlotte wasn't sure how to react. Finally she settled on a simple supportive comment that I call the Standard Positive Response, which is useful on many occasions when adoptive parents feel at a loss for words. Charlotte simply said, "I'm glad you told me. And you know, I think if I were adopted I'd feel the same way."

Adoptive parents represent not only themselves. They are also, in their child's eyes, stand-ins for the missing birth parents. Soon An at seventeen exhibited this thought process when she told her mother that she thought her birth mother was "like you, Mom. Maybe she even had blond hair." Rather than laughing at the confusion of such a comment, parents can appreciate how much they mean to their child and how fully they, the adoptive parents, are the model of what parenthood means to their teenager.

Last Words

INTERNATIONAL ADOPTION is an adventure for life. Although this book is filled with challenges and how to meet them, these challenges are not the whole story. High points and triumphs abound daily when you are raising an internationally adopted child. These peaks emerge not only when challenges are overcome but also when your child departs for school without complaint or when calm reigns during an ordinary evening at home. At those times the beauty, the connection, the pleasures of family life feel like the blessings they truly are. Recognize and relish these magical moments.

International adoption is an adventure for life, an adventure of learning about yourself as well about your child. Take time to celebrate your accomplishments. No matter how small these changes seem to you, they are large in the life of your child and your family. When your child became frustrated, you tried a new strategy that worked: *Bravo!* Your child pitched in to do a family chore without being asked: *Success!*

International adoption means learning about your own connections to others, including family and friends. It is about making new connections with new people and reshaping old connections in new ways. Take time to be nurtured by others. Such shared experiences bring a quiet joy. Take time to think about your own changes and growth. Take time to reflect and rejoice. Savor your own and your child's successes. Find ways to make each success a family celebration. The sweetness you share as a family will smooth the road ahead.

Appendix: Teaching Your Child Your Language

Pronounce words clearly, separately, and slowly. Remember that your child's brain has been prepared to hear some sounds but not others. Asian languages lack the *r* sound; Spanish substitutes a soft *b* for *v*. Do not run words together. For example, "Areya readyet?" ("Are you ready yet?") is hard to decipher when a language is new.

Repeat and emphasize key words. Avoid pronouns and use proper names even if this sounds oddly repetitive.

Use physical examples to explain a concept or idea.

Use multiple forms of communication, including signs, gestures, facial expressions, and pantomime.

Focus the majority of conversation on what a child does and feels or on immediate events so that he can relate language to the here and now.

Avoid long words. Replace them with simpler words.

Avoid nonsense games and rhymes unless your child enjoys them.

Avoid rhetorical questions, ambiguous or vague questions, and more than one question in a single sentence.

Make sure your child grasps basic numbers, colors, days of the week, and so on before moving on to more abstract concepts. Rely on teaching materials for preschool and ESL students to help cover concepts thoroughly.

Talk about holidays using context and hands-on examples. For example, internationally adopted children may have no background about Halloween, the Fourth of July, New Year's, birthdays, or religious holidays such as Christmas, Hanukkah, Easter, or Passover. Use hands-on demonstrations with objects to acquaint your child with the basic elements of cultural and religious events.

Teach "first, next, and last." Many children who have complex backgrounds have not learned the concept of sequence. The easiest way to teach these related ideas is to talk about things that happen during the day. For example, "First we woke up. Next we ate breakfast, and last we went to the park to play." Another effective method to teach sequence is to tell the "story of the day" at bedtime or the dinner table.

Teach your child to listen and remember a sequence of items. Many parents think their child fails to follow directions because he is stubborn or lazy or oppositional. In fact, many children have difficulty with "auditory memory" because they were never expected to remember more than one thing at a time.

Teach cause and effect in daily life. Once a child learns about sequence you can begin teaching cause and effect. The idea that something happens *because* of something else is often a new idea to internationally adopted children. Their lives have been topsy-turvy with no apparent reasons or causes. Use simple things around the house, and begin with your child's causing something to happen, especially something good. For example, point out that because your child turned on the faucet, water came out, or that the light went on because your child pressed the light switch: "You made the light turn on when you moved the switch." (You do not have to use the phrase *cause and effect* to teach the concept.)

WHEN TO GET ASSESSMENT AND PROFESSIONAL HELP

Early language assessment should be as standard as an initial pediatric checkup, because nearly all children adopted internationally have some speech and/or language issues. A first speech and language assessment for a child should be done between two and a half and three years of age.

If a child has difficulty with swallowing or eating solid food by one year old (or older), an assessment of oral proficiency is important. Look for a therapist who has experience with very young children, with feeding issues, and with internationally adopted children. The closest children's hospital is a good source of referrals.

If your child does not seem to be making progress in language for a short period, she may be busy learning some other new skill or be stressed by a new situation. However, it is time to get an assessment if your child's language acquisition seems to stall or moves slowly for more than two months without cause.

Bibliography

I have divided the bibliography into three sections. The first section consists of books or articles written for parents, teachers, or the general public. I have included some very readable articles from clinical journals as well. The second section includes the children's books and the music to which I have referred; it is not meant to be a definitive list of children's books about adoption. The final section consists of lengthy clinical texts or articles written primarily for adoption professionals. These books reflect my object-relations, psycho-neurological developmental perspective.

FOR PARENTS AND TEACHERS

Blechner, Maris. "Inducement: Adoption Language We Must Understand." *Adoptalk* (Fall 2004), a publication of the North American Council on Adoptable Children (NACAC).
> *This article is one to read and reread. The article can be accessed at http://www. nacac.org/adoptalk/adoptalkarticles.html#parenting.*

Brazelton, T. Berry. *Touchpoints: Your Child's Emotional and Behavioral Development.* Cambridge, MA: Perseus Books, 2000.
> *A parent-friendly book about how the onset of new developmental stages offers important parenting opportunities for connection.*

Brodzinksy, David M., Marshall D. Schecter, and Robin Marantz Henig. *Being Adopted: The Lifelong Search for Self.* New York: Doubleday, 1992.
> *A classic in the field worth reading.*

Cederblad, Marianne. *Adoption—But at What Price?* Stockholm, Sweden: National Board for Intercountry Adoptions, 2003 (http://www.mia.eu/english/ utredneng.pdf).
> *A thorough summary of all the research on intercountry adoptions as of 2003.*

Clark, Pamela, Sally Thigpen, and Amy Moeller Yates. "Integrating the Older/ Special Needs Adoptive Child into the Family." *Journal of Marital and Family Therapy* (April 2006), 181–194.
> *A clear description of the key family qualities that make adoption work.*

Department of Community Services, Government of New South Wales, Australia. *Adoption Act 2000.* http://www.community.nsw.gov.au/DOCS/ STANDARD/PC_101099.htm.
>   *Worth looking at on the Web.*

Eldridge, Sherrie. *Twenty Things Adopted Kids Wish Their Adoptive Parents Knew.* New York: Dell Publishing, 1999.

Federici, Ronald. "Raising the Post-Institutionalized Child: Risks, Challenges and Innovative Treatment." http://www.drfederici.com/raising_child.htm.
>   *An excellent article, except for his endorsement of "holding time."*

Fulbeck, Kip. *Part Asian, 100% Hapa.* San Francisco, CA: Chronicle Books, 2006.
>   *A visual experience, not to be missed if you have an Asian or mixed-race child.*

Hughes, Daniel A. *Facilitating Developmental Attachment: The Road to Emotional Recovery and Behavioral Change in Foster and Adopted Children.* Northvale, NJ: Jason Aronson, Inc., 1997.
>   *If your child is out of control, buy this book and go directly to chapter 11, "Principles of Parenting," and chapter 12, "Day-to-Day Parenting."*

James, John W., and Russell Friedman. *When Children Grieve.* With Leslie Landon Matthews. New York: HarperCollins, 2001.
>   *An immensely readable, practical guide; the best strategies for helping a child cope with grief that I've found for parents.*

Jarratt, Claudia Jewett. *Helping Children Cope with Separation and Loss,* revised edition. Boston, MA: Harvard Common Press, 1994.

———. *Adopting the Older Child.* Boston, MA: Harvard Common Press, 1978.

Kaplan, Louise J. *Oneness and Separateness: From Infant to Individual.* New York: Simon and Schuster, 1978.
>   *This beautifully written book describes the uninterrupted development of a child, enabling parents to recognize what is working or missing with an adopted child.*

Keefer, Betsy, and Jayne E. Schooler. *Telling the Truth to Your Adopted or Foster Child: Making Sense of the Past.* Westport, CT: Bergin & Garvey, 2000.
>   *A good guide for talking about the realities of adoption life stories.*

Kranowitz, Carol Stock. *The Out-of-Sync Child: Recognizing and Coping with Sensory Integration Dysfunction.* New York: Perigee Books, 1998.
>   *The most popular book on sensory integration.*

MacLeod, Jean, and Sheena Macrae, PhD, eds. *Adoption Parenting: Creating a Toolbox, Building Connections.* Warren, NJ: EMK Press, 2006.
> *A wonderful collection by many knowledgeable writers. Contains great summaries of developmental information about non-adopted children and traditional parenting strategies followed by explanations of how adoption alters these ("the adoption twist"). An excellent companion to this book!*

Maskew, Trish. *Our Own: Adopting and Parenting the Older Child.* Morton Grove, IL: Snowcap Press, 1999.
> *An excellent resource which is written in parent-friendly language, providing a good balance between clinical and practical information, including school issues, explanations of psychological diagnoses, and medical issues.*

Melina, Lois. "Carefully Crafted Explanation Won't Eliminate Questions of Self-Worth Raised by Adoption." *Adopted Child Newsletter* 17, no. 4 (1998).
> *An extremely thoughtful analysis of a no-win situation.*

Moline, Karen. "Get Rid of 'Gotcha.'" *Adoptive Families* (March 2006), 29. Or see http://www.adoptivefamilies.com/articles.php?aid=1266.
> *This article makes the point powerfully from a child's viewpoint.*

Muhamedrahimov, Rifkat J., Oleg I. Palmov, and others. "Institution-Based Early Intervention Program." *Infant Mental Health Journal* 25, no. 5 (2004).
> *An account of staffing and life in a Russian orphanage that pulls no punches.*

Riley, Debbie. *Beneath the Mask: Understanding Adopted Teens.* With John Meeks. Silver Spring, MD: C.A.S.E. Publications, 2005.
> *Written for parents and clinicians, this book helps parents look behind a teen's troubling behavior to find the fears and concerns.*

Root, Maria P. P., and Matt Kelley, eds. *Multiracial Child Resource Book: Living Complex Identities.* Seattle, WA: MAVIN Foundation, 2003.
> *A fascinating and informative book with great photos, with two chapters on adoptees.*

Roseberry-McKibbin, Celeste. *Multicultural Students with Special Language Needs: Practical Strategies for Assessment and Intervention.* Oceanside, CA: Academic Communication Associates, 1995.
> *If your child has language difficulties, this book will help you identify the problems clearly.*

Schoettle, Marilyn. *W.I.S.E. Up! Powerbook.* Silver Spring, MD: C.A.S.E. Publications, 2000.

A workbook format to help kids choose how to deal with uncomfortable, intrusive questions. For children starting at age four with assistance from parents.

Siegel, Daniel J. *The Developing Mind: How Relationships and the Brain Interact to Shape Who We Are.* New York: Guilford Press, 1999.
   A readable description of brain research and development.

———— and Mary Hartzell. *Parenting from the Inside Out.* New York: Guilford Press, 2003.
   In nonclinical language, the brain researcher (Siegel) teams with his child's preschool teacher (Hartzell) to discuss how a parent's brain influences the child's developing mind.

Tepper, Thais, Lois Hannon, and Dorothy Sandstrom, eds. *International Adoption: Challenges and Opportunities.* Meadowlands, PA: Parents Network for the Post Institutionalized Child, 1999.
   An excellent resource on difficulties covered only cursorily in other works, including central auditory processing disorder and fetal alcohol syndrome.

Trott, Maryann Colby. *SenseAbilities: Understanding Sensory Integration.* Tucson, AZ: Communication Skill Builders, 1993. Available from Harcourt Assessment, (800) 211-8378.
   The best description I know of sensory difficulties. Short, but to the point.

Wilbarger, Patricia and Julia Wilbarger. "Sensory Defensiveness in Children Aged 2–12: An Intervention Guide for Parents and Other Caretakers." Available from Avanti Educational Programs, 14547 Titus Street, Suite 109, Panorama City, CA 91402. (818) 414-4230 or (818) 782-7366. http://avanti-ed.com/3.html.

Winnicott, D. W. *The Family, the Child, and the Outside World.* London: Penguin Books, 1964. Reprint, Reading, MA: Perseus Publishing, a member of the Perseus Books Group, 1987.
   Elegant and readable, tender and brilliantly insightful by a gifted psychiatrist.

CHILDREN'S BOOKS AND REFERENCED SONGS

Cole, Joanna. *How You Were Born.* William Morrow and Co., 1984.

Keller, Holly. *Horace.* New York: Greenwillow Books, 1991.

Mitchell, Joni. "The Circle Game." *Ladies of the Canyon.* Los Angeles: Siquomb Publishing Corp., 1970.

No Vacancy. "Heal Me, I'm Heartsick." *School of Rock.* Los Angeles: Paramount Pictures, 2003.

Ruffin, Jimmy. "What Becomes of the Broken Hearted?" *Standing in the Shadows of Motown.* Santa Monica, CA: Artisan Home Entertainment, 2001.

Sachar, Louis. *Holes.* New York: Scholastic, 1998.

Slote, Alfred. *Finding Buck McHenry.* New York: HarperCollins, 1991.

CLINICAL WORKS

Bourne, Victoria, and Brenda Todd. "When Left Means Right: An Explanation of the Left Cradling Bias in Terms of Right Hemisphere Specialization." *Developmental Science* 7, no. 1 (February 2004), 19–24.

Brodzinsky, David M. and David M. Steiger. "Prevalence of Adoptees among Special Education Populations." *Journal of Learning Disabilities* 24 (1991), 484–89.

Bruce, Elizabeth J., and Cynthia L. Schultz. *Nonfinite Loss and Grief: A Psychoeducational Approach.* Baltimore, MD: Paul H. Brookes Publishing Co., Inc., 2001.

Cassidy, Jude, and Phillip R. Shaver, eds. *Handbook of Attachment: Theory, Research, and Clinical Applications.* New York: Guilford Press, 1999.
    A gold mine of information.

Dozier, Mary. "Attachment-Based Treatment for Vulnerable Children." *Attachment & Human Development* 5, no. 3 (2003), 253–57.

———, Elizabeth Higley, Kathleen Albus, and Anna Nutter. "Interviewing with Foster Infant's Caregivers: Targeting Three Critical Needs." *Infant Mental Health Journal* 23, no. 5 (2002), 541–44.

Fahlberg, Vera I., MD. *A Child's Journey through Placement.* Indianapolis, IN: Perspectives Press, 1991.

Hamlin, J. Kiley, Karen Wynn, and Paul Bloom. "Social Evaluation by Preverbal Infants." *Nature 450,* November 22, 2007, 557–559.

James, Beverly. *Handbook for Treatment of Attachment-Trauma Problems in Children.* New York: The Free Press, 1994.
    One of the few authors willing to take on "coercive therapies."

Lester, Barry M., and T. Berry Brazelton. "Cross-Cultural Assessment of Neonatal Behavior." In *Cultural Perspectives on Child Development,* edited by Daniel A. Wagner and Harold W. Stevenson. New York: W. H. Freeman & Company, 1982.

Lieberman, Alicia F. "The Treatment of Attachment Disorder in Infancy and Early Childhood: Reflections from Clinical Intervention with Later-Adopted Foster Care Children." In *Attachment and Human Development* 5, no. 3 (September 2003), 279–82.

————. "Child Parent Psychotherapy with Trauma and Bereavement," presented at the National Training Institute of Zero to Three, Sacramento, CA, 2004.

Lieberman, Alicia F., Nance C. Compton, Patricia Van Horn, and Chandra Ghosh Ippen. *Losing a Parent to Death in the Early Years: Guidelines for the Treatment of Traumatic Bereavement in Infancy and Early Childhood.* Washington, DC: Zero to Three Press, 2003.
    Elegantly written, with wonderful strategies and case studies.

Mahler, Margaret S., Fred Pine, and Anni Bergman. *The Psychological Birth of the Human Infant: Symbiosis and Individuation.* New York: Basic Books, 1975.

Mandel-Emer, Denise, and Peter W. Jusczyk. "What's in a Name? How Infants Respond to Some Familiar Sound Patterns." In *Jusczyk Lab Final Report,* edited by D. Houston, A. Seidl, G. Hollich, E. Johnson, and A. Jusczyk, 2003. Available online at http://hincapie.psych.purdue.edu/Jusczyk/pdf/Name.pdf.

Nelson, Eric E., and Jaak Panskepp. "Brain Substrates of Infant-Mother Attachment: Contributions of Opioids, Oxytocin and Norepinephrine." *Neuroscience and Biobehavioral Review* 22, no. 3 (1998), 437–52.

Osofsky, Joy, D. *Young Children and Trauma: Intervention and Treatment.* New York: Guilford Press, 2004.

Porges, Stephen W. "Physiological Regulation in High Risk Infants: A Model for Assessment and Potential Intervention." *Development and Pyschopathology* 8 (1996), 43–58.

Schore, Allan N. *Affect Regulation and the Origin of the Self: The Neurobiology of Emotional Development.* Mahwah, NJ: Lawrence Erlbaum and Associates, 1994.

————. *Affect Dysregulation and Disorders of the Self.* New York: W. W. Norton, 2003.

Sroufe, L. Alan. "Early Relationships and the Development of Children. *Infant Mental Health Journal* 21, nos. 1–2 (2000), 67–74.

Teiman, Wendy, Jan van der Ende, and Frank Verhulst. "Psychiatric Disorders in Young Adult Intercountry Adoptees: An Epidemiological Study." *American Journal of Psychiatry* 162 (2005), 592–98.

van der Kolk, Bessel. "The Body Keeps Score: Memory and the Evolving Psychobiology of Post Traumatic Stress." In *Traumatic Stress*, edited by B. A. van der Kolk, 214–41. New York: Guilford Press, 1996.

van der Vegt, Erasmus, Erasmus van der Ende, Frank Verhulst, and Henning Tiemeir. "Early Childhood Adversities and Cortisol Secretion in Adults—A Study of International Adoptees." Presentation at the 6th World Congress on Stress. Oct. 2007.

Verhulst, Frank, Monika Althaus, and Herman J. Versluis-Den Beiman. "Problem Behavior in International Adoptees I: An Epidemiological Study." *Journal of the American Academy of Child & Adolescent Psychiatry* 29, no. 1 (January 1990), 94–103.

———. "Problem Behavior in International Adoptees III: Diagnosis of Child Psychiatric Disorders." *Journal of the American Academy of Child & Adolescent Psychiatry* 29, no. 3 (May 1990), 420–28.

Verhulst, Frank, and H. J. Versluis-Den Beiman. "Developmental Course of Problem Behaviors in Adolescent Adoptees." *Journal of the American Academy of Child & Adolescent Psychiatry* 34. no. 2 (February 1995), 151–59.

Wismer Fries, Alison B., and Seth Pollack. "Early Experience in Humans Is Associated with Changes in Neuropeptides Critical for Regulating Social Behavior." *Proceedings of the National Academy of Sciences* (PNAS) 102, no. 47 (2005), 17237–40.

Zero to Three. *Diagnostic Classification of Mental Health and Developmental Disorders of Infancy and Early Childhood*, rev. ed. Washington, DC: Zero to Three Press, 2005.

Ziegler, David. *Traumatic Experience and the Brain*. Phoenix, AZ: Acacia Publishing Inc., 2002.

Index

July 24/09